Montréal & Québec City

"When it comes to information on regional history, what to see and do, and shopping, these guides are exhaustive."

—USAir Magazine

"Usable, sophisticated restaurant coverage, with an emphasis on good value."

—Andy Birsh, *Gourmet Magazine* columnist

"Valuable because of their comprehensiveness."

—Minneapolis Star-Tribune

"Fodor's always delivers high quality...thoughtfully presented...thorough."

—Houston Post

"An excellent choice for those who want everything under one cover."

—Washington Post

Reprinted from *Fodor's Canada '97*
Fodor's Travel Publications, Inc.
New York • Toronto • London • Sydney • Auckland
http://www.fodors.com/

Fodor's Montréal & Québec City '97

Editor: Anastasia Redmond Mills

Editorial Contributors: Steven K. Amsterdam, Robert Andrews, David Brown, Susan Brown, Audra Epstein, Dorothy Guinan, Laura M. Kidder, Patricia Lowe, Donna Nebenzahl, Alice H. Oshins, Heidi Sarna, Helayne Schiff, Linda K. Schmidt, Mary Ellen Schultz, M. T. Schwartzman (Gold Guide editor), Dinah Spritzer, Julie Waters, Paul A. R. Waters

Creative Director: Fabrizio La Rocca

Associate Art Director: Guido Caroti

Photo Researcher: Jolie Novak

Cartographer: David Lindroth

Cover Photograph: Bob Krist

Text Design: Between the Covers

Copyright

Special Sales

Fodor's Travel Publications are available at special discounts for bulk purchases for sales promotions or premiums. Special editions, including personalized covers, excerpts of existing guides, and corporate imprints, can be created in large quantities for special needs. For more information, contact your local bookseller or write to Special Markets, Fodor's Travel Publications, 201 East 50th Street, New York, NY 10022. Inquiries from Canada should be directed to your local Canadian bookseller or sent to Random House of Canada, Ltd., Marketing Department, 1265 Aerowood Drive, Mississauga, Ontario L4W 1B9. Inquiries from the United Kingdom should be sent to Fodor's Travel Publications, 20 Vauxhall Bridge Road, London, England SW1V 2SA.

PRINTED IN THE UNITED STATES OF AMERICA

10 9 8 7 6 5 4 3 2 1

CONTENTS

Maps and Plans

ON THE ROAD WITH FODOR'S

W E'RE ALWAYS THRILLED to get letters from readers, especially one like this:

It took us an hour to decide what book to buy and we now know we picked the best one. Your book was wonderful, easy to follow, very accurate, and good on pointing out eating places, informal as well as formal. When we saw other people using your book, we would look at each other and smile.

Our editors and writers are deeply committed to making every Fodor's guide "the best one"—not only accurate but always charming, brimming with sound recommendations and solid ideas, right on the mark in describing restaurants and hotels, and full of fascinating facts that make you view what you've traveled to see in a rich new light.

About Our Writers

Our success in achieving our goals—and in helping to make your trip the best of all possible vacations—is a credit to the hard work of our extraordinary writers.

Québec is the preserve of writers associated with *The Gazette* of Montréal. **Dorothy Guinan,** who wrote the Province of Québec chapter, does political research for the daily; **Donna Nebenzahl,** who edits the *Woman News* section, updated the Québec City and Province of Québec chapters. **Paul Waters,** the paper's travel editor, is the expert who handled the Montréal chapter.

We'd also like to thank the Canadian Consulate General office in New York; Tourism Québec, particularly Pierre Tougas and Marie Dubé; and the Greater Québec Area Tourism and Convention Bureau, especially Richard Séguin and Monique Després.

New This Year

This year we've reformatted our guides to make them easier to use. Each chap-

ter of *Montréal & Québec City* begins with brand-new recommended itineraries to help you decide what to see in the time you have; a section called When to Tour points out the optimal time of day, day of the week, and season for your journey. You may also notice our fresh graphics, new in 1996. More readable and more helpful than ever? We think so—and we hope you do, too.

Also check out Fodor's Web site (http:// www.fodors.com/), where you'll find travel information on major destinations around the world and an ever-changing array of travel-savvy interactive features.

How to Use This Book

Organization

Up front is the **Gold Guide.** Its first section, **Important Contacts A to Z,** gives addresses and telephone numbers of organizations and companies that offer destination-related services and detailed information and publications. **Smart Travel Tips A to Z,** the Gold Guide's second section, gives specific information on how to accomplish what you need to in Montréal and Québec City as well as tips on savvy traveling. Both sections are in alphabetical order by topic.

The book starts with the urban landscapes of Montréal and Québec City. Each city chapter begins with an Exploring section, which is subdivided by neighborhood; each subsection recommends a walking or driving tour and lists sights in alphabetical order. The Province of Québec chapter guides you to and through the countryside near both cities. It is divided by geographical area; within each area, towns are covered in logical geographical order, and attractive stretches of road and minor points of interest between them are indicated by the designation En Route. Throughout, Off the Beaten Path sights appear after the places from which they are most easily accessible. And within town sections, all restaurants and lodgings are grouped together.

To help you decide what to visit in the time you have, all chapters begin with recommended itineraries. The A to Z section that ends all chapters covers getting there, getting around, and helpful contacts and resources.

Icons and Symbols

★ Our special recommendations
✕ Restaurant
🏠 Lodging establishment
✕🏠 Lodging establishment whose restaurant warrants a detour
🏕 Campground
🦆 Rubber duckie (good for kids)
☞ Sends you to another section of the guide for more information
✉ Address
☎ Telephone number
FAX Fax number
⊙ Opening and closing times
💲 Admission prices (those we give apply only to adults; substantially reduced fees are almost always available for children, students, and senior citizens)

Numbers in white and black circles—②
and ❷, for example—that appear on the maps, in the margins, and within the tours correspond to one another.

Currency

Unless otherwise stated, prices are quoted in Canadian dollars.

Dining and Lodging

The restaurants and lodgings we list are the cream of the crop in each price range. Price charts appear in the Pleasures and Pastimes section that follows each chapter introduction.

Hotel Facilities

We always list the facilities that are available—but we don't specify whether they cost extra: When pricing accommodations, always ask what's included.

Assume that hotels operate on the **European Plan** (EP, with no meals) unless we note that they use the **American Plan** (AP, with all meals), the **Modified American Plan** (MAP, with breakfast and dinner daily), or the **Continental Plan** (CP, with a Continental breakfast daily).

Restaurant Reservations and Dress Codes

Reservations are always a good idea; we note only when they're essential or when they are not accepted. Book as far ahead as you can, and reconfirm when you get to town. Unless otherwise noted, the restaurants listed are open daily for lunch and dinner. We mention dress only when men are required to wear a jacket or a jacket and tie.

Credit Cards

The following abbreviations are used: **AE,** American Express; **DC,** Diners Club; **MC,** MasterCard; and **V,** Visa.

Don't Forget to Write

You can use this book in the confidence that all prices and opening times are based on information supplied to us at press time; Fodor's cannot accept responsibility for any errors. Time inevitably brings changes, so always confirm information when it matters—especially if you're making a detour to visit a specific place. In addition, when making reservations be sure to mention if you have a disability or are traveling with children, if you prefer a private bath or a certain type of bed, or if you have specific dietary needs or any other concerns.

Were the restaurants we recommended as described? Did our hotel picks exceed your expectations? Did you find a museum we recommended a waste of time? If you have complaints, we'll look into them and revise our entries when the facts warrant it. If you've discovered a special place that we haven't included, we'll pass the information along to our correspondents and have them check it out. So send your feedback, positive *and* negative, to the Montréal & Québec City Editor at 201 East 50th Street, New York, New York 10022—and have a wonderful trip!

Karen Cure
Editorial Director

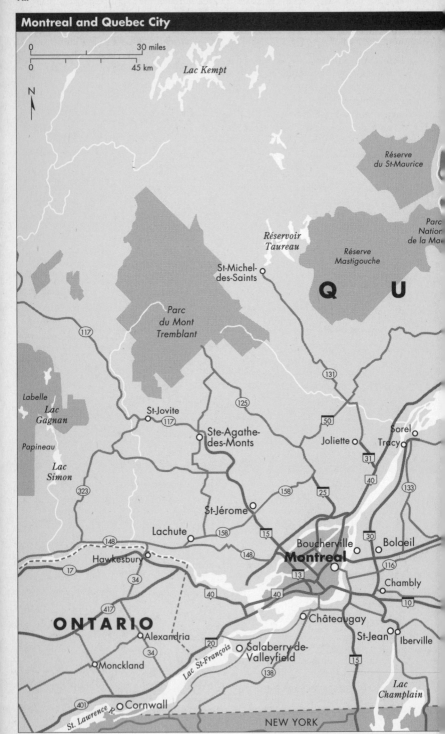

0   30 miles
0   45 km

Lac Kempt

N

Réserve du St-Maurice

Réserve Mastigouche

Réservoir Taureau

St-Michel-des-Saints

Parc Nation de la Mat

Q   U

Parc du Mont Tremblant

117

125

131

Labelle

Lac Gagnan

St-Jovite

117

50

Sorel

Papineau

Ste-Agathe-des-Monts

Joliette

Tracy

31

Lac Simon

323

158

25

40

133

St-Jérome

Lachute

158

15

30

Boucherville

Boloeil

148

Hawkesbury

148

Montreal

116

17

34

13

Chambly

40

40

10

417

ONTARIO

Châteaugay

Alexandria

20

St-Jean

Iberville

34

Lac St-François

Salaberry-de-Valleyfield

15

Monckland

138

Lac Champlain

401

Cornwall

St. Lawrence R.

NEW YORK

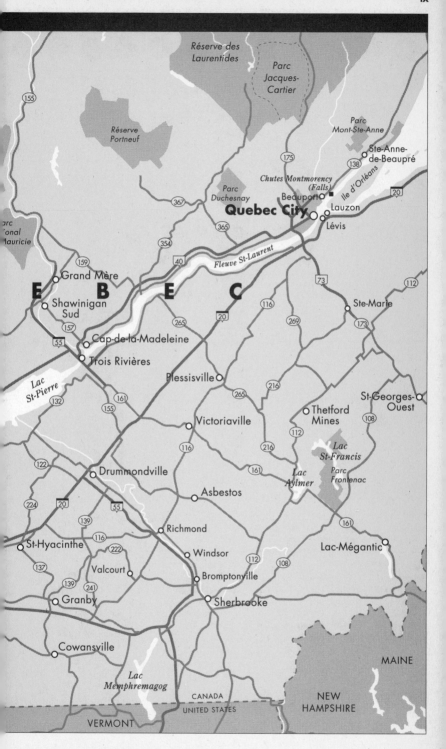

Réserve des Laurentides

Parc Jacques-Cartier

Parc Mont-Ste-Anne

Ste-Anne-de-Beaupré

155

Réserve Portneuf

175

138

arc onal lauricie

Chutes Montmorency (Falls)

Parc Duchesnay

Beauport

Île d'Orléans

367

Quebec City

Lauzon

20

365

Lévis

354

40

Fleuve St-Laurent

159

73

112

E **B** **E** **C**

Grand Mère

116

Ste-Marie

Shawinigan Sud

265

20

269

173

157

55

Cap-de-la-Madeleine

216

St-Georges-Ouest

Trois Rivières

Plessisville

108

Lac St-Pierre

161

265

112

132

155

Victoriaville

Thetford Mines

Lac St-Francis

122

116

216

Parc Frontenac

Drummondville

161

Lac Aylmer

224

20

Asbestos

161

55

139

Lac-Mégantic

St-Hyacinthe

116

Richmond

137

222

Windsor

112

108

139

Valcourt

241

Bromptonville

Granby

Sherbrooke

Cowansville

MAINE

Lac Memphrémagog

CANADA

NEW HAMPSHIRE

UNITED STATES

VERMONT

World Time Zones

MONDAY
SUNDAY

International Date Line

+12 +13

-9

-10

-11

-10

+11

+12

-4

-3

0

25

3

7

4

-5 -4

-7

14 15

-3:30

8

9

13

5 -8

16

-6

17

6

10

18

12

11

-4

19

22

-5

-4

-3

20

23

21

24

-3

+11   +12 -   -11   -10   -9   -8   -7   -6   -5   -4   -3   -2

Numbers below vertical bands relate each zone to Greenwich Mean Time (0 hrs.).
Local times frequently differ from these general indications,
as indicated by light-face numbers on map.

Algiers, **29**	Berlin, **34**	Delhi, **48**	Istanbul, **40**
Anchorage, **3**	Bogotá, **19**	Denver, **8**	Jerusalem, **42**
Athens, **41**	Budapest, **37**	Djakarta, **53**	Johannesburg, **44**
Auckland, **1**	Buenos Aires, **24**	Dublin, **26**	Lima, **20**
Baghdad, **46**	Caracas, **22**	Edmonton, **7**	Lisbon, **28**
Bangkok, **50**	Chicago, **9**	Hong Kong, **56**	London
Beijing, **54**	Copenhagen, **33**	Honolulu, **2**	(Greenwich), **27**
	Dallas, **10**		Los Angeles, **6**
			Madrid, **38**
			Manila, **57**

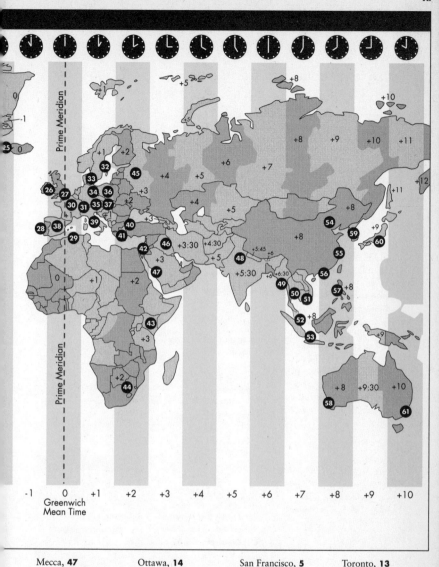

-1 0 +1 +2 +3 +4 +5 +6 +7 +8 +9 +10
Greenwich
Mean Time

Mecca, **47**
Mexico City, **12**
Miami, **18**
Montréal, **15**
Moscow, **45**
Nairobi, **43**
New Orleans, **11**
New York City, **16**

Ottawa, **14**
Paris, **30**
Perth, **58**
Reykjavík, **25**
Rio de Janeiro, **23**
Rome, **39**
Saigon (Ho Chi Minh City), **51**

San Francisco, **5**
Santiago, **21**
Seoul, **59**
Shanghai, **55**
Singapore, **52**
Stockholm, **32**
Sydney, **61**
Tokyo, **60**

Toronto, **13**
Vancouver, **4**
Vienna, **35**
Warsaw, **36**
Washington, D.C., **17**
Yangon, **49**
Zürich, **31**

IMPORTANT CONTACTS A TO Z

*An Alphabetical Listing of Publications,
Organizations, and Companies that Will Help You
Before, During, and After Your Trip*

A

AIR TRAVEL

The major gateways to Montréal are **Dorval Airport** (☎ 514/633–3105), 22½ kilometers (14 miles) west of the city, and **Mirabel International** (☎ 514/393–3333), 54½ kilometers (31 miles) northwest of the city. Québec City's **Jean Lesage International Airport** (☎ 418/640–2600) is in the suburb of Ste-Foy, 19 kilometers (12 miles) from downtown. You usually have to stop in Montréal, Toronto, or Ottawa and take one of the regional commuter lines.

CARRIERS

To Montréal➤ Contact **Air Canada** (☎ 800/776–3000), **American Airlines** (☎ 800/433–7300), **Continental** (☎ 800/525–0280), **Delta** (☎ 514/337–5520 or 800/221–1212; in Québec province, 800/361–1970), **Northwest** (☎ 800/225–2525), **United** (☎ 800/722–5243), or **USAir** (☎ 800/428–4322).

To Québec City➤ Commuter airlines that serve the city include Air Canada's **Air Alliance** (☎ 418/692–0770 or 800/361–8620), which has a daily flight direct from Newark, New Jersey, and **Canadian Airlines International** (☎ 418/692–1031).

From the U.K.➤ **British Airways** (☎ 0181/897–4000; outside London, 0345/222–111) flies daily to Montréal where connections can be made to Québec City.

FLYING TIME

Flying time to Montréal is 1½ hours from New York, 2 hours from Chicago, 6 hours from Los Angeles, 6½ hours from London.

COMPLAINTS

To register complaints about charter and scheduled airlines, contact the U.S. Department of Transportation's **Aviation Consumer Protection Division** (✉ C-75, Washington, DC 20590, ☎ 202/366–2220). Complaints about lost baggage or ticketing problems and safety concerns may also be logged with the **Federal Aviation Administration (FAA) Consumer Hotline** (☎ 800/322–7873).

CONSOLIDATORS

For the names of reputable air-ticket consolidators, contact the **United States Air Consolidators Association** (✉ 925 L St., Suite 220, Sacramento, CA 95814, ☎ 916/441–4166, ℻ 916/441–3520). For discount air-ticketing agencies, *see* Discounts & Deals, *below.*

PUBLICATIONS

For information about charter carriers, ask for the Department of Transportation's free brochure **"Plane Talk: Public Charter Flights"** (✉ Aviation Consumer Protection Division, C-75, Washington, DC 20590, ☎ 202/366–2220). The department also publishes a 58-page booklet, **"Fly Rights,"** available from the Consumer Information Center (✉ Supt. of Documents, Dept. 136C, Pueblo, CO 81009; $1.75).

For other tips and hints, consult the Consumers Union's monthly **"Consumer Reports Travel Letter"** (✉ Box 53629, Boulder, CO 80322, ☎ 800/234–1970; $39 1st year).

B

BETTER BUSINESS BUREAU

For contacts in the hometown of a tour operator you may be considering, consult the **Council of Better Business Bureaus** (✉ 4200 Wilson Blvd., Suite 800, Arlington, VA 22203, ☎ 703/276–0100, ℻ 703/525–8277).

BUS TRAVEL

Greyhound (✉ 222 1st Ave. SW, Calgary, Alberta, T2P 0A6, ☎ 403/265–9111 or 800/231–2222) has the most widespread bus service to Canada, and you can get from almost any point in the United

States to almost any point in Canada on its extensive network.

WITHIN CANADA

The bus is an essential form of transportation in Canada, especially if you want to visit out-of-the-way towns that do not have airports or rail lines. Two major bus companies, **Greyhound** (☞ *above*) and **Voyageur** (✉ 505 E. Boulevard Maisonneuve Montréal, H2L 1Y4, ☎ 514/843–4231), offer interprovincial service. In the United Kingdom, contact **Greyhound International** ✉ Sussex House, London Road, E. Grinstead, East Sussex, RHI9 1LD (☎ 01342/317317).

C

CAR RENTAL

The major car-rental companies represented in Montréal and Québec are **Alamo** (☎ 800/327–9633; in the U.K., 0800/272–2000), **Avis** (☎ 800/331–1084; in Canada, 800/879–2847), **Budget** (☎ 800/527–0700; in the U.K., 0800/181181), **Dollar** (☎ 800/800–4000; in the U.K., 0990/565656, where it is known as Eurodollar), **Hertz** (☎ 800/654–3001; in Canada, 800/263–0600; in the U.K., 0345/555888), and **National InterRent** (sometimes known as Europcar InterRent outside North America; ☎ 800/227–3876; in the U.K., 01345/222525). In Montréal, rates begin at $29 a day and $203 a week for an economy car with unlimited mileage. This does not include tax on car rentals, which is 14%.

CHILDREN & TRAVEL

FLYING

Look into **"Flying with Baby"** (✉ Third Street Press, Box 261250, Littleton, CO 80163, ☎ 303/595–5959; $4.95 includes shipping), cowritten by a flight attendant. **"Kids and Teens in Flight,"** free from the U.S. Department of Transportation's Aviation Consumer Protection Division (✉ C-75, Washington, DC 20590, ☎ 202/366–2220), offers tips on children flying alone. Every two years the February issue of *Family Travel Times* (☞ Know-How, *below*) details children's services on three dozen airlines. **"Flying Alone, Handy Advice for Kids Traveling Solo"** is available free from the American Automobile Association (AAA) (✉ send stamped, self-addressed, legal-size envelope: Flying Alone, Mail Stop 800, 1000 AAA Dr., Heathrow, FL 32746).

KNOW-HOW

Family Travel Times, published quarterly by Travel with Your Children (✉ TWYCH, 40 5th Ave., New York, NY 10011, ☎ 212/477–5524; $40 per year), covers destinations, types of vacations, and modes of travel.

CUSTOMS

U.S. CITIZENS

The **U.S. Customs Service** (✉ Box 7407, Washington, DC 20044, ☎ 202/927–6724) can answer questions on duty-free

limits and publishes a helpful brochure, "Know Before You Go." For information on registering foreign-made articles, call 202/927–0540 or write U.S. Customs Service, Resource Management, 1301 Constitution Ave. NW, Washington DC, 20229.

COMPLAINTS➤ Note the inspector's badge number and write to the commissioner's office (✉ 1301 Constitution Ave. NW, Washington, DC 20229).

U.K. CITIZENS

HM Customs and Excise (✉ Dorset House, Stamford St., London SE1 9NG, ☎ 0171/202–4227) can answer questions about U.K. customs regulations and publishes a free pamphlet, **"A Guide for Travellers,"** detailing standard procedures and import rules.

D

DISABILITIES & ACCESSIBILITY

COMPLAINTS

To register complaints under the provisions of the Americans with Disabilities Act, contact the U.S. Department of Justice's **Disability Rights Section** (✉ Box 66738, Washington, DC 20035, ☎ 202/514–0301 or 800/514–0301, ℻ 202/307–1198, TTY 202/514–0383 or 800/514–0383). For airline-related problems, contact the U.S. Department of Transportation's **Aviation Consumer Protection Division** (☞ Air Travel, *above*). For complaints about surface transportation, contact the

Department of Transportation's **Civil Rights Office** (⌗ 400 7th St. SW, Room 10215, Washington DC, 20590 ☎ 202/366–4648).

ORGANIZATIONS

TRAVELERS WITH HEARING IMPAIRMENTS➤ The **American Academy of Otolaryngology** (⌗ 1 Prince St., Alexandria, VA 22314, ☎ 703/836–4444, FAX 703/683–5100, TTY 703/519–1585) publishes a brochure, "Travel Tips for Hearing Impaired People."

TRAVELERS WITH MOBILITY PROBLEMS➤ Contact **Mobility International USA** (⌗ Box 10767, Eugene, OR 97440, ☎ and TTY 541/343–1284, FAX 541/343–6812), the U.S. branch of a Belgium-based organization (☞ *below*) with affiliates in 30 countries; **MossRehab Hospital Travel Information Service** (☎ 215/456–9600, TTY 215/456–9602), a telephone information resource for travelers with physical disabilities; the **Society for the Advancement of Travel for the Handicapped** (⌗ 347 5th Ave., Suite 610, New York, NY 10016, ☎ 212/447–7284, FAX 212/725–8253; membership $45); and **Travelin' Talk** (⌗ Box 3534, Clarksville, TN 37043, ☎ 615/552–6670, FAX 615/552–1182), which provides local contacts worldwide for travelers with disabilities.

TRAVELERS WITH VISION IMPAIRMENTS➤ Contact the **American Council of the Blind** (⌗ 1155 15th St. NW, Suite

720, Washington, DC 20005, ☎ 202/467–5081, FAX 202/467–5085) for a list of travelers' resources or the **American Foundation for the Blind** (⌗ 11 Penn Plaza, Suite 300, New York, NY 10001, ☎ 212/502–7600 or 800/232–5463, TTY 212/502–7662), which provides general advice and publishes "Access to Art" ($19.95), a directory of museums that accommodate travelers with vision impairments.

IN THE U.K.

Contact the **Royal Association for Disability and Rehabilitation** (⌗ RADAR, 12 City Forum, 250 City Rd., London EC1V 8AF, ☎ 0171/250–3222) or **Mobility International** (⌗ rue de Manchester 25, B-1080 Brussels, Belgium, ☎ 00–322–410–6297, FAX 00–322–410–6874), an international travel-information clearinghouse for people with disabilities.

PUBLICATIONS

Several publications for travelers with disabilities are available from the **Consumer Information Center** (⌗ Box 100, Pueblo, CO 81009, ☎ 719/948–3334). Call or write for its free catalog of current titles. The Society for the Advancement of Travel for the Handicapped (☞ Organizations, *above*) publishes the quarterly magazine **"Access to Travel"** ($13 for 1-year subscription).

The 500-page *Travelin' Talk Directory* (⌗ Box 3534, Clarksville, TN 37043, ☎ 615/552–

6670, FAX 615/552–1182; $35) lists people and organizations who help travelers with disabilities. For travel agents worldwide, consult the *Directory of Travel Agencies for the Disabled* (⌗ Twin Peaks Press, Box 129, Vancouver, WA 98666, ☎ 360/694–2462 or 800/637–2256, FAX 360/696–3210; $19.95 plus $3 shipping).

TRAVEL AGENCIES & TOUR OPERATORS

The Americans with Disabilities Act requires that all travel firms serve the needs of all travelers. That said, you should note that some agencies and operators specialize in making travel arrangements for individuals and groups with disabilities, among them **Access Adventures** (⌗ 206 Chestnut Ridge Rd., Rochester, NY 14624, ☎ 716/889–9096), run by a former physical-rehab counselor.

TRAVELERS WITH MOBILITY PROBLEMS➤ Contact **Hinsdale Travel Service** (⌗ 201 E. Ogden Ave., Suite 100, Hinsdale, IL 60521, ☎ 708/325–1335), a travel agency that benefits from the advice of wheelchair traveler Janice Perkins; and **Wheelchair Journeys** (⌗ 16979 Redmond Way, Redmond, WA 98052, ☎ 206/885–2210 or 800/313–4751), which can handle arrangements worldwide.

TRAVELERS WITH DEVELOPMENTAL DISABILITIES➤ Contact the nonprofit **New Directions** (⌗ 5276 Hollister Ave., Suite 207, Santa

Barbara, CA 93111,
☎ 805/967–2841).

TRAVEL GEAR

The **Magellan's** catalog
(☎ 800/962–4943,
FAX 805/568–5406),
includes a section
devoted to products
designed for travelers
with disabilities.

AIRFARES

For the lowest airfares
to Montréal and
Québec, call 800/
FLY–4–LES.

CLUBS

Contact **Entertainment
Travel Editions** (✉ Box
1068, Trumbull, CT
06611, ☎ 800/445–
4137; $28–$53, de-
pending on destination),
Great American Traveler
(✉ Box 27965, Salt
Lake City, UT 84127,
☎ 800/548–2812;
$49.95 per year), **Mo-
ment's Notice Discount
Travel Club** (✉ 7301
New Utrecht Ave.,
Brooklyn, NY 11204,
☎ 718/234–6295; $25
per year, single or fam-
ily), **Privilege Card
International** (✉ 3391
Peachtree Rd. NE,
Suite 110, Atlanta, GA
30326, ☎ 404/262–
0222 or 800/236–9732;
$74.95 per year), **Travel-
ers Advantage** (✉ CUC
Travel Service, 49 Music
Sq. W, Nashville, TN
37203, ☎ 800/548–
1116 or 800/648–4037;
$49 per year, single or
family), or **Worldwide
Discount Travel Club**
(✉ 1674 Meridian Ave.,
Miami Beach, FL
33139, ☎ 305/534–
2082; $50 per year for
family, $40 single).

PASSES

See Train Travel, *below.*

STUDENTS

Members of Hostelling
International–American
Youth Hostels (☞
Students, *below*) are
eligible for discounts on
car rentals, admissions
to attractions, and other
selected travel expenses.

PUBLICATIONS

Consult *The Frugal
Globetrotter,* by Bruce
Northam (✉ Fulcrum
Publishing, 350 Indiana
St., Suite 350, Golden,
CO 80401, ☎ 800/
992–2908; $16.95 plus
$4 shipping). For publi-
cations that tell how to
find the lowest prices
on plane tickets, *see* Air
Travel, *above.*

AUTO CLUBS

Members of the Auto-
mobile Association of
America (AAA) can
contact the **Canadian
Automobile Association**
(✉ 1775 Courtwood
Crescent, Ottawa,
Ontario K2C 3J2, ☎
613/226–7631; emer-
gency road service, ☎
800/336–4357). Mem-
bers of the Automobile
Association of Great
Britain, the Royal Auto-
mobile Club, the Royal
Scottish Automobile
Club, the Royal Irish
Automobile Club and
the automobile clubs of
the Alliance Interna-
tionale de Tourisme
(AIT) and Fédération
Internationale de l'Auto-
mobile (FIA) are entitled
to all the services of the
CAA on presentation of
a membership card.

ORGANIZATIONS

The **International Gay
Travel Association** (✉

Box 4974, Key West,
FL 33041, ☎ 800/448–
8550, FAX 305/296–
6633), a consortium of
more than 1,000 travel
companies, can supply
names of gay-friendly
travel agents, tour
operators, and accom-
modations.

PUBLICATIONS

The 16-page monthly
newsletter **"Out &
About"** (✉ 8 W. 19th
St., Suite 401, New
York, NY 10011, ☎
212/645–6922 or 800/
929–2268, FAX 800/
929–2215; $49 for 10
issues and quarterly
calendar) covers gay-
friendly resorts, hotels,
cruise lines, and air-
lines.

TOUR OPERATORS

Toto Tours (✉ 1326 W.
Albion Ave., Suite 3W,
Chicago, IL 60626, ☎
312/274–8686 or 800/
565–1241, FAX 312/
274–8695) offers group
tours to worldwide
destinations.

TRAVEL AGENCIES

The largest agencies
serving gay travelers
are **Advance Travel**
(✉ 10700 Northwest
Fwy., Suite 160, Hous-
ton, TX 77092, ☎ 713/
682–2002 or 800/292–
0500), **Club Travel** (✉
8739 Santa Monica
Blvd., West Hollywood,
CA 90069, ☎ 310/
358–2200 or 800/429–
8747), **Islanders/
Kennedy Travel** (✉ 183
W. 10th St., New York,
NY 10014, ☎ 212/
242–3222 or 800/988–
1181), **Now Voyager**
(✉ 4406 18th St., San
Francisco, CA 94114,
☎ 415/626–1169 or
800/255–6951), and
Yellowbrick Road (✉
1500 W. Balmoral Ave.,
Chicago, IL 60640,

☎ 312/561–1800 or 800/642–2488). **Skylink Women's Travel** (✉ 2460 W. 3rd St., Suite 215, Santa Rosa, CA 95401, ☎ 707/570–0105 or 800/225–5759) serves lesbian travelers.

H
HEALTH

MEDICAL ASSISTANCE COMPANIES

The following companies are concerned primarily with emergency medical assistance, although they may provide some insurance as part of their coverage. For a list of full-service travel insurance companies, *see* Insurance, *below.*

Contact **International SOS Assistance** (✉ Box 11568, Philadelphia, PA 19116, ☎ 215/244–1500 or 800/523–8930; Box 466, Pl. Bonaventure, Montréal, Québec H5A 1C1, ☎ 514/874–7674 or 800/363–0263; 7 Old Lodge Pl., St. Margarets, Twickenham TW1 1RQ, England, ☎ 0181/744–0033), **Medex Assistance Corporation** (✉ Box 5375, Timonium, MD 21094, ☎ 410/453–6300 or 800/537–2029), **Near Travel Services** (✉ Box 1339, Calumet City, IL 60409, ☎ 708/868–6700 or 800/654–6700), **Traveler's Emergency Network** (✉ 1133 15th St. NW, Suite 400, Washington DC, 20005, ☎ 202/828–5894 or 800/275–4836, FAX 202/828–5896), **TravMed** (✉ Box 5375, Timonium, MD 21094, ☎ 410/453–6380 or 800/732–5309), or **Worldwide Assistance Services**

(✉ 1133 15th St. NW, Suite 400, Washington, DC 20005, ☎ 202/331–1609 or 800/821–2828, FAX 202/828–5896).

I
INSURANCE

IN CANADA

Contact **Mutual of Omaha** (✉ Travel Division, 500 University Ave., Toronto, Ontario M5G 1V8, ☎ 800/465–0267 in Canada or 416/598–4083).

IN THE U.S.

Travel insurance covering baggage, health, and trip cancellation or interruptions is available from **Access America** (✉ 6600 W. Broad St., Richmond, VA 23230, ☎ 804/285–3300 or 800/334–7525), **Carefree Travel Insurance** (✉ Box 9366, 100 Garden City Plaza, Garden City, NY 11530, ☎ 516/294–0220 or 800/323–3149), **Tele-Trip** (✉ Mutual of Omaha Plaza, Box 31716, Omaha, NE 68131, ☎ 800/228–9792), **Travel Guard International** (✉ 1145 Clark St., Stevens Point, WI 54481, ☎ 715/345–0505 or 800/826–1300), **Travel Insured International** (✉ Box 280568, East Hartford, CT 06128, ☎ 203/528–7663 or 800/243–3174), and **Wallach & Company** (✉ 107 W. Federal St., Box 480, Middleburg, VA 22117, ☎ 540/687–3166 or 800/237–6615).

IN THE U.K.

The **Association of British Insurers** (✉ 51

Gresham St., London EC2V 7HQ, ☎ 0171/600–3333) gives advice by phone and publishes the free pamphlet **"Holiday Insurance and Motoring Abroad,"** which sets out typical policy provisions and costs.

L
LODGING

APARTMENT & VILLA RENTAL

Among the companies to contact are **Property Rentals International** (✉ 1008 Mansfield Crossing Rd., Richmond, VA 23236, ☎ 804/378–6054 or 800/220–3332, FAX 804/379–2073) and **Rent-a-Home International** (✉ 7200 34th Ave. NW, Seattle, WA 98117, ☎ 206/789–9377 or 800/488–7368, FAX 206/789–9379, rentahomeinternational @msn.com). Members of the travel club **Hideaways International** (✉ 767 Islington St., Portsmouth, NH 03801, ☎ 603/430–4433 or 800/843–4433, FAX 603/430–4444, info@hideaways.com; $99 per year) receive two annual guides plus quarterly newsletters and arrange rentals among themselves.

HOME EXCHANGE

One of the principal clearinghouses is **Home-Link International/ Vacation Exchange Club** (✉ Box 650, Key West, FL 33041, ☎ 305/294–1448 or 800/638–3841, FAX 305/294–1148; $78 per year), which sends members five annual directories, with a listing in one, plus updates.

HOTELS

The major hotel chains in Canada include **Best Western International** (☎ 800/528–1234, in the U.K., 0181/541–0033), **CP (Canadian Pacific) Hotels & Resorts** (☎ 800/828–7447, in the U.K., 0800/898852), **Choice Hotels International** (☎ 800/424–6423, in the U.K. 0800/444–4444), **Days Inns** (☎ 800/325–2525, in the U.K. 01483/440470), **Delta Hotels** (☎ 800/877–1133, in the U.K., 0171/937–8033), **Four Seasons Hotels** (☎ 800/332–3442, in the U.K., 0800/526648), **Holiday Inns** (☎ 800/465–4329, in the U.K., 0800/897121), **Hyatt Hotels** (☎ 800/223–1234, in the U.K. 0171/580–8197), **Marriott Hotels and Resorts** (☎ 800/228–9290, in the U.K., 0800/282811), **Radisson Hotels** (☎ 800/333–3333, in the U.K., 0800/891999), **Ramada** (☎ 800/228–2828, in the U.K., 0181/688–1418), **Relais & Châteaux** (☎ 800/743–8033; 800/677–3524 for reservations), **Sheraton** (☎ 800/325–3535, in the U.K., 0800/353535), **Travelodge** (☎ 800/255–3050, in the U.K., 0345/404040), and **Westin Hotels** (☎ 800/228–3000, in the U.K., 0171/408–0636).

M

ATMS

For specific **Cirrus** locations in the United States and Canada, call 800/424–7787. For U.S. **Plus** locations, call 800/843–7587 and enter the area code and first three digits of the number from which you're calling (or of the calling area in which you want to locate an ATM).

CURRENCY EXCHANGE

If your bank doesn't exchange currency, contact **Thomas Cook Currency Services** (☎ 800/287–7362 for locations). **Ruesch International** (☎ 800/424–2923 for locations) can also provide you with foreign banknotes before you leave home and publishes a number of useful brochures, including a "Foreign Currency Guide" and "Foreign Exchange Tips."

WIRING FUNDS

Funds can be wired via **MoneyGram℠** (for locations and information in the U.S. and Canada, ☎ 800/926–9400) or **Western Union** (for agent locations or to send money using MasterCard or Visa, ☎ 800/325–6000; in Canada, 800/321–2923; in the U.K., 0800/833833; or visit the Western Union office at the nearest major post office).

P

For strategies on packing light, get a copy of *The Packing Book,* by Judith Gilford (⊠ Ten Speed Press, Box 7123, Berkeley, CA 94707, ☎ 510/559–1600 or 800/841–2665, FAX 510/524–4588; $7.95 plus $3.50 shipping).

U.K. CITIZENS

For fees, documentation requirements, and to request an emergency passport, call the **London Passport Office** (☎ 0990/210410).

The **Kodak Information Center** (☎ 800/242–2424) answers consumer questions about film and photography. The *Kodak Guide to Shooting Great Travel Pictures* (available in bookstores; or contact Fodor's Travel Publications, ☎ 800/533–6478; $16.50 plus $4 shipping) explains how to take expert travel photographs.

S

"Trouble-Free Travel," from the AAA, is a booklet of tips for protecting yourself and your belongings when away from home. Send a stamped, self-addressed, legal-size envelope to Trouble-Free Travel (⊠ Mail Stop 75, 1000 AAA Dr., Heathrow, FL 32746).

CLUBS

Sears's **Mature Outlook** (⊠ Box 10448, Des Moines, IA 50306, ☎ 800/336–6330; annual membership $14.95) includes a lifestyle/travel magazine and membership in ITC-50 travel club, which offers discounts of up to 50% at participating hotels and restaurants. (☞ Discounts & Deals *in*

THE GOLD GUIDE / IMPORTANT CONTACTS

Smart Travel Tips A to Z).

EDUCATIONAL TRAVEL

The nonprofit **Elderhostel** (⊠ 75 Federal St., 3rd Floor, Boston, MA 02110, ☎ 617/426–7788), for people 55 and older, has offered inexpensive study programs since 1975. Courses cover everything from marine science to Greek mythology and cowboy poetry. Fees for programs in the United States and Canada, which usually last one week, run about $300, not including transportation.

ORGANIZATIONS

Contact the **American Association of Retired Persons** (⊠ AARP, 601 E St. NW, Washington, DC 20049, ☎ 202/434–2277; annual dues $8 per person or couple). Its Purchase Privilege Program secures discounts for members on lodging, car rentals, and sightseeing, and the AARP Motoring Plan (☎ 800/334–3300) furnishes domestic trip-routing information and emergency road-service aid for an annual fee of $39.95 ($59.95 for a premium version). Senior citizen travelers can also join the AAA for emergency road service and other travel benefits (☞ Driving, *above, and* Discounts & Deals *in* Smart Travel Tips A to Z).

GROUPS

A major tour operator specializing in student travel is **Contiki Holidays** (⊠ 300 Plaza Alicante, Suite 900,

Garden Grove, CA 92640, ☎ 714/740–0808 or 800/266–8454).

HOSTELING

In the United States, contact **Hostelling International–American Youth Hostels** (⊠ 733 15th St. NW, Suite 840, Washington, DC 20005, ☎ 202/783–6161, FAX 202/783–6171); in Canada, **Hostelling International–Canada** (⊠ 205 Catherine St., Suite 400, Ottawa, Ontario K2P 1C3, ☎ 613/237–7884); and in the United Kingdom, the **Youth Hostel Association of England and Wales** (⊠ Trevelyan House, 8 St. Stephen's Hill, St. Albans, Hertfordshire AL1 2DY, ☎ 01727/855215 or 01727/845047). Membership (in the U.S., $25; in Canada, C$26.75; in the U.K., £9.30) gives you access to 5,000 hostels in 77 countries that charge $5–$40 per person per night.

ORGANIZATIONS

A major contact is the **Council on International Educational Exchange** (⊠ mail orders only: CIEE, 205 E. 42nd St., 16th Floor, New York, NY 10017, ☎ 212/822–2600, FAX 212/822–2699, info@ciee.org). The **Educational Travel Centre** (⊠ 438 N. Frances St., Madison, WI 53703, ☎ 608/256–5551 or 800/747–5551, FAX 608/256–2042) offers rail passes and low-cost airline tickets, mostly for flights that depart from Chicago.

In Canada, also contact **Travel Cuts** (⊠ 187 College St., Toronto,

Ontario M5T 1P7, ☎ 416/979–2406 or 800/667–2887).

T

Among the companies that sell tours and packages to Montréal and Québec, the following are nationally known, have a proven reputation, and offer plenty of options.

GROUP TOURS

DELUXE➤ **Globus** (⊠ 5301 S. Federal Circle, Littleton, CO 80123-2980, ☎ 303/797-2800 or 800/221–0090, FAX 303/795–0962), **Maupintour** (⊠ Box 807, 1515 St. Andrews Dr., Lawrence, KS 66047, ☎ 913/843–1211 or 800/255–4266, FAX 913/843–8351), and **Tauck Tours** (Box 5027, 276 Post Rd. W, Westport, CT 06881, ☎ 203/226–6911 or 800/468–2825, FAX 203/221–6828).

FIRST-CLASS➤ **Brennan Tours** (⊠ 1402 3rd Ave., #717, Seattle, WA 98101, ☎ 206/622–9155 or 800/237–7249) and **Collette Tours** (⊠ 162 Middle St., Pawtucket, RI 02860, ☎ 401/728-3805 or 800/832–4656).

BUDGET➤ **Cosmos** (☞ Globus, *above*).

PACKAGES

Independent vacation packages are available from major tour operators and airlines. Contact **Adventure Vacations** (⊠ 10612 Beaver Dam Rd., Hunt Valley, MD 21030-2205, ☎ 410/785–3500 or 800/638–9040, FAX 410/584–2771), **Air Canada Vacations** (☎

514/876–4141), **Delta Dream Vacations** (☎ 800/872–7786), and **USAir Vacations** (☎ 800/455–0123). **Gogo Tours**, based in Ramsey, New Jersey, sells packages to Montréal and Québec only through travel agents.

FROM THE U.K.

Travel agencies that offer cheap fares to Canada include **Trailfinders** (✉ 42–50 Earl's Court Rd., London W8 6FT, ☎ 0171/937–5400), **Travel Cuts** (✉ 295A Regent St., London W1R 7YA, ☎ 0171/637–3161; ☞ Students, *above*), and **Flightfile** (✉ 49 Tottenham Court Rd., London W1P 9RE, ☎ 0171/700–2722).

For independent self-drive itineraries, contact **Budget WorldClass Drive** (☎ 800/527–0700; in the U.K., 0800/181181).

ORGANIZATIONS

The **National Tour Association** (✉ NTA, 546 E. Main St., Lexington, KY 40508, ☎ 606/226–4444 or 800/755–8687) and the **United States Tour Operators Association** (✉ USTOA, 211 E. 51st St., Suite 12B, New York, NY 10022, ☎ 212/750–7371) can provide lists of members and information on booking tours.

PUBLICATIONS

Contact the USTOA (☞ Organizations, *above*) for its **"Smart Traveler's Planning Kit."** Pamphlets in the kit include the "Worldwide Tour and Vacation Package Finder," "How to Select a Tour or Vacation

Package," and information on the organization's consumer protection plan. Also get a copy of the Better Business Bureau's **"Tips on Travel Packages"** (✉ Publication 24-195, 4200 Wilson Blvd., Arlington, VA 22203; $2). The National Tour Association will send you **"On Tour,"** a listing of its member operators, and a personalized package of information on group travel in North America.

TRAIN TRAVEL

Amtrak (☎ 800/872–7245) currently has service from New York to Montréal, providing connections between Amtrak's U.S.-wide network and VIA Rail's Canadian routes.

Transcontinental rail service is provided by **VIA Rail Canada** (☎ 800/665–0200). In the United Kingdom, **Long-Haul Leisurail** (☎ 01733/335599) represents VIA Rail.

TRAVEL GEAR

For travel apparel, appliances, personal-care items, and other travel necessities, get a free catalog from **Magellan's** (☎ 800/962–4943, FAX 805/568–5406), **Orvis Travel** (☎ 800/541–3541, FAX 540/343–7053), or **TravelSmith** (☎ 800/950–1600, FAX 415/455–0554).

TRAVEL AGENCIES

For names of reputable agencies in your area, contact the **American Society of Travel Agents** (✉ ASTA, 1101 King St., Suite 200, Alexandria, VA 22314, ☎ 703/739–2782), the

Association of Canadian Travel Agents (✉ Suite 201, 1729 Bank St., Ottawa, Ontario K1V 7Z5, ☎ 613/521–0474, FAX 613/521–0805) or the **Association of British Travel Agents** (✉ 55-57 Newman St., London W1P 4AH, ☎ 0171/637–2444, FAX 0171/637–0713).

U
U.S.
GOVERNMENT
TRAVEL BRIEFINGS

The U.S. Department of State's American Citizens Services office (✉ Room 4811, Washington, DC 20520; enclose SASE) issues **Consular Information Sheets** on all foreign countries. These cover such issues as crime, security, political climate, and health risks as well as listing embassy locations, entry requirements, currency regulations, and providing other useful information. For the latest information, stop in at any U.S. passport office, consulate, or embassy; call the interactive hot line (☎ 202/647–5225, FAX 202/647–3000); or, with your PC's modem, tap into the department's computer bulletin board (☎ 202/647–9225).

V
VISITOR
INFORMATION

Contact **Tourisme Québec** (✉ 60 Rue D'Auteuil, Québec, PQ G1R 4C4, ☎ 800/363–7777).

IN THE U.K.

In the United Kingdom contact the **Visit Canada**

THE GOLD GUIDE / IMPORTANT CONTACTS

Center (✉ 62–65 Trafalgar Sq., London, WC2 5DT, ☎ 0891/715–000) or **Québec Tourism** (✉ 59 Pall Mall, London SW1Y 5JH, ☎ 0171/930–8314).

W
WEATHER

For current conditions and forecasts, plus the local time and helpful travel tips, call the **Weather Channel Connection** (☎ 900/932–8437; 95¢ per minute) from a Touch-Tone phone.

Environment Canada's local weather offices can provide forecasts and weather reports over the telephone.

The *International Traveler's Weather Guide* (✉ Weather Press, Box 660606, Sacramento, CA 95866, ☎ 916/974–0201 or 800/972–0201; $10.95 includes shipping), written by two meteorologists, provides month-by-month information on temperature, humidity, and precipitation in more than 175 cities worldwide.

SMART TRAVEL TIPS A TO Z

Basic Information on Traveling in Montréal and Québec and Savvy Tips to Make Your Trip a Breeze

A

AIR TRAVEL

If time is an issue, **always look for nonstop flights,** which require no change of plane. If possible, **avoid connecting flights,** which stop at least once and can involve a change of plane, even though the flight number remains the same; if the first leg is late, the second waits.

For better service, **fly smaller or regional carriers,** which often have higher passenger satisfaction ratings. Sometimes they have such in-flight amenities as leather seats or greater legroom and they often have better food.

CUTTING COSTS

The Sunday travel section of most newspapers is a good place to look for deals.

MAJOR AIRLINES➤ The least-expensive airfares from the major airlines are priced for round-trip travel and are subject to restrictions. Usually, you must **book in advance and buy the ticket within 24 hours** to get cheaper fares, and you may have to **stay over a Saturday night.** The lowest fare is subject to availability, and only a small percentage of the plane's total seats is sold at that price. It's smart to **call a number of airlines,** and **when you are quoted a good price, book it on the spot**—the same fare may not be available on the same flight the next day. Airlines generally allow you to change your return date for a $25 to $50 fee. If you don't use your ticket, you can apply the cost toward the purchase of a new ticket, again for a small charge. However, most low-fare tickets are nonrefundable. To get the lowest airfare, **check different routings.** If your destination has more than one gateway, **compare prices to different airports.**

FROM THE U.K.➤ To save money on flights, **look into an APEX or Super-Pex ticket.** APEX tickets must be booked in advance and have certain restrictions. Super-PEX tickets can be purchased right at the airport.

CONSOLIDATORS➤ Consolidators buy tickets for scheduled flights at reduced rates from the airlines, then sell them at prices below the lowest available from the airlines directly—usually without advance restrictions. Sometimes you can even get your money back if you need to return the ticket. Carefully read the fine print detailing penalties for changes and cancellations. If you doubt the reliability of a consolidator, **confirm your reservation with the airline.**

ALOFT

AIRLINE FOOD➤ If you hate airline food, **ask for special meals when booking.** These can be vegetarian, low-cholesterol, or kosher, for example; commonly prepared to order in smaller quantities than standard fare, they can be tastier.

JET LAG➤ To avoid this syndrome, which occurs when travel disrupts your body's natural cycles, try to maintain a normal routine. At night, **get some sleep.** By day, move about the cabin to **stretch your legs, eat light meals, and drink water—not alcohol.**

SMOKING➤ Smoking is not allowed on flights of six hours or less within the continental United States. Smoking is also prohibited on flights within Canada. For U.S. flights longer than six hours or international flights, **contact your carrier regarding their smoking policy.** Some carriers have prohibited smoking throughout their system; others allow smoking only on certain routes or even certain departures of that route.

B

BUSINESS HOURS

Stores, shops, and supermarkets are usually open Monday through Saturday from 9 to 6—although in major cities, supermarkets are often open from 7:30 AM until 9 PM. Blue laws are in effect in much of Canada, but a growing number of provinces have stores with limited Sunday hours, usually from noon to 5 (shops in areas highly frequented by tourists are usually open on Sunday). Retail stores are generally open on Thursday and Friday evenings, most shopping malls until 9 PM. Most banks in Canada are open Monday through Thursday from 10 to 3, and from 10 to 5 or 6 on Friday. Some banks are open longer hours and also on Saturday morning. All banks are closed on national holidays. Drugstores in major cities are often open until 11 PM, and convenience stores are often open 24 hours a day, seven days a week.

NATIONAL HOLIDAYS

National holidays for 1997 are: New Year's Day, Good Friday (March 28), Easter Monday (March 31), Victoria Day (May 19), Canada Day (July 1), Labor Day (September 1), Thanksgiving (October 13), Remembrance Day (November 11), Christmas, and Boxing Day (December 26).

St. Jean Baptiste Day (June 24) is a provincial holiday.

C

CAMERAS, CAMCORDERS, & COMPUTERS

IN TRANSIT

Always **keep your film, tape, or disks out of the sun;** never put these on the dashboard of a car.

Carry an extra supply of batteries, and **be prepared to turn on your camera, camcorder, or laptop computer for security personnel** to prove that it's real.

X-RAYS

Always **ask for hand inspection at security.** Such requests are virtually always honored at U.S. airports, and are usually accommodated abroad. Photographic film becomes clouded after successive exposure to airport X-ray machines. Videotape and computer disks are not harmed by X-rays, but **keep your tapes and disks away from metal detectors.**

CUSTOMS

Before departing, **register your foreign-made camera or laptop with U.S. Customs.** If your equipment is U.S.-made, call the consulate of the country you'll be visiting to find out whether it should be registered with local customs upon arrival.

CAR RENTAL

CUTTING COSTS

To get the best deal, **book through a travel agent who is willing to shop around.** Ask your agent to **look for fly-drive packages,** which also save you money, and **ask if local taxes are included** in the rental or fly-drive price. These can be as high as 20% in some destinations. Don't forget to find out about required deposits, cancellation penalties, drop-off charges, and the cost of any required insurance coverage.

Also **ask your travel agent about a company's customer-service record.** How has it responded to late plane arrivals and vehicle mishaps? Are there often lines at the rental counter, and—if you're traveling during a holiday period—does a confirmed reservation guarantee you a car?

Always **find out what equipment is standard** at your destination before specifying what you want; automatic transmission and air-conditioning are usually optional—and very expensive.

INSURANCE

When driving a rented car, you are generally responsible for any damage to or loss of the rental vehicle, as well as any property damage or personal injury that you cause. Before you rent, **see what coverage you already have** under the terms of your personal auto insurance policy and credit cards.

If you do not have auto insurance or an umbrella insurance policy that covers damage to third parties, purchasing CDW or LDW is highly recommended.

LICENSE REQUIREMENTS

In Canada your own driver's license is acceptable. If you have rented in the United States, be sure to keep the rental contract with you to indicate that use in Canada is authorized by the rental agency.

SURCHARGES

Before you pick up a car in one city and leave it in another, **ask about** drop-off charges or one-way service fees, which can be substantial. Note, too, that some rental agencies charge extra if you return the car before the time specified on your contract. To avoid a hefty refueling fee, **fill the tank just before you turn in the car**—but be aware that gas stations near the rental outlet may overcharge.

CHILDREN &
TRAVEL

When traveling with children, **plan ahead** and **involve your youngsters** as you outline your trip. When packing, **include a supply of things to keep them busy** en route (☞ Children & Travel *in* Important Contacts A to Z). On sightseeing days, try to **schedule activities of special interest to your children,** like a trip to a zoo or a playground. If you **plan your itinerary around seasonal festivals,** you'll never lack for things to do. In addition, **check local newspapers for special events** mounted by public libraries, museums, and parks.

BABY-SITTING

For recommended local sitters, **check with your hotel desk.**

DRIVING

If you are renting a car, don't forget to **arrange for a car seat when you reserve.** Sometimes they're free.

FLYING

As a general rule, infants under two not occupying a seat fly at greatly reduced fares and occasionally for

free. If your children are two or older **ask about special children's fares.** Age limits for these fares vary among carriers. Rules also vary regarding unaccompanied minors, so again, check with your airline.

BAGGAGE➤ In general, the adult baggage allowance applies to children paying half or more of the adult fare. If you are traveling with an infant, **ask about carry-on allowances** before departure. In general, for infants charged 10% of the adult fare you are allowed one carry-on bag and a collapsible stroller, which may have to be checked; you may be limited to less if the flight is full.

SAFETY SEATS➤ According to the FAA, it's a good idea to **use safety seats aloft** for children weighing less than 40 pounds. Airline policies vary. U.S. carriers allow FAA-approved models but usually require that you buy a ticket, even if your child would otherwise ride free, since the seats must be strapped into regular seats. However, some U.S. and foreign-flag airlines may require you to hold your baby during takeoff and landing—defeating the seat's purpose. Other foreign carriers may not allow infant seats at all, or may charge a child rather than an infant fare for their use.

FACILITIES➤ When making your reservation, **request children's meals or freestanding bassinets** if you need them; the latter are available only to those

seated at the bulkhead, where there's enough legroom. If you don't need a bassinet, **think twice before requesting bulkhead seats**—the only storage space for in-flight necessities is in inconveniently distant overhead bins.

GAMES

Milton Bradley and Parker Brothers have travel versions of some of their most popular games, including Yahtzee, Trouble, Sorry, and Monopoly. Prices run $5 to $8. Look for them in the travel section of your local toy store.

LODGING

Most hotels allow children under a certain age to stay in their parents' room at no extra charge; others charge them as extra adults. Be sure to **ask about the cutoff age.**

CUSTOMS &
DUTIES

To speed your clearance through customs, **keep receipts for all your purchases abroad** and **be ready to show the inspector what you've bought.** If you feel that you've been incorrectly or unfairly charged a duty, you can **appeal assessments in dispute.** First ask to see a supervisor. If you are still unsatisfied, **write to the port director** at your point of entry, sending your customs receipt and any other appropriate documentation. The address will be listed on your receipt. If you still don't get satisfaction, you can take your case to customs headquarters in Washington.

THE GOLD GUIDE / SMART TRAVEL TIPS

ON ARRIVAL

American and British visitors may bring in the following items duty-free: 200 cigarettes, 50 cigars, and 14 ounces of tobacco; 1 bottle (1.1 liters or 40 imperial ounces) of liquor or wine, or 24 355-milliliter (12-ounce) bottles or cans of beer for personal consumption; gifts up to the value of C$60 per gift. A deposit is sometimes required for trailers (refunded upon return). Cats and dogs must have a certificate issued by a licensed veterinarian that clearly identifies the animal and certifies that it has been vaccinated against rabies during the preceding 36 months. Plant material must be declared and inspected. With certain restrictions (some fruits and vegetables), visitors may bring food with them for their own use, providing the quantity is consistent with the duration of the visit.

Canada's firearms laws are significantly stricter than the United States's. All handguns, semi-automatic, and fully automatic weapons are prohibited and cannot be brought into the country. Sporting rifles and shotguns may be imported provided they are to be used for sporting, hunting, or competition while in Canada. All firearms must be declared to Canada Customs at the first point of entry. Failure to declare firearms will result in their seizure, and criminal charges may be made. (New legislation has just been introduced in Parliament to further tighten Canada's gun laws).

IN THE U.S.

You may bring home $400 worth of foreign goods duty-free if you've been out of the country for at least 48 hours and haven't already used the $400 allowance, or any part of it, in the past 30 days.

Travelers 21 or older may bring back 1 liter of alcohol duty-free, provided the beverage laws of the state through which they reenter the United States allow it. In addition, regardless of their age, they are allowed 100 non-Cuban cigars and 200 cigarettes. Antiques, which the U.S. Customs Service defines as objects more than 100 years old, are duty-free. Original works of art done entirely by hand are also duty-free. These include, but are not limited to, paintings, drawings, and sculptures.

Duty-free, travelers may mail packages valued at up to $200 to themselves and up to $100 to others, with a limit of one parcel per addressee per day (and no alcohol or tobacco products or perfume valued at more than $5); on the outside, the package must be labeled as being either for personal use or an unsolicited gift, and a list of its contents and their retail value must be attached. Mailed items do not affect your duty-free allowance on your return.

IN THE U.K.

From countries outside the EU, including Canada, you may import, duty-free, 200 cigarettes, 100 cigarillos, 50 cigars, or 250 grams of tobacco; 1 liter of spirits or 2 liters of fortified or sparkling wine or liqueurs; 2 liters of still table wine; 60 milliliters of perfume; 250 milliliters of toilet water; plus £136 worth of other goods, including gifts and souvenirs.

D

DISABILITIES & ACCESSIBILITY

When discussing accessibility with an operator or reservationist, ask hard questions. Are there any stairs, inside *or* out? Are there grab bars next to the toilet *and* in the shower/tub? How wide is the doorway to the room? To the bathroom? For the most extensive facilities, meeting the latest legal specifications, **opt for newer accommodations,** which more often have been designed with access in mind. Older properties or ships must usually be retrofitted and may offer more limited facilities as a result. Be sure to **discuss your needs before booking.**

DISCOUNTS & DEALS

You shouldn't have to pay for a discount. In fact, you may already be eligible for all kinds of savings. Here are some time-honored strategies for getting the best deal.

LOOK IN YOUR WALLET

When you **use your credit card to make travel purchases,** you may get free travel-accident insurance, collision damage insurance, medical or legal assistance, depending on the card and bank that issued it. American Express, Visa, and MasterCard provide one or more of these services, so **get a copy of your card's travel benefits.** If you are a member of the AAA or an oil-company-sponsored road-assistance plan, always **ask hotel or car-rental reservationists for auto-club discounts.** Some clubs offer additional discounts on tours, cruises, or admission to attractions. And don't forget that auto-club membership entitles you to free maps and trip-planning services.

SENIORS CITIZENS & STUDENTS

As a senior-citizen traveler, you may be eligible for special rates, but you should mention your senior-citizen status up front. If you're a student or under 26 you can also get discounts, especially if you have an official ID card (☞ Senior-Citizen Discounts *and* Students on the Road, *below*).

DIAL FOR DOLLARS

To save money, **look into "1-800" discount reservations services,** which often have lower rates. These services use their buying power to get a better price on hotels, airline tickets, and sometimes even car rentals. When booking a room, always **call the hotel's local toll-free number** (if one is available) rather than the central reservations

number—you'll often get a better price. Ask the reservationist about special packages or corporate rates, which are usually available even if you're not traveling on business.

JOIN A CLUB?

Discount clubs can be a legitimate source of savings, but you must use the participating hotels and visit the participating attractions in order to realize any benefits. Remember, too, that you have to pay a fee to join, so **determine if you'll save enough to warrant your membership fee.** Before booking with a club, **make sure the hotel or other supplier isn't offering a better deal.**

GET A GUARANTEE

When shopping for the best deal on hotels and car rentals, **look for guaranteed exchange rates,** which protect you against a falling dollar. With your rate locked in, you won't pay more even if the price goes up in the local currency.

DRIVING

By law, you are required to **wear seat belts** (and use infant seats). Some provinces have a statutory requirement to drive with vehicle headlights on for extended periods after dawn and before sunset.

Speed limits vary from province to province, but they are usually within the 90–100 kph (50–60 mph) range outside the cities. The price of gasoline varies more than the speed limit, from 44¢ to 63¢ a

liter. (There are 3.8 liters in a U.S. gallon, 4.5 liters in a Canadian Imperial gallon.) Distances are now always shown in kilometers, and gasoline is always sold in liters. The Imperial gallon is seldom used.

FROM THE U.S.

Drivers must have proper owner registration and proof of insurance coverage, which is compulsory in Canada. The Canadian Non-Resident Inter-Provincial Motor Vehicle Liability Insurance Card, available from any U.S. insurance company, is accepted as evidence of financial responsibility anywhere in Canada. The minimum liability coverage in Canada is $200,000, except in Québec where the minimum is $50,000. For more information, contact the Insurance Bureau of Canada (181 University Ave., Toronto, Ontario, M5H 3M7, ☎ 416/362–2301). If you are driving a car that is not registered in your name, carry a letter from the owner that authorizes your use of the vehicle.

The U.S. Interstate Highway System leads directly into Canada: I–95 from Maine to New Brunswick; I–91 and I–89 from Vermont to Québec; I–87 from New York to Québec; I–81 and a spur off I–90 from New York to Ontario; I–94, I–96, and I–75 from Michigan to Ontario; I–29 from North Dakota to Manitoba; I–15 from Montana to Alberta; and I–5 from Washington state to British Columbia.

Most of these connections hook up with the Trans-Canada Highway within a few miles. There are many smaller highway crossings between the two countries as well. From Alaska, take the Alaska Highway (from Fairbanks), the Klondike Highway (from Skagway), and the Top of the World Highway (to Dawson City).

I
INSURANCE

Travel insurance can protect your monetary investment, replace your luggage and its contents, or provide for medical coverage should you fall ill during your trip. Most tour operators, travel agents, and insurance agents sell specialized health-and-accident, flight, trip-cancellation, and luggage insurance as well as comprehensive policies with some or all of these coverages. Comprehensive policies may also reimburse you for delays due to weather—an important consideration if you're traveling during the winter months. Some health-insurance policies do not cover preexisting conditions, but waivers may be available in specific cases. Coverage is sold by the companies listed in Important Contacts A to Z; these companies act as the policy's administrators. The actual insurance is usually underwritten by a well-known name, such as The Travelers or Continental Insurance.

Before you make any purchase, **review your existing health and homeowner's policies** to find out whether they cover expenses incurred while traveling.

BAGGAGE

Airline liability for baggage is limited to $1,250 per person on domestic flights. On international flights, it amounts to $9.07 per pound or $20 per kilogram for checked baggage (roughly $640 per 70-pound bag) and $400 per passenger for unchecked baggage. Insurance for losses exceeding the terms of your airline ticket can be bought directly from the airline at check-in for about $10 per $1,000 of coverage; note that it excludes a rather extensive list of items, shown on your airline ticket.

COMPREHENSIVE

Comprehensive insurance policies include all the coverages described above plus some that may not be available in more specific policies. If you have purchased an expensive vacation, especially one that involves travel abroad, comprehensive insurance is a must; **look for policies that include trip delay insurance,** which will protect you in the event that weather problems cause you to miss your flight, tour, or cruise. A few insurers will also sell you a waiver for preexisting medical conditions. Some of the companies that offer both these features are Access America, Carefree Travel, Travel Insured International, and Travel Guard.

FLIGHT

You should **think twice before buying flight insurance.** Often purchased as a last-minute impulse at the airport, it pays a lump sum when a plane crashes, either to a beneficiary if the insured dies or sometimes to a surviving passenger who loses his or her eyesight or a limb. Supplementing the airlines' coverage described in the limits-of-liability paragraphs on your ticket, it's expensive and basically unnecessary. Charging an airline ticket to a major credit card often automatically provides you with coverage that may also extend to travel by bus, train, and ship.

HEALTH

Medicare generally does not cover health care costs outside the United States; nor do many privately issued policies. If your own health insurance policy does not cover you outside the United States, **consider buying supplemental medical coverage.** It can reimburse you for $1,000–$150,000 worth of medical and/or dental expenses incurred as a result of an accident or illness during a trip. These policies also may include a personal-accident, or death-and-dismemberment, provision, which pays a lump sum ranging from $15,000 to $500,000 to your beneficiaries if you die or to you if you lose one or more limbs or your eyesight, and a medical-assistance provision, which may either reimburse you for the cost of referrals, evacuation, or repatriation and other services, or automatically enroll you as a member of a particular medical-assistance company.

TRIP

Without insurance, you will lose all or most of your money if you cancel your trip regardless of the reason. Especially if your airline ticket, cruise, or package tour is nonrefundable and cannot be changed, it's essential that you **buy trip-cancellation-and-interruption insurance.** When considering how much coverage you need, look for a policy that will cover the cost of your trip plus the nondiscounted price of a one-way airline ticket should you need to return home early. Read the fine print carefully, especially sections that define "family member" and "preexisting medical conditions." Also **consider default or bankruptcy insurance,** which protects you against a supplier's failure to deliver. Be aware, however, that if you buy such a policy from a travel agency, tour operator, airline, or cruise line, it may not cover default by the firm in question.

U.K. TRAVELERS

You can buy an annual travel insurance policy valid for most vacations during the year in which it's purchased. If you are pregnant or have a preexisting medical condition make sure you're covered before buying such a policy.

L

LANGUAGE

Canada's two official languages are English and French. Though English is widely spoken, it may be useful to **learn a few French phrases.** Canadian French, known as Québecois or *joual,* is a colorful language often quite different from that spoken in France.

LODGING

Besides the quaint hotels of Québec, Canada's range of accommodations closely resembles that of the United States. In the cities you'll have a choice of luxury hotels, moderately priced modern properties, and smaller older hotels with perhaps fewer conveniences but a bit more charm. Canada's answer to the small European family-run hotel is the mom-and-pop motel, but even though Canada is as attuned to automobile travel as the United States, you won't find these motels as frequently. Even here you'll need to make reservations at least on the day on which you're planning to pull into town.

There is no national government rating system for hotels, but many provinces rate their accommodations. Expect accommodations to cost more in summer than in the off-season. When making reservations, **ask about special deals** and packages when reserving. Big city hotels that cater to business travelers often offer weekend packages, and many

city hotels offer rooms at up to 50% off in winter. If you're planning to visit a major city or resort area in high season, **book well in advance.** Also be aware of any special events or festivals that may coincide with your visit and fill every room for miles around. For resorts and lodges, consider the winter ski-season high as well and plan accordingly.

APARTMENT & VILLA RENTAL

If you want a home base that's roomy enough for a family and comes with cooking facilities, **consider taking a furnished rental.** This can also save you money, but not always—some rentals are luxury properties (economical only when your party is large). Home-exchange directories list rentals—often second homes owned by prospective house swappers—and some services search for a house or apartment for you (even a castle if that's your fancy) and handle the paperwork. Some send an illustrated catalog; others send photographs only of specific properties, sometimes at a charge; up-front registration fees may apply.

B&BS

One way to save on lodging and spend some time with native Canadians is to stay at a bed-and-breakfast. They can be found in both the country and the cities. Every provincial tourist board either has a listing of B&Bs or can refer you to an associa-

THE GOLD GUIDE / SMART TRAVEL TIPS

tion that will help you secure reservations. Rates range from $20 to upwards of $70 a night and include a Continental or a full breakfast. Because most bed-and-breakfasts are in private homes, you might not have your own bathroom. Some B&B hosts lock up early; be sure to ask. Room quality varies from house to house as well, so don't be bashful about asking to see a room before making a choice. **Fodor's Canada's Great Country Inns** lists places to stay from coast to coast. You can buy it in most bookstores or ask to have it ordered.

DORMS AND HOSTELS

There are a few alternatives to camping if you're on a budget. Among them are hostels, which are open to young and old, families and singles (☞ Students on the Road, *below*), and university campuses, which open their dorms to travelers for overnight stays from May through August.

HOME EXCHANGE

If you would like to find a house, an apartment, or some other type of vacation property to exchange for your own while on holiday, **become a member of a home-exchange organization,** which will send you its updated listings of available exchanges for a year, and will include your own listing in at least one of them. Arrangements for the actual exchange are made by the two parties

involved, not by the organization.

M
MAIL

In Canada you can buy stamps at the post office or from automatic vending machines in most hotel lobbies, railway stations, airports, bus terminals, many retail outlets, and some newsstands. Within Canada, postcards and letters up to 30 grams cost 46¢; between 30 grams and a kilogram, the cost is $3.75. Letters and postcards to the United States cost 52¢ for up to 30 grams, and $3.40 for up to 250 grams. Prices include GST.

International mail and postcards run 92¢ for up to 30 grams, and $2.10 for up to 100 grams.

Telepost is a fast "next day or sooner" service that combines the CN/CP Telecommunications network with letter-carrier delivery service. Messages may be telephoned to the nearest CN/CP Public Message Centre for delivery anywhere in Canada or the United States. Telepost service is available 24 hours a day, seven days a week, and billing arrangements may be made at the time the message is called in. Intelpost allows you to send documents or photographs via satellite to many Canadian, American, and European destinations. This service is available at main postal facilities in Canada, and is paid for in cash.

RECEIVING MAIL

Visitors may have mail sent to them c/o General Delivery in the town they are visiting, for pickup in person within 15 days, after which it will be returned to the sender.

MONEY

American money is accepted in much of Canada (especially in communities near the border). However, visitors are encouraged to exchange at least some of their money into Canadian funds at a bank or other financial institution in order to get the most favorable exchange rate. Traveler's checks (some are available in Canadian dollars) and major U.S. credit cards are accepted in most areas.

The units of currency in Canada are the Canadian dollar (C$) and the cent, in almost the same denominations as U.S. currency—the $1 and $2 bill are no longer used; instead they have been replaced by $1 and $2 coins ($5, $10, $20, 1¢, 5¢, 10¢, 25¢, etc.). The use of $2 currency is common here although rare in the United States. At press time the exchange rate was C$1.37 to US$1 and C$2.15 to £1.

ATMS

CASH ADVANCES➣ Before leaving home, **make sure that your credit cards have been programmed for ATM use.** Note that Discover is accepted mostly in the United States.

TRANSACTION FEES➣ Although fees charged

for ATM transactions may be higher abroad than at home, Cirrus and Plus exchange rates are excellent, because they are based on wholesale rates offered only by major banks.

EXCHANGING CURRENCY

For the most favorable rates, **change money at banks.** You won't do as well at exchange booths in airports or rail and bus stations, in hotels, in restaurants, or in stores, although you may find their hours more convenient. To avoid lines at airport exchange booths, **get a small amount of the local currency before you leave home.**

TAXES

A goods and services tax of 7% (GST) applies on virtually every transaction in Canada except for the purchase of basic groceries.

HOTEL➤ Québec charges a 6.5% tax on hotel rooms.

SALES➤ In addition to the GST, there is a sales tax from 4% to 12% on most items purchased in shops, on restaurant meals, and sometimes on hotel rooms. Québec offers a sales-tax rebate system similar to the federal one; call the provincial toll-free information lines for details (☞ Visitor Information *in* Important Contacts A to Z, *above*). Most provinces do not tax goods shipped directly by the vendor to the visitor's home address.

VAT➤ You **can get a full GST refund** on any purchase taken out of

the country and on short-term accommodations (but not on food, drink, tobacco, car or motorhome rentals, or transportation); rebate forms, which must be submitted within 60 days of leaving Canada, may be obtained from certain retailers, duty-free shops, customs officials or from Revenue Canada (✉ Visitor's Rebate Program, Ottawa, Ontario K1A 1J5, ☎ 800/668-4748 in Canada). Instant rebates are provided by some duty-free shops when leaving Canada, and most provinces do not tax goods that are shipped directly by the vendor to the purchaser's home. You'll need your receipts.

TRAVELER'S CHECKS

Whether or not to buy traveler's checks depends on where you are headed; **take cash to rural areas and small towns, traveler's checks to cities.** The most widely recognized checks are issued by American Express, Citicorp, Thomas Cook, and Visa. These are sold by major commercial banks for 1%–3% of the checks' face value—it pays to **shop around.** Both American Express and Thomas Cook issue checks that can be countersigned and used by either you or your traveling companion. So you won't be left with excess foreign currency, **buy a few checks in small denominations** to cash toward the end of your trip. Before leaving home, **contact your issuer for information on where to cash your**

checks without incurring a transaction fee. Record the numbers of all your checks, and keep this listing in a separate place, crossing off the numbers of checks you have cashed.

WIRING MONEY

For a fee of 3%–10%, depending on the amount of the transaction, you can have money sent to you from home through Money-Gram^{SM} or Western Union (☞ Money *in* Important Contacts A to Z). The transferred funds and the service fee can be charged to a MasterCard or Visa account.

P
PACKING FOR MONTRÉAL AND QUÉBEC

Layering is the best defense against Canada's cold winters; a hat, scarf, and gloves are essential. For summer travel, loose-fitting natural-fiber clothes are best; bring a wool sweater and light jacket. Pack both casual clothes for day touring and more formal wear for evenings out. If your visit includes a stay at a large city hotel, bring a bathing suit in any season to take advantage of the indoor pool.

Bring an extra pair of eyeglasses or contact lenses in your carry-on luggage, and if you have a health problem, **pack enough medication** to last the trip or have your doctor write you a prescription using the drug's generic name, because brand names vary from country to country (you'll then need a duplicate prescription from a local doctor). It's important that you **don't put prescription drugs or valuables in luggage to be checked,** for it could go astray. To avoid problems with customs officials, carry medications in the original packaging. Also, don't forget the addresses of offices that handle refunds of lost traveler's checks.

LUGGAGE

Airline baggage allowances depend on the airline, the route, and the class of your ticket; ask in advance. In general, on domestic flights and on international flights between the United States and foreign destinations, you are entitled to check two bags. A third piece may be brought on board, but it must fit easily under the seat in front of you or in the overhead compartment. In the United States, the FAA gives airlines broad latitude regarding carry-on allowances, and they tend to tailor them to different aircraft and operational conditions. Charges for excess, oversize, or overweight pieces vary.

If you are flying between two foreign destinations, note that baggage allowances may be determined not by piece but by weight—generally 88 pounds (40 kilograms) in first class, 66 pounds (30 kilograms) in business class, and 44 pounds (20 kilograms) in economy. If your flight between two cities abroad *connects* with

your transatlantic or transpacific flight, the piece method still applies.

SAFEGUARDING YOUR LUGGAGE➤ Before leaving home, **itemize your bags' contents** and their worth, and label them with your name, address, and phone number. (If you use your home address, cover it so that potential thieves can't see it readily.) Inside each bag, **pack a copy of your itinerary.** At check-in, **make sure that each bag is correctly tagged** with the destination airport's three-letter code. If your bags arrive damaged—or fail to arrive at all—file a written report with the airline before leaving the airport.

PASSPORTS & VISAS

U.S. CITIZENS

Citizens and legal residents of the United States do not need a passport or a visa to enter Canada, but proof of citizenship (a birth certificate or valid passport) and proof of identity may be requested. Naturalized U.S. residents should carry their naturalization certificate or "green card." U.S. residents entering Canada from a third country must have a valid passport, naturalization certificate, or "green card."

U.K. CITIZENS

Citizens of the United Kingdom need only a valid passport to enter Canada for stays of up to six months. Applications for new and

renewal passports are available from main post offices and at the passport offices in Belfast, Glasgow, Liverpool, London, Newport, and Peterborough. You may apply in person at all passport offices, or by mail to all except the London office. Children under 16 may travel on an accompanying parent's passport. All passports are valid for 10 years. Allow a month for processing.

It is advisable that you **leave one photocopy of your passport's data page** with someone at home and keep another with you, separated from your passport, while traveling. If you lose your passport, promptly call the nearest embassy or consulate and the local police; having the data page information can speed replacement.

S

SENIOR-CITIZEN DISCOUNTS

To qualify for age-related discounts, **mention your senior-citizen status up front** when booking hotel reservations, not when checking out, and before you're seated in restaurants, not when paying the bill. Note that discounts may be limited to certain menus, days, or hours. When renting a car, **ask about promotional car-rental discounts**—they can net even lower costs than your senior-citizen discount.

VIA Rail Canada (☞ Rail Travel *in* Important Contacts A to Z, *above*) offers those 60 and over a 10% discount on basic transportation for travel any time and with no advance-purchase requirement. This 10% discount can also apply to off-peak reduced fares that have advance-purchase requirements.

STUDENTS ON THE ROAD

Persons under 18 years of age who are not accompanied by their parents should bring a letter from a parent or guardian giving them permission to travel to Canada.

To save money, **look into deals available through student-oriented travel agencies.** To qualify, you'll need to have a bona fide student ID card. Members of international student groups are also eligible (☞ Students *in* Important Contacts A to Z).

T

TELEPHONES

LONG-DISTANCE

The long-distance services of AT&T, MCI, and Sprint make calling home relatively convenient and let you avoid hotel surcharges; typically, you dial an 800 number in the United States.

TIPPING

Tips and service charges are not usually added to a bill in Canada. In general, tip 15% of the total bill. This goes for waiters, waitresses,

barbers and hairdressers, taxi drivers, etc. Porters and doormen should get about 50¢–$1 a bag ($1 or more in a luxury hotel). For maid service, $1 a day is sufficient ($2 in luxury hotels).

TOUR OPERATORS

A package or tour to Montréal and Québec can make your vacation less expensive and more hassle-free. Firms that sell tours and packages reserve airline seats, hotel rooms, and rental cars in bulk and pass some of the savings on to you. In addition, the best operators have local representatives available to help you at your destination.

A GOOD DEAL?

The more your package or tour includes, the better you can predict the ultimate cost of your vacation. Make sure you know exactly what is covered, and **beware of hidden costs.** Are taxes, tips, and service charges included? Transfers and baggage handling? Entertainment and excursions? These can add up.

Most packages and tours are rated deluxe, first-class superior, first class, tourist, or budget. The key difference is usually accommodations. If the package or tour you are considering is priced lower than in your wildest dreams, **be skeptical.** Also, **make sure your travel agent knows the accom-**

modations and other services. Ask about the hotel's location, room size, beds, and whether it has a pool, room service, or programs for children, if you care about these. Has your agent been there in person or sent others you can contact?

BUYER BEWARE

Each year a number of consumers are stranded or lose their money when operators—even very large ones with excellent reputations—go out of business. To avoid becoming one of them, take the time to **check out the operator**—find out how long the company has been in business and ask several agents about its reputation. Next, **don't book unless the firm has a consumer-protection program.** Members of the USTOA and the NTA are required to set aside funds for the sole purpose of covering your payments and travel arrangements in case of default. Nonmember operators may instead carry insurance; look for the details in the operator's brochure—and for the name of an underwriter with a solid reputation. Note: When it comes to tour operators, **don't trust escrow accounts.** Although there are laws governing those of charter-flight operators, no governmental body prevents tour operators from raiding the till.

Next, **contact your local Better Business Bureau and the attorney general's offices** in both your own state and the operator's; have any complaints been filed? Finally, **pay with a major credit card.** Then you can cancel payment, provided that you can document your complaint. Always **consider trip-cancellation insurance** (☞ Insurance, *above*).

BIG VS. SMALL➢ Operators that handle several hundred thousand travelers per year can use their purchasing power to give you a good price. Their high volume may also indicate financial stability. But some small companies provide more personalized service; because they tend to specialize, they may also be more knowledgeable about a given area.

USING AN AGENT

Travel agents are excellent resources. In fact, large operators accept bookings made only through travel agents. But it's good to **collect brochures from several agencies** because some agents' suggestions may be skewed by promotional relationships with tour and package firms that reward them for volume sales. If you have a special interest, **find an agent with expertise in that area;** ASTA can provide leads in the United States. (Don't rely solely on your agent, though; agents may be unaware of small-niche operators, and some special-interest travel companies only sell direct.)

SINGLE TRAVELERS

Prices are usually quoted per person, based on two sharing a room. If traveling solo, you may be required to pay the full double-occupancy rate. Some operators eliminate this surcharge if you agree to be matched up with a roommate of the same sex, even if one is not found by departure time.

TRAVEL GEAR

Travel catalogs specialize in useful items that can **save space when packing** and make life on the road more convenient. Compact alarm clocks, travel irons, travel wallets, and personal-care kits are among the most common items you'll find.

U
U.S.
GOVERNMENT

The U.S. government can be an excellent source of travel information. Some of this is free and some is available for a nominal charge. When planning your trip, **find out what government materials are available.** For just a couple of dollars, you can get a variety of publications from the Consumer Information Center in Pueblo, Colorado. Free consumer information also is available from individual government agencies, such as the Department of Transportation or the U.S. Customs Service. For specific titles, see the appropriate publications entry in Important Contacts A to Z, *above*.

W
WHEN TO GO

Québec has hot, steamy summers and severe winters, with snow lasting from mid-December to mid-March. The whole of eastern Canada enjoys blooming springs and brilliant autumns.

CLIMATE

The following are average daily maximum and minimum temperatures for Montréal and Québec City.

MONTRÉAL

Jan.	23F	− 5C	May	65F	18C	Sept.	68F	20C
	9	−13		48	9		53	12
Feb.	25F	− 4C	June	74F	23C	Oct.	57F	14C
	12	−11		58	14		43	6
Mar.	36F	2C	July	79F	26C	Nov.	42F	6C
	23	− 5		63	17		32	0
Apr.	52F	11C	Aug.	76F	24C	Dec.	27F	− 3C
	36	2		61	16		16	− 9

QUÉBEC CITY

Jan.	20F	− 7C	May	62F	17C	Sept.	66F	19C
	6	−14		43	6		49	9
Feb.	23F	− 5C	June	72F	22C	Oct.	53F	12C
	8	−13		53	12		39	4
Mar.	33F	1C	July	78F	26C	Nov.	39F	4C
	19	− 7		58	14		28	− 2
Apr.	47F	8C	Aug.	75F	24C	Dec.	24F	− 4C
	32	0		56	13		12	−11

THE GOLD GUIDE / SMART TRAVEL TIPS

1 Destination: Montréal & Québec City

FRANCOPHONES IN THE NEW WORLD

QUÉBEC IS the largest and oldest of Canada's provinces, covering 600,000 square miles of land and waterways, one-sixth of Canada's land. Of Québec's 6,627,000 inhabitants, 5,300,000 are French-speaking, 81.3 percent of the French-speaking population of Canada. Although Montréal and Québec City are linked by their history and culture, no two cities could be more different.

History buffs and romantics will want to roam the winding cobblestone streets of Québec City, the capital of the province. Its French colonial history is evident in its architecture, silver-spired churches, and grand cathedrals. In Montréal the Old World meets the New with French bistros and postmodern skyscrapers vying for the limelight. Québec may be the center of the province's government, but Montréal is the business center. Much like New York City, Montréal has attracted a large immigrant population. Its ethnic diversity can be seen in its wide range of restaurants and enclaves. It is not only considered the Canadian center for book publishing, the film industry, and architecture and design; it is also considered the unrivaled bagel capital of Canada.

Québec History

Montréal's and Québec City's histories are inextricably linked. Montréal sits on the site that was called Hochelaga by the Indians who lived there. Québec City was known as Stadacona. In 1534 Jacques Cartier, a young sea captain setting out to find a passage to China, instead came upon Canada and changed the course of events in that region forever. He returned in the following year seeking gold. But this time he found a wide river, sailed down it, and arrived at Stadacona, an Indian village. He admired the location of the village perched on the cliffs overlooking a *kebec,* the Algonquin word for a narrowing of the waters. He continued along to Hochelaga, which eventually became Montréal.

More than 1,000 surprised Iroquois greeted the Frenchman. It would take two centuries of fierce battles before the French made peace with the Iroquois people. Perhaps the violent meeting of the French explorers and the Canadian natives discouraged the French, because no more exploring was done until 1608, when Samuel de Champlain established a French settlement at Stadacona.

Throughout the 17th century, the French opened up Canada and some of what became the United States, using both Montréal and Québec City as convenient trading posts and strategic military locations. They discovered and mapped a vast area stretching from Hudson Bay to the Gulf of Mexico. *Coureurs de bois* (fur traders), missionaries, and explorers staked out this immense new territory.

During this time, France tamed and populated its new colonies across the ocean with the firm hand of *seigneurs,* aristocrats to whom the king distributed land. In turn, the seigneurs swore loyalty to the king, served in the military, maintained manor houses, ceded land to tenant farmers, and established courts to settle local grievances. Seigneuries were close knit, with sons and fathers able to establish farms within the same territory. In addition, the Roman Catholic Church's influence was strong in these communities. Priests and nuns acted as doctors, educators, and overseers of business arrangements among the farmers and between French-speaking traders and English-speaking merchants. An important doctrine of the church in Québec was *survivance,* the survival of the French people and their culture. Couples were told to have large families, and they did. Ten to 12 children in a family was the norm, not the exception.

The Seven Years' War between England and France marked the second half of the 18th century. In 1756, France sent the commander Louis-Joseph, Marquis de Montcalm, to secure the frontier of New France and consolidate the new territory of Louisiana. Although Montcalm, leading a French and Indian expedition, was able to secure the Ohio Valley, turn Lake Ontario into a French waterway, and secure Fort Carillon (now Ticonderoga) on Lake Champlain, the tides began to turn in 1759 with the arrival of a large British fleet to the shores of Québec City, commanded by James Wolfe.

After bombarding the city for several weeks, Wolfe and his 4,000 men decided the fate of Canada in a vicious battle that lasted 20 minutes. The British won, but both leaders were mortally wounded. Today, in Québec City's Governors Park, there is a unique memorial to these two army men—the only statue in the world commemorating both victor and vanquished of the same battle. A year later the French regained the city of Québec, but they were soon forced to withdraw when English ships arrived with supplies and reinforcements. The French were driven back to Montréal, where a large British army defeated them in 1760. In 1763, the Treaty of Paris ceded Canada to Britain. France preferred to give up the new country to preserve its sugar islands, which it believed were of greater value. At that time, all the French civil administrators, as well as the principal landowners and businessmen, returned to France. Of the leaders of New France, only the Roman Catholic clergy remained, and they became more important to the peasant farmers than ever before.

Québec's trouble was in no way over with the Treaty of Paris. In 1774, the British Parliament passed the Québec Act. It extended Québec's borders, hemming in the northernmost of the independence-minded British colonies to the south. The Roman Catholic Church's authority and the seigneurial landlord system were maintained under the act, leaving traditional Québecois life fairly intact. But the American colonists were furious with the passing of the Québec Act and hoped to incite a revolt in Québec against British rule. After the American War of Independence broke out in 1775, Generals Richard Montgomery and Benedict Arnold led American troops that took over Montréal and set up headquarters in the Château de Ramezay, home of the British governor (and now a museum). The Americans then attempted to capture Québec City, but they had misunderstood the Catholic Royalist heritage of the Canadians. Québecois did not share the Americans' love of independence and republicanism. Rather than incite a revolt, the Americans managed to draw the Canadians and British together. The Canadians stood with the British in Québec City to fight off the invasions. Montgomery died in the attack and Arnold fled. The following year, British forces arrived and recaptured Montréal.

The Creation of Upper and Lower Canada

A number of British and American settlers left Albany in New York and settled in Montréal. They began to press the authorities, as did other British colonists west of the Ottawa River, to introduce representative government.

The British responded with the Constitutional Act of 1791, which divided Québec into two provinces, Upper and Lower Canada, west and east of the Ottawa River. The act provided for nominated legislative councils and elected assemblies, like those that had existed in the English colonies. The first election was held the following year.

Elected government was a novelty to the French Canadians, who had never known democracy and had been shielded from the French Revolution of 1789. But democracy suited them well, and before long there was a rising demand for more rights. Heading the movement for greater rights was Louis Joseph Papineau, who was also leader of the French-speaking majority in the legislative assembly. He demanded that the English *château clique,* which made up the governor's council, should be subject to elections as the assembly was. In 1834, he and his associates issued a long list of grievances, "The 92 Resolutions." Papineau lost the support of many of his own associates, and that of the leaders of the church. The British responded with their own "10 resolutions" and refused elections to the council. That same year crops failed and unemployment spread. General unrest led to clashes between the English and young French *Patriotes* in Montréal. Soon a general insurrection broke out. Patriote irregulars fought British troops at St. Charles and St. Eustache near Montréal.

In spite of bad feelings, the upheavals led to major legislative changes in 1841. England passed the Act of Union, which produced a united Canada. Québec was now known as Canada East, while Upper Canada became Canada West. Each sent an equal number of representatives to the elected assembly; the governor was not responsible to the assembly, but rather to the Colonial Office in London. This continued to bridle both English and French members of the assembly.

The Growth of Montréal

Toward the end of the 1700s, the fur trade declined so much that Montréal almost faced economic disaster. But in Europe the demand for lumber increased, and Québec had lots of it. As a result, Montréal became the major trading center in British North America, helped by the fact that New York and New England had seceded from Britain.

Then the flood of immigration from Britain started, so much so that by the mid-1800s, Montréal was transformed into a predominantly English city. About 100,000 Irish immigrants came to work in Montréal's flour mills, breweries, and shipyards, which had sprung up on the shores of the river and the Lachine Canal, begun in 1821. By 1861, working-class Irish made up a third of Montréal's population. Within the next 80 years, Polish, Hungarian, Italian, Chinese, Ukrainian, Greek, Armenian, Spanish, Czech, Japanese, German, and Portuguese immigrants, escaping from poverty and political hardships, arrived by the thousands, seeking freedom in the New World. By 1867, more than a half-million immigrants had arrived from Europe, pushing Canada's population to more than 2 million. The demand for union came from all the provinces of British North America to increase trade and economic prosperity, to increase their military strength in case of attack from the United States, to create a government capable of securing and developing the Northwest (the vast lands west of Canada West), and to make possible the building of a railway that would contribute to the realization of all these ambitions.

The Dominion of Canada was created on July 1, 1867, by an act of the British Parliament, known as the British North American (BNA) Act. It divided the province of Canada into Québec and Ontario and brought in Nova Scotia and New Brunswick. Manitoba joined in 1870, British Columbia in 1871, Prince Edward Island in 1873, Alberta and Saskatchewan in 1905, and Newfoundland in 1949. The BNA Act also enshrined French as an official language. The province of Québec, like the other provinces, was given far-reaching responsibilities in social and civil affairs.

The Conscription Crisis

The entente between the French and the English in Canada was viable until World War I strained it. At the outbreak of the war, the two groups felt equally supportive of the two European motherlands. Many volunteered, and a totally French regiment, the Royal 22nd, was created. But two things ended the camaraderie.

On the battlefields of Europe, Canadians, along with Australians, formed the shock troops of the British Empire and died horribly, by the thousands. More than 60,000 Canadians died in the war, a huge loss for a country of 7.5 million. In 1915, Ontario passed Regulation 17, severely restricting the use of French in its schools. It translated into an anti-French stand and created open hostility. The flow of French Canadians into the army became a trickle. Then Prime Minister Robert Borden ordered the conscription of childless males to reinforce the ailing Canadian corps. A wider conscription law loomed in Ottawa, resulting in an outcry in Québec led by nationalist, journalist, and politician Henry Bourassa (grandson of patriot Louis Joseph Papineau). The nationalists claimed that conscription was a device to diminish the French-speaking population. When, in 1917, conscription did become law, Québec was ideologically isolated from the rest of Canada.

The crisis led to the formation of the Union Nationale provincial party in 1936, initially a reformist party. Under its leader Maurice Duplessis, it held control until 1960 and was characterized by lavish patronage, strong-arm methods, fights with Ottawa, and nationalistic sloganeering. Duplessis believed that to survive, Québecois should remain true to their traditions. Duplessis deterred industrial expansion in Québec, which went to Ontario, and slowed the growth of reformist ideas until his death and the flowering of the Quiet Revolution.

The Quiet Revolution

The population of Québec had grown to 6 million, but the province had fallen economically and politically behind Canada's English majority. Under Duplessis and the Union Nationale party, French-language schools and universities were supervised by the church and offered courses in the humanities rather than in science and economics. Francophones (French-speaking Québeckers) were denied any chance of real business education unless they attended English institutions. As a result, few of them held top positions in industry or finance. On a general cultural basis, the country overwhelmingly reflected Anglo-Saxon attitudes rather than an Anglo-French mixture.

In 1960, the Liberal Party under Jean Lesage swept to power. Though initially occupied with social reform, it soon turned to economic matters. In 1962, Lesage's minister of natural resources, René Lévesque, called for the nationalization of most of the electricity industry, which up to then had been in private hands. This was the first step toward economic independence for Québec. The financiers of Montréal's St. James Street, the heart of the business district, opposed it, but ordinary Québecois were enthusiastic. In 1965, Lévesque's ministry established a provincial mining company to explore and develop the province's mineral resources.

Meanwhile U.S. capital poured into Québec, as it did everywhere else in Canada. With it came American cultural influence, which increased Québecois' expectations of a high standard of living. English-speaking citizens remained in firm control of the large national corporations headquartered in Montréal. Indeed it became clear that they had no intention of handing power over to the French. Few Francophones were promoted to executive status. Successive provincial governments became increasingly irritated by the lack of progress.

The discontent led to a dramatic radicalization of Québec politics. A new separatist movement arose that hoped to make Québec a distinct state by breaking away from the rest of the country. The most extreme faction of the movement was the Front de Libération du Québec (FLQ). It backed its demands with bombs and arson, culminating in the kidnapping and murder of Québec Cabinet Minister Pierre Laporte in October 1970.

The federal government in Ottawa, under Prime Minister Pierre Elliott Trudeau, himself a French-speaking Québecois, imposed the War Measures Act. This permitted the police to break up civil disorders and arrest hundreds of suspects and led to the arrest of the murderers of Laporte.

The political crisis calmed down, but it left behind vibrations that affected all of the country. The federal government redoubled its efforts to correct the worst grievances of the French Canadians. Federal funds flowed into French schools outside Québec to support French-Canadian culture in the other provinces. French Canadians were appointed to senior positions in the government and crown corporations. The federal government dramatically increased its bilingual services to the population.

In Québec from the mid-1970s, the Liberal government and then the Parti Québecois, elected in 1976 and headed by René Lévesque (who had left the Liberal party in 1967 and helped found the Parti Québecois), replaced the English language with the French language in Québec's economic life. In 1974, French was adopted as the official language of Québec. This promoted French-language instruction in the schools and made French the language of business and government. The Parti Québecois followed up in 1977 with the Charter of the French Language, which established deadlines and fines to help enforce the program to make French the chief language in all areas of Québec life. The charter brought French into the workplace; it also accelerated a trend for English companies to relocate their headquarters outside Québec, particularly in and near Toronto. The provincial government is working to attract new investment to Québec to replace those lost jobs and revenues.

The Parti Québecois proposed to go further by taking Québec out of the confederation, provided that economic ties with the rest of Canada could be maintained. Leaders in the other provinces announced that such a scheme would not be acceptable. A referendum was held in 1980 for the authority to negotiate a sovereignty association with the rest of Canada. Québec voters rejected the proposal by a wide margin. In 1985, the Parti Québecois government was defeated at the polls by the Liberal Party, headed by Robert Bourassa.

Bourassa was committed to keeping Québec within Canada until the collapse of the Meech-Lake Accord, a three-year attempt to integrate Québec into the Canadian constitution, in 1990. Bourassa then vowed to put the interests of the province before those of the country, even if this meant separation. The Québec Bélanger-Campeau commission, set up to study the future of Québec in Canada, concluded that the province should be recognized as a "sovereign state," although it would remain part of the Canadian Federation given certain conditions. However, the federal and provincial governments did not reach an agreement. In a 1995 referendum, Québecois decided by a narrow margin to remain in the Federation.

The People of Québec

Although French is the official language of Québec, Québec also has a large English-speaking population (676,000), particularly in Montréal, the Ottawa Valley, and l'Estrie. They are descendants of those English, Irish, and Scots who landed here after the conquest of New France, and of immigrants from other nations whose main language is English. English-speaking Montréalers founded and financed a variety of such great institutions as universities, museums, hospitals, orchestras, and social agencies, as well as a number of national and multinational corporations in the worlds of banking and finance, transportation, natural resources, and distilled spirits.

Half a million immigrants from Europe, Asia, Latin America, and the Caribbean also live in Québec. People from 80 different countries have made their new homes in the province. In proportion to its population, this land, along with the rest of Canada, has welcomed the greatest number of fugitives from political and economic unrest over the past 20 years.

Between 1968 and 1982, for example, 60,000 immigrants arrived from Czechoslovakia, Haiti, Uganda, Lebanon, Chile, and Southeast Asia. A much larger wave of immigrants—from Italy, Greece, and Eastern Europe—had arrived following World War II.

The native people of Québec number more than 40,000. Nearly 30,000 of Québec's Amerindians live in villages within reserved territories in various parts of Québec, where they have exclusive fishing and hunting rights. The Inuit people (Eskimo) number over 5,000 and live in villages scattered along the shores of James Bay, Hudson Bay, Hudson Strait, and Ungava Bay. They have abandoned their igloos for prefabricated houses, but they still make their living by trapping and hunting.

The French Canadians of Québec, often called Latins of the North, have an ever-sparkling joie de vivre, especially at the more than 400 festivals and carnivals they celebrate each year. Even the long winter does not dampen their good spirits. The largest festival splash is on June 24, which was originally the Feast of Saint John the Baptist. Now it is called La Fête Nationale (National Day). Everyone celebrates the long weekend by building roaring bonfires and dancing in the streets.

February brings Québec City's Winter Carnival, a two-week-long noisy and exciting party. Chicoutimi also has a winter carnival in which residents of the city celebrate and dress up in period costumes. In September international canoe races are held in Mauricie, and in August an international swim gets under way across Lac-Saint-Jean. Trois-Rivières celebrates the summer with automobile races through its streets, and Valleyfield is the scene of international regattas.

WHAT'S WHERE

Montréal

This island city—Canada's most romantic metropolis—seems to favor grace and elegance over order and even prosperity. It is a city full of music, art, and joie de vivre.

Québec City

Québec City, which enjoys one of the most beautiful natural settings in North America, perched on a cliff above a narrow point in the St. Lawrence River, is the capital of and the oldest municipality in the province.

Province of Québec

Québec is set apart by its strong French heritage, a matter not only of language but of customs, religion, and political structure. Defining the land outside the cities are innumerable lakes, streams, and rivers; farmlands and villages; great mountains, such as the Laurentians with their ski resorts, and deep forests; and a rugged coastline along the Gulf of St. Lawrence.

PLEASURES AND PASTIMES

Baseball

If you're missing a bit of Americana, don't fret. Baseball has been a favorite in Canada since the major leagues expanded into Montréal in 1969 with the Montréal Expos.

Biking

Bikers favor the hilly terrain of the Gaspé Peninsula. Write to the provincial tourist board for road maps (which are more detailed than the maps available at gas stations) and information on local cycling associations.

Curling

For a true taste of Canadian sportsmanship you might want to watch a curling match, which is not unlike a shuffleboard game on ice. Two teams of four players each compete by sliding large polished granite stones toward the center of a bull's-eye, or "house."

Dining

Although the earliest European settlers of Canada—the British and the French—bequeathed a rather bland diet of meat and potatoes, vestiges of what the European settlers learned from the Native Americans are evident in the hearty ingredients that make up the French-Canadian cuisine. You'll find the best of the province's hearty meat pies and pâtés in Québec City; Montréal dining tends to be more classic French than French-Canadian.

Fishing

Anglers can find their catch in virtually any region of the country, though restrictions, seasons, license requirements, and catch limits vary from province to province. In addition, a special fishing permit is required to fish in all national parks; it can be obtained at any national park site, for a nominal fee. The lakes of Québec hold trout, bass, pike, and landlocked salmon, called *ouananiche* (pronounced *wah*-nah-nish).

Football

The Canadian Football League, which dates from the 1800s, plays with three downs, a 110-yard field, and 12 players per side. Montréal has a team. The Grey Cup, which Canadians take as seriously as we do our Super Bowl, is played every November.

Hockey

Officially, Canada's national sport is lacrosse, but ice hockey is the national favorite. It's played by children and professionals alike, with leagues and teams organized everywhere. The National Hockey League teams in the province of Québec are the Montréal Canadiens and the Québec Nordiques. The season runs from October to April.

Shopping

ANTIQUES➤ On the whole, prices for antiques are lower in Canada than in the United States. Shops along Montréal's rue Sherbrooke Ouest stock everything from ancient maps to fine crystal; Vieux-Montréal and the rue Notre-Dame sell antiques and collectibles ranging from Napoléonic-period furniture to 1950s bric-a-brac.

ARTS AND CRAFTS➤ The craftspeople of Québec are known for producing beautiful wood carvings.

MAPLE SYRUP➤ Eastern Canada is famous for its sugar maples. The trees are tapped in early spring, and the sap is collected in buckets to be boiled down into maple syrup. This natural confection is sold all year. Avoid the tourist shops and department stores; for the best prices, stop at farm stands and markets. A small can of syrup costs between $6 and $9.

NATIVE CANADIAN ART➤ Interest has grown in the highly collectible art and sculpture of the Inuit, usually rendered in soapstone. For the best price and a guarantee of authenticity, purchase Inuit and other native crafts in the province where they originate. Many styles are now attributed to certain tribes and are mass-produced for sale in galleries and shops miles away from their regions of origin. At the very top galleries you can be assured of getting pieces done by individual artists, though the prices will be higher than in the provinces of origin. The Canadian government has registered the symbol of an igloo as a mark of a work's authenticity. Be sure this Canadian government sticker or tag is attached before you make your purchase.

Skiing

Skiing is probably the most popular winter sport in Canada. For downhill skiing the slopes in Québec province are among the best. For cross-country skiing, almost any provincial or national park will do.

Winter Sports

Canadians flourish in winter, as the range of winter sports attests. In addition to the sports already mentioned, at the first drop of a snowflake Canadians will head outside to ice skate, toboggan, snowmobile, dogsled, snowshoe, and ice fish.

NEW AND NOTEWORTHY

In October 1995, Montréal survived yet another **referendum** on the independence of Québec. Separatists lost by the narrowest possible margins with more than 49% of the vote, and so the city faces at least one more nerve-wracking debate in the future. But this island city has never let politics get in the way of a good time. Its summer **festivals** of jazz, film, fireworks, and comedy are among the most important in the world. And the Canadiens hockey team moved into a brand-new downtown home, **Centre Molson.**

FODOR'S CHOICE

No two people will agree on what makes a perfect vacation, but it's fun and helpful to know what others think. We hope you'll have a chance to experience some of Fodor's Choices yourself in Montréal and Québec City. For detailed information about each entry, refer to the appropriate chapter.

Historic Sites

★**Basilique Notre-Dame de Montréal, Montréal.** The enormous (3,800-seat) rectangular neo-Gothic church, opened in 1829 and has a medieval-style interior with stained-glass windows, a stunning vaulted blue ceiling, and pine and walnut-wood carving.

★**Basilica of Ste-Anne de Beaupré, Québec City.** The monumental and inspiring church is an important shrine that draws hordes of pilgrims. According to local legend, St. Anne was responsible over the years for saving voyagers from shipwrecks in the harsh waters of the St. Lawrence; she is also believed to have healing powers.

★**Plains of Abraham, Québec City.** The site of the famous 1759 battle between the French and the British that decided the fate of New France is now part of a large park overlooking the St. Lawrence River.

★**Vieille Ville, Québec City.** The Old Town is small and dense, steeped in four centuries of history and French tradition. Immaculately preserved as the only fortified city in North America, it is a UNESCO World Heritage Site.

Park and Garden

★**Jardin Botanique de Montréal** (Botanical Gardens), **Montréal.** This park, with 181 acres of gardens in summer and 10 greenhouses open all year, has one of the best bonsai collections in the West and the largest Ming-style garden outside Asia.

Restaurants

★**Toqué, Montréal.** This is the most fashionable and the most zany restaurant in Montréal. The menu depends on what the two chefs found fresh that day and on which way their ever-creative spirit moved them. $$$

★**Aux Anciens Canadiens, Québec City.** The house, dating from 1675, has four dining rooms with varying historical themes. The cooking is authentic, hearty French-Canadian. *$$$*

★**L'Eau à la Bouche, Ste-Adèle, Québec.** At this Bavarian-style property you'll find a superb marriage of nouvelle cuisine and traditional Québec cooking in such dishes as roast partridge stuffed with oyster mushrooms and cream sauce. *$$$$*

Hotels

★**Auberge les Passants du Sans Soucy, Montréal.** A tiny gem, the only inn in Vieux-Montréal, has rooms with brass beds, bare stone walls, exposed beams, soft lighting, and lots of fresh-cut flowers. *$$*

★**Hostellerie Les Trois Tilleuls, St-Marc-sur-Richelieu, Québec.** This romantic little inn on a quiet country road near Montréal has modern rooms, each with a balcony or terrace facing the lovely Rivière Richelieu. *$$$–$$$$*

FESTIVALS AND SEASONAL EVENTS

Contact tourist boards for more information about these and other festivals.

WINTER

FEBRUARY➤ *La Fête des Neiges* is winter carnival in Montréal. **Winter Carnival** in Québec City is an 11-day festival of winter sports competitions, ice-sculpture contests, and parades. Cross-country skiers race between Lachute and Gatineau in the **Canadian Ski Marathon.**

SPRING

APRIL➤ **Sugaring-off parties** celebrate the beginning of the maple syrup season.

SUMMER

JUNE➤ Some of the world's best drivers compete in the **Molson Grand Prix** in Montréal. Québec City hops with the **International Jazz Festival.** Beauport hosts the **International Children's Folklore Festival.**

JULY➤ **Festival International de Jazz de Montréal** draws more than 2,000 musicians from all over the world for this 11-day series. **Québec International Summer Festival** offers entertainment in the streets and parks of old Québec City. Montréal's **Juste pour Rire** (Just for Laughs) comedy festival features comics from around the world, in French and English. Drummondville **World Folklore Festival** brings troupes from more than 20 countries to perform in the streets and parks. At **Festival Orford** international artists perform in Orford Park's music center (through August). **Matinée Ltd. International** spotlights the best male tennis players in Montréal.

AUGUST➤ Montréal hosts a **World Film Festival.** St-Jean-sur-Richelieu's **Hot Air Balloon Festival** is the largest gathering of hot air balloons in Canada.

AUTUMN

SEPTEMBER➤ **Québec International Film Festival** screens in Québec City. The **Gatineau Hot Air Balloon Festival** brings together hot air balloons from across Canada, the United States, and Europe.

OCTOBER➤ **Festival of Colors** celebrates foliage throughout the province.

2 Montréal

Montréal is Canada's most romantic metropolis, an island city that seems to favor grace and elegance over order and even prosperity; a city full of music, art, and joie de vivre.

By Patricia
Lowe

Updated by
Paul and Julie
Waters

MONTRÉAL IS CANADA'S MOST ROMANTIC
metropolis, an island city that seems to favor
grace and elegance over order and even pros-
perity; a city full of music, art, and joie de vivre. It is rather like the
European capital Vienna—past its peak of power and glory, perhaps,
but still a vibrant and beautiful place full of memories, dreams, and
festivals.

That's not to say Montréal is ready to fade away. It may not be so young
anymore—it celebrated its 350th birthday in 1992—but it remains
Québec's largest city and an important port and financial center. Its
office towers are full of young Québécois entrepreneurs, members of
a new breed who are ready and eager to take on the world.

Montréal is the only French-speaking metropolis in North America and
the second-largest French-speaking city in the world, but it's a toler-
ant place that over the years has made room for millions of immigrants
who speak dozens of languages. Today about 15% of the 3.1 million
people who live in the metropolitan area claim English as their mother
tongue and another 15% claim a language that's neither English nor
French. The city's gentle tolerance has won recognition: Several times
it has been voted one of the world's most livable cities.

The city's grace, however, has been sorely tested in recent decades. Since
1976, Montréal has twice weathered the election of a separatist provincial government, a law banning all languages but French on virtually
all public signs and billboards, and four referendums on the future of
Québec and Canada.

The latest chapter in this long constitutional drama was the cliffhanger
referendum on Québec independence on October 30, 1995. In that show-
down between federalists and independents, Québécois voters chose
to remain part of Canada, but by the thinnest of possible margins. More
than 98% of eligible voters participated, and the final province-wide
result was 49.42% in favor of independence and 50.58% against. In
fact, 60% of the province's francophones voted in favor of establish-
ing an independent Québec. But Montréal, where most of the province's
anglophones and immigrants live, bucked the separatist trend. Voters
in the metropolitan region voted nearly 70% against independence. And
the drama continues. The separatist Parti-Québécois still controls the
provincial government and has a new and revered leader in Lucien
Bouchard, so it's likely there will be another referendum in 1997. And
there's no respite in Ottawa. The Bloc-Québécois, an allied separatist
party that Mr. Bouchard founded, dominates the official opposition
in Canada's federal parliament. All this has prompted some Montrealers to begin talking about seceding from Québec and forming their
own province or city-state.

But in spite of uncertainty about the future, most Montrealers still delight in their city, which has weathered all these storms with aplomb.
It is, after all, a city that's used to turmoil. It was founded by the French,
conquered by the British, and occupied by the Americans. It has a long
history of reconciling contradictions, and even today is a city of contrasts. The flamboyant glass office tower of La Maison des Coopérants,
for example, soars above a Gothic-style Anglican cathedral that squats
gracefully in its shadow. The neo-Gothic facade of the Basilique Notre-
Dame-de-Montréal glares across Place d'Armes at the pagan temple
that is the head office of the Bank of Montréal. And while pilgrims
still climb the steps to the Oratoire St-Joseph's on their knees on one

side of the mountain, thousands of their fellow Catholics line up to get into the very chic Casino de Montréal on the other side—certainly not what the earnest French settlers who founded Montréal envisioned when they landed on the island in May 1642.

Those 54 pious men and women under the leadership of Paul Chomedy Sieur de Maisonneuve, hoped to do nothing less than create a new Christian society. They named their settlement Ville-Marie in honor of the mother of Christ and set out to convert the Indians. Those early years were marked by the heroism of two remarkable women— Jeanne Mance, a French noblewoman who arrived with de Maisonneuve, and Marguerite Bourgeoys, who came 11 years later. Jeanne Mance, working alone, established the Hôpital Hôtel Dieu de St-Joseph, still one of the city's major hospitals. In 1659, she invited members of a French order of nuns to help her in her efforts. That order, the Religieuses Hospitalières de St-Joseph, now has its motherhouse in Montréal and is the oldest nursing group in the Americas. Marguerite Bourgeoys, with Jeanne Mance's help, established the colony's first school and taught both French and Indian children how to read and write. Bourgeoys founded the Congrégation de Notre Dame, a teaching order that still has schools in Montréal, across Canada, and around the world. She was canonized a saint by the Roman Catholic church in 1982.

Piety wasn't the settlement's only raison d'être, however. Ville Marie was ideally located to be a commercial success, as well. It was at the confluence of two major transportation routes—the St. Lawrence and Ottawa rivers—and fur trappers used the town as a staging point for their expeditions. But the city's religious roots were never forgotten. Until 1854, long after the French lost possession of the city, the island of Montréal remained the property of the Sulpicians, an aristocratic order of French priests. The Sulpicians were responsible for administering the colony and for recruiting colonists. They still run the Basilique Notre-Dame-de-Montréal, and are still responsible for training priests for the Roman Catholic archdiocese.

The French regime in Canada ended with the Seven Years' War—what Americans call the French and Indian Wars. British troops took Québec City in 1759 and Montréal fell less than a year later. The Treaty of Paris ceded all New France to Britain in 1763, and soon English and Scottish settlers poured into Montréal to take advantage of the city's geography and economic potential. By 1832, Montréal was a leading colonial capital of business, finance, and transportation, and had grown far beyond the walls of the old settlement. Much of that business and financial leadership has since moved to Toronto, the upstream rival Montrealers love to hate.

Pleasures and Pastimes

Churches

Montréal's two most popular and most enduring attractions are a pair of monuments dedicated to a Jewish couple who lived 2,000 years ago—the oratory dedicated to St. Joseph on the north side of Mont-Royal and the Basilique Notre-Dame-de-Montréal dedicated to his wife in the heart of the old city. But these are just two of the dozens of beautiful churches built in the days when the Québécois were among the most devout adherents to the Roman Catholic church. In fact, Mark Twain, novelist and anticleric, once complained (or perhaps boasted) that you couldn't throw a rock in Montréal without breaking a church window. Other gems of ecclesiastical architecture are St. Patrick's Basilica, the Jesuit-run Le Gésu, the Chapelle Notre Dame des Lourdes,

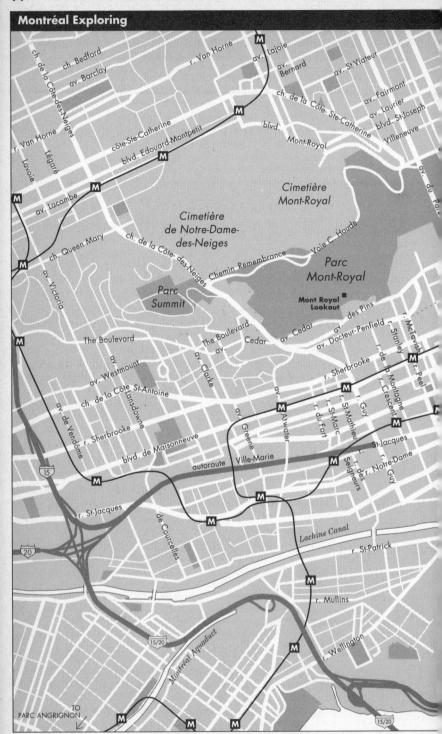

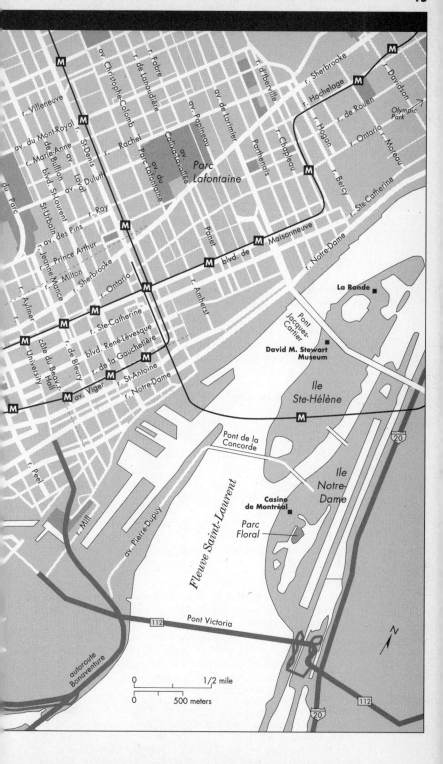

r. Villeneuve

av. du Mont-Royal

r. Marie-Anne

de la Bullion

av. Anne

av. Laval

St-Denis

blvd. St-Laurent

St-Urbain

av. des Pins

Jeanne-Mance

Milton

Prince Arthur

Sherbrooke

Ontario

Aylmer

University

côte du Beaver Hall

r. de Bleury

av. Viger

r. Notre-Dame

r. St-Antoine

de la Gauchetière

blvd. René-Lévesque

r. Ste-Catherine

av. Christophe-Colomb

r. de Lanaudière

r. Fabre

Rachel

Duluth

Roy

av. du Parc Lafontaine

av. Calixa-Lavallée

av. Papineau

av. de Lorimier

Parc Lafontaine

Panet

blvd. de Maisonneuve

r. Amherst

Parthenais

r. d'Iberville

r. Chapleau

r. Sherbrooke

Hochelaga

r. Hogan

r. de Rouen

Ontario

r. Bercy

Ste-Catherine

r. Notre-Dame

Davidson

r. Moreau

Olympic Park

La Ronde ■

Pont Jacques-Cartier

David M. Stewart Museum ■

Ile Ste-Hélène

20

Pont de la Concorde

Ile Notre-Dame

r. Peel

Mill

av. Pierre-Dupuy

Fleuve Saint-Laurent

Casino de Montréal ■

Parc Floral

112

Pont Victoria

autoroute Bonaventure

20

112

N

0		1/2 mile

0 ——— 500 meters

and in the distant north end of the city, the Église de la Visitation, the oldest extant church on the island and a jewel box of baroque decoration. But even humble parish churches in working-class neighborhoods are as grand as some cathedrals.

Dining

Montrealers are passionate about food. They love to dine on classic dishes in restaurants like Les Halles and the Beaver Club, or swoon over culinary innovations in places like Toqué, but they can get equally passionate about humbler fare. They'll argue with some heat about where to get the juiciest smoked meat, the crispiest barbecued chicken, and the soggiest *stimés* (steamed hot dogs). The city has more than 4,500 restaurants, representing more than 75 ethnic groups.

CATEGORY	COST*
$$$$	over $30
$$$	$20–$30
$$	$10–$20
$	$5–$10

per person without tax (combined GST of 7% and provincial tax of 4% on all meals), service, or drinks

Festivals

Summer and fall are just one long succession of festivals that begins in late June with a 10-day Jazz Festival when as many as a million fans descend on the city to hear more than 1,000 musicians, including such giants as guitarist John Scofield and tenor saxophonist Joe Lovano, play in concert halls, on street stages, and on the sidewalks. In August there's the World Film Festival and the lively Just for Laughs Comedy Festival in the Vieux-Port area. Other festivals celebrate beer, alternative films, French-language music and song from around the world, and international cuisine. Every Saturday in June and every Sunday in July the skies over the city waterfront erupt in color and flame as fireworks teams from around the world compete for prizes in the International Fireworks Competition.

History

Montréal is one of the oldest European settlements in North America, and traces of its long history are found everywhere. Some buildings in Vieux-Montréal date to the 17th century. Other parts of the city are full of wonderful examples of Victorian architecture. Such museums as the McCord Museum of Canadian History, the Musée d'Archéologie de la Pointe-à-Callière, and the Stewart Museum in the Old Fort on Ile Ste-Hélène attest to the city's fascination with its past.

Lodging

On the island of Montréal alone there are rooms available in every type of accommodation, from world-class luxury hotels to youth hostels, from student dormitories to budget executive motels. Keep in mind that during peak season (May–August) it may be difficult to find a bed without reserving, and most, but not all, hotels raise their prices. Rates often drop from mid-November to early April. Throughout the year a number of the better hotels have two-night, three-day, double-occupancy packages that offer substantial discounts.

The Ritz-Carlton Kempinski has been setting standards of luxury since 1912, and the nearby Westin Mont-Royal is one of the best modern luxury hotels in the country. But the city also offers more intimate charm, at the Château Versailles on rue Sherbrooke, for example, or the tiny Auberge les Passants du Sans Soucy in the heart of Vieux-Montréal.

CATEGORY	COST*
$$$$	over $160
$$$	$120–$160
$$	$85–$120
$	under $85

All prices are for a standard double room, excluding an optional service charge.

Nightlife

Montréal's reputation as a fun place to visit for a night on the town dates at least to Prohibition days in the United States, when hordes of thirsty Americans would flood the city every weekend to eat, drink, and be merry. The city has dozens of discos, bistros, show-bars, and jazz clubs, not to mention hundreds of bars where you can go to argue about sports, politics, and religion until the early hours of the morning. Much of the action takes place along rue St-Denis and adjacent streets in the eastern part of the city or rues Bishop, Crescent, and de la Montagne in the downtown area. The night scene is constantly shifting—last year's hot spot can quickly become this year's dive. The best and easiest way to figure out what's in is to stroll down rue St-Denis or rue Bishop at about 10:30 and look for the place with the longest lineup and the rudest doorman.

Shopping

The development of the Underground City has made shopping a year-round sport in Montréal. That vast complex linked by underground passageways and the Métro includes two major department stores, at least a dozen huge shopping malls, and more than 1,000 boutiques. Add to this Montréal's status as one of the fur capitals of the world, and you have a city that was born to be shopped.

EXPLORING MONTRÉAL

The Ile de Montréal is an island in the St. Lawrence River, roughly equidistant (256 kilometers, or 160 miles) from Lake Ontario and the point where the river widens into the Gulf of St. Lawrence. The island is 51 kilometers (32 miles) long and 14 kilometers (9 miles) wide and is bounded on the north by the narrow Rivière des Prairies and on the south by the St. Lawrence. The only rise in the landscape is the 764-foot Mont-Royal, which gave the island its name and which residents call simply "the mountain." The city of Montréal is the oldest and by far the largest of the 24 municipalities on the island, which together make up the Communauté Urbaine de Montréal (the Montréal Urban Community), the regional government that runs, among other things, the police department and the transit system. There is a belt of off-island suburbs on the South Shore of the St. Lawrence and just to the north across the narrow Rivière-des-Prairies, on an island of its own, is Laval, a suburb that has grown to be the second-largest city in the province. But the countryside is never far away. The pastoral Eastern Townships, first settled by Loyalists fleeing the American Revolution, are less than an hour's drive away, and the Laurentians, an all-season playground full of lakes and ski hills, are even closer.

For a good overview of the city, head for the lookout at the Chalet du Mont-Royal. You can drive most of the way, park, and walk ½ kilometer (¼ mile) or hike all the way up from chemin de la Côte-des-Neiges or avenue des Pins. If you look directly out—southeast—from the belvedere, at the foot of the hill will be the McGill University campus and, surrounding it, the skyscrapers of downtown Montréal. Just beyond, along the banks of the river, are the stone houses of Vieux-

Montréal. Hugging the South Shore on the other side of the river are the Iles Ste-Hélène and Notre-Dame, sites of La Ronde amusement park, the Biosphere, the Casino de Montréal, acres of parkland, and the Lac de l'Ile Notre-Dame public beach—all popular excursions. To the east is rue St-Denis and the Latin Quarter with its rows of French and ethnic restaurants, bistros, chess hangouts, designer boutiques, antiques shops, and art galleries. Even farther east you can see the flying-saucer-shape Olympic Stadium with its leaning tower.

Montréal is easy to explore. Streets, subways, and bus lines are clearly marked. The city is divided by a grid of streets roughly aligned east–west and north–south. (This grid is tilted about 40 degrees off—to the left of—true north, so west is actually southwest and so on.) North–south street numbers begin at the St. Lawrence River and increase as you head north. East–west street numbers begin at boulevard St-Laurent, which divides Montréal into east and west halves. The city is not so large that seasoned walkers can't see all the districts around the base of Mont-Royal on foot. Nearly everything else is easily accessible by the city's quiet, clean, and very safe bus and Métro (subway) system.

Great Itineraries

In Prohibition days, thirsty Americans often came to Montréal for one-night jaunts, and were happy with the experience, but getting any real feel for this bilingual, multicultural city takes a lot longer. An ideal stay would be seven days, but a modern visitor should spend at least three days walking and soaking up the atmosphere. That's enough time to visit Mont-Royal, explore Vieux-Montréal, do some shopping downtown, and perhaps visit the Parc Olympique. It also includes enough nights for an evening of bar-hopping on rue St-Denis or rue Crescent and another for a long, luxurious dinner at a restaurant such as Nuances or Toqué.

IF YOU HAVE 3 DAYS

Any visit to Montréal should start with Mont-Royal. The mountain is Montréal's most enduring symbol and the view from the big, flag-stoned terrace in front of the Chalet du Mont-Royal is both magnificent and helpful for orientation. Afterward wander down to avenue des Pins and then through McGill University to the Centre-Ville (downtown). Make an effort to stop at the Musée des Beaux-Arts and St. Patrick's Basilica. Day 2 should be spent exploring Vieux-Montréal, with special emphasis on the Basilique Notre-Dame-de-Montréal and the Musée d'Archéologie de Pointe de la Pointe-à-Callière. On Day 3 you can either visit the Parc Olympique (recommended for children) or stroll through the Quartier Latin (Latin Quarter).

IF YOU HAVE 5 DAYS

Once again start with a visit to Parc Mont-Royal, but instead of going downtown after you've viewed the city from the Chalet du Mont-Royal, visit the Oratoire St-Joseph. You should still have enough time to visit the Musée des Beaux-Arts before dinner. That will leave time on Day 2 to get in more shopping as you explore downtown with perhaps a visit to the Centre Canadien d'Architecture. Spend all of Day 3 in Vieux-Montréal, and on Day 4 stroll through the Quartier Latin. On Day 5, visit the Parc Olympique and then do one of three things: visit the islands, take a ride on the Lachine Rapids, or revisit some of the sights you missed in Vieux-Montréal or downtown.

IF YOU HAVE 7 DAYS

A week will give you enough time to do the five-day itinerary, expanding your Vieux-Montréal explorations to two days and adding a shopping spree on rue Chabanel and a visit to the Casino.

Vieux-Montréal (Old Montréal)

Numbers in the text below correspond to numbers in the margin and on the maps.

When Montréal's first European settlers arrived by river in 1642 they stopped to build their houses just below the treacherous Lachine Rapids that blocked the way upstream. They picked a site near an old Iroquois settlement on the bank of the river nearest Mont-Royal. In the mid-17th century Montréal consisted of a handful of wood houses clustered around a pair of stone buildings, all flimsily fortified by a wood stockade. For the next three centuries this district—bounded by rues Berri and McGill on the east and west, rue St-Jacques on the north, and the river to the south—was the financial and political heart of the city. Government buildings, the largest church, the stock exchange, the main market, and the port were there. The narrow but relatively straight streets were cobblestone and lined with solid, occasionally elegant houses, office buildings, and warehouses—also made of stone. Exiting the city meant using one of four gates through the thick stone wall that protected against native people and marauding European powers. Montréal quickly grew past the bounds of its fortifications, however, and by World War I the center of the city had moved toward Mont-Royal. The new heart of Montréal became Dominion Square (now Square Dorchester). For the next two decades Vieux-Montréal, as it became known, was gradually abandoned, the warehouses and offices emptied. In 1962 the city began studying ways to revitalize Vieux-Montréal, and a decade of renovations and restorations began.

Today, Vieux-Montréal is a center of cultural life and municipal government. Most of the summer activities revolve around Place Jacques-Cartier, which becomes a pedestrian mall with street performers and outdoor cafés. This lovely square is a good place to view the annual fireworks festival at La Ronde, and it's adjacent to the Vieux-Port, one of the city's most popular recreation grounds. Classical music concerts are staged all year long at Basilique Notre-Dame, which has one of the finest organs in North America, and English-language plays are staged in the Centaur Theatre in the old stock-exchange building. This district has six museums devoted to history, religion, and arts.

A Good Walk

Take the Métro to the Square-Victoria Station and follow the signs to the **Centre de Commerce Mondial de Montréal** ①, one of the most pleasant enclosed spaces in Montréal, with a fountain and frequent art exhibits. Exit on the east side of the complex and turn right on rue St-Pierre, walk south to rue St-Jacques, and turn left. This was once the financial heart, not just of Montréal, but of Canada. As you walk east, note the fine decorative stone flourishes—grapevines, nymphs, angels, and goddesses—on the Victorian office buildings. This part of Vieux-Montréal can seem almost tomblike on weekends when the business and legal offices in the district close down, but don't worry, things get livelier as you get closer to the waterfront.

Stop at **Place d'Armes** ②, a square that was the site of battles with the Iroquois in the 1600s and later became the center of Montréal's "Upper Town." There are calèches at the south end of the square; the north side is dominated by the **Bank of Montréal** ③, an impressive building with Corinthian columns, built in 1847 and remodeled by renowned architects McKim, Mead & White in 1905. The soaring towers of the **Basilique Notre-Dame-de-Montréal** ④, one of the most beautiful and ornate churches in North America, dominate the south end of Place d'Armes. The low, more retiring stone building behind a wall to the

west of the basilica is the **Vieux Séminaire** ⑤, Montréal's oldest building. This elegant example of 17th-century Québec architecture is unfortunately closed to the public. Moving back toward the basilica, visit
rue St-Sulpice, one of the the first streets in Montréal. On the eastern
side of the street a plaque marks the spot where Jeanne Mance built
Hôpital Hôtel-Dieu, the city's first hospital, in 1644. Now cross rue
St-Sulpice—the Art Deco **Aldred Building** sits on the far left corner—
and take rue Notre-Dame Est. One block farther, just past boulevard
St-Laurent, on the left, rises the black-glass-sheathed **Palais de Justice**
(1971), the main courthouse for the judicial district of Montréal. The
large domed building at 155 rue Notre-Dame Est, is the Classical Revival–style **Old Courthouse** ⑥ (1857), now municipal offices. Across
the street, at 160 rue Notre-Dame Est, is the **Maison de la Sauvegarde**
(1811), one of the oldest houses in the city and now home to the European sausage restaurant, Chez Better (☞ *Dining, below*). The Old
Courthouse abuts the small **Place Vauquelin** ⑦, named after the 18th-
century naval hero who is memorialized by a statue in its center. North
of this square is **Champs-de-Mars,** the former site of a colonial military parade ground and now a public park. The ornate building on
the east side of Place Vauquelin is the Second Empire–style **Hôtel de
Ville** ⑧, or City Hall, built in 1878. On July 24, 1967, President Charles
de Gaulle of France stood on the central balcony here and made his
famous *"Vive le Québec libre"* speech.

You are in a perfect spot to explore **Place Jacques-Cartier** ⑨, the square
that is the heart of Vieux-Montréal. At the western corner of rue
Notre-Dame is the **Greater Montréal Convention and Tourism Bureau** ⑩. Both sides of the square are lined with two- and three-story
stone buildings that were originally homes or hotels. In the summer,
the one-block **rue St-Amable** ⑪ near the bottom of the square becomes
a marketplace for local jewelers, artists, and craftspeople.

Retrace your steps to the north end of Place Jacques-Cartier and continue east on rue Notre-Dame. On the right, at the corner of rue St-
Claude, is **Château Ramezay** ⑫, built as the residence of the 11th
governor of Montréal, Claude de Ramezay, and now a museum. Continue east to rue Berri. On the corner are two houses from the mid-
19th century that have been transformed into the **George-Étienne
Cartier Museum** ⑬, honoring the most important French-Canadian
statesman of his day and one of the leading figures in founding the Canadian federation in 1867.

When you come out of the museum, walk south on rue Berri to rue
St. Paul and then start walking west again toward the center of the city.
The first street on your right is rue Bonsecours, one of the oldest in
the city. On the corner is the charming Maison du Calvet, now a
restaurant and small bed-and-breakfast. Opposite it is the small but
beautiful **Chapelle Notre-Dame-de-Bonsecours** ⑭, built by St. Marguerite Bourgeoys, Montréal's first schoolteacher. The long, domed building to the west of the chapel is the **Marché Bonsecours** ⑮ (1845), for
many years Montréal's main produce, meat, and fish market, and now
municipal offices. The market has been transformed into a cultural center with exhibits on Montréal.

Rue St-Paul is the most fashionable street in Vieux-Montréal. For almost 20 blocks it is lined with restaurants, shops filled with Québécois handicrafts, and nightclubs. In an old stone building on rue St-Paul
Ouest is an exhibit that focuses on the very new: **Images du Futur** ⑯
is devoted to interactive art and the information superhighway. Eight
blocks west of Place Jacques-Cartier, rue St-Paul leads to **Place Royale** ⑰,
the site of the first permanent settlement in Montréal.

Behind the Old Customs House you will find **Pointe-à-Callière** ⑱, a small park that commemorates the settlers' first landing and is the site of **Musée d'Archéologie Pointe-à-Callière,** Montréal's dazzling museum of history and archeology. A 1½-block walk down rue William takes you to the **Youville Stables** ⑲ on the left. These low stone buildings enclosing a garden were originally built as warehouses in 1825 (they never were stables). They now house offices, shops, and Gibby's restaurant (☞ Dining, *below*).

Across rue William from the stables is the old fire station that houses the **Centre d'Histoire de Montréal** ⑳, a museum that chronicles the day-to-day life of Montrealers throughout the years. Now walk back east on rue William and turn right down rue du Port to rue de la Commune. Across the street is the **Vieux-Port-de-Montréal** ㉑. This once seedy area has been transformed into a very pleasant and popular waterfront park, and makes a fitting close to any walk in Vieux-Montréal. If you have time, you can arrange for a harbor excursion or a daring ride on the Lachine Rapids. The Vieux-Port is also home to the **Cinéma IMAX** ㉒, which shows films on a seven-story screen. The impact can be more terrifying than the rapids.

TIMING

If you walk briskly and don't stop, you could get through this route in under an hour. A more realistic and leisurely pace would take about 90 minutes—still without stopping—longer in winter when the streets are icy. The Basilique Notre-Dame is one of Montréal's most famous landmarks and deserves at least a 45-minute visit; Château de Ramezay deserves the same. Pointe-à-Callière could keep an enthusiastic history buff occupied for a whole day, but give it at least two hours.

Sights to See

Numbers in the margin correspond to points of interest on the Vieux-Montréal map.

❹ **Basilique Notre-Dame-de-Montréal** (Notre-Dame Basilica). The first church called Notre-Dame was a bark-covered structure built in 1642, the year the first settlers arrived. Three times it was torn down and rebuilt, each time in a different spot, each time larger and more ornate. The present church is an enormous (3,800-seat), neo-Gothic structure that opened in 1829. Its architect was an American Protestant named James O'Donnell, who converted to Catholicism during construction and is buried in the church crypt. The twin towers are 228 feet high, and the western one holds one of North America's largest bells. The interior of the church is neo-Gothic, with stained-glass windows, a stunning vaulted blue ceiling studded with thousands of 24-carat gold stars, and pine and walnut wood carving in traditional Québec style. If the church interior looks familiar, that might be because you've seen it on television. In 1978, Luciano Pavarotti sang a program of Christmas music in the church, which is still often rebroadcast in December in the United States. With more than 7,000 pipes, the pipe organ is one of the largest on the continent. If you just want to hear the organ roar, drop in for the 11 AM solemn Mass on Sunday and pay special attention to the recessional. Behind the main altar is the Sacré-Coeur Chapel, which was destroyed by fire in 1978 and rebuilt in five different styles. The chapel is often called the Wedding Chapel because of the hundreds of Montrealers who get married in it every year. When pop star Céline Dion married her manager in 1994, however, the lavish and elaborate ceremony was in the main church. Also in the back of the church is a small museum of religious paintings and historical objects. Please note: Notre-Dame is an active house of worship and visitors should dress accordingly. Also, it is advisable to plan your visit around the daily 12:15

PM Mass in the chapel and the 5 PM Mass in the main church. ✉ *116 rue Notre-Dame Ouest; basilica,* ☎ *514/849–1070; museum, 514/842–2925.* ✒ *Basilica donation requested, tour free; museum $1.* ☉ *Basilica Labor Day–June 24, daily 7–6, and June 25–Labor Day, daily 7 AM–8 PM; guided tour daily (except Sun. morning) May–June 24, daily 9–4, and June 25–Labor Day, daily 8:30–4:30, and Labor Day–mid-Oct., daily 9–4; museum weekends 9:30–5.*

❶ Centre de Commerce Mondial de Montréal (Montréal World Trade Center). This is one of the most pleasant enclosed spaces in Montréal, with a fountain, frequent art exhibits, and some surprisingly comfortable benches. It also has Montréal's own chunk of the Berlin Wall, complete with colorful grafitti. The center covers a block of the rundown ruelle des Fortifications, a narrow lane that marks the place where the city walls once stood. Developers glassed it in and sandblasted and restored 11 of the 19th-century buildings that lined it. It's home to the Hôtel Inter-Continental (☞ Lodging, *below*), a growing number of boutiques and restaurants, and an imaginative food court. *Métro: Square-Victoria Station and follow signs.*

❷⓿ Centre d'Histoire de Montréal. This museum uses video games, soundtracks, models, and more than 300 artifacts to re-create the day-to-day life of the ordinary men and women who have lived in Montréal, from the Indians of precolonial time to modern factory workers. Some of the most touching exhibits are the ones depicting family life in Montréal's working-class tenements during the 20th century. ✉ *335 Place d'Youville,* ☎ *514/872–3207.* ✒ *$4.50.* ☉ *Tues.–Sun. 10–5.*

⓮ Chapelle Notre-Dame-de-Bonsecours. The indomitable Marguerite Bourgeoys dedicated this chapel to the Virgin Mary in 1657. It became known as a sailor's church, and small wood models of sailing ships hang from the ceiling. In the basement there's a small museum that tells the story of the saint's life with a series of little tableaux. A gift shop sells Marguerite Bourgeoys souvenirs. From the museum you can climb to the rather precarious bell tower (beware of the slippery metal steps in winter) for a fine view of Vieux-Montréal and the port. ✉ *400 rue St-Paul Est,* ☎ *514/845–9991.* ✒ *Museum $2.* ☉ *Museum May–Nov., Tues.–Sat. 9–4:30, Sun. 11:30–4:30, and Dec.–Apr., Tues.–Fri. 10:30–2:30, Sat. 10–4:30, Sun. 11:30–4:30; chapel May–Nov., daily 9–5, and Dec.–Apr., daily 10–3.*

⓬ Château Ramezay. This charming little castle is one of the most elegant colonial buildings in Montréal. It was built as the residence of the 11th governor of Montréal, Claude de Ramezay. In 1775–76 it was the headquarters for American troops seeking to conquer Canada; Benjamin Franklin stayed here during that winter occupation. The château became a museum of city and provincial history in 1895, and it has been restored to the style of Governor de Ramezay's day. ✉ *280 rue Notre-Dame Est,* ☎ *514/861–3708.* ✒ *$5.* ☉ *June–Sept., daily 10–6; Oct.– May, Tues.–Sun. 10–4:30.*

NEED A BREAK? In summer there are few places in the city that are lovelier and livelier than Place Jacques Cartier. You could stop at a *terasse* (sidewalk café) for a beer or a coffee or just sit on a bench amid the flower vendors and listen to the street musicians or watch a juggler perform. If you're peckish, there are several snack bars and ice cream stands. If you're really daring, you could try *poutine,* Québec's very own contribution to junk-food culture. It consists of french fries covered with cheese curds and smothered in gravy—an acquired taste.

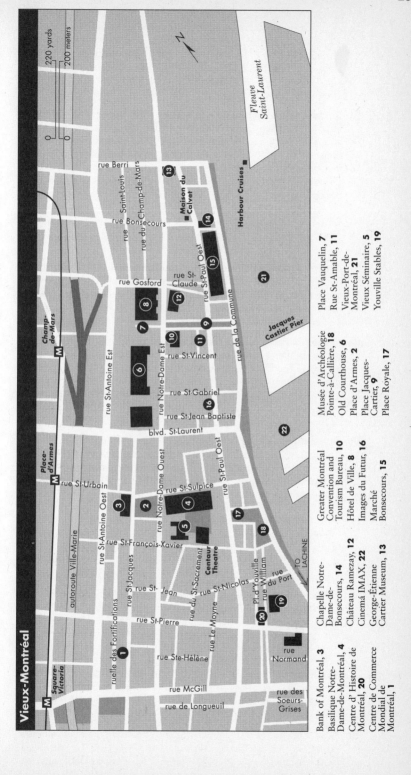

Vieux-Montréal

Bank of Montréal, **3**
Basilique Notre-Dame-de-Montréal, **4**
Centre d' Histoire de Montréal, **20**
Centre de Commerce Mondial de Montréal, **1**

Chapelle Notre-Dame-de-Bonsecours, **14**
Château Ramezay, **12**
Cinemá IMAX, **22**
George-Étienne Cartier Museum, **13**

Greater Montréal Convention and Tourism Bureau, **10**
Hôtel de Ville, **8**
Images du Futur, **16**
Marché Bonsecours, **15**

Musée d'Archéologie Pointe-à-Callière, **18**
Old Courthouse, **6**
Place d'Armes, **2**
Place Jacques-Cartier, **9**
Place Royale, **17**

Place Vauquelin, **7**
Rue St-Amable, **11**
Vieux-Port-de-Montréal, **21**
Vieux Séminaire, **5**
Youville Stables, **19**

🖐 ㉒ **Cinéma IMAX.** Nausea, panic, and vertigo are some of the more negative things people experience the first time they see an IMAX film roar at them from a seven-story screen. Wonder and excitement are among the more positive. The content of the films—most under an hour long—is decidedly educational. It's best to reserve ahead. ⊠ *Vieux-Port, Shed No. 7,* ☎ *514/496–3519 or 514/790–1245.* ▣ *$11.75.* ⏰ *Tues.–Sun. from 9:45 AM.*

⑬ **Georges-Étienne Cartier Museum.** This exhibit honors one of the most important French Canadians of the 19th century, a leader in bringing about the Canadian federation in 1867. The museum comprises two houses. The west house was the Cartiers's home in 1862 and has been meticulously restored to the style of that period, with plush Victorian furniture and decorations. The house on the east focuses on Sir Georges's political career. One delightful exhibit that runs every year from mid-November to mid-December is the Victorian Christmas, when the Cartiers's home is festooned with period decorations. ⊠ *458 rue Notre-Dame Est,* ☎ *514/283–2282.* ▣ *$3.* ⏰ *Late May–Labor Day, daily 10–6; Labor Day–mid-May, Wed.–Sun. 10–noon and 1–5.*

⑩ **Greater Montréal Convention and Tourism Bureau.** This small building (1811) was the site of the old Silver Dollar Saloon, so named because there were 350 silver dollars nailed to the floor. Today it's now one of two tourist information offices operated by Info-Touriste. ⊠ *174 rue Notre-Dame Est,* ☎ *514/873–2015.*

⑯ **Images du Futur.** Make a virtual dog growl and a virtual jungle grow in this exhibit devoted to interactive art and the information superhighway. There are also exhibits of the latest in CD-ROMs and computerized animation. In the electronic café, visitors can have coffee and a sandwich and plug into the Internet on one of 40 computers. ⊠ *85 rue St-Paul Ouest,* ☎ *514/849–1612.* ▣ *$11.75.* ⏰ *Sun.–Thurs. 10–6, Fri.–Sat. 10–9; call for show times.*

🖐 ⑱ **Musée d'Archéologie Pointe-à-Callière.** Here you can get to the very foundations of New France. This museum in the ☞ **Pointe-à-Callière** park was built around the excavated remains of structures dating to Montréal's beginnings, including the city's first Catholic cemetery. It's a labyrinth of stone walls and corridors, illuminated by spotlights and holograms of figures from the past. An audiovisual show gives a historical overview of the area. It also has an excellent gift shop, full of interesting books on Montréal's history, as well as pictures and reproductions of old maps, engravings, and other artifacts. ⊠ *350 pl. Royale,* ☎ *514/872–9150.* ▣ *$7.* ⏰ *June 24–Labor Day, Tues.–Sun. 10–8; Sept. 6–June 23, Tues. and Thur.–Sun. 10–5, Wed. 10–8.*

Palais de Justice. Built in 1971, this black glass building is the main courthouse for the judicial district of Montréal. Criminal law in Canada falls under federal jurisdiction and is based on British common law, but civil law is a provincial matter and Québec's is based on France's Napoleonic Code, which governs all the minutiae of private life—from setting up a company and negotiating a mortgage to drawing up a marriage contract and registering the names of children. Lawyers and judges in Québec courts wear the same elaborate gowns as their British counterparts, but not the wigs. This building is not open for tours. ⊠ *1 rue Notre-Dame Est.*

❷ **Place d'Armes.** This square was the site of battles with the Iroquois in the 1600s and later became the center of Montréal's "Upper Town." In the middle of the square is a statue of Paul de Chomedey, the founder of Montréal. In 1644 he was wounded here in a battle with Indians. There are tunnels beneath the square, which protected the colonists from the extremes of winter weather and provided an escape route. Unfortunately, the tunnels are too small and dangerous to visit. ⊠ *Bordered by rues Notre-Dame Ouest and St-Jacques.*

⑨ Place Jacques-Cartier. This two-block-long square, at the heart of Vieux-Montréal, opened in 1804 as a municipal market, and every summer it is transformed into a flower market. The 1809 monument at the top of the square celebrates Lord Nelson's victory over Napoléon Bonaparte's French navy at Trafalgar. It was built, not as you might expect, by patriotic British residents of Montréal, but by the Sulpician priests, who didn't have much love for the Corsican emperor, either.⊠ *Bordered by rues Notre-Dame Est and de la Commune.*

⑱ Pointe-à-Callière. This small park commemorates the settlers' first landing and is the site of ☞ **Musée d'Archéologie Pointe-à-Callière,** Montréal's dazzling museum of history and archeology. A small stream used to flow into the St. Lawrence here, and it was on the point of land between the two waters that the colonists landed their four boats on May 17, 1642. The settlement was almost washed away the next Christmas by a flood. When it was spared, de Maisonneuve placed a cross on top of Mont-Royal as thanks to God. ⊠ *Bordered by rues de la Commune and William.*

㉑ Vieux-Port-de-Montréal. This port was once the very heart and soul of the city's commercial life. But bigger ships and a longer shipping season made the port obsolete. Now the area is a popular waterfront park with a promenade and benches with views of the river. In summer, there's a giant flea market (☞ Shopping, *below*) in one of the warehouses. Several companies offer boat excursions on the river (☞ Outdoor Activities and Sports, *below*). Cruise ships dock here and so do visiting naval vessels. The port also marks the start of one of the city's most popular bicycle paths. Every weekend, hundreds of Montrealers follow the route of the old Lachine Canal (built in 1825 to bypass the Lachine Rapids and rendered obsolete by the St. Lawrence Seaway) to Parc René Lévesque in Lachine, a narrow spit of land with a great views of Lac St-Louis.

⑤ Vieux Séminaire. This is Montréal's oldest building, which is considered the finest, most elegant example of 17th-century Québec architecture. It was built in 1685 as a headquarters for the Sulpician priests who owned the island of Montréal until 1854, and it is still a residence the Sulpicians who administer the basilica. The clock on the roof over the main doorway is the oldest (pre-1701) public timepiece in North America. Behind the seminary building is a small but beautiful garden, which is unfortunately closed to the public as is the seminary itself. ⊠ *116 rue Notre-Dame Ouest, behind wall west of Basilique Notre-Dame-de-Montréal.*

Centre-Ville (Downtown)

On the surface, Montréal's Centre-Ville is much like the downtown core of many other major cities—full of life and noisy traffic, its streets lined with department stores, boutiques, bars, restaurants, strip clubs, amusement arcades, and bookstores. But, in fact, much of the area's activity goes on beneath the surface, in Montréal's Underground City. Development of this unique endeavor began in 1966 when the Métro opened. Now it includes (at last count) seven hotels, 1,500 offices, 30 movie theaters, more than 1,600 boutiques, 200 restaurants, three universities, two colleges, two train stations, a skating rink, 40 banks, a bus terminal, an art museum, a complex of concert halls, the home ice of the Montréal Canadiens, and a church. All this is linked by Métro lines and more than 30 kilometers (19 miles) of well-lit, boutique-lined passages that protect shoppers and workers from the hardships of winter and the sweltering heat of summer. A traveler arriving by train could book into a fine hotel and spend a week in Montréal shopping, dining, and going to a long list of movies, plays, concerts, sports events, and discos, without once stepping outside.

Aboveground, the downtown core is a sprawling 30-by-8-block area bounded by avenue Atwater and boulevard St-Laurent on the west and east, respectively, avenue des Pins on the north, and rue St-Antoine on the south. In the early days of European settlement, this area was a patchwork of farms, pastures, and woodlots. After 1700, however, Montréal was growing too big for the walled confines of Vieux-Montréal. In 1701 the French administration signed a peace treaty with the Iroquois, and the colonists began to feel safe about building outside Montréal's fortifications. The city inched northward, toward Mont-Royal, particularly after the British conquest in 1760. By the end of the 19th century, rue Ste-Catherine was the main commercial thoroughfare, and the city's elite built mansions on the slope of the mountain. Since 1960 city planners have made a concerted effort to move the focus eastward. With the opening of Place des Arts (1963) and the Complexe Desjardins (1976), the city center shifted in that direction.

A Good Walk

Numbers in the text below correspond to numbers in the margin and on the maps.

Our downtown walk begins underground at the McGill Métro station, one of the central points in the Underground City. It's linked to half a dozen office towers and two of the "Big Three" department stores, **Eaton** ㉓ and La Baie (the other is Ogilvy). Passages also link the station to such major shopping malls as Le Centre Eaton, Les Promenades de la Cathédrale, and Les Cours Mont-Royal.

A tunnel links the Centre Eaton to **Place Ville-Marie** ㉔. This 1962 office tower was Montréal's first modern skyscraper and the mall complex underneath it was the first link in the Underground City. From here head south via the passageways toward **Le Reine Elizabeth** ㉕, or Queen Elizabeth, hotel. The **Gare Centrale** (Central Railway Station), just behind the hotel, is where most trains from the United States and the rest of Canada arrive. Follow the signs marked "Métro/Place Bonaventure" to **Place Bonaventure** ㉖. On the lower floors of this building are shops, restaurants, and offices, which are topped by the Bonaventure Hilton International and 2½ acres of gardens.

When you've finished exploring Place Bonaventure, go to the northwest corner of the building and descend the escalator into the Underground City. This time follow the signs for **Le 1000 rue de la Gauchetière** ㉗, a skyscraper that's home to the Amphithéâtre Bell, a $5-million indoor ice rink that's open year-round. Return to the tunnels, and follow signs to the Bonaventure Métro station and then to the Canadian Pacific Railway Company's **Windsor Station** ㉘, with its massive stone exterior and amazing steel-and-glass roof. The rail station and the Place Bonaventure métro station below it are all linked to **Centre Molson** ㉙, the new home of the Montréal Canadiens.

Exit the Underground City at the north end of Windsor Station and cross rue de la Gauchetière to **St. George's** ㉚ (1872), a jewel of neo-Gothic architecture and the prettiest Anglican church in the city. Just to the east across rue Peel is **Place du Canada** ㉛, a park with a statue of Sir John A. Macdonald, Canada's first prime minister. Cross the park and rue de la Cathédrale to **Mary Queen of the World Cathedral** ㉜, which is modeled after St. Peter's Basilica in Rome. People sometimes call the massive gray granite building across boulevard René-Lévesque from the cathedral the "Wedding Cake," because it rises in tiers of decreasing size and has lots of columns, but its real name is the **Sun Life Building** ㉝ (1914). At one time it was the largest building in the British Commonwealth. During World War II, much of England's financial reserves and national treasures were stored in Sun Life's vaults. The park that faces the Sun Life Building just north of boulevard René-Lévesque is **Square Dorchester** ㉞, for many years the heart of Montréal. Walk east along boulevard René-Lévesque to **St. Patrick's Basilica** ㉟ (1847). This beautiful old church is to Montréal's English-speaking Catholics what Notre-Dame is to the city's French-speaking Catholics.

After visiting the church, backtrack a half block, cross boulevard René-Lévesque, and walk north on rue Phillips (which becomes rue Aylmer) to rue **Ste-Catherine,** the main retail shopping street of Montréal. Here you'll see the exteriors of some of the places you've already visited underground. At the northwest corner of rues Ste-Catherine and Aylmer is **La Baie** department store. The church just west of La Baie is **Christ Church Cathedral** ㊱ (1859), the main church of the Anglican diocese of Montréal.

As you continue your walk west, pause briefly to admire the **view** at the corner of rue Ste-Catherine and avenue McGill College. Look north up this broad boulevard and you can see the Victorian-era buildings of the McGill University campus with Mont-Royal looming in the background. The grim-looking gray castle you can see high on the slopes to the right is the Royal Victoria Hospital.

Another six blocks farther west is **Ogilvy** ㊲, the last of the Big Three department stores. **Rue de la Montagne,** and rues **Crescent** and **Bishop,** the two streets just west of it, constitute the heart of Montréal's downtown nightlife and restaurant scene. This area once formed the playing fields of the Montréal Lacrosse and Cricket Grounds, and later it became an exclusive suburb lined with millionaires' row houses. Since then these three streets between rues Sherbrooke and Ste-Catherine have become fertile ground for trendy bars, restaurants, and shops ensconced in those old row houses.

While you're in the vicinity, take in **Le Centre Canadien d'Architecture** ㊳, the Canadian Center for Architecture, just four blocks west at rue St-Marc on rue Baile. Walk north on rue Fort three blocks to rue Sherbrooke. On the north side of the street you will see a complex of fine neoclassical buildings in a shady garden. This is the **Grand Séminaire de Montréal** ㊴, a former seminary and girls' school.

Three blocks east at rue Bishop you'll enter a very different environment: the exclusive neighborhood known as the **Golden Square Mile** ㊵. In the heart of this district at the corner of rues Sherbrooke and de Musée is the **Musée des Beaux-Arts de Montréal** ㊶, the Museum of Fine Arts. The oldest museum in the country, it was founded by a group of Anglophone Montrealers in 1860 and has a large collection of art, artifacts, and decorative art from around the world. Walking east on rue Sherbrooke brings you to the small and exclusive **Holt Renfrew** ㊷ department store, perhaps the city's fanciest, at the corner of rue de la Montagne. One block farther east at rue Drummond stands the **Ritz-Carlton** ㊸, the grande dame of Montréal hotels.

The grassy campus of **McGill University** ㊹ is on the north side of rue Sherbrooke just three blocks west of the Ritz-Carlton. Just across rue

Sherbrooke from the campus is the **McCord Museum of Canadian History** ㊺, one of the best history museums in Canada. Turn right on rue University and walk a block to the McGill Métro station. Take the train one stop in the direction of Honoré-Beaugrand to the **Place des Arts** ㊻ station and follow the signs to the theater complex of the same name. The **Musée d'Art Contemporain** ㊼, the city's modern art museum, is in Place des Arts. While still in Place des Arts, follow the signs to the **Complexe Desjardins** ㊽, an office building, hotel, and mall along the lines of Place Ville-Marie (☞ *above*). The next development south is the **Complexe Guy-Favreau,** a huge federal office building named after the Canadian minister of justice in the early '60s. If you continue in a straight line, you will hit the **Palais des Congrès de Montréal Convention Centre** ㊾ above the Place d'Armes Métro stop. But if you take a left out of Guy-Favreau onto rue de la Gauchetière, you will be in **Chinatown** ㊿, a relief after all that enclosed retail space.

TIMING

Just to walk this route briskly will take a minimum of two hours, even on a fine day. Several of the musuems along the route—the McCord, the Centre Canadien d'Architecture, the Musée d'Art Contemporain, and the Musée des Beaux-Arts—are worthy of visits of at least two hours each. So if you want to see everything, it would be wise to spread the tour of downtown over two days, stopping the first day after the Musée des Beaux-Arts. Another possibility is to walk the route in one day, stopping briefly at places like St. Patrick's Basilica and perhaps going for a skate at the Amphithéâtre Bell, and then doing the museums on another day.

Sights to See

Numbers in the margin correspond to points of interest on the Downtown Montréal map.

☝ **Amphithéâtre Bell.** Skating is a passion in Montréal and you can do it year-round in this $5-million indoor ice rink on the ground floor of
㉗ the skyscraper Le **1000 rue de la Gauchetière.** The rink is bathed in natural light and surrounded by cafés, a food court, and a winter garden. It's open to skaters of all levels of experience; skate rentals and lockers are available. There are also skating lessons, Saturday-night skating to rock music, and scheduled ice shows. To find the rink once you're inside the building, remember the French word for skating rink is *patinoire.* ⊠ *1000 rue de la Gauchetière,* ☏ *514/395–0555, Ext. 237.* ⊠ *$5, skate rental $4.* ⊙ *Weekdays 11:30–10, Sat. 11:30–7, Sun. 11:30–6; dancing on ice for those 18 or over, Sat. 7 PM—midnight.*

NEED A
BREAK?

The formerly grim passageways at the back of Central Station just below the escalators leading to Place Ville-Marie have been transformed into one of Montréal's trendiest food courts, Les Halles de la Gare. This is not a burger-and-fried-chicken emporium—the dining area is set up like a library with wooden tables and trompe l'oeil bookshelves. The food available includes some of the best bread and baked goods in the city, salads, sandwiches made with fresh terrine and pâté, and homemade pastries and ice cream. If it's nice out, you can take your snack and go up the escalator to the mall under Place Ville-Marie and then up the stairs in the middle of its food court to the terrace, a wide area with a fine view much favored by office workers on their lunch break or coffee break.

㉙ **Centre Molson.** Opened in spring 1996, this arena is the new home of the Montréal Canadiens, the hockey team devoted hometown fans call simply *les Glorieux.* The brown-brick building replaces the old Forum that had been the Canadiens's home since 1917. The new

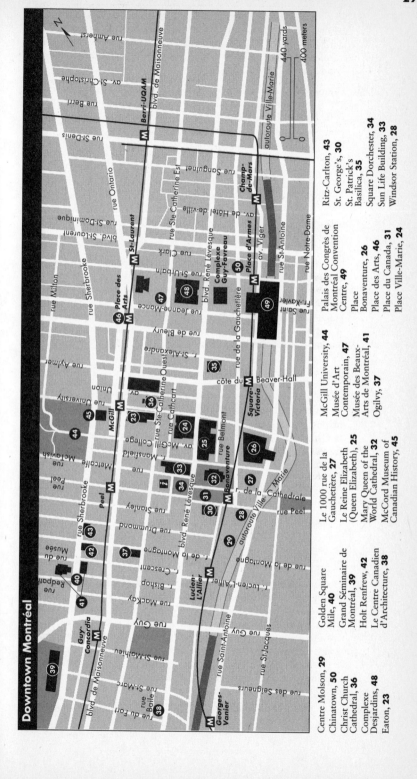

Downtown Montréal

Centre Molson, **29**
Chinatown, **50**
Christ Church
Cathedral, **36**
Complexe
Desjardins, **48**
Eaton, **23**

Golden Square
Mile, **40**
Grand Séminaire de
Montréal, **39**
Holt Renfrew, **42**
Le Centre Canadien
d'Architecture, **38**

Le 1000 rue de la
Gauchetière, **27**
Le Reine Elizabeth
(Queen Elizabeth), **25**
Mary Queen of the
World Cathedral, **32**
McCord Museum of
Canadian History, **45**

McGill University, **44**
Musée d'Art
Contemporain, **47**
Musée des Beaux-
Arts de Montréal, **41**
Ogilvy, **37**

Palais des Congrès de
Montréal Convention
Centre, **49**
Place
Bonaventure, **26**
Place des Arts, **46**
Place du Canada, **31**
Place Ville-Marie, **24**

Ritz-Carlton, **43**
St. George's, **30**
St. Patrick's
Basilica, **35**
Square Dorchester, **34**
Sun Life Building, **33**
Windsor Station, **28**

name refers to the Molson family who established Montréal's first brewery in the 18th century and whose present company, Molson-O'Keefe, owns the hockey team. So far, however, Montrealers stubbornly call the place the New Forum. ⊠ *1260 rue de la Gauchetière Ouest,* ☎ *517/932–2582.*

㊿ **Chinatown.** The Chinese first came to Montréal in large numbers after 1880, following the construction of the transcontinental railroad. They settled in an 18-block area between boulevard René-Lévesque and avenue Viger to the north and south, and near rues Hôtel de Ville and Bleury on the west and east, an area that became known as Chinatown, where there are many restaurants, food stores, and gift shops. If you have enough energy you may want to stroll south on rue St-Urbain for a block to rue St-Antoine. Half a block east is **Steve's Music Store** (⊠ 51 rue St-Antoine Ouest), a shabby warren of five storefronts jammed with just about everything you need to be a rock star except talent. Sooner or later every musician and wanna-be musician in the city wanders through it.

NEED A
BREAK?

For a huge bowl of beef soup full of noodles, vegetables, and big slices of beef, stop at **Pho Bang New York** (⊠ 970 blvd. St-Laurent, ☎ 514/954–2032), a Vietnamese restaurant on the edge of Chinatown. This small-white-tiled place specializes in traditional Vietnamese soups that are served in bowls big enough to bathe a small dog. And it's cheap, too—for less than $5, you get soup, a plate of crispy vegetables, and a small pot of tea. The restaurant does not accept credit cards.

㊱ **Christ Church Cathedral.** This is the main church (1859) of the Anglican diocese of Montréal. In early 1988, the diocese leased the land and air rights to a consortium of developers for 99 years. The consortium then built **La Maison des Coopérants,** a 34-story office tower, behind the cathedral, and a huge retail complex, **Les Promenades de la Cathédrale,** under it. The church has a quiet graceful interior and frequent organ recitals and concerts. ⊠ *535 rue Ste-Catherine Ouest.* ⊙ *Daily 8–6.*

㊽ **Complexe Desjardins.** Built in 1976, this is an office building, hotel, and mall development along the lines of Place Ville-Marie. The luxurious **Le Meridien** hotel (☞ Lodging, *below*) rises from its northwest corner. The large galleria space is the scene of all types of performances, from lectures on Japanese massage techniques to pop music, as well as avid shopping in the dozens of stores. ⊠ *Bounded by rues Ste.-Catherine, Jeanne-Mance, and St.-Urbain and blvd. René Lévesque.*

㊵ **Golden Square Mile.** This was once the richest neighborhood in Canada. At the turn of the century, the people who lived here—mostly of Scottish descent—controlled 70 percent of the country's wealth. Their baronial homes filled an area that stretched from avenue Atwater in the west to rue de Bleury in the east and from rue de la Gauchetière in the south to avenue des Pins halfway up the mountain. Most of those palatial homes have been leveled to make way for high rises and office towers, and the few left are either consulates or conference centers associated with McGill University.

㊴ **Grand Séminaire de Montréal.** This seminary run by the Sulpicians, is housed in buildings that date to 1860; two squat towers in the extensive gardens date to the 17th century. It was in one of these that St. Marguerite Bourgeoys set up her first school for native girls. The towers, which are among the oldest buildings on the island, are visible from the street; there is a little area just by the gates with three plaques that explain the towers and their history in French. The seminary is private, but the public can go to Mass at 10:30 on Sunday morning from September to June in the newly restored chapel. This is a lovely example of 19th-century neoclassical design with choir seating and a magnificent French-style organ. ⊠ *2065 rue Sherbrooke Ouest.*

38 **Le Centre Canadien d'Architecture** (Canadian Center for Architecture). Architect Phyllis Lambert transformed one of the city's grand old mansions into the centerpiece of what is probably the world's premier architectural collection. The center traces the history and development of all architecture (not just Canadian), with exhibits that include blueprints, photographs, scale models, and hands-on demonstrations. The main exhibit is in the Shaughnessy Mansion, a grand 19th-century home that gave its name to Shaughnessy Village, the surrounding neighborhood of homes and apartments. ⊠ *1920 rue Baile,* ☎ *514/939–7000.* ☒ *$5.* ☉ *Wed. and Fri. 11–6, Thurs. 11–8, weekends 11–5.*

32 **Mary Queen of the World Cathedral.** Seat of the Roman Catholic archbishop of Montréal, this church (1894), is modeled after St. Peter's Basilica in Rome. Victor Bourgeau, the same architect who did the interior of Notre-Dame in Vieux-Montréal, thought the idea of the cathedral's design terrible but completed it after the original architect proved incompetent. Inside there is even a canopy over the altar that is a miniature copy of Bernini's *baldacchino* in St. Peter's. ⊠ *1085 rue Cathédral; through main doors on blvd. René Lévesque.*

45 **McCord Museum of Canadian History.** A grand, eclectic attic of a museum, the McCord documents the life of ordinary Canadians, using costumes and textiles, decorative arts, paintings, prints and drawings, and the 700,000-print-and-negative Notman Photographic Archives, which highlights 19th-century life in Montréal. The McCord is the only museum in Canada with a permanent costume gallery. There are guided tours (call for times), a reading room and documentation center, a gift shop and bookstore, and a tearoom. ⊠ *690 rue Sherbrooke Ouest,* ☎ *514/398–7100.* ☒ *$5.* ☉ *Tues., Wed., and Fri. 10–6; Thurs. 10–9; weekends 10–5; closed Mon. except statutory holidays.*

44 **McGill University.** James McGill, a wealthy Scottish fur trader, bequeathed the money and the land for this institution, which opened in 1828 and is perhaps the finest English-language university in the nation. The student body numbers 15,000, and the university is best known for its medical and engineering schools. Most of the campus buildings are fine examples of Victorian architecture. ⊠ *845 rue Sherbrooke Ouest.*

NEED A BREAK? The McGill University campus is an island of green in a sea of traffic and skyscrapers. On a fine day you can sit on the grass in the shade of a 100-year-old tree and just let the world drift by.

47 **Musée d'Art Contemporain.** The museum's large permanent collection of modern art represents works by Québécois, Canadian, and international artists in every medium. The museum often has weekend programs, with many child-oriented activities, and almost all are free. There are guided tours; hours vary. ⊠ *185 rue Ste-Catherine Ouest,* ☎ *514/847–6226.* ☒ *$5, Wed. evening free.* ☉ *Tues. and Thurs.–Sun. 11–6, Wed. 11–9.*

41 **Musée des Beaux-Arts de Montréal** (Museum of Fine Arts). Montréal's main art museum houses its permanent collection and displays its special exhibits in the older Benaiah-Gibb Pavilion on the north side of rue Sherbrooke and in the glittering Pavilion Jean-Noël-Desmarais right across the street. The newer pavilion, with a dramatic glass front that incorporates the redbrick facade of a former apartment building, was designed by architect Moshe Safdie, and more than doubles the size of the museum. The two buildings are connected by underground tunnels and hold a large collection of European and North American fine and decorative art; ancient treasures from Europe, the Near East, Asia, Africa, and America; art from Québec and Canada; and Native American and Inuit artifacts. The museum has a gift shop, an art-book store, a restaurant, a cafeteria, and a gallery from which you can buy or rent paintings by local artists. ⊠ *1380 rue Sherbrooke Ouest,* ☎ *514/285–1600.* ✆ *Permanent collection free, special exhibitions $10.* ☉ *Tues. and Thurs.–Sun. 11–6, Wed. 11–9.*

⓴ Place des Arts. The Place des Arts theater complex, which opened in 1963, is reminiscent of New York's Lincoln Center in that it is a government-subsidized complex of three very modern theaters. Guided tours of the halls and backstage are available. The **Musée d'Art Contemporain,** the city's modern art museum, moved here in 1991 (☞ *above*). ⊠ *183 rue Ste.-Catherine Ouest,* ☎ *514/842–2112; guided tour, 514/285– 4275.*

㉛ Place du Canada. This park has a statue of Sir John A. Macdonald, Canada's first prime minister. In October 1995, this area was the site of a huge rally for Canadian unity that drew more than 300,000 participants from across the country. That patriotic demonstration was at least partly responsible for blunting the separatist drive and preserving a slim victory for the pro-unity forces in the subsequent referendum on independence for Québec. At the south end of Place du Canada is **Le Marriott Château Champlain** (☞ Lodging, *below*), known as the Cheese Grater because of its rows and rows of half-moon-shape windows. ⊠ *Bordered by blvd. Réne Lévesque and rue de la Gauchetière.*

㉟ St. Patrick's Basilica. This basilica (1847), is one of the purest examples of the Gothic Revival style in Canada. St. Patrick's is off the tourist trail and lacks some of Notre-Dame's grandeur, but it makes up for it in warmth. The colors are soft and the vaulted ceiling over the sanctuary glows with green and gold mosaics. The old pulpit has panels depicting the Apostles and the huge lamp is decorated with six 6-foot-high angels that hangs over the main altar. If you're named after some obscure saint, you might find his or her portrait in one of the 150 painted panels that decorate the oak wainscoting along the walls of the nave. The church has a strong musical tradition: solemn Mass is sung every Sunday at 11 AM (in Latin, the third week of every month) from September to June. ⊠ *460 blvd. René-Lévesque Ouest,* ☎ *514/866–0491.* ☉ *Daily 8:30–6.*

㉞ Square Dorchester. Until 1870, a Catholic burial ground occupied this block (and there are still bodies buried beneath the grass); but with the rapid development of the area, the city decided to turn it into a park. The statuary includes a monument to the Boer War in the center and a statue of the Scottish poet Robert Burns near rue Peel. ⊠ *Bordered by rues Peel and Metcalfe McTavish.*

Quartier Latin (Latin Quarter)

Numbers in the text below correspond to numbers in the margin and on the maps.

Early in this century, rue St-Denis cut through a bourgeois neighborhood of large, comfortable residences. The Université de Montréal was established here in 1893, and the students and academics who moved into the area dubbed it the Quartier Latin, or Latin Quarter. The university eventually moved to a larger campus on the north side of Mont-Royal, and the area went into decline. It revived in the early 1970s, and then boomed, largely as a result of the 1969 opening of the Université du Québec à Montréal and the launch of the International Jazz Festival in the summer of 1980. Plateau Mont-Royal, the neighborhood just north of the Quartier Latin, shared in this revival. Its residents are now a mix of immigrants, working-class Francophones, and young professionals eager to find a home they can renovate close to the city center. The Quartier Latin and Plateau Montréal are home to rows of French and ethnic restaurants, charming bistros, coffee shops, designer boutiques, antiques shops, and art galleries. When night falls, these streets are always full of omnilingual hordes—young and not so young, rich and poor, established and still studying.

Many of the older residences in this area have graceful wrought-iron balconies and twisting staircases that are typical of Montréal. They were built that way for practical reasons. The buildings are what Montrealers call duplexes or triplexes, that is, two or three residences stacked on top of each other. To save interior space, the stairs to reach the upper floors were put outside. The stairs and balconies are treacherous in winter, but in summer they are often full of families and couples, gossiping, picnicking, and partying. If Montrealers tell you they spend the summer in Balconville, they mean they don't have the money or the time to leave town and won't get any farther than their balcony.

A Good Walk

Begin at the **Berri-UQAM** Métro stop, perhaps the most important in the whole city, because three lines intersect here. The "UQAM" in the subway name is pronounced "oo-kam" by local Francophones and "you-kwam" by local Anglophones. It refers to the **Université du Québec à Montréal** ⑤①, which has no traditional campus. It has some splendid fragments of Gothic grandeur you can see sprouting up among the modern brick hulks, and the ornate **Chapelle Notre-Dame-de-Lourdes** ⑤②.

Rue St-Denis is lined with cafés, bistros, and restaurants that attract the academic crowd. On rue Ste-Catherine there are a number of low-rent nightclubs popular with avant-garde rock-and-roll types. Just west of rue St-Denis you find the **Cinémathèque Québécoise** ⑤③, which houses one of the largest cinematic reference libraries in the world.

Around the corner and a half block north on rue St-Denis stands the 2,500-seat **Théâtre St-Denis** ⑤④, the second-largest auditorium in Montréal (after Salle Wilfrid Pelletier in Place des Arts). Sarah Bernhardt and many other famous actors have graced its stage. On the next block north you see the Beaux-Arts **Bibliothèque Nationale du Québec** (1915), a library that houses Québec's official archives (✉ 1700 rue St-Denis, ☎ 514/873–1100), which are open Tuesday–Saturday 9–5.

Turn left on Sherbrooke and left again on boulevard St-Laurent for the **Musée Juste pour Rire** ⑤⑤, the world's first museum of humor. Backtrack east on rue Sherbrooke and turn left on rue St-Denis. Above the Sherbrooke Métro station is the **Institut de Tourisme et d'Hôtellerie du Québec,** where students learn the art of cooking and serving food, mixing drinks, and managing a hotel in a singularly ugly building that overlooks **Square St-Louis** ⑤⑥, one of the most graceful green spaces in Montréal.

The stretch of **rue Prince Arthur** ⑤⑦, beginning at the western end of ☞ Square St-Louis and continuing several blocks west, is a center of youth culture. When you reach **boulevard St-Laurent** ⑤⑧, take a right and stroll north on the street that cuts through Montréal life in a number of ways. First, this is the east–west dividing street; like the Greenwich meridian, boulevard St-Laurent is where all the numbers begin.

The street is also lined with shops and restaurants that represent the ethnic diversity of Montréal.

This area was still partly rural in the mid-19th century, with lots of open space and fresh air, which made it healthier than overcrowded Vieux-Montréal. So in 1861, the Hôpital Hôtel-Dieu, the hospital Jeanne Mance founded in the 17th century, moved into a new building at what is now the corner of avenue des Pins and rue St-Urbain, just a block west of boulevard St-Laurent. Hôtel-Dieu, one of the city's major hospitals, is still there, and right next to it is the **Musée des Hospitalières** 59, which gives a remarkable picture of the early days of colonization.

Just 30 years after the hospital moved, the first electric tramway that could climb the slope to Plâteau Mont-Royal was installed on boulevard St-Laurent. Working-class families, who couldn't afford a horse and buggy to pull them up the hill, began to move in. In the 1880s the first of many waves of Russian-Jewish immigrants escaping the pogroms arrived and settled here. Boulevard St-Laurent became known as the Main, as in "Main Street," and Yiddish was the primary language spoken along some stretches. The Russian Jews were followed by Greeks, Eastern Europeans, Portuguese, and, most recently, Latin Americans.

The 10 blocks north of rue Sherbrooke are filled with delis, junk stores, restaurants, luncheonettes, and clothing stores, as well as fashionable boutiques, bistros, cafés, bars, nightclubs, bookstores, and galleries exhibiting the work of the latest wave of "immigrants" to the area—gentrifiers and artists. The block between rues Roy and Napoléon is particularly rich in delights.

Merchants are attempting to re-create rue Prince Arthur on **rue Duluth** 60. Turn right and walk four blocks east to rue St-Denis, where you will find Greek and Vietnamese restaurants and boutiques and art galleries on either side of the street. Walk east another nine blocks and you come to **Parc Lafontaine.** At about 100 acres, it's the smallest of Montréal's three major parks, but it's a lively place and is much loved by area residents.

After exploring the park, walk south to rue Sherbrooke Est and then turn right and walk west on rues Sherbrooke and Cherrier to the Sherbrooke Métro station to complete the walk. Or head west to begin the Parc du Mont-Royal tour (☞ *below*).

TIMING
This is a comfortable afternoon walk, lasting perhaps two hours, longer if you linger for an hour or so in the Musée des Hospitallières and spend some time shopping. There's a bit of a climb from boulevard de Maisonneuve to rue Sherbrooke.

Sights to See
Numbers in the margin correspond to points of interest on the Latin Quarter and Mount Royal Park map.

52 **Chapelle Notre-Dame-de-Lourdes.** This tiny Roman Catholic chapel is one of the most ornate pieces of religious architecture in the city. It was built in 1876 and decorated with brightly colored murals by artist Napoléon Bourassa, who lived nearby. It's a mixture of Roman and Byzantine styles, and its beautifully restored interior is a must-see, despite the panhandlers that cluster at its doors and the somewhat eccentric devotees it attracts. ⊠ *430 rue Ste-Catherine Est.* ⊙ *Daily 8–5.*

53 **Cinémathèque Québécoise.** This museum and repertory movie house is one of Montréal's great bargains. For $3 you can visit the perma-

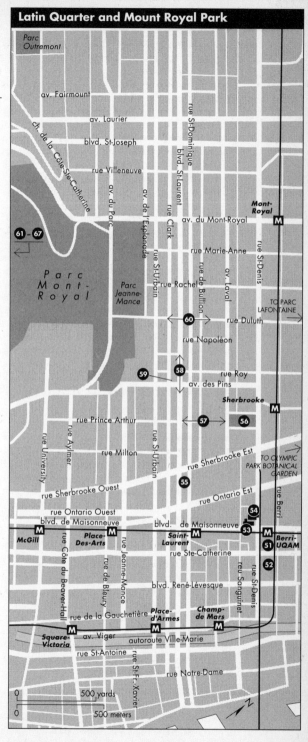

Latin Quarter and Mount Royal Park

nent exhibition on the history of filmmaking equipment and see two movies. ✉ *335 blvd. de Maisonneuve Ouest,* ☎ *514/842–9763.*

59 Musée des Hospitalières. France in the 17th century was consumed with religious fervor, and aristocratic men and women often built hospitals, schools, and churches in distant lands. The nuns of the Religieuses Hospitalières de St-Joseph who came to Montréal in the mid-17th century to help Jeanne Mance run the Hôpital Hôtel Dieu were good examples of this fervor, and much of their spirit is evident in the letters, books, and religious artifacts displayed here. Pay special attention to the beautiful wooden stairway in the museum's entrance hall. There's a fascinating and sometimes chilling exhibit on the history of medicine and nursing. ✉ *201 av. des Pins Ouest,* ☎ *514/849–2919.* ✚ *$5.* ☉ *Mid-June–mid-Oct., Tues.–Fri. 10–5, weekends 1–5; mid-Oct.–mid-June, Wed.–Sun. 1–5.*

NEED A
BREAK?

Café Santropol (✉ 3990 St-Urbain, ☎ 514/842–3110) serves hearty soups, cake, salads, a huge selection of teas, and unusual high-rise sandwiches garnished with fruit (the Jeanne Mance mixes pineapples and chives in cream cheese). The atmosphere is, well, homey, with a molded tin ceiling and a private little *terasse* out back—all under the watchful eye of a plaster statue of St. Francis of Assisi. One percent of the profits go to charity. Credit cards are not accepted.

55 Musée Juste pour Rire (International Humor Museum). This is the first museum in the world to be dedicated to laughter. Its multimedia exhibits explore and celebrate humor by drawing visitors into their plots. And some of the visiting exhibits have a serious side. There is a large collection of humor videos, a cabaret where budding comics can test their material, and a restaurant where you can watch old tapes while you eat. ✉ *2111 blvd. St-Laurent,* ☎ *514/845–4000,* ✚ *$9.95.* ☉ *Tues.–Sun. 1–8.*

Parc Lafontaine. Montréal's two main cultures are reflected in this park's layout: the eastern half is pure French with paths, gardens, and lawns laid out in rigid geometric shapes; the western half is based on the English model with meandering paths and irregularly shaped ponds that follow the natural contours of the land. For summer visitors there are two artificial lakes where you can rent paddleboats, bowling greens, tennis courts, and an open-air theater with free arts events. In winter, the two artificial lakes form a large skating rink. ✉ *3933 av. Parc Lafontaine,* ☎ *514/872–6211.* ☉ *Daily 9 AM–10 PM.*

57 Rue Prince Arthur. In the 1960s, the young people who moved to the neighborhood transformed this street into a small hippie bazaar of clothing, leather, and smoke shops. It remains a center of youth culture, although it's now much tamer and more commercial. The city turned the blocks between avenue Laval and boulevard St-Laurent into a pedestrian mall. Hippie shops have metamorphosed into inexpensive Greek, Vietnamese, Italian, Polish, and Chinese restaurants and little neighborhood bars. ✉ *Beginning at western end of sq. St-Louis and stretching a few blocks west.*

56 Square St-Louis. This is one of the most graceful squares in Montréal. It has a fountain and trees and is surrounded by 19th-century homes built in the large, comfortable style of the Second Empire. Originally a reservoir, these blocks became a park in 1879 and attracted upper-middle-class families and artists to the area. French Canadian poets were among the most famous creative people to occupy the houses back then, and the neighborhood is now home to painters, filmmakers, musicians, and writers. On the wall of 336 Square St-Louis you can see—

and read, if your French is good—a long poem by Michel Bujold. ⊠ *Bordered by av. Laval and rue St-Denis.*

NEED A BREAK? On a pleasant sunny day there is no finer place to rest your feet than on one of the park benches near the fountain in Square St-Louis. There are plenty of take-out restaurants nearby if you want a coffee or a pastry.

🗿 **Université du Québec à Montréal.** Part of a network of provincial campuses set up by the provincial government in 1969, UQAM, which anchors the academic life of the surrounding Latin Quarter, has no traditional campus, but is housed in a series of massive, modern brick buildings that clog much of the three city blocks bordered by rues Sanguinet and Berri and boulevards de Maisonneuve and René-Lévesque. The splendid fragments of Gothic grandeur that you can see sprouting up among the modern brick hulks like flowers in a swamp are all that's left of the once magnificent Eglise St. Jacques. A more substantial religious monument that has survived right in UQAM's resolutely secularist heart is the Chapelle Notre-Dame-de-Lourdes (☞ *above*).

Parc du Mont-Royal (Mount Royal Park)

Parc du Mont-Royal (Mount Royal Park) is 494 acres of forest and paths in the heart of the city. It was designed by Frederick Law Olmsted, the celebrated architect of New York's Central Park. He believed that communion with nature could cure body and soul, and the park follows the natural topography and accentuates its features, in the English style. You can go skating on Beaver Lake in the winter, visit one of the two lookouts and scan the horizon. Horse-drawn transport is popular year-round: sleigh rides in winter and calèche rides in summer. On the eastern side of the hill stands the 100-foot steel cross that is the symbol of the city. Not far away from the park and perched on a neighboring crest of the same mountain is the Oratoire St-Joseph, a shrine that draws millions of tourists every year.

A Good Walk

Begin by taking the Métro's Orange Line to the Mont-Royal station and transfer to a No. 11 bus (be sure to get a transfer [*correspondance* in French] from a machine before you get on the Métro). The No. 11 drives right through the park on the Voie Camilien Houde. Get off at the **Obsérvatoire de l'Est** ㉛, a lookout that gives a spectacular view of the east end of the city and the St. Lawrence River. Climb the stone staircase at the end of the parking lot and follow the trails to the **Chalet du Mont-Royal** ㉜, a large, baronial building with a wide semicircular, flagstone terrace in front of it overlooking downtown Montréal. The next stop is **Lac aux Castors** ㉝, or Beaver Lake, and there are at least three ways to get there. You can take the long way and walk down the steep flight of stairs at the east end of the terrace and then turn right to follow the gravel road that circles the mountain. The shortest way is to leave the terrace at the west end of the terrace and follow the crowds along the road. The middle way is to leave at the east end, but then to turn off the main road and follow one of the shaded paths that leads through the woods and along the southern ridge of the mountain. Lac aux Castors was reclaimed from boggy ground and so violates Olmstead's purist vision of a natural environment. But children like to float boats on it in summer, and it makes a fine skating rink in winter.

Across Chemin Remembrance from Lac aux Castors is what looks like one vast cemetery. It is in fact, two cemeteries—one Protestant and the other Catholic. The **Cimetière Mont-Royal** ㉞ is toward the east in a little valley that cuts off the noise of the city; it is the final resting place of Anna Leonowens, the real-life heroine of *The King and I*. The yellow-brick buildings and tower you can see on the north side of the mountain beyond Mount Royal Cemetery belong to the **Université de Montréal,** the second-largest French-language university in the world with nearly 60,000 students. If you're now humming "Getting to Know You," you'll probably change your tune to Canada's national anthem when you enter the **Cimetière Notre-Dame-des-Neiges** ⑥⑤, as the song's composer, Calixa Lavallée, is buried here.

Wander northwest through the two cemeteries, and you will eventually emerge on Chemin Queen Mary on the edge of a decidedly lively area of street vendors, ethnic restaurants, and boutiques. Walk west on Queen Mary across Chemin Côte-des-Neiges, and you come to Montréal's most grandiose religious monument, the **Oratoire St-Joseph** ⑥⑥. This huge domed church perched high on a ridge of Mont-Royal is the largest shrine in the world dedicated to the earthly father of Jesus. Across the street is the ivy-covered **Collège Notre Dame** ⑥⑦, where the oratory's founder, Brother André, worked as a porter. It's still an important private school, and one of the few in the city that still accepts boarders. Its students these days, however, include girls, a situation that would have shocked Brother André.

After visiting the church, retrace your steps to Chemin Côte-des-Neiges, and walk through the lively neighborhood to the Côte-des-Neiges station to catch the Métro home.

TIMING
Allot at least the better part of a day for this tour; longer if you plan on catching some rays or ice skating in the park.

Sights to See

⑥② **Chalet du Mont-Royal.** This large, baronial building with a wide semicircular, flagstone terrace in front of it overlooks downtown Montréal. In the distance you can see Mont-Royal's sister mountains—Mont St-Bruno, Mont St-Hilaire, and Mont St-Grégoire. These isolated peaks—called the Montétrégies or Mountains of the King—rise quite dramatically from flat surrounding countryside. Be sure to take a look inside the chalet, especially at the murals that depict scenes from Canadian history. There's a snack bar in the back. ☉ *Daily 9–5.*

⑥④ **Cimetière Mont-Royal.** This cemetery was established in 1852 by the Anglican, Presbyterian, Unitarian, and Baptist churches, and was laid out like a landscaped garden with monuments that are genuine works of art. Many prominent families have mausoleums and plots here, but the cemetery's most famous permanent guest is Anna Leonowens, who was governess to the children of the King of Siam and is the real-life model for the heroine of the musical *The King and I*. There are no tours of the cemetery. ✉ *1297 Chemin de la Forêt.*

⑥⑤ **Cimetière Notre-Dame-des-Neiges.** This Catholic graveyard is the largest in the city, and the final resting place of hundreds of prominent artists, poets, intellectuals, politicians, and clerics. Among them is Calixa Lavallée, who wrote "O Canada." Many of the monuments and mausoleums—scattered along 55 kilometers (more than 30 miles) of paths and roadways—are the work of leading artists. There are no tours of the cemetery. ✉ *4601 Côte-des-Neiges.*

⑥⑥ **Oratoire St-Joseph** (St. Joseph's Oratory). This huge church is the result of the persistence of a remarkable little man named Brother André, who was a porter in the school that his religious order ran. He dreamed of building a shrine dedicated to St. Joseph—Canada's patron saint—

and began in 1904 by building a little chapel. Miraculous cures were reported and attributed to St. Joseph's intercession, and Brother André's project caught the imagination of Montréal. The result is one of the most important shrines in North America. The oratory dome is one of the biggest in the world and the church has a magnificent setting. It's also home to Les Petits Chanteurs de Mont-Royal, the city's finest boys' choir. But alas, the interior is oppressive and drab. There's a more modest and quite undistinguished crypt church at the bottom of the structure, and right behind it is a room that glitters with hundreds of votive candles lit in honor of St. Joseph. The walls are festooned with crutches discarded by the cured. Right behind that is the simple tomb of Brother André, who was beatified in 1982. Brother André's heart is displayed in a glass case upstairs in a small museum depicting events in his life. From early December through February the oratory features a display of crèches (nativity scenes) from all over the world. High on the mountain beside the main church is a beautiful garden, commemorating the passion of Christ with life-sized representations of the 14 traditional Stations of the Cross. Carillon, choral, and organ concerts are held weekly at the oratory during the summer. To visit the church you can either climb the more than 300 steps to the front door (many pilgrims do so on their knees, pausing to pray at each step) or you can take the shuttle bus that runs from the front gate. ✉ *3800 Chemin Queen Mary, near Côte-des-Neiges Métro station,* ☎ *514/733–8211.* ☉ *Sept.–May, daily 6 AM–9:30 PM; June–Aug., daily 6 AM—10 PM.*

Parc Olympique (Olympic Park) and Jardin Botanique (Botanical Garden)

Olympic Park and Botanical Garden are in the east end of the city. You can reach them via the Pie-IX or Viau Métro stations (the latter is nearer the stadium entrance).

The giant, mollusk-shape Stade Olympique (Olympic Stadium) and the leaning tower that supports its roof are probably the preeminent symbols of modern Montréal—they dominate the skyline of the eastern end of the city. But the area has a lot more to recommend it than just the stadium complex: Montréal's world-class Jardin Botanique (Botanical Garden) is nearby, as are Parc Maisonneuve and the Insectarium, the world's largest museum dedicated to bugs (visit at the right time, and you can even taste a few delicacies like deep-fried bumblebees).

There are daily guided tours of the entire complex, which leave from the **Tourist Hall** (☎ 514/252–8687) in the base of the Tower. The tours at 12:40 and 3:40 are in English and the ones at 11 and 2 are in French.

A Good Walk

Numbers in the text below correspond to numbers in the margin and on the maps.

Start with a ride on the Métro's Green Line and get off at the Viau station, which is only a few steps from the main entrance to the 70,000-seat **Stade Olympique** ⑱, built for the 1976 summer games. A trip to the top of the **Tour Olympique** ⑲, or Olympic Tower, the world's tallest tilting structure, on the funicular is very popular with visitors; a two-level cable car can whisk 90 people up the exterior of the 890-foot tower. On a clear day you can see up to 80 kilometers (50 miles) from the tower-top observatory. Under the base of the tower is the **Centre Aquatique** ⑳ (☎ 514/252–4622), the Aquatic Center, a complex of six swimming pools that's a good place for a refreshing dip.

Right next to the tower is what used to be the Velodrome, where the Olympic bicycle races were held. It has been converted into the very popular **Biodôme** ⑦, where you can explore both a rain forest and an arctic landscape. Continuing your back-to-nature experience, cross rue Sherbrooke to the north of the Olympic Park (or take the free shuttle bus) to reach the **Jardin Botanique** ⑦. This park, with 181 acres of gardens in summer and 10 exhibition greenhouses open all year, is the second-largest attraction of its kind in the world (after England's Kew Gardens). It includes the **Insectarium** ⑦ and the 5-acre **Montréal-Shanghai Lac de Rêve** ⑦, or Montréal-Shanghai Dream Lake Garden, an elegant Ming-style garden.

After you've looked at the flowers and the bugs, return to boulevard Pie IX, which runs along the eastern border of the gardens. The name of this main traffic artery (and the adjoining Métro station) puzzles thousands of tourists every year. The street is named for the 19th-century pope, Pius IX, or Pie IX in French. It's pronounced Pee-neuf, however, which isn't at all how it looks from an English-speaker's standpoint.

Walk south, crossing rues Rachel and Sherbrooke, to the **Musée des Arts Décoratifs** ⑦ on the west side of rue Sherbrooke. This exhibit of furniture and home decoration is in one of the best examples of Beaux-Arts architecture in Montréal.

TIMING
To see all the sights at a leisurely pace, you'll need a full day.

Sights to See
Numbers in the margin correspond to points of interest on the Olympic Park and the Botanical Garden map.

⑦ **Biodôme.** Not everyone thought it was a great idea to change a bicycle-racing stadium into a natural-history exhibit, but the result is one of the city's most popular attractions, with both residents and visitors. It combines four ecosystems—the boreal forest, tropical forest, polar world, and St. Lawrence River—under one climate-controlled dome. Visitors follow protected pathways through each environment, observing indigenous flora and fauna of each ecosystem. A word of warning: the tropical forest really is tropical. If you want to stay comfortable, dress in layers. ⊠ *4777 av. Pierre-de-Coubertin,* ☎ *514/868–3000.* ⌧ *$9.50.* ⊙ *June 18–Sept. 9, daily 9–8; Sept. 10–June 17, daily 9–6.*

⑦ **Jardin Botanique** (Botanical Garden). The garden was founded in 1931, and has more than 26,000 species of plants. The poisonous plant garden is a perennial favorite. Visitors can see a traditional tea ceremony in the Japanese Garden, which also has one of the best bonsai collections in the West. The 5-acre **Montréal-Shanghai Dream Lake Garden** is the largest Ming-style garden outside Asia, with seven elegant pavilions and a 30-foot rockery built around a reflecting pool. The **Insectarium**, a bug-shape building, houses more than 250,000 insect specimens. ⊠ *4101 rue Sherbrooke Est,* ☎ *514/872–1400.* ⌧ *May 15–Oct. 15 $6.50; combined ticket for Biodôme and Botanical Garden $14.75; Oct. 16–May 14 free.* ⊙ *Daily 9–6. Metro: Pie-IX.*

⑦ **Musée des Arts Décoratifs** (Montréal Museum of Decorative Arts). Stroll into this elegant Beaux-Arts building and you step back into another age. The Château Dufresne comprises two adjoining mansions built in 1916 for a pair of prosperous brothers, shoe manufacturers Marius and Oscar Dufresne. It is decorated much as it was when the Dufresnes lived there, with a Moorish smoking room and a Louis XVI drawing room. Some of the rooms have unusual allegorical murals. ⊠ *2929 rue Jeanne-d'Arc,* ☎ *514/259–2575,* ⌧ *$3.* ⊙ *Wed.–Sun., 11–5.*

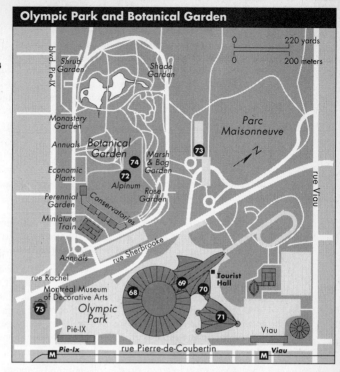

Olympic Park and Botanical Garden

68 **Stade Olympique** (Olympic Stadium). The stadium, built for the 1976 summer games, is beautiful to look at but not very practical. It's hard to heat and the retractable fabric roof, supported by the tower, has never worked properly. Nevertheless, it's home to the National League's Expos and is used for things like Montréal's annual car show. ✉ *4141 av. Pierre-de-Coubertin,* ☎ *514/252–8687.*

Les Iles (The Islands)

Expo '67—the world fair staged to celebrate the centennial of the Canadian federation—was the biggest party in Montréal's history, and it marked a defining moment in the city's evolution as a modern metropolis. That party was held on two islands in the middle of the St. Lawrence River—Ile Ste-Hélène, which was formed by nature, and Ile Notre-Dame, which was created by humans out of the stone rubble excavated for Montréal's Métro. The two islands are still a playground—the Parc des Iles has a major amusement park with one of the biggest roller coasters in the world, acres of flower gardens, a beach with clean filtered water, and the wildly successful Casino de Montréal. There's history, too, at the Old Fort where soldiers in colonial uniforms display the military skills of ancient wars. In winter, you can skate on the old Olympic rowing basin or slide down iced trails on an inner tube. You can get information on most of the activities and attractions at Parc des Iles by phoning (☎ 514/872–6222).

A Good Walk

Start at the Ile Ste-Hélène station on the Métro's Yellow Line. The first thing you'll see when you emerge will be the huge geodesic dome that houses **Biosphere,** an environmental exhibition center. From the Biosphere walk to the northern shore and then east through the Parc des Iles to the **Old Fort,** now a museum of colonial life and a parade ground. Just east of the Old Fort past the Pont Jacques-Cartier (Jacques Cartier Bridge) is **La Ronde,** an amusement park.

Now cross over to the island's southern shore and walk back along the waterfront to the Cosmos Footbridge that leads to Ile Notre-Dame. On the way you'll pass the Restaurant Hélène de Champlain, which probably has the prettiest setting of any restaurant in Montréal, and the military cemetery of the British garrison stationed on Ile Ste-Hélène from 1828 to 1870.

Ile Notre-Dame is laced by a network of canals and ponds and the grounds are brilliant with flower gardens left from the 1980 Floralies Internationales flower show. Most of the Expo '67 buildings are gone, the victims of time and weather. One that has remained, however, is the fanciful French Pavilion, now the very successful **Casino de Montréal** and site of Nuances, one of the city's best restaurants. A five-minute walk west of the Casino is the Lac de l'Ile Notre-Dame, site of **Plage de l'Ile Notre Dame,** Montréal's only beach. In mid-June, Ile Notre-Dame is the site of the Molson Grand Prix du Canada, a top Formula I international auto race at the **Circuit Gilles Villeneuve.**

After your walk you can either return to the Métro or walk back to the city via the Pont de la Concorde and the Parc de la Cité du Havre to Vieux-Montréal. If you walk, you'll see what looks like an updated version of a Hopi cliff dwelling. This irregular pile of prefabricated concrete blocks is **Habitat '67,** a private apartment complex, designed by Moshe Safdie and built as an experiment in housing for Expo.

TIMING

This is a comfortable two-hour stroll, but the Biosphere and the Old Fort (try to time your visit to coincide with a drill display by the colonial troops of the Fraser Highlanders and the Compagnie Franche de la Marine) deserve at least an hour each, and you should leave another half hour to admire the flowers. Children will want to spend a whole day at La Ronde, but the best time to go is in the evening when it's cooler. Try to visit the casino during a weekday when the crowds are at their thinnest.

Sights to See

Biosphere. This center, in the huge geodesic dome designed by Buckminster Fuller as the American Pavilion at Expo '67, successfully brings fun to an earnest project—heightening awareness of the St. Lawrence River system and its problems. ⊠ *Ile St-Hélène,* ☎ *514/283–5000.* ☜ *$6.50.* ☼ *June 1–Sept. 30 daily 10–8; Oct. 1–May 31, Tues.–Sun., 10–6.*

Casino de Montréal. When the provincial government decided to get into the casino business, it elected to pursue the elegance of Monte Carlo rather than the flash of Las Vegas. It trained its croupiers in politeness as well as math and instituted a strict dress code. The dramatic interior glitters with glass and modern murals, the views of the city skyline across the river are stunning, and the three restaurants are all good. In fact, Nuances is among the city's best (☞ Dining, *below*). The minimum age to enter is 18 and the dress code—no jeans, shorts, or sneakers—is strictly enforced. ⊠ *1 av. du Casino, Ile Notre-Dame,* ☎ *514/392–2746 or 800/665–2274.* ☜ *Free.* ☼ *Daily 11 AM–3 AM.*

☾ **La Ronde.** This world-class amusement park has Ferris wheels, boat rides, simulator-style rides, and the second-highest roller coaster in the world. It is also the site of the annual Benson & Hedges International Fireworks Competition, one of the city's most popular festivals, which takes place every weekend in June and July. You can buy a ticket, which includes an amusement park pass, to watch the display from a reserved seat, but thousands of Montrealers take their lawn chairs and blankets down to the Vieux-Port or across the river to the park along the South Shore and watch the show for nothing. ☎ *514/935–5161 or 800/361–8020; fireworks in the U.S., 800/678–5440; fireworks in Canada, 800/361–4595.* ✆ *$24.75, grounds only (no rides) $13.* ☉ *May 11–June 20, daily 10–9; June 21–Sept. 2, daily 11–11; days of fireworks displays 10 AM–midnight.*

Ⓒ **Old Fort.** In summer the grassy parade square of this fine stone fort comes alive with the crackle of musket fire as the volunteer members of French and British colonial forces show off their skills. The French are represented by the Compagnie Franche de la Marine and the British by the kilted 78th Fraser Highlanders, one of the regiments that participated in the conquest of Québec in 1759. The fort itself, built to protect Montréal from American invasion, is now Stewart Museum at the Fort, which tells the story of colonial life in Montréal through displays of old firearms, maps, and uniforms. The fort is also the site of Le Festin du Gouverneur, a re-creation of a 17th-century banquet. The two companies of colonial soldiers raise the flag every day at 11 am, practice their maneuvers at 1 pm, put on a combined display of precision drilling and musket fire at 2:30, and lower the flag at 5. Children can participate. ☎ *514/861–6701.* ✆ *$5.* ☉ *Summer, Wed.–Mon. 10–6; winter, Wed.–Mon. 10–5.*

Plage de l'Ile Notre-Dame. This strip of sand is often filled to capacity in summer. The swimming beach is an oasis, with clear, filtered lake water, and an inviting stretch of lawn and trees. Lifeguards are on duty; there is a shop that rents swimming and boating paraphernalia, and there are picnic areas and a restaurant. ✆ *$3.* ☉ *Daily.*

DINING

Montréal has more than 4,500 restaurants of every price range, representing more than 75 ethnic groups. When you dine out, you can, of course, order à la carte, choosing each course yourself. But many of the better restaurants offer a table d'hôte menu as well, a kind of two- to four-course package deal selected by the chef. It's usually cheaper, often offers interesting special dishes, and may also take less time to prepare. If you want to splurge with your time and money, indulge yourself with the *menu de dégustation,* a five- to seven-course dinner executed by the chef. It usually includes soup, salad, fish, sherbet (to refresh the taste buds), a meat dish, dessert, and coffee or tea. At the city's finest restaurants, such a meal for two, along with a good bottle of wine, can easily cost close to $200 and last three or four hours; done well, it's worth every cent and every second.

A word about language. Menus in many restaurants are bilingual, but some are in French only. If you don't understand what a dish is, don't be shy about asking; a good server will be delighted to explain. If you feel brave enough to order in French, remember that in French an entrée is an appetizer and what English-speakers call an entrée is a *plat principal,* or main dish.

Chinese

$$–$$$ ✕ **Chez Chine.** The restaurant sits beside a miniature lake full of fat goldfish and is crossed by little stone bridges that zig and zag to fool evil spirits; there's also a huge skylight and a waterfall. The impressive menu has a whole page of specialties for shark-fin fans, along with such delicacies as a clay pot full of sautéed beef slices that have been stir-fried with fresh

44

Montréal Dining

45

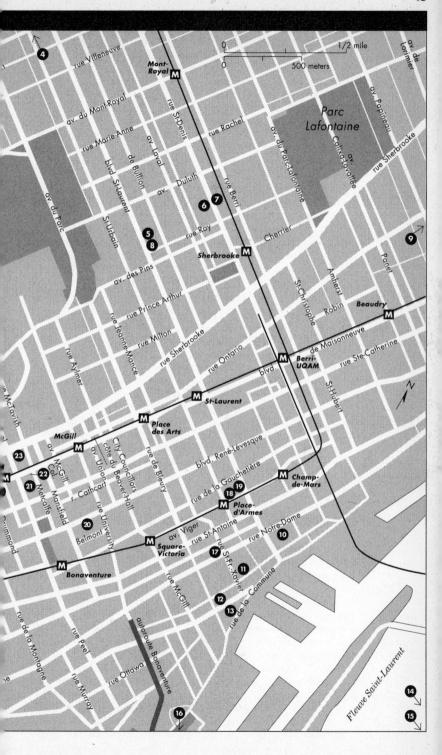

ginger, green onions, and oyster sauce. ⊠ *Holiday Inn Centre-Ville, 99 rue Viger Ouest,* ☎ *514/878–9888. AE, D, DC, MC, V.*

$$–$$$ ✕ **Zen.** This mod establishment has a prix-fixe menu that should not be missed. Called the "Zen Experience," the meal is a kind of all-you-can-eat extravaganza, except that instead of helping yourself to a buffet of precooked dishes, you are presented with a menu of 45 magnificently prepared Szechuan items and asked to select one at a time until you can't possibly eat any more. If that doesn't suit your fancy, for the same price you can try the Chinese fondue, which features delicate Chinese cooking with some Thai, Malaysian, and Indonesian dishes mixed in for variety. Try the fillet of chicken with crispy spinach or the chicken with black bean sauce. This is very fine Chinese cuisine. ⊠ *Le Westin Mont-Royal, 1050 rue Sherbrooke Ouest,* ☎ *514/499–0801. Reservations essential. AE, DC, MC, V.*

$$ ✕ **Maison Kam Fung.** This bright, airy restaurant offers the most reliable dim sum lunch in Chinatown. Every day from 10 to 3, waiters push a parade of trolleys through the restaurant, carting treats like firm dumplings stuffed with pork and chicken, stir-fried squid, and delicate pastry envelopes filled with shrimp. Evening meals include delicacies like roast suckling pig. ⊠ *1008 rue Clark,* ☎ *514/878–2888. Reservations not accepted for dim sum. AE, MC, V.*

Continental

$$$ ✕ **Nuances.** The Québec government wanted the Casino de Montréal
★ on Ile Notre-Dame to be classy rather than flashy, and the casino's main restaurant is stunning. Diners sit amidst burnished rosewood paneling and have a magnificent view of Montréal. Start with sautéed duck foie gras with exotic fruits and progress to lightly grilled red tuna with vegetables marinated in balsamic vinegar and olive oil. Even dishes that have been approved by the Québec Heart and Stroke Foundation sound exciting, like the saddle of rabbit pot-au-feu served with mushrooms. ⊠ *1 av. de Casino,* ☎ *514/392–2708. Reservations essential. Jacket and tie. AE, DC, MC, V. No lunch weekends.*

Delicatessens

$ ✕ **Bens.** On the menu of this large, efficient deli, all the items with "Bens" in the name are red or are covered in red: "Bens Cheesecake" is smothered in strawberries; "Bens Ice Cold Drink" is the color of electric cherry juice; and the specialty, the "Big Ben Sandwich," is two slices of rye bread enclosing a seductive, pink pile of juicy smoked meat (Montréal's version of corned beef). The decor is strictly '50s, with yellow and green walls and institutional furniture. The waiters are often wisecracking characters but are, nonetheless, incredibly efficient. Beer, wine, and cocktails are served. ⊠ *990 blvd. de Maisonneuve Ouest,* ☎ *514/844–1000. Reservations not accepted. MC, V.*

$ ✕ **Schwartz's Delicatessen.** Its proper name is the Montreal Hebrew Delicatessen, but everyone calls it Schwartz's. The sandwiches are huge; the steaks are tender and come with grilled liver appetizers. To drink you'll find nothing stronger than a Coke. The furniture looks like it was rescued from a Salvation Army depot and the waiters are briskly efficient. Don't ask for a menu (there isn't one) and avoid the lunch hour unless you don't mind long lines. ⊠ *3895 blvd. St-Laurent,* ☎ *514/842–4813, Reservations not accepted. No credit cards.*

$ ✕ **Wilensky's Light Lunch.** Since 1932 the Wilensky family has served up its special: salami and bologna on a "Jewish" (kaiser) roll, generously slathered with mustard. You can also get hot dogs or a chopped-egg sandwich, which comes with a pickle and an old-fashioned soda fountain drink like a cherry or pineapple cola (there's no liquor license).

The regulars at the counter are among the most colorful in Montréal—a visit here is a must. This neighborhood haunt was a setting for the film *The Apprenticeship of Duddy Kravitz*, from the novel by Mordecai Richler. The service does not prompt one to linger, but the prices make up for it. ✉ *34 rue Fairmount Ouest,* ☎ *514/271–0247. Reservations not accepted. No credit cards. Closed weekends.*

French

$$$$ ✗ **Beaver Club.** Early fur traders started the Beaver Club in a shack during Montréal's colonial days. In the 19th century it became a social club for the city's business and political elite, and it still has the august atmosphere of a men's club. Today, it's a gourmet French restaurant and open to anyone with a reservation. The luncheon table d'hôte often includes an exotic dish, such as terrine of duckling with pistachios and onion, and always includes one or two health-conscious selections. The restaurant also specializes in such meaty dishes as roast prime rib of beef au jus. The waitstaff are veterans, and the service is as excellent as the food. ✉ *La Reine Elizabeth hotel, 900 blvd. René-Lévesque Ouest,* ☎ *514/861–3511. Reservations essential. Jacket and tie. AE, D, DC, MC, V.*

$$$$ ✗ **Les Halles.** This restaurant took its name from the celebrated Parisian market, and the mirrors and murals of the decor reflect the market theme. The wine cellar is exceptional. The menu shows a lot of imagination without ignoring the classics: main dishes like Grapefruit Marie-Louise with scallops and lobster or roasted duck with pears sit comfortably beside the chef's ventures into nouvelle cuisine, such as his lobster with ginger and coconut. The desserts are classic, delicious, and remarkably fresh. The Paris-Brest, a puff pastry with praline cream inside, is one of the best in town. ✉ *1450 rue Crescent,* ☎ *514/844–2328. Reservations essential. AE, DC, MC, V. Closed Sun. and some holidays. No lunch Mon. or Sat.*

$$$$ ✗ **Les Trois Tilleuls.** Just 30 minutes southeast of town, you can lunch or dine on delectable food right on the Rivière Richelieu. This small, romantic inn, one of the prestigious Relais et Châteaux chain, has a terrace and a large, airy dining room with beautiful sunset views. The chef specializes in cream of onion soup, sweetbreads, and game dishes. ✉ *290 rue Richelieu, Saint Marc sur Richelieu,* ☎ *514/584–2231. Reservations essential. AE, DC, MC, V.*

$$$ ✗ **Guy and Dodo Morali.** This comfortable room with pale yellow walls
★ and lots of art is in the very exclusive Cours Mont-Royal shopping plaza. In summer, dining spills out onto a little terrace on rue Metcalfe. Guy's cooking is classic French with a splash of modern flair; his menu is 70% seafood. His daily table d'hôte menu is the best bet, with openers such as excellent lobster bisque followed by beef Wellington (a house specialty), poached salmon, or fillet of halibut with leeks. Desserts are exquisite—try the *tatan,* apples and caramel with crème anglaise. ✉ *Les Cours Mont-Royal, 1444 rue Metcalfe,* ☎ *514/842–3636. Reservations essential. AE, D, DC, MC, V.*

$$$ ✗ **Hélène de Champlain.** The food here is good if unadventurous (rack of lamb, filet of sole amandine), but people come for the setting. The restaurant is in the middle of the park on Ile Ste-Hélène, with views over the river and the city. The large dining room with its fireplace and antique furnishings is delightful. ✉ *Ile Ste-Hélène near Métro station,* ☎ *514/395–2424. Reservations essential. AE, DC, MC, V.*

$$$ ✗ **Le Café de Paris.** Patrons sit at large, well-spaced tables in a room ablaze with flowers and with light streaming through the French windows. The Ritz garden, with its picturesque duck pond, is open for summer dining alfresco. The menu opens with a selection of fresh caviar.

You can then choose from such classics as escalope de veau Viennoise or steak tartare. At meal's end the waiter will trundle over the dessert cart; the royale chocolat and the *îles flottant* (puffs of soft meringue in custard) are favorites. ⊠ *Ritz-Carlton, 1228 rue Sherbrooke Ouest,* ☎ *514/842–4212. Reservations essential. Jacket required. AE, D, DC, MC, V.*

$$$ ✕ Le Passe-Partout. New York–born James MacGuire might make the
★ best bread in Montréal—moist but airy with a tight, crispy crust. He and his wife, Suzanne Baron-Lafrenière, sell this delicacy, along with homemade pâtés and terrines, in a storefront bakery next door to their restaurant. The handwritten menu is short and changes according to mood and availability, but each dish is a gem. You might start with smoked salmon, a potage of curried sweet potatoes, or perhaps a venison terrine. Entrées include swordfish steak served with a purée of red cabbage or a loin of veal with poached cucumbers and house-made noodles. ⊠ *3857 blvd. Décarie (5-min walk south from Ville-Marie Métro),* ☎ *514/487–7750. Reservations required. AE, DC, MC, V. No lunch Sat.–Mon., no dinner Sun.–Wed.*

$$$ ✕ Toqué. This is both the zaniest and most fashionable restaurant in
★ Montréal. Its name means "a bit crazy." Its appeal lies not just in its market-fresh ingredients whipped into dazzling combinations and colors, but also in the funky and eccentric ambience. The decor is a mix of florid red velvet, plain gray, and electric yellow that somehow works. The young and innovative chef-owner, Normand Laprise, and partner Christin LaMarche are among the best chefs in the city. The menu often features tournedos de saumon, smoked salmon, and warm foie gras, all flavored with fresh ingredients like red peppers, thinly shredded leeks, celery roots, and Québec goat cheese. The portions don't look big but they are surprisingly filling. ⊠ *3842 rue St-Denis,* ☎ *514/ 499–2084. Reservations essential. MC, V.*

$$–$$$ ✕ L'Express. This favorite Paris-style bistro is often crammed with popular media figures who come here to be seen—a task made easier by the mirrored walls. The atmosphere is smoky, and the noise level peaks on weekend evenings. The cuisine is always impeccable, the service is fast, and the prices are very good. The steak tartare with French fries, the salmon with sorrel, and the calves' liver with tarragon are marvelous. Jars of gherkins, fresh baguettes, and cheeses aged to perfection make the pleasure last longer. L'Express has one of the best and most original wine cellars in town. ⊠ *3927 rue St-Denis,* ☎ *514/845–5333. Reservations essential. AE, DC, MC, V.*

$ ✕ Bonaparte. In this wonderful little restaurant in the heart of Vieux-
★ Montréal, piped-in Mozart serenades diners surrounded by exposed brick walls. The traditional French dishes here have a light touch. You could start with a wild-mushroom ravioli seasoned with fresh sage and move on to a lobster stew flavored with vanilla and served with a spinach fondue, or a roast rack of lamb in a Port wine sauce. Lunch is a particularly good value. ⊠ *443 rue St-François-Xavier,* ☎ *514/844–4368. Reservations essential. AE, D, DC, MC, V. No lunch Sat.*

Greek

$$$$ ✕ Milos. Nets, ropes, floats, and lanterns—the usual cliché symbols of the sea—hang from Milos's walls and ceilings. The real display, however, in the refrigerated cases and on the beds of ice in the back by the kitchen, is fresh fish from all over the world: octopus, squid, shrimp, crabs, oysters, and sea urchins. The main dish at Milos is usually fish—pick whatever looks freshest—grilled over charcoal and seasoned with parsley, capers, and lemon juice. It's done to a turn and is achingly delicious. The fish are priced by the pound, and you can order one large fish to serve two or more. You'll also find lamb, steaks, chicken, cheeses, and olives. Milos is a healthy walk from Métro Laurier. You can also take Bus 51 from the same Métro stop and ask the driver to let you off at avenue du Parc; Milos is halfway up the block to the right. ⊠ *5357 av. du Parc,* ☎ *514/272–3522. Reservations essential. AE, D, DC, MC, V. No lunch Sat.*

Indian

$$–$$$ ✕ **Le Taj.** The cuisine of the north of India is produced here, less spicy and more refined than that of the south. The tandoori ovens seal in the flavors of the grilled meat and fish. Vegetarian dishes include the *taj-thali,* made of lentils; chili *pakoras;* basmati rice; and *saag panir*—spicy white cheese with spinach. A nine-course buffet is served daily at lunch for under $10, and in the evening there's an "Indian feast" for $20. The desserts—pistachio ice cream or mangoes—are often decorated with pure silver leaves. The Taj has a gift shop that sells Indian delicacies and objets d'art, as well as some of the ingredients used in the preparation of Taj dishes. ⊠ *2077 rue Stanley,* ☎ *514/845–9015. Reservations essential. AE, MC, V.*

Italian

$$$ ✕ **Bocca d'Oro.** This restaurant next to Métro Guy has a huge menu. One pasta specialty is *tritico di pasta:* one helping each of spinach ravioli with salmon and caviar, shellfish marinara, and spaghetti primavera. Also recommended is the *pasta mistariosa*—no cream, no butter, no tomatoes, but delicious nonetheless. With dessert and coffee, the waiters bring out a bowl of walnuts for you to crack at your table. The two-floor dining area is inexplicably decorated with a huge display of golf pictures, and Italian pop songs play in the background. The staff is extremely friendly and professional; if you're in a hurry, they'll serve your meal in record time. ⊠ *1448 rue St-Mathieu,* ☎ *514/933–8414. Reservations essential. AE, DC, MC, V. Closed Sun.*

$$ ✕ **Pizzaiole.** Pizzaiole brought the first wood-fired pizza ovens to Montréal, and it's still the best in the field. Whether you choose a simple tomato-cheese or a ratatouille on a whole-wheat crust—there are about 30 possible combinations—all the pizzas are made to order and brought to your table piping hot. The calzone is worth the trip. ⊠ *1446-A rue Crescent,* ☎ *514/845–4158;* ⊠ *5100 rue Hutchison,* ☎ *514/274–9349. AE, DC, MC, V.*

Japanese

$$$–$$$$ ✕ **Katsura.** This cool, elegant Japanese restaurant introduced sushi to Montréal and is the haunt of businesspeople who equate raw food with power. The sushi chefs create an assortment of raw seafood delicacies, as well as their own delicious invention, the cone-shape Canada roll (smoked salmon and salmon caviar) at the sushi bar in the rear. The service is excellent, but if you sample all the sushi, the tab can be exorbitant. ⊠ *2170 rue de la Montagne,* ☎ *514/849–1172. Reservations essential. AE, DC, MC, V. No lunch weekends.*

Polish

$$–$$$ ✕ **Café Stash.** On chilly nights many Montrealers turn to Café Stash for sustenance—for roast pork or duck, hot borscht, pierogis, or cabbages and sausage—in short, for all the hearty specialties of a Polish kitchen. Diners sit on pews from an old chapel at refectory tables from an old convent. ⊠ *200 rue St-Paul Ouest,* ☎ *514/845–6611. AE, MC, V.*

Québécois

$$$$ ✕ **La Sucrerie de la Montagne.** On the road to Rigaud, toward Ottawa, maple syrup flows from carafes year-round and seasons plates of pork and beans, *tourtière* (meat pie flavored with cloves), ham, omelet soufflés, and crepes cooked over wood fires at this old-fashioned sugar hut. Pierre Faucher, the owner of this immense sugar cabin, who looks more like a lumberjack than a restaurateur, greets the Sunday passersby as well as the buses overflowing with tourists in the middle of July. An old-fashioned general store sells Québec handicrafts and maple syrup. ⊠ *300 rang St-Georges, Rigaud (Rte. 40, Exit 17),* ☎ *514/451–5204. Reservations essential. AE, MC, V.*

$$ ✕ **Chez Clo.** Deep in the heart of east-end Montréal in a neighborhood where seldom is heard an English word, lies that rarest of Montréal culinary finds—authentic Québécois food. A meal here could start with a bowl of the best pea soup in the city, followed by a slab of *tourtière,* a mound of mashed potatoes, another of carrots and turnips, and a bowl of gloopy gravy on the side. And the best is yet to come. Desserts include bread pudding, egg pudding, and several flavors of *renversées* (upside-down cakes). But the restaurant is most famous for its *pudding au chomeur* (literally, pudding for the unemployed), a kind of shortcake smothered in a sauce thick with brown sugar. The service is noisy and friendly and the clientele mostly local. ⊠ *3199 rue Ontario Est,* ☎ *514/522–5348. No credit cards.*

Sausages

$ ✕ **Chez Better.** The rustic fieldstone walls of historic Maison Sauvegarde create a fitting ambience for this North American branch of a popular European sausage house. Although the decor—exposed stone walls, casement windows, and dimmed lighting—is upscale, the limited nature of the menu keeps prices down, to only $3.95 in the case of the "Better Special," a satisfying sandwich of one mild sausage on freshly baked bread. It's a convenient refueling stop for visitors touring Vieux-Montréal, only a few steps from Place Jacques-Cartier. This Notre-Dame restaurant is the most elegant of the five "Betters." ⊠ *160 rue Notre-Dame Est,* ☎ *514/861–2617;* ⊠ *5400 chemin Côte-des-Neiges;* ⊠ *1310 blvd. de Maisonneuve;* ⊠ *4382 blvd. St-Laurent;* ⊠ *1430 rue Stanley. Reservations essential. AE, MC, V.*

Seafood

$$$ ✕ **Chez Delmo.** Chez Delmo was founded at this address on rue Notre-Dame in 1910. Today, its location, halfway between the courts and the stock exchange, means that lunchtime finds it crammed with legal types gobbling oysters and fish. In the back is a more relaxed and cheerful dining room. A good first course is the seafood salad, a delicious mix of shrimp, lobster, crab, and artichoke hearts on a bed of Boston lettuce, sprinkled with a scallion vinaigrette. The poached salmon with hollandaise is a nice slab of perfectly cooked fish served with potatoes and broccoli. The service is efficient and low-key. ⊠ *211–215 rue Notre-Dame Ouest,* ☎ *514/849–4061. Reservations essential. AE, DC, MC, V. Closed Sun., 2 wks in midsummer, and Christmas week.*

Steak

$$$ ✕ **Gibby's.** While the extensive menu here is rich in items like broiled
★ lobster, Dover sole meunière, and Cajun-blackened grouper, it was Gibby's first-class steaks—some say the best in the city—that made this magnificent restaurant famous. Gibby's also boasts its own on-site bak-

ery and makes its own ice cream. The thick gray stone walls and fireplaces here date to 1825, and the attention to service and detail also
seems to belong to another age. ⊠ *298 Pl. d'Youville,* ☎ *514/282–
1837. AE, D, DC, MC, V.*

$$$ ✕ **Moishe's.** The steaks here are big and marbled, and the Lighter broth-
ers still age them in their own cold rooms for 21 days before charcoal
grilling them, just the way their father did when he opened Moishe's
more than 50 years ago. There are other things on the menu, such as
lamb, veal sweetbreads, and grilled Arctic char—but people come for
the beef. There's an exquisite selection of single-malt Scotches. ⊠
3961 blvd. St-Laurent, ☎ *514/845–3509. Reservations essential. AE,
DC, MC, V. No lunch.*

$ ✕ **Magnan.** Women finally got free run (they were restricted to the up-
stairs dining room) of this tavern in working-class Pointe St-Charles
in 1988, but the atmosphere remains decidedly and defiantly mascu-
line. The decor is upscale warehouse and the half-dozen television sets
are noisily stuck on professional sports. You can't beat the roast beef
and the huge, industrial-strength steaks that range from 6 to 22 ounces.
The tavern is right on the belt of parkland and bicycle paths that line
the Lachine Canal, and is a great place to refuel after a strenuous pedal
from downtown. It also has excellent beer from several local micro-
breweries on tap. ⊠ *2602 rue St-Patrick,* ☎ *514/935–9647. Reser-
vations essential. AE, DC, MC, V.*

Thai

$$ ✕ **Sawatdee Thai.** The seedy stretch of rue Notre-Dame running west
from avenue Atwater is one of the last places you'd expect to find a
charming little restaurant decorated with exquisite Thai art and serving terrific Thai food. *Tom yam gay* is a spicy hot-and-sour chicken
soup with lemongrass. *Som Tum* is a salad of papaya, dried shrimp,
chili peppers, and lime juice. ⊠ *3453 rue Notre-Dame Ouest,* ☎ *514/
938–8188. Reservations essential. AE, MC, V.*

LODGING

If you arrive in Montréal without a hotel reservation, the information
booths at either airport can provide you with a list of hotels and room
availability. You must, however, make the reservation yourself. Alter-
natively, there is a room reservation service at Info-touriste (☞ Contacts and Resources, *below*), which can find you a room in one of 80
hotels, motels, and bed-and-breakfasts.

Downtown

$$$$ 🏨 **Bonaventure Hilton International.** This large Hilton occupies the top
★ three floors of the Place Bonaventure exhibition center. From the outside the massive building is uninviting, but you step off the elevator
into an attractive reception area flanked by an outdoor swimming pool
(heated year-round) and 2½ acres of gardens. Also on this floor is Le
Castillon restaurant, known for its three-course, 55-minute busi-
nessperson's lunch. All rooms have sleek modern furniture, pastel
walls, and TVs in the bathrooms. The Bonaventure has excellent access to the Métro and the Underground City. ⊠ *1 Pl. Bonaventure,
H5A 1E4,* ☎ *514/878–2332 or 800/267–2575,* FAX *514/028–1442.
393 rooms. 3 restaurants, minibars, room service, pool, business services, shops. AE, D, DC, MC, V.*

$$$$ 🏨 **Hotel Inter-Continental Montréal.** This luxury hotel on the edge of
★ Vieux-Montréal is part of the Centre de Commerce Mondiale, a block-
long retail and office development. Rooms are in a modernly built 24-

Montréal Lodging

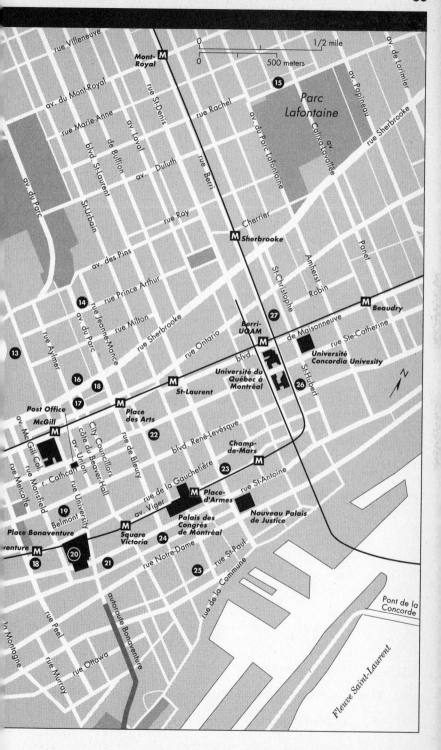

rue Villeneuve

Mont-
Royal Ⓜ

0   1/2 mile
0   500 meters

av. du Mont-Royal

rue Marie-Anne

⑮

Parc
Lafontaine

rue Rachel

rue St-Denis

av. de Lorimier

av. Papineau

av. Duluth

de Bullion

av. Laval

blvd. St-Laurent

av. du Parc

St-Urbain

rue Roy

av. du Parc Lafontaine

av. Calix-Lavallée

rue Sherbrooke

Cherrier

av. des Pins

Ⓜ Sherbrooke

rue Prince Arthur

St-Christophe

Panet

⑭

rue Milton

av. du Parc

rue Jeanne-Mance

rue Sherbrooke

Amherst

Robin

Ⓜ Beaudry

rue Ontario

Berri-
UQAM

de Maisonneuve

rue Ste-Catherine

⑬

rue Aylmer

blvd.

⑯

⑱

Ⓜ
St-Laurent

⑰

Ⓜ

Place-
des-Arts

⑳

Ⓜ
McGill

Post Office

av. McGill Col.

McGill Col.

City Councillors
côte du Beaver-Hall

av. Union

rue de Bleury

⑳

⑳

⑳

⑳

Université du
Québec à
Montréal

Université
Concordia Univesity

St-Hubert

㉖

㉗

N

blvd. René-Lévesque

Champ-
de-Mars
Ⓜ

rue St-Antoine

r. Cathcart

rue Mansfield

rue University

Belmont

⑲

Ⓜ
Square
Victoria

rue de la Gauchetière

Ⓜ
Place-
d'Armes

㉓

av. Viger

Palais des
Congrés
de Montréal

Nouveau Palais
de Justice

Place Bonaventure

㉔

㉑

Ⓜ
Bonaventure

⑱

⑳

rue Notre-Dame

rue St-Paul

㉕

rue de la Commune

Pont de la
Concorde

rue Peel

autoroute Bonaventure

la Montagne

rue Peel

rue Ottawa

rue Murray

Fleuve Saint-Laurent

story brick tower with fanciful turrets and pointed roofs. They're large, with lush carpets, pastel walls, heavy drapes, and big windows overlooking either downtown or Vieux-Montréal and the waterfront. The main lobby is home to Le Continent Restaurant, which serves fine international cuisine. ⊠ *360 rue St-Antoine Ouest, H2Y 3X4,* ☎ *514/987–9900 or 800/327–0200; in the U.S. and Canada, 800/361–3600;* FAX *514/847–8550. 335 rooms, 22 suites. 2 restaurants, room service, indoor pool, sauna, health club, concierge, meeting facilities. AE, D, DC, MC, V.*

$$$$ 🏨 **Le Centre Sheraton.** This hotel is a favorite with celebrities. In a huge 37-story complex well placed between the downtown business district and the restaurant-lined streets of Crescent and Bishop, it offers services to both the business and tourist crowds. Rooms have coffee makers, irons, and ironing boards. The elite, 10-story Towers section is geared toward business travelers. The Sheraton caters to conventions. The rooms are typical hotel modern—beige, comfortable, and unremarkable, but the bar in the busy lobby is in a pleasant forest of potted trees, some of them 30 feet tall. ⊠ *1201 blvd. René-Lévesque Ouest, H3B 2L7,* ☎ *514/878–2000 or 800/325–3535,* FAX *514/878–3958. 784 rooms, 40 suites. 2 restaurants, 2 bars, indoor pool, beauty salon, sauna, health club with whirlpool and sauna, baby-sitting, business services, parking (fee). AE, D, DC, MC, V.*

$$$$ 🏨 **Le Meridien.** This Air France property rises 12 stories from the center of the Complexe Desjardins, a boutique-rich mall in the middle of the Underground City. The hotel caters to those who want ultramodern style like blonde wood and leather chairs in a huge lobby with patterned stone floors and potted plants overlooking a glassed-in swimming pool; a stainless-steel-and-glass elevator that looks like a space module to whisk guests from the ground floor to the fourth-floor lobby; and big rooms with lots of that sleek modern furniture with rounded edges and shiny finish. For instance, within Le Café Fleuri French restaurant there's a chicer, pricier enclave called Le Club. If you feel like a stroll, you can head to Chinatown, a five-minute walk away. ⊠ *4 Complexe Desjardins, C.P. 130, H5B 1E5,* ☎ *514/285–1450 or 800/543–4300,* FAX *514/285–1243. 572 rooms, 28 suites. 3 restaurants, piano bar, indoor pool, exercise room, sauna, whirlpool, baby-sitting, business services. AE, D, DC, MC, V.*

$$$$ 🏨 **Le Reine Elizabeth.** Le Reine Elizabeth, or Queen Elizabeth, is built
★   like a battleship—massive and gray. This Canadian Pacific hotel sits on top of the Gare Centrale train station in the very heart of the city, across the street from Place Ville-Marie. The lobby is a bit too much like a railway station—hordes march this way and that—to be attractive and personal, but upstairs the rooms are modern, spacious, and spotless, with lush pale carpets, striped Regency wallpapers, and chintz bedspreads. The Penthouse floors—20 and 21—have business services. The hotel is home to the Beaver Club (☞ Dining, *above*), a flagship restaurant that is considered an institution. Conventions are a specialty here. ⊠ *900 blvd. René-Lévesque Ouest, H3B 4A5,* ☎ *514/861–3511 or 800/441–1414,* FAX *514/954–2256. 1,020 rooms. 2 restaurants, 4 lounges, indoor pool, health club, children's programs, beauty salon. AE, D, DC, MC, V.*

$$$$ 🏨 **Le Westin Mont-Royal.** Service and hospitality make this establish-
★   ment stand out among Montréal's best hotels. Its concierge desk can organize anything. The clientele here is primarily corporate, and the large rooms are decorated to serve that market: floral chintzes, plush carpeting, and English traditional furnishings. One of the city's best Chinese restaurants is the Zen (☞ Dining, *above*), downstairs. ⊠ *1050 rue Sherbrooke Ouest, H3A 2R6,* ☎ *514/284–1110 or 800/228–3000,* FAX *514/845–3025. 300 rooms, 28 suites. Restaurant, lounge,*

minibar, room service, pool, health club, whirlpool, 2 saunas. AE, D, DC, MC, V.

$$$$
★ **⛻ Loew's Hôtel Vogue.** The Vogue opened in late 1990, transforming a drab office tower into a chic, elegant hotel with tall windows and a facade of polished rose granite and deep aqua trim. It is in the heart of downtown, right across the street from Ogilvy department store. The lobby's focal point, the L'Opéra Bar, has an expansive bay window overlooking the trendy rue de la Montagne. Room furnishings are upholstered with striped silk, and the beds are draped with lacy duvets. Fax machines and multiline telephones in rooms appeal to business travelers; the bathrooms—with whirlpool baths, televisions, and phones—appeal to everyone. The Société Café on the lobby level is a favorite among downtowners. ⊠ *1425 rue de la Montagne, H3G 1Z3,* ☎ *514/285–5555 or 800/465–6654,* ℻ *514/849–8903. 126 rooms, 16 suites. Restaurant, bar, exercise room. AE, D, DC, MC, V.*

$$$$
★ **⛻ Ritz-Carlton Kempinski.** This property was opened in 1912 by locals who wanted a hotel where their rich European friends could indulge their champagne-and-caviar tastes. Since then, many earthshaking events have occurred here, including the marriage of Elizabeth Taylor and Richard Burton. Power meals are the rule at the elegant Le Café de Paris (☞ Dining, *above*). Guest rooms are a successful blend of Edwardian style—some suites have working fireplaces—with such modern accessories as electronic safes. Careful and personal attention are hallmarks of the Ritz-Carlton's service: your shoes get shines, there's fresh fruit in your room, and everyone calls you by name. Even if you're not a guest, stop by the Ritz's Hotel Courtyard during the summer for afternoon tea and to see the duck pond, a Ritz tradition. At press time, the hotel was in the middle of a multiphase restoration. ⊠ *1228 rue Sherbrooke Ouest, H3G 1H6,* ☎ *514/842–4212 or 800/223–6800,* ℻ *514/842–3383. 201 rooms, 39 suites. 3 restaurants, bar, piano bar, room service, barbershop. AE, DC, MC, V.*

$$$
⛻ Delta Montréal. The Delta has the most complete exercise and pool facility in Montréal and an extensive business center. The hotel's public areas are spread over two stories and are decorated to look a bit like a French château, with a huge baronial chandelier and thick, gold patterned carpets. Rooms are big with plush broadloom, pastel walls, mahogany-veneer furniture, and huge windows that overlook the mountain or downtown. The jazz bar serves lunch on weekdays. ⊠ *475 av. President-Kennedy, H3A 1J7,* ☎ *514/286–1986 or 800/268–1133,* ℻ *514/284–4306. 453 rooms, 10 suites. 2 restaurants, bar, indoor and outdoor pools, sauna, health club, aerobics, 2 squash courts, whirlpool, recreation room, video games, children's programs, business services. AE, DC, MC, V.*

$$$
★ **⛻ Holiday Inn Centre-Ville.** This Chinatown hotel is full of surprises, from the two pagodas on the roof to the waterfall and fish pond in the Chinese garden in the lobby. The hotel is one of the city's most charming, and its restaurant, Chez Chine (☞ Dining, *above*), is one of the best Chinese restaurants in Montréal. There's an executive floor with all the usual business facilities. The hotel has a pool and a small exercise room, but guests also have access to a plush private health and leisure club downstairs with a whirlpool, saunas, a billiard room, and a bar. The hotel is catercorner to the Palais des Congrès and a five-minute walk from the Centre de Commerce Mondiale. ⊠ *99 av. Viger Ouest, H2Z 1E9,* ☎ *514/878–9888 or 800/465–4329,* ℻ *514/878–6341. 325 rooms. Restaurant, lobby bar, pool, exercise room, business services. AE, D, DC, MC, V.*

$$$
★ **⛻ Hôtel de la Montagne.** Upon entering the reception area you'll be greeted by a naked, butterfly-winged nymph who rises out of a fountain; an enormous crystal chandelier hangs from the ceiling. The decor

resembles Versailles rebuilt with a dash of Art Nouveau, although management prefers to describe it as a mix of Early American and Rococo. The rooms are tamer, large, and comfortable. There's a piano bar and a rooftop terrace, and a tunnel connects the hotel to Thursday's/Les Beaux Jeudis—a popular singles bar, restaurant, and dance club. The clientele is a bilingual mixture of French-speaking Montrealers stopping by for a drink and Torontans in town on business. If you're staying elsewhere, the reception area is at least worth a visit. ⊠ *1430 rue de la Montagne, H3G 1Z5,* ☎ *514/288–5656 or 800/361–6262,* FAX *514/288–9658. 135 rooms. 2 restaurants, bar, pool, concierge. AE, D, DC, MC, V.*

$$$ 🏨 **Le Marriott Château Champlain.** In the heart of downtown Montréal, at the southern end of Place du Canada, is this 36-floor skyscraper with distinctive half moon–shape windows. The decor inside is formal, with only 20 rooms per floor. The floor-to-ceiling windows give the rooms a Moorish feel, but the furniture is elegantly French and the bedspreads are brightly patterned. Underground passageways connect the Champlain with the Bonaventure Métro station and Place Ville-Marie. ⊠ *1050 rue de la Gauchetière, H3B 4C9,* ☎ *514/878–9000 or 800/200–5909,* FAX *514/878–6761. 616 rooms, 33 suites. Restaurant, bar, indoor pool, sauna, health club, no-smoking rooms. AE, DC, MC, V.*

$$–$$$ 🏨 **Auberge de la Fontaine.** The decor of this small hotel in the heart
★ of the trendy Plateau Mont-Royal district sounds wild—contrasting purple and bare-brick walls, a red molding separating yellow walls from a green ceiling, dark green doors with mauve frames—but the hotel is restful and delightful. Its 21 rooms are scattered over three floors in two turn-of-the-century residences. Some of them have whirlpool baths and a few have private balconies. Guests can use the little ground-floor kitchen and take whatever they like from its fridge full of snacks. The hotel is right on one of the city's bicycle paths and just across the street from Parc Lafontaine. ⊠ *1301 rue Rachel Est, H2J 2K1,* ☎ *800/597–0597 or 514/597–0166,* FAX *514/597–0496. 21 rooms with bath. Meeting room. CP. AE, DC, MC, V.*

$$–$$$ 🏨 **Hôtel du Fort.** All rooms here have good views of the city, the river, or the mountain, and have hair dryers, microwaves, refrigerators, and coffee makers, as well as comfortable desks with extra phone lines for modems and faxes. It's in the west end of downtown in a residential neighborhood known as Shaughnessy Village, close to shopping at the Faubourg Ste-Catherine and Square Westmount, and just around the corner from the Centre Canadien d'Architecture. Rates include Continental breakfast served in the charming Louis XV Lounge, which doubles as a bar in the evening. There is no restaurant on the premises, but the hotel is linked to Complexe du Fort where there are two good restaurants—Le Fuchsia and Café Suprême. ⊠ *1390 rue du Fort, H3H 2R7,* ☎ *514/938–8333 or 800/565–6333,* FAX *514/938–2078. 127 rooms. Exercise room. CP. AE, DC, MC, V.*

$$–$$$ 🏨 **Hôtel du Parc.** This hotel's greatest virtue is its location. It's an L-shape brick tower that faces northwest over Parc du Mont-Royal, just half a block away. The McGill University campus is a 5-minute walk to the west and the nightlife of rue Prince Arthur is just six blocks south. The hotel sits on top of a shopping mall with many stores and movie theaters. The hotel itself is a briskly efficient operation that caters to corporate clients. The rooms are large, and the decor is modern with lots of blonde wood and pastel shades. The lobby is dominated by a large and comfortable bar. ⊠ *3625 av. du Parc, H2X 3P8,* ☎ *514/288–6666 or 800/448–8355; in Canada, 800/363–0735;* FAX *514/288–2469. 358 rooms, 20 suites. Restaurant, bar, café, no-smoking floors,*

2 outdoor pools, 1 indoor pool, tennis court, health club, squash. AE, D, DC, MC, V.

$$ ⊞ **Auberge Les Passants du Sans Soucy.** This gem is the only inn in
★ Vieux-Montréal. The building, on rue St-Paul behind the Basilique Notre-Dame, is a former fur warehouse dating to 1836; the foundations date to 1684. The lobby is also an art gallery that opens onto the street. Behind it are a living room and a dining room separated by a fireplace that crackles with burning hardwood in winter and lit by two skylights. The suite is on the ground floor, with a sitting room window overlooking the street. The rest of the rooms—all with private baths and discreetly hidden television sets—are on the second floor. This is one of the most romantic city hostelries you'll find anywhere, with brass beds, bare stone walls, exposed beams, soft lighting, whirlpool baths, and lots of fresh-cut flowers. But it's also a practical place for businesspeople, with fax machines at the front desk, and only a short walk from the financial district. ⊠ *171 rue St. Paul Ouest, H2Y 1Z5,* ☎ *514/842–2634,* 🖷 *514/842–2912. 8 rooms, 1 suite. CP. AE, DC, MC, V.*

$$ ⊞ **Château Versailles.** This charming hotel is unassuming, classy, and
★ not too expensive. It occupies a row of four converted mansions on rue Sherbrooke Ouest near Métro Guy-Concordia. The owners have decorated it with antique paintings, tapestries, and furnishings; some rooms have ornate moldings and plaster decorations on the walls and ceilings. All rooms have king-size beds and curtains and bedspreads with colorful Victorian prints. Across the street, at 1808 rue Sherbrooke, is a former apartment hotel that the Villeneuve family added as an annex to the original town houses. Called La Tour Versailles, it has 107 larger, more modern rooms—at the same reasonable price. There is a fine French restaurant, the Champs-Elysées, in La Tour, and a breakfast room in the Château. The staff is extremely helpful and friendly. ⊠ *1659 rue Sherbrooke Ouest, H3H 1E3,* ☎ *514/933–3611 or 800/361–3664; in Canada, 800/361–7199;* 🖷 *514/933–7102. 70 rooms in Château; 105 rooms, 2 suites in La Tour. Restaurant, breakfast room. AE, DC, MC, V.*

$$ ⊞ **Days Inn Old Montréal.** This is a moderately priced hotel near the restaurants and nightlife of rue St-Denis. Rooms have brightly colored bedspreads, modern furniture, and in-room movies. The restaurant, Il Cavaliere, serves Italian food and is popular with locals. The hotel is next to the Université du Québec à Montréal; the Berri-UQAM Métro stop is a block away. ⊠ *1199 rue Berri, H2L 4C6,* ☎ *514/845–9236 or 800/932–5985,* 🖷 *514/849–9855. 154 rooms. Restaurant, no-smoking floors, 3 meeting rooms. AE, DC, MC, V.*

$$ ⊞ **Hôtel Radisson des Gouverneurs de Montréal.** Abutting the stock exchange, this property rises above a three-story atrium-reception area and is attractive to convention crowds. It's near Place Bonaventure, the western fringe of Vieux-Montréal, and the Square Victoria Métro (accessible via an underground passage). There's an exclusive floor for higher-paying guests and a shopping arcade on the underground level. The Tour de Ville on the top floor is the city's only revolving restaurant, and its bar has live jazz nightly. Chez Antoine, an art nouveau–style bistro, serves gourmet salads and sandwiches. ⊠ *777 rue University, H3C 3Z7,* ☎ *514/879–1370 or 800/361–8155,* 🖷 *514/879–1761. 550 rooms, 23 suites. 2 restaurants, bar, indoor pool, steam room, health club. AE, DC, MC, V.*

$$ ⊞ **Howard Johnson Hôtel Plaza.** This medium-size, medium-price hotel, next to the McGill campus, caters to businesspeople and families. There are exercise machines and a spa with sauna, and the lobby is decorated in Art Deco style with dark-green leather furniture, brass trim, and marble tables. Rooms have chintz furniture and brass lamps. There are also several two-story suites with tall, dramatic windows overlooking downtown. The restaurant, La Découverte, is decorated with brass and marble and has bay windows overlooking the street and a terrace for outdoor dining. The Hôtel Plaza is handy to downtown business and shopping areas. ⊠ *475 rue Sherbrooke Ouest, H3A 2L9,* ☎ *514/842–3961 or 800/446–4656,* 𝖥𝖠𝖷 *514/842–0945. 194 rooms. Restaurant, café, sauna, exercise room. AE, DC, MC, V.*

$$ 🏨 **Le Nouvel Hôtel.** In its four towers this hotel has a mix of brightly colored and functional studios and 2½-room apartments. It is near the restaurants and bars on rues Crescent, de la Montagne, and Bishop, six blocks from the heart of downtown, and two blocks from the Guy-Concordia Métro station. ⊠ *1740 blvd. René-Lévesque Ouest, H3H 1R3,* ☎ *514/931–8841 or 800/363–6063,* 𝖥𝖠𝖷 *514/931–3233. 126 rooms, 60 2½-room units. Restaurant, bar, pool. AE, DC, MC, V.*

$ 🏨 **Hôtel Thrift Lodge.** This hotel is adjacent to the Terminus Voyageur bus station (buses park directly beneath one wing of the hotel), and some of the bus-station aura has rubbed off on the place: It's a little dingy. But if you're stumbling after a long bus ride and want somewhere to stay *now,* the Roussillon's rooms are large and clean, the service is friendly, and the price is right. It's also handy to the Berri-UQAM Métro station. ⊠ *1600 rue St-Hubert, H2L 3Z3,* ☎ *514/849–3214,* 𝖥𝖠𝖷 *514/849–9812. 147 rooms. Restaurant. AE, MC, V.*

$ 🏨 **YMCA.** This clean Y is downtown, next to Peel Métro station. Men should book at least two days in advance; women should book seven days ahead because there are fewer rooms with showers for them. Anyone staying summer weekends must book at least a week ahead. There is a full gym facility and a typical Y cafeteria. ⊠ *1450 rue Stanley, H3A 2W6,* ☎ *514/849–8393,* 𝖥𝖠𝖷 *514/849–8017. 331 rooms, 429 beds. Cafeteria, health club. AE, MC, V.*

$ 🏨 **YWCA.** Very close to dozens of restaurants, the Y is right downtown, one block from rue Ste-Catherine. Although men can eat at the café, the overnight facilities and health club are for women only. If you want a room with any amenities you must book in advance; not all of the rooms come with a sink and bath. ⊠ *1355 blvd. René-Lévesque, H3G 1P3,* ☎ *514/866–9941,* 𝖥𝖠𝖷 *514/861–1603. 107 rooms. Café, pool, sauna, aerobics, exercise room, shops. MC, V.*

McGill University Area

$ 🏨 **Auberge de Jeunesse Internationale de Montréal.** This youth hostel is in the heart of downtown just a two-minute walk from Windsor Station and the Centre Molson, home of the Montréal Canadiens. It charges $16 per person, per night, for members, and $18 for Canadian nonmembers. Other nonmembers have to buy a membership ($25). Rooms sleep 3–10 people (same sex); some rooms are available for couples and families. There are kitchen facilities and lockers for valuables. Reserve early during summer. ⊠ *1030 rue Mackay, H3G 2H1,* ☎ *514/843–3317,* 𝖥𝖠𝖷 *514/934–3251. 263 beds. Coin laundry. DC, MC, V.*

$ 🏨 **McGill Student Apartments.** From mid-May to mid-August, when McGill is on summer recess, you can stay in its dorms on the grassy, quiet campus in the heart of the city. Nightly rates are $28 students, $36.75 nonstudents (single rooms only). As a visitor, you may use the campus swimming pool and gym facilities for a fee. The university cafeteria is also open during the week, serving breakfast and lunch. ⊠ *3935 rue University, H3A 2B4,* ☎ *514/398–6367,* 𝖥𝖠𝖷 *514/398–6770. 1,000 rooms. MC, V.*

Université de Montréal Area

$ ⊞ **Université de Montréal Residence.** The university's student housing accepts visitors from early May to late August. It's on the other side of Mont-Royal from downtown and Vieux-Montréal, but is right next to the Edouard Monpetit Métro station. The rooms have phones for local calls; common lounges have microwaves and TVs. For a fee, visitors may use the campus sports facilities. Nightly rates are $21 per night and $100 per week for students, and $31 per night and $141 per week for nonstudents. ✉ *2350 blvd. Edouard-Montpetit, H3C 3J7,* ☎ *514/343–6531,* FAX *514/343–2353. 750–800 rooms. AE, MC, V.*

NIGHTLIFE AND THE ARTS

The entertainment section of the *Gazette,* the English-language daily paper, is a good place to find out about upcoming events in Montréal. The Friday Preview section has an especially good list of all events at the city's concert halls, theaters, clubs, dance spaces, and movie houses. Other publications listing what's on include the *Mirror, Hour, Scope,* and *Voir* (in French), distributed free at restaurants and other public places. You can also phone **Info-Arts (Bell)** (☎ 514/790–2787) for events information.

For tickets to major pop and rock concerts, shows, festivals, and hockey and baseball games, go to the individual box offices or call **Admission** (☎ 514/790–1245 or 800/361–4595) or **Ticketmaster** (☎ 514/790–1111) for tickets to Théâtre St-Denis. Place des Arts tickets may be purchased at its box office underneath the Salle Wilfrid-Pelletier, next to the Métro station.

The Arts

Dance

Traditional and contemporary dance companies thrive in Montréal, though many take to the road or are on hiatus in the summer. **Ballets Classiques de Montréal** (☎ 514/866–1771) performs mostly classical programs. **Les Grands Ballets Canadiens** is the leading Québec company (☎ 514/849–8681 or 514/849–0269). **Ouest Vertigo Danse** (☎ 514/251–9177) stages innovative, postmodern performances. **Montréal Danse** (☎ 514/845–2031). **LaLaLa Human Steps** (☎ 514/277–9090) is an avant-garde, exciting powerhouse of a company. **Les Ballets Jazz de Montréal** (☎ 514/982–6771) experiments with new musical forms. **Margie Gillis Fondation de Danse** (☎ 514/845–3115) gives young dancers and choreographers opportunities to develop their art. **Tangente** (☎ 514/525–1860) is a nucleus for many of the more avant-garde dance troupes. When not on tour, many of these artists can be seen at Place des Arts or at any of the **Maisons de la Culture** (☎ 514/872–6211) performance spaces around town. Montréal's dancers have a downtown performance and rehearsal space, the **Agora Dance Theatre** (✉ 840 rue Chérrier Est, ☎ 514/525–1500), affiliated with the Université de Montréal dance faculty. Every other September (that is, in the odd-numbered years, such as 1997), the **Festival International de Nouvelle Danse** brings "new" dance to various venues around town. Tickets for this event always sell quickly.

Music

The **Orchestre Symphonique de Montréal** (☎ 514/842–9951) has gained world renown under the baton of Charles Dutoit. When not on tour, its regular venue is the Salle Wilfrid-Pelletier at the Place des Arts. The orchestra also gives Christmas and summer concerts in the

Basilique Notre-Dame and pop concerts at the Arena Maurice Richard in Olympic Park. Also check the *Gazette* listings for its free summertime concerts in Montréal's city parks. Montréal's other orchestra, the **Orchestre Métropolitain de Montréal** (☎ 514/598–0870), also stars at Place des Arts most weeks during the October–April season. McGill University's **Pollack Concert Hall** (☎ 514/398–4547) is the site of concerts, notably by the **McGill Chamber Orchestra.** The city is home to one of the best chamber orchestras in Canada, I Musici de Montréal (☎ 514/982–6037). **L'Opéra de Montréal** (☎ 514/985–2258) stages four productions a year at Place des Arts.

The **Montréal Forum** (✉ 2313 rue Ste-Catherine Ouest, ☎ 514/932–2582 or 800/678–5440) has 20,000 seats. **Stade Olympique** (✉ Parc Olympique, ☎ 514/252–8687), much larger than the Forum, hosts rock and pop concerts. The 2,500-seat **Théâtre St-Denis** (✉ 1594 rue St-Denis, ☎ 514/849–4211) is the second-largest auditorium in Montréal (after Salle Wilfrid-Pelletier in Place des Arts). Sarah Bernhardt and many other famous actors have graced its stage. The **Spectrum** (✉ 318 rue Ste-Catherine Ouest, ☎ 514/861–5851) is an intimate concert hall.

Theater

French-speaking theater lovers will find a wealth of dramatic productions. There are at least 10 major companies in town, some that have an international reputation. **Théâtre de Quat'Sous** (✉ 100 av. des Pins Est, ☎ 514/845-7277) performs modern, experimental, and cerebral plays. **Théâtre du Nouveau Monde** (✉ 84 rue Ste-Catherine Ouest, ☎ 514/866–8667) is the North American temple of French classics. **Théâtre du Rideau Vert** (✉ 4664 rue St-Denis, ☎ 514/844–1793) specializes in modern French repertoire. Anglophones have less to choose from. **Centaur Theatre** (✉ 453 rue St-François-Xavier, ☎ 514/288–3161), the best-known English theatrical company, stages Beaux-Arts–style productions in the former stock exchange building in Vieux-Montréal. English-language plays can also be seen at the **Saidye Bronfman Centre** (✉ 5170 chemin de la Côte Ste-Catherine, ☎ 514/739–2301 or 514/739–7944), a multidisciplinary institution that is a focus of cultural activity for Montréal as a whole and for the Jewish community in particular. The center was a gift from the children of Saidye Bronfman in honor of their mother's lifelong commitment to the arts. The Mies van der Rohe–inspired building was originally designed by Mrs. Bronfman's daughter, Montréal architect Phyllis Lambert. Many of its activities, such as gallery exhibits, lectures on public and Jewish affairs, performances, and concerts, are free to the public. The center is home to the **Yiddish Theatre Group,** one of the few Yiddish companies performing today in North America. Michel Tremblay is Montréal's premier playwright, and all of his plays are worth seeing, even if in the English translation. Touring companies of Broadway productions can often be seen at the **Théâtre St-Denis** (✉ 1594 rue St-Denis, ☎ 514/849–4211), as well as at Place des Arts (☎ 514/842–2112)—especially during the summer months.

Nightlife

Comedy

The **Comedy Nest** (✉ 1740 blvd. René-Lévesque Ouest, ☎ 514/932–6378) has shows by name performers, up-and-comers, and new talent.

Discos

What was the glitziest disco in town, **Metropolis** (✉ 59 rue Ste-Catherine Est, ☎ 514/288–2020), now has occasional theme evenings for a young, primarily French-speaking crowd. Most popular is Toro Toro, an evening of Latin dance the first Friday of every month. **Club 737**

(✉ 1 Place Ville Marie, ☎ 514/397–0737) on top of Place Ville-Marie does the disco number every Thursday, Friday, and Saturday night. This has become very popular with the upscale, mid-20s to mid-30s crowd. The view is magnificent and there is an open-air rooftop bar to cool off. The **Zoo** (✉ 3556 blvd. St-Laurent, ☎ 514/848–6398) is *the* place for the beautiful people. **Hard Rock Café** (✉ 1458 rue Crescent, ☎ 514/987–1420). **Thursday's** (✉ 1449 rue Crescent, ☎ 514/288–5656) is a popular disco.

Folk

Hurley's Irish Pub (✉ 1225 rue Crescent, ☎ 514/861–4111) attracts some of the city's best Celtic musicians and dancers. An enthusiastic crowd sings along with Québécois performers at the **Deux Pierrots Boîte aux Chansons** (✉ 104 rue St-Paul Est, ☎ 514/861–1270).

Jazz

Montréal has a very active local jazz scene. The best-known club is Vieux-Montréal's **L'Air du Temps** (✉ 191 rue St-Paul Ouest, ☎ 514/842–2003). This small, smoky club presents 90% local talent and 10% international acts from 5 PM on into the night. Downtown, duck into **Biddle's** (✉ 2060 rue Aylmer, ☎ 514/842–8656), where bassist Charles Biddle holds forth most evenings when he's not appearing at a local hotel. Biddle's serves pretty good ribs and chicken. You might also try the **Quai des Brumes Dancing** (✉ 4481 rue St-Denis, ☎ 514/499–0467).

The annual **Festival International de Jazz de Montréal** (Montréal International Jazz Festival) brings together 2,000 musicians from 20 countries who enjoy more than 400 concerts over 11 days, from the end of June to the beginning of July. Festival dates for 1997 are June 26 to July 6. The biggest of the big names have played, including B.B. King, Buddy Guy, Etta James, Al Jareau, Charlie Haden, and Pat Metheny. And 75% of concerts are presented free of charge on the outdoor stages of the festival site: four city blocks that are closed to traffic. In addition to jazz, you can hear blues, Latin rhythms, gospel, Cajun, and world music as you wander from stage to stage. **Bell Info-Jazz** (☎ 514/871–1881 or 888/515–0515) answers all queries about the festival and about travel packages. Leave your name and address and they'll send you a program. You can charge tickets over the phone (☎ 514/790–1245 or 800/678–5440; in Canada, 800/361–4595).

Rock

Rock clubs seem to spring up, flourish, then fizzle out overnight. **Club Soda** (✉ 5240 av. du Parc, ☎ 514/270–7848), the granddaddy of them all, sports a neon martini glass complete with neon effervescence outside. Inside it's a small hall with a stage, three bars, and room for about 400 people. International rock acts play here, as does local talent. It's also a venue for the comedy and jazz festivals. The club is open only for shows. Phone the box office to find out what's on. **Déjà Vu** (✉ 1224 rue Bishop, ☎ 514/866–0512), a rock club with a nostalgia theme, is popular with young English-speakers. **L'Ours Qui Fume** (✉ 2019 rue St-Denis, ☎ 514/845–6998), or the Smoking Bear, is loud, raucous, and very Francophone.

OUTDOOR ACTIVITIES AND SPORTS

Most Montrealers would probably claim they hate winter, but the city is rich in cold-weather activities—skating rinks, cross-country ski trails, toboggan runs, and even a downhill ski run. In summer, there are tennis courts, miles of bicycle trails, golf courses, and two lakes on the island for boating and swimming.

Participant Sports

Bicycling

The island of Montréal—except for Mont-Royal itself—is quite flat, and there are more than 20 cycling paths in the metropolitan area. Bikes are welcome on the first and last cars of Métro trains during non-rush hours. Ferries at the Vieux-Port will take you to Ile Ste-Hélène and the south shore of the St. Lawrence River. You can rent 10-speed bicycles at **Cyclo-Touriste at the Centre Info-Touriste** (✉ 1001 sq. Dorchester, ☎ 514/393–1528). One of the most interesting paths follows the **Lachine Canal** (1825) from Vieux-Montréal to the shores of Lac St.-Louis in suburban Lachine. Along the way you can stop at the bustling **Atwater Farmer's Market** (✉ 110 av. Atwater) to buy the makings of a picnic. In Lachine you can visit the **Fur Trade at Lachine Historic Site** (✉ 1255 blvd. St-Joseph, Lachine, ☎ 514/637–7433). **Parks Canada** (☎ 514/283–6054 or 514/637–7433) conducts guided cycling tours along the Lachine Canal every summer weekend.

Fishing

The lakes and rivers around Montréal teem with fish, and a number of guides offer day trips, but you'll need a provincial license first. For complete information, call **Tourisme-Québec** (☎ 514/873–2015 or 800/363–7777).

Golf

For a complete listing of the many golf courses in the Montréal area, call **Tourisme-Québec** (☎ 514/873–2015 or 800/363–7777).

Ice Skating

There are at least 195 outdoor and 21 indoor rinks in the city. There are huge ones on Ile Ste-Hèlène and at the Vieux-Port. Call the **Parks and Recreation Department** (☎ 514/872–6211) for further information. There is year-round skating in the **Amphithéatre Bell** (☎ 514/395–0555, Ext. 237) in Le 1000 Rue de la Gauchetière.

Jogging

Montréal became a runner's city following the 1976 Olympics. There are paths in most city parks, but for running with a panoramic view, head to the dirt track in **Parc du Mont-Royal** (take rue Peel, then the steps up to the track).

Rafting

French settlers built Montréal where they did because they couldn't get their boats safely past the Lachine Rapids—which means Montréal is one of the few cities in the world where you can get in a boat at a downtown wharf and be crashing through Class V white water minutes later. For more than a decade, Jack Kowalski has been taking thrill-seekers on a 45-minute voyage through the rapids in big, sturdy aluminum jet boats. He supplies heavy-water gear, but it's impossible to stay dry—or have a bad time. He also offers speed-lovers a half-hour trip around the islands in smaller, 10-passenger boats that can go 60 miles an hour. Reservations are required; trips are narrated in French and English. ✉ *Lachine Rapids Tours Ltd., 105 rue de la Commune (Quai de l'Horloge or Clock Tower Pier),* ☎ *514/284–9607.* ⊡ *$48.* ☉ *5 trips through rapids May–Sept., daily at 10, noon, 2, 4, and 6.*

Skiing

Trails crisscross most of the city's parks, including Parc des Iles, Maisonneuve, and Mont-Royal. Parc Angrignon in the nearby suburb of LaSalle is good for skiers as well, but the best is probably the 900-acre **Cap St-Jacques Regional Park** in suburban Pierrefonds on the west end of Montréal Island.

For the big slopes you'll have to go northwest to the Laurentians (☞ Chapter 4), or south to the Eastern Townships (☞ Chapter 4), an hour or two away by car. There is a small slope in Parc du Mont-Royal. Pick up the "Ski-Québec" brochure at **Tourisme-Québec** offices (☎ 514/873–2015 or 800/363–7777).

Squash

Reserve court time three days ahead at **Nautilus Centre St-Laurent Côte-de-Liesse Racquet Club** (✉ 8305 chemin Côte-de-Liesse, ☎ 514/739–3654).

Swimming

There is a large indoor pool at the Olympic Park's **Centre Aquatique** (Métro Viau, ☎ 514/252–4622) and at **Centre Sportif et des Loisirs Claude-Robillard** (✉ 1000 av. Emile Journault, ☎ 514/872–6900). The outdoor pool on Ile Ste-Hélène is an extremely popular (and crowded) summer gathering place, open June–Labor Day. The city-run beach at Ile Notre-Dame is the only natural swimming hole in Montréal (☎ 514/872–6211).

Tennis

There are public courts in the Jeanne-Mance, Kent, Lafontaine, and Somerled parks. For details, call the **Parks and Recreation department** (☎ 514/872–6211).

Windsurfing and Sailing

Sailboards and small sailboats can be rented at **L'Ecole de Voile de Lachine** (✉ 2105 blvd. St-Joseph, Lachine, ☎ 514/634–4326) and the **Société du Parc des Iles** (☎ 514/872–6093).

Spectator Sports

Baseball

The National League's **Montréal Expos** (☎ 514/253–3434 or 800/463–9767) play at the Olympic Stadium from April through September.

Cycling

Le Tour de l'Ile de Montréal (☎ 514/521–8356) has made the *Guinness Book of World Records* for attracting the greatest number of participants. More than 30,000 amateur cyclists participate in "North America's most important amateur cycling event" each June, wending their way 70 kilometers (38 miles) through the streets and parks of Montréal.

Grand Prix

The annual **Molson Grand Prix du Canada** (☎ 514/392–0000 or 514/392–4731), which draws top Formula 1 racers from around the world, takes place every June at the **Gilles Villeneuve Race Track** on Ile Notre-Dame.

Hockey

The **Montréal Canadiens,** winners of 23 Stanley Cups, meet National Hockey League rivals at the Centre Molson (✉ 1250 rue de la Gauchetière Ouest, ☎ 514/932–2582), which opened in spring 1996.

SHOPPING

Montrealers *magasinent* (go shopping) with a vengeance, so it's no surprise that the city has 160 multifaceted retail areas encompassing some 7,000 stores.

The law allows shops to stay open weekdays 9–9 and weekends 9–5. However, many merchants close Monday–Wednesday evenings and on Sunday. You'll find many specialty service shops closed on Monday, particularly in predominantly French neighborhoods. Stores in designated tourist zones, such as Vieux-Montréal, remain open on Sunday.

Just about all stores, with the exception of some bargain outlets and a few selective art and antiques galleries, accept major credit cards. Buying with plastic usually gets you the best daily exchange rate on the Canadian dollar. If you're shopping with cash, buy your Canadian money at a bank or exchange bureau beforehand. Most purchases are subject to a federal goods and services tax (GST) of 7% as well as a provincial tax of 8%.

Montréal Specialties

Visitors usually reserve at least one day to hunt for either exclusive fashions along rue Sherbrooke or bargains at the Vieux-Montréal flea market. But there are specific items that the wise shopper seeks out in Montréal.

Fine English bone china, crystal, and woolens are more readily available and cheaper in metropolitan stores than in their U.S. equivalents, thanks to Canada's tariff status as a Commonwealth country.

CHINA AND CRYSTAL

Collectors of china and crystal will find reasonable prices at **Caplan Duval** (✉ Cavendish Mall, Côte-St-Luc, ☎ 514/483–4040; ✉ Plaza Côte-des-Neiges, Montréal, ☎ 514/345–0000), which has an overwhelming variety of patterns.

FUR

Montréal is one of the fur capitals of the world. Close to 85% of Canada's fur manufacturers are based in the city, as are many of their retail outlets. Many of them are clustered along rue Mayor and rue de Maisonneuve between rue Bleury and rue Aylmer. **McComber** (✉ 402 blvd. de Maisonneuve Ouest, ☎ 514/845–1167) has been in business for 100 years and its present owner has a flair for mink designs. **Shuchat** (✉ 418 blvd. de Maisonneuve Ouest, ☎ 514/849–2113) has been in the same family for more than 40 years and has a pleasant showroom full of the latest fashions. **Grosvenor** (✉ 400 blvd. de Maisonneuve Ouest, ☎ 514/288–1255) caters more to the wholesale trade, but has several showrooms where customers can view its decidedly European styles. **Alexandor** (✉ 2055 rue Peel, ☎ 514/288–1119), is nine blocks west of the main fur trade area and its storefront showroom caters to the downtown trade. **Birger Christensen at Holt Renfrew** (✉ 1300 rue Sherbrooke Ouest, ☎ 514/842–5111) is perhaps the most exclusive showroom of the lot with prices to match.

If you think you might be buying fur, it is wise to check with your country's customs officials before leaving to find out which animals are considered endangered and cannot be imported. Do the same if you think you might be buying Inuit carvings, many of which are made of whalebone and ivory and cannot be brought into the United States.

Centre-Ville

Downtown is Montréal's largest retail district. It takes in rue Sherbrooke, boulevard de Maisonneuve, rue Ste-Catherine, and the side streets between them. Because of the proximity and variety of shops, it's the best shopping bet for visitors in town overnight or over a weekend. The area bounded by rues Sherbrooke and Ste-Catherine, and rues de la Montagne and Crescent has antiques and art galleries in addition to designer salons. Rue Sherbrooke is lined with an array of art and antiques galleries. Rue Crescent is a tempting blend of antiques, fashions, and jewelry displayed beneath colorful awnings.

Complexe Desjardins

Complexe Desjardins (⊠ blvd. René-Lévesque and rue Jeanne Mance) is filled with splashing fountains and exotic plants, which give it a Mediterranean joie de vivre, even when it's below freezing outside. To get here take the Métro to the Place des Arts and follow the tunnels to Desjardins's multitiered atrium mall. The roughly 80 stores include budget outlets like Le Château for clothing as well as the exclusive Jonathan Roche Monsieur for men's fashions.

Department Stores

Eaton (⊠ 677 rue Ste-Catherine Ouest, ☎ 514/284–8411) is the city's leading department store and part of Canada's largest chain. Founded in Toronto by Timothy Eaton, the first Montréal outlet appeared in 1925. It now sells everything—from fashions and furniture to meals in the Art Deco top-floor restaurant and zucchini loaves in the basement bakery. Everything, that is, except tobacco. Timothy was a good Methodist and his descendants honor his principles.

La Baie—The Bay in English—(⊠ 585 rue Ste. Catherine Ouest) has been a department store since 1891. It was originally named Morgan's, but in 1960 it was bought by the Hudson Bay Company and acquired its present name. La Baie is known for its duffel coats and its Hudson Bay red-, green-, and white-striped blankets. It also sells the typical department store fare.

Exclusive **Holt Renfrew** (⊠ 1300 rue Sherbrooke Ouest, ☎ 514/842–5111), is known for its furs. The city's oldest store, it was established in 1837 as Henderson, Holt and Renfrew Furriers, and made its name supplying coats to four generations of British royalty. When Queen Elizabeth II married Prince Phillip in 1947, Holt's created a priceless Labrador mink as a wedding gift. Holt's carries the exclusive and pricey line of furs by Denmark's Birger Christensen, as well as the haute-couture and prêt-à-porter collections of Yves St-Laurent.

A kilted piper regales shoppers at **Ogilvy** (⊠ 1307 rue Ste-Catherine Ouest, ☎ 514/942–7711) every day at noon. An institution with Montrealers since 1865, the once-homey department store has undergone a miraculous face-lift. Fortunately, it preserved its delicate pink glass chandeliers and still stocks traditional apparel by retailers like Aquascutum and Jaeger. The store has been divided into individual designer boutiques selling pricier lines than La Baie or Eaton. It used to be Ogilvy's (just as Eaton used to be Eaton's) before Québec's French-only sign laws made apostrophes illegal.

Faubourg Ste-Catherine

A good place to start is the **Faubourg Ste-Catherine** (⊠ 1616 rue Ste-Catherine Ouest, at rue Guy), a vast bazaar abutting the Grey Nuns' convent grounds. There are three levels of clothing and crafts boutiques, as well as food counters and kiosks. You can pick up Québec maple syrup at a street-level boutique or a fine French wine for about $30 at the government-run Société d'Alcools du Québec. Prices at most stores here are generally reasonable, especially if you're sampling the varied ethnic cuisine of the snack counters.

Les Cours Mont-Royal

Les Cours Mont-Royal (⊠ 1550 rue Metcalfe) is *très élégant*. It's linked to both the Peel and McGill Métro stations and caters to expensive tastes, but even bargain hunters find it an intriguing spot for window shopping. Beware: The interior layout can be disorienting.

Les Promenades de la Cathédrale

The unusual location of **Les Promenades de la Cathédrale** (⊠ rues Ste-Catherine Ouest and University) makes it a sightseeing adventure as well as a shopping destination: It's directly beneath stately Christ Church Cathedral, the seat of Montréal's Anglican (Episcopalian) bishop. Les Promenades, which is connected to the McGill Métro station, has Canada's largest Linen Chest outlet, with hundreds of bedspreads and duvets draped over revolving racks plus aisles of china, crystal, linen, and silver. It's also home to the Anglican Church's Diocesan Book Room, which sells an unusually good and ecumenical selection of books as well as tasteful religious objects.

Place Bonaventure

Place Bonaventure (⊠ rues de la Gauchetière and University), is one of Canada's largest commercial exhibition centers. It's directly above the Bonaventure Métro station and has a mall with some 120 stores, including the trendy Au Coton and Bikini Village and the practical Bata Shoes. There are also a number of fun shops: Ici-Bas for outrageous hose, Le Rouet for handicrafts, and Miniatures Plus for exquisite dolls' furniture and tiny gifts.

Place Montréal Trust

Place Montréal Trust (⊠ 1600 rue McGill College, at rue Ste-Catherine Ouest) is the lively entrance to an imposing glass office tower. Shoppers, fooled by the aqua and pastel decor, may think they have stumbled into a California mall. Prices at the 110 outlets range from hundreds (for designs by Alfred Sung, haute couture at Gigi, or men's fashions at Rodier) to only a few dollars (for sensible cotton T-shirts or steak-and-kidney pies at the outpost of famed British department store Marks & Spencer). This shopping center is linked to the McGill Métro station.

Place Ville-Marie

Weatherproof shopping began in 1962 beneath the 42-story cruciform towers of **Place Ville-Marie** (⊠ blvd. René-Lévesque and rue Université). It's linked to the Bonaventure Métro station via Place Bonaventure, Central Station, and Le Reine Elizabeth and to the McGill station via the Centre Eaton, another major downtown shopping mall reached by taking the corridor from Centre Eaton south to Place Ville-Marie. Renovations opened Place Ville-Marie to the light, creating a more cheerful ambience.

Stylish women head to Place Ville-Marie's 100-plus retail outlets for the clothes (haute couture at Tristan & Iseut and Cactus). The upscale department store Holt Renfrew has an outlet here, and traditionalists will love Aquascutum. More affordable clothes shops include Dalmys and Reitmans. For shoes, try Mayfair, Brown's, François Villon, and French.

Notre-Dame Ouest

The place for antiquing is Notre-Dame Ouest, beginning at rue Guy and continuing west to avenue Atwater (a five-minute walk south from the Lionel-Groulx Métro station). Once a shabby strip of run-down secondhand stores, this area has blossomed beyond its former nickname of Attic Row. It now has the highest concentration of antiques, collectibles, and curiosity shops in Montréal. Collectors can find Canadian pine furniture—armoires, cabinets, spinning wheels, rocking chairs—for reasonable prices here. Consider a Sunday tour, beginning with brunch at **Salon de Thé Ambiance** (⌧ 1874 rue Notre-Dame Ouest, ☎ 514/939–2609), a charming restaurant that also sells antiques. Try **Antiquités Landry** (⌧ 1726 rue Notre-Dame Ouest, ☎ 514/937–7040) for solid pine furnitrue. **Viva Gallery** (⌧ 1970 rue Notre-Dame Ouest, ☎ 514/952–3200) specializes in Asian antiques. **Héritage Antique Métropolitain** has elegant English and French furniture. **Deux-ième** (⌧ 1880 rue Notre-Dame Ouest, ☎ 514/933–8560) sells a fascinating jumble of objects from every age.

Rue Chabanel

And now for something completely different. **Rue Chabanel,** in the north end of the city, is the soul of Montréal's extensive garment industry. Every Saturday, from about 8:30 to 1, many of the manufacturers and importers in the area open their doors to the general public. At least, they do if they feel like it. What results is part bazaar, part circus, and often all chaos—but quite friendly chaos. When Montrealers say "Chabanel," they mean the eight-block stretch just west of boulevard St-Laurent. The factories and shops there are tiny—dozens of them are crammed into each building. The goods seem to get more stylish and more expensive the farther west you go. For really cheap leather goods, sportswear, children's clothes, and linens, try the shops at 99 rue Chabanel. For more deluxe options, drop into 555 rue Chabanel. The manufacturers and importers here have their work areas on the upper floors and have transformed the mezzanine into a stylish mall with bargains in men's suits, winter coats, knitted goods, and very stylish leather jackets. A few places on Chabanel accept credit cards, but bring cash, anyway. It's easier to bargain if you can flash bills, and if you pay cash, the price will often "include the tax."

Rue Wellington

Two sturdy institutions that bear witness to the working-class origins of much of Montréal's English-speaking population anchor the ends of this lively thoroughfare crammed with bargain clothing stores, grocery stores, and tanning salons near the de l'Eglise Métro station in the Verdun neighborhood. **Muirs** (⌧ 3651 rue Wellington, ☎ 514/768–2422), which supplies haggis for dozens of Robert Burns dinners every January, is a tiny shop decorated in early-Depression that makes and sells Scottish meat pies, potato scones, sausage rolls, egg custards, shortbread, and Empire biscuits (jam-filled, glazed cookies that are to die for). **Stilwells** (⌧ 5123 rue Wellington, ☎ 514/766–4481) has been at the same seedy little shopfront since 1926, making chocolate creams, truffles, peanut brittle, and the best humbugs (a striped hard candy that tastes of carmelized sugar and mint) in the known universe. (The place closes down every July and August because, the Stilwells say, chocolate doesn't set worth a darn in summer. But rumor has it they spend those months on a huge yacht called the S.S. *Humbug.*) The sparkling, modern **Chez Gaumond** (⌧ 3725 rue Wellington, ☎ 514/768–2564) is one of the best pastry shops on Montréal Island, with a wonderful array of desserts, cakes, pâtés, and homemade ice cream and sherbet. If you get peckish looking at all this food, try the Peruvian specialties at **Villa Wellington** (⌧ 4701 rue Wellington, ☎ 514/768–0102) or, for something a bit grander, the excellent Italian food at **Casa Rossi** (✉ 5145 rue Wellington, ☎ 514/761–2578).

Square Westmount and Avenue Greene

Square Westmount (✉ rue Ste-Catherine Ouest and av. Greene) has some of the city's finest shops (and the most luxurious public washrooms on the island), which is hardly surprising—it serves the mountainside suburb of Westmount, home to executives and former prime ministers. Humbler types can get there easily by taking the Métrovia to the Atwater station, and following the tunnel to Square Westmount. **Collange** (☎ 514/933–4634) sells lacy lingerie. **Ma Maison** (☎ 514/933–0045) stocks quality housewares. **Hugo Nicholson** (☎ 514/937–1937) sells exclusive fashions for men and women. The very elegant **Marché de Westmount** has an array of gourmet boutiques that sell pastries, cheeses, pâtés, fruits, cakes, chocolates, etc. You can assemble your own picnic and eat it at one of the little tables scattered among the stalls. If all this tires you out, you can stop in at the **Spade Westmount** (☎ 514/933–9966) for a massage. The square opens onto **avenue Greene,** two flower-lined blocks of restored redbrick row houses full of boutiques, restaurants, and shops. **Double Hook** (✉ 1235A av. Greene, ☎ 514/932–5093) sells only Canadian books. And try the **Coach House** (✉ 1325 av. Greene, ☎ 514/937–6191) for antique silverware.

Upper Boulevard St-Laurent and Avenue Laurier Ouest

Upper boulevard St-Laurent—which runs roughly from avenue du Mont-Royal north to rue St-Viateur and climbs the mountain to rue Bernard—has blossomed into one of Montréal's chicest *quartiers*. It's not entirely surprising, given that much of this area lies within or adjacent to Outremont, an enclave of wealthy Francophone Montrealers, with restaurants, boutiques, nightclubs, and bistros catering to the upscale visitor. **Scandale** (✉ 3639 blvd. St-Laurent, ☎ 514/842–4707) has designs for the very hip as well as great lingerie and a second-hand clothes store. **J. Schrecter** (✉ 4350 blvd. St-Laurent, ☎ 514/845–4231) had been supplying work duds for blue-collar workers for decades when the grunge look suddenly made the store trendy.

Shoppers flock to the two blocks of avenue Mont-Royal just east of boulevard St-Laurent for a series of shops that sell secondhand clothes and recycled clothes (things like housecoats chopped into sassy miniskirts). **Scarlett O'Hara** (✉ 254 av. Mont-Royal Est, ☎ 514/844–9435) started the whole trend. **Eva B** (✉ 2013 blvd. St-Laurent, ☎ 514/849–8246) sells new clothes as well as used. **Hatfield & McCoy** (✉ 156 av. Mont-Royal Est, ☎ 514/982–0088) recycles clothes from the '30s, '40s, and '50s.

Avenue Laurier Ouest, from boulevard St-Laurent to chemin de la Côte-Ste-Catherine, is roughly an eight-block stretch; you'll crisscross it many times as you explore its fashionable and trendy shops, which carry everything from crafts and clothing to books and paintings. **Tilley Endurables** (✉ 158 av. Laurier Ouest, ☎ 514/272–7791) sells the famous Canadian-designed Tilley hat and other easy-care travel wear. **Boutique Gabriel Filion** (✉ 1127 av. Laurier Ouest, ☎ 514/274–0697) sells interesting imported toys and a marvelous array of dolls, doll clothes, stuffed animals, and music boxes. For Asian and African crafts, try **Artefact** (✉ 102 av. Laurier Ouest, ☎ 514/278–6575).

Vieux-Montréal

Despite Vieux-Montréal's abundance of garish souvenir shops, a shopping spree there can be worthwhile. Both rues Notre-Dame and St-Jacques, from rue McGill to Place Jacques-Cartier, are lined with low to moderately priced fashion boutiques and shoe stores. **Tripps** (⊠ 389 rue Notre-Dame Ouest, ☎ 514/845–1979), a pioneer clothes discounter, sells boxes full of end-of-the-line, brand-name goods in its huge, cluttered shop. **Desmarais et Robitaille** (⊠ 60 rue Notre-Dame Ouest, ☎ 514/845–3194), a store that supplies churches with vestments and liturgical aids, has Québécois carvings and handicrafts as well as tasteful religious articles. **Rue St-Paul** also has some interesting shops and art galleries. **Drags** (⊠ 367 rue St-Paul Est, ☎ 514/866–0631) is crammed with fragments of military uniforms and loads of clothes, shoes, hats, and accessories from the '30s and '40s. **L'Empreinte Coopérative** (⊠ 272 rue St-Paul Est, ☎ 514/861–4427) has a fine collection of Québec handicrafts. **Rita R. Giroux** (⊠ 206 rue St-Paul Ouest, ☎ 514/8444714) makes flamboyant dried flower creations. At the **Cerf Volanterie** (⊠ 224 rue St-Paul Ouest, ☎ 514/845–7613), Claude Thibaudeau makes sturdy, gloriously colored kites that he signs and guarantees for three years. The **Galerie Art & Culture** (⊠ 227 rue St-Paul Ouest, ☎ 514/843–5980) specializes in Canadian landscapes. **Galerie des Arts Relais des Epoques** (⊠ 234 rue St-Paul Ouest, ☎ 514/844–2133) sells some fascinating work by contemporary Montréal painters.

The Vieux-Port hosts a sprawling flea market, the **Marché aux Puces.** Dealers and pickers prowl through the huge hangar searching for secondhand steals and antique treasures. ⊠ *King Edward Pier,* ☉ *May 5–28, Fri. and Sun. 11–9, Sat. 11–10; May 31–Aug. 27, Wed., Thurs., and Sun. 11–9, Sat. 11–10; July and Aug., Tues. 11–9.*

MONTRÉAL A TO Z

Arriving and Departing

By Bus

For information about the following three companies, contact Terminus Voyageur (☞ *below*). **Greyhound** has coast-to-coast service and serves Montréal with buses arriving from and departing for various cities in North America. **Vermont Transit** serves Montréal via Boston, New York, and other points in New England. **Voyageur** and Voyageur-Colonial service destinations primarily within Québec and Ontario. The city's downtown bus terminal, **Terminus Voyageur** (⊠ 505 blvd. de Maisonneuve Est, ☎ 514/842–2281), connects with the Berri-UQAM Métro station.

By Car

Montréal is accessible from the rest of Canada via the Trans-Canada Highway, which enters the city from the east and west via Routes 20 and 40. The New York State Thruway (I–87) becomes Route 15 at the Canadian border, and then it's 47 kilometers (30 miles) to the outskirts of Montréal. U.S. I–89 becomes two-lane Route 133, which eventually joins Route 10, at the border. From I–91 from Massachusetts, you must take Routes 55 and 10 to reach Montréal. At the border you must clear Canadian Customs, so be prepared with proof of citizenship and your vehicle's ownership papers. On holidays and during the peak summer season, expect waits of a half hour or more at the major crossings.

Once you're in Québec, the road signs will be in French, but they're designed so you shouldn't have much trouble understanding them. The speed limit is posted in kilometers; on highways the limit is 100 kph (about 62 mph). There are extremely heavy penalties for driving while intoxicated, and drivers and front-seat passengers must wear over-the-shoulder seat belts. Gasoline is sold in liters (3¾ liters equal 1 U.S. gallon), and lead-free is called *sans plomb*. If you're traveling in winter, remember that your car may not start on extra-cold mornings unless it has been kept in a heated garage. All Montréal parking signs are in French, so brush up on your *gauche* (left), *droit* (right), *ouest* (west), and *est* (east).

Montréal police have a diligent tow-away and fine system for cars double-parked or stopped in no-stopping zones in downtown Montréal during rush hours and business hours. A parking ticket will cost between $35 and $40. If your car is towed away while illegally parked, it will cost an additional $35 to retrieve it. Be especially alert during winter: Montréal's snow-clearing crews are the best in the world and a joy to watch in action after a major blizzard—but they're ruthless in dealing with any parked cars that get in their way. If they don't tow them, they'll bury them. New York, Maine, and Ontario residents should drive with extra care in Québec: Traffic violations in the province are entered on their driving records back home (and vice versa).

And if you drive in the city, remember two things: Québec law forbids you to turn right on a red light and Montrealers are notorious jaywalkers.

By Plane

Montréal is served by two airports. **Dorval International,** 22½ kilometers (14 miles) west of the city, handles domestic and most U.S. flights. **Mirabel International,** 54½ kilometers (34 miles) northwest of the city, is a hub for the rest of the international trade.

Air Canada (☎ 514/393–3333 or 800/361–8620) offers nonstop service from New York, Miami, and Tampa and from Boston via its connector airline, Air Alliance. Direct service is available from Los Angeles and San Francisco. **American Airlines** (☎ 800/433–7300) has nonstop service from Chicago with connections from the rest of the United States. **Canadian Airlines International** (☎ 514/847–2211 or 800/426–7000; in Canada, 800/363–7530) has a nonstop charter from Fort Lauderdale and direct or connecting service from Hawaii and Los Angeles. **Delta Air Lines** (☎ 514/337–5520 or 800/221–1212; in Québec Province, 800/361–1970) has nonstops from Boston, Hartford, Connecticut, and Miami and connecting service from most major U.S. cities. **USAir** (☎ 800/428–4322) has services from Philadelphia and Pittsburgh.

Flying time from New York is 1½ hours; from Chicago, two hours; from Los Angeles, 6½ hours (with a connection).

A **taxi** from Dorval to downtown will cost $25, from Mirabel about $56. All taxi companies in Montréal must charge the same rates by law. It is best to have Canadian money with you, because the exchange rate for U.S. dollars is at the driver's discretion. **Autobus Connaisseur** (☎ 514/934–1222) is a much cheaper alternative to taxis into town from Mirabel and Dorval. **Shuttle service** from Mirabel to the terminal next to the **Gare Centrale** (✉ 777 rue de la Gauchetière) is frequent and costs only $14.50. The shuttle from Dorval runs about every half hour and stops at Le Centre Sheraton, Le Château Champlain, Le Reine Elizabeth, and the Voyageur terminal. It costs $9. If you know you are going to use the bus to go back to either airport, you can save $8 by buying a round-trip ticket. Connaisseur also runs a shuttle between Dorval and Mirabel.

By Train

The Gare Centrale (Central Station), on rue de la Gauchetière between rues University and Mansfield (behind Le Reine Elizabeth), is the rail terminus for all trains from the United States and from other Canadian provinces. It is connected by underground passageway to the Bonaventure Métro station.

Budget cuts killed **Amtrak's** (☎ 800/878–7245) overnight *Montrealer* from Washington and New York, but the *Adirondack* still leaves New York's Penn Station every morning for the 10½–hour trip through the spectacular scenery of upstate New York to Montréal. It has a snack car but no dinner service or sleepers. A round-trip ticket is usually cheaper than two one-way fares.

VIA Rail (☎ 514/871–1331 or 800/561–3949; in Québec Province, 800/361–5390) connects Montréal with all the major cities of Canada, including Québec City, Halifax, Ottawa, Toronto, Winnipeg, Edmonton, and Vancouver.

Getting Around

By Bus and Métro

Public transportation is easily the best and cheapest way to get around. The Métro (subway) is clean, quiet (it runs on rubber wheels), and safe, and it's heated in winter and cooled in summer. Métro hours on the Orange, Green, and Yellow lines are weekdays 5:30 AM–12:58 AM, Saturday 5:30 AM–1:28 AM, and Sunday 5:30 AM–1:58 AM. The Blue Line runs daily from 5:30 AM to 11 PM. Trains run as often as every three minutes on the most crowded lines—Orange and Green at rush hours. The Métro is also connected to the 29 kilometers (18 miles) of the Underground City, so you may not need to go outside during bad weather. Each of the 65 Métro stops has been individually designed and decorated; Berri-UQAM has stained glass, and at Place d'Armes a small collection of archaeological artifacts is exhibited. The stations between Snowdon and Jean-Talon on the Blue Line are worth a visit, particularly Outremont, with its glass-block design. Each station connects with one or more bus routes, which cover the rest of the island. The STCUM (Société de Transport de la Communauté Urbaine de Montréal) administers both the Métro and the buses, so the same tickets and transfers are valid on either service. You should be able to get within a few blocks of anywhere in the city on one fare. At press time rates were: single ticket, $1.85; six tickets, $7.75; monthly pass, $44.50. Visitors can buy a day pass for $5 or a three-day pass for $12. They're available at most major hotels and at Info-Touriste.

Free maps may be obtained at Métro ticket booths. Try to get the *Carte Réseau* (system map); it's the most complete. Transfers from Métro to buses are available from the dispenser just beyond the ticket booth inside the station. Bus-to-bus and bus-to-Métro transfers may be obtained from the bus driver. For more information on reaching your destination call the **Société de Transport de la Communauté de Montréal** (☎ 514/288–6287).

By Taxi

Taxis in Montréal all run on the same rate: $2.25 minimum and $1 a kilometer. They're usually reliable, although they may be hard to find on rainy nights after the Métro has closed. Each carries on its roof a white or orange plastic sign that is lit when available and off when occupied.

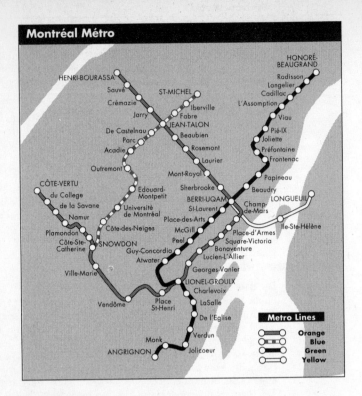

Montréal Métro

Metro Lines
Orange
Blue
Green
Yellow

Contacts and Resources

Car Rentals
Avis (☎ 514/866–7906 or 800/321–3652). **Budget** (☎ 514/938–1000). **Discount** (☎ 514/286–1554). **Dollar** (☎ 514/990–0074 or 800/800–4000). **Hertz** (☎ 514/842–8537 or 800/263–0678). **Tilden** (☎ 514/878–2771 or 800/387–4747). **Via Route** (☎ 514/521–5221).

Consulates
United States (⊠ 1155 rue St-Alexandre, ☎ 514/398–9695). Open weekdays 8:30–4:30. **United Kingdom** (⊠ 1000 rue de la Gauchetière Ouest, ☎ 514/866–5863). Open weekdays 9–5.

Doctors and Dentists
The U.S. Consulate cannot recommend specific doctors and dentists but does provide a list of various specialists in the Montréal area. Call in advance (☎ 514/398–9695) to make sure the consulate is open.

Dental clinic (☎ 514/342–4444) open 24 hours, Sunday emergency appointments only. **Montréal General Hospital** (☎ 514/937–6011). **Québec Poison Control Centre** (☎ 800/463–5060). **Touring Club de Montréal–AAA, CAA, RAC** (☎ 514/861–7111).

Emergencies
Dial 911 to reach the **police, fire,** and **ambulance.**

English-Language Bookstores
Coles (⊠ 1171 rue Ste-Catherine Ouest, ☎ 514/849–8825). **Double Hook** (⊠ 1235A av. Greene, ☎ 514/932–5093) sells only Canadian books. **Paragraphe** (⊠ 2065 rue Mansfield, ☎ 514/845–5811) has a café.

Guided Tours

BOAT

Amphi Tour Ltée (☎ 514/386–1298) offers a unique tour of Vieux-Montréal and the Vieux-Port on both land and water in an amphibious bus. The one-hour tours run from May to October. **Bateau-Mouche** (☎ 514/849–9952) runs four harbor excursions and an evening supper cruise every day from May to October. The boats are reminiscent of the ones that cruise the canals of the Netherlands—wide-beamed and low-slung, with a glassed-in passenger deck. Boats leave from the Jacques Cartier Pier at the foot of Place Jacques-Cartier in the Vieux-Port (Métro Champs-de-Mars).

CALÈCHE RIDES

Open horse-drawn carriages—fleece-lined in winter—leave from Place Jacques-Cartier, Square Dorchester, Place d'Armes, and rue de la Commune. An hour-long ride costs about $50 (☎ 514/653–0751).

ORIENTATION

Gray Line (☎ 514/934–1222) has nine different tours of Montréal in the summer and one tour during the winter. It offers pickup service at the major hotels, or you may board the buses at Info-Touriste (⊠ 1001 sq. Dorchester). **Murray Hill Trolley Buses** (☎ 514/871–4733) follow a 14-stop circuit of the city. Passengers can get off and on as often as they like and stay at each stop as long as they like. There's pickup service at major hotels.

Late-Night Pharmacies

Many pharmacies are open until midnight, including the following two. **Jean Coutu** (⊠ 501 Mont-Royal Est, ☎ 514/521–3481; ⊠ 5510 Côte-des-Neiges, ☎ 514/344–8338). **Pharmaprix** (⊠ 1500 rue Ste-Catherine Ouest, ☎ 514/933–4744; ⊠ 5157 rue Sherbrooke Ouest, ☎ 514/484–3531). **Pharmaprix** (⊠ Promenades du Musée; ⊠ 5122 Côte-des-Neiges, ☎ 514/738–8464; ⊠ 901 rue Ste-Catherine Est, ☎ 514/842–4915) is open 24 hours.

Lodging Reservations

Bed and Breakfast à Montréal represents more than 50 homes in downtown and in the elegant neighborhoods of Westmount and Outremont. Singles run $40–$55; doubles $55–$85. ⊠ *Marian Kahn, Box 575, Snowdon Station, H3X 3T8,* ☎ *514/738–9410,* FAX *514/735–7493.*

Downtown B&B Network represents 75 homes and apartments, mostly around the downtown core and along rue Sherbrooke, that have one or more rooms available for visitors. Singles are $25–$40, doubles $35–$55. Even during the height of the tourist season, this organization has rooms open. ⊠ *Bob Finkelstein, 3458 av. Laval (at rue Sherbrooke), H2X 3C8,* ☎ *514/289–9749 or 800/267–5180.*

There is a room reservation service at **Info-Touriste** (☎ 800/665–1528), which can find you a room in one of 80 hotels, motels, and bed-and-breakfasts.

Passes

The Montréal museum pass allows you access to 19 major museums, including most of the ones mentioned in this chapter. A day pass costs $15, a three-day pass $28; family passes are $30 for one day and $60 for three days. They are available at museums or **Centre Info-Touriste** (⊠ 1001 sq. Dorchester).

Travel Agencies

American Express (⊠ 1141 blvd. de Maisonneuve Ouest, ☎ 514/284–3300). **Canadian Automobile Club** (⊠ 1180 rue Drummond, ☎ 514/

861–5111). **Vacances Tourbec** (✉ 595 blvd. de Maisonneuve Ouest, ☎ 514/842–1400). **Voyages Campus** (✉ McGill University, 3480 rue McTavish, ☎ 514/398–0647).

Visitor Information

Centre Info-Touriste (✉ 1001 sq. Dorchester, ☎ 514/873–2015 or 800/363–7777) on Square Dorchester is open June 10–Labor Day, daily 8:30–7:30, and Labor Day–June 9, daily 9–6. A second branch (✉ 174 rue Notre-Dame Est, at pl. Jacques-Cartier, ☎ 514/873–2015) is open Labor Day–mid-May, daily 9–1 and 2–5, and mid-May–Labor Day, daily 9–7.

3 Québec City

With Side Trips to Côte de Beaupré, Montmorency Falls, and Île d'Orléans

Québec City, which enjoys one of the most beautiful natural settings in North America, perched on a cliff above a narrow point in the St. Lawrence River, is the capital of, as well as the oldest municipality in, Québec province.

NO EXCURSION TO FRENCH-SPEAKING Canada is complete without a visit to exuberant, romantic Québec City, which enjoys one of the most beautiful natural settings in North America. The well-preserved Vieille Ville (Old City) is small and dense, steeped in four centuries of history and French tradition. Here you can explore 17th- and 18th-century buildings, the ramparts that once protected the city, and numerous parks and monuments. The Québec government has completely restored many of the centuries-old buildings of Place Royale, one of the oldest districts on the continent. Because of its immaculate preservation as the only fortified city remaining in North America, UNESCO has designated the Vieille Ville a World Heritage Site.

By Alice H. Oshins

Updated by Donna Nebenzahl

Perched on a cliff above a narrow point in the St. Lawrence River, Québec City is the oldest municipality in Québec province. During the 17th century the first French explorers, fur trappers, and missionaries came here to establish the colony of New France. Today it still resembles a French provincial town in many ways; its family-oriented residents have strong ties to their past. More than 95% of its metropolitan population of 650,000 are French-speaking.

In 1535 French explorer Jacques Cartier first came upon what the Algonquin Indians called "Kebec," meaning "where the river narrows." New France, however, was not actually founded in the vicinity of what is now Québec City until 1608, when another French explorer, Samuel de Champlain, recognized the military advantages of the location and set up a fort. On the banks of the St. Lawrence, on the spot now called Place Royale, this fort developed into an economic center for fur trade and shipbuilding. Twelve years later, Champlain realized the French colony's vulnerability to attacks from above and expanded its boundaries to the top of the cliff, where he built the fort Château St-Louis on the site of the present-day Château Frontenac.

During the early days of New France, the French and British fought for control of the region. In 1690, when an expedition led by Admiral Sir William Phipps arrived from England, Comte de Frontenac, New France's most illustrious governor, defied him with the statement, "Tell your lord that I will reply with the mouth of my cannons."

The French, preoccupied with scandals at the courts of kings Louis XV and Louis XVI, gave only grudging help to their possessions in the New World. The French colonists built walls and other military structures and had the advantage of the defensive position on top of the cliff, but they still had to contend with Britain's naval supremacy. On September 13, 1759, the British army, led by General James Wolfe, scaled the colony's cliff and took the French troops led by General Louis-Joseph Montcalm by surprise. The British defeated the French in a 20-minute battle on the Plains of Abraham, and New France came under British rule.

The British brought their mastery of trade to the region. During the 18th century, Québec City's economy prospered because of the success of the fishing, fur-trading, shipbuilding, and timber industries. Wary of new invasions, the British continued to expand upon the fortifications left by the French. They built a wall encircling the city and a star-shape citadel, both of which mark the city's urban landscape today. The constitution of 1791 established Québec City as the capital of Lower Canada until the 1840 Act of Union that united Upper and Lower Canada and made Montréal the capital. The city remained under British rule until 1867, when the Act of Confederation united several

Canadian provinces (Québec, Ontario, New Brunswick, and Nova Scotia) and established Québec City as capital of the province of Québec.

In the mid-19th century, the economic center of eastern Canada shifted west from Québec City to Montréal and Toronto. Today government is Québec City's main business: About 30,000 civil-service employees work and live in the area. Office complexes continue to spring up outside the older part of town; modern malls, convention centers, and imposing hotels now cater to an established business clientele.

Pleasures and Pastimes

Dining

Québec City reveals its French heritage most obviously in its cuisine. You'll discover a French touch in the city's numerous cafés and brasseries and in the artful presentation of dishes at local restaurants. This is the best place in the province to sample French-Canadian cuisine, composed of robust, uncomplicated dishes that make use of the region's bounty of foods, including fowl and wild game (quail, caribou, venison), maple syrup, and various berries and nuts. Because Québec has a cold climate for a good portion of the year, it has a traditionally heavy cuisine, with such specialties as *cretons* (pâtés), *tourtière* (meat pie), and *tarte au sucre* (maple-syrup pie).

Most dining establishments usually have a selection of dishes à la carte, but you'll often discover more creative specialties by opting for the table d'hôte, a two- to four-course meal chosen daily by the chef. At dinner, many restaurants will offer a *menu de dégustation,* a five- to seven-course dinner of the chef's finest creations. If you're budget-conscious, try the more expensive establishments at lunchtime. Lunch usually costs about 30% less than dinner, and many of the same dishes are available. Lunch is usually served 11:30 through 2:30; dinner, 6:30 until about 11. You should tip about 15% of the bill.

CATEGORY	COST*
$$$$	over $30
$$$	$20–$30
$$	$10–$20
$	under $10

*per person, excluding drinks, service, 7% federal sales tax, and 6.5% provincial sales tax

Lodging

With more than 35 hotels within its walls and countless family-run bed-and-breakfasts, Québec City has a range of lodging options. Landmark hotels stand as prominent as the city's most historic sites; modern high rises outside the ramparts offer spectacular views of the Old City. Visitors can immerse themselves in the city's historic charm by staying in one of the many old-fashioned inns where no two rooms are alike.

Be sure to make a reservation if you visit during peak season (May through September) or during the Winter Carnival, in February. During busy times, hotel rates usually rise 30%. From November through April, many lodgings offer discount weekend packages and other promotions.

CATEGORY	COST*
$$$$	over $140
$$$	$85–$140
$$	$50–$85
$	under $50

*All prices are for a standard double room, excluding 7% federal sales tax, 6.5% provincial sales tax, and an optional service charge.

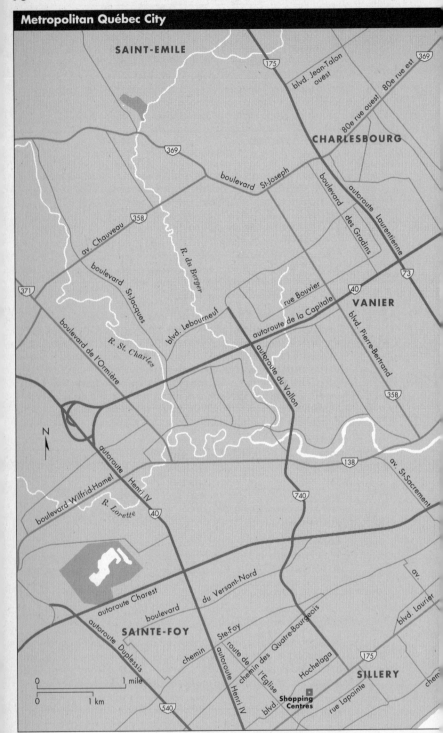

Metropolitan Québec City

SAINT-EMILE

175

blvd. Jean-Talon ouest

80e rue ouest

80e rue est

369

CHARLESBOURG

369

boulevard St-Joseph

boulevard des Gradins

autoroute Laurentienne

358

av. Chauveau

R. du Berger

rue Bouvier

73

371

boulevard St-Jacques

blvd. Lebourneuf

autoroute de la Capitale

VANIER

blvd. Pierre-Bertrand

boulevard de l'Ormière

R. St. Charles

autoroute du Vallon

358

N

138

av. St-Sacrement

autoroute Henri IV

740

boulevard Wilfrid-Hamel

R. Lorette

40

autoroute Charest

du Versant-Nord

av.

boulevard

blvd. Laurier

autoroute Duplessis

SAINTE-FOY

chemin

Ste-Foy

route de l'Église

chemin des Quatre-Bourgeois

Hochelaga

175

SILLERY

chem

autoroute Henri IV

blvd.

Shopping
Centres

rue Lapointe

0   1 mile

0   1 km

540

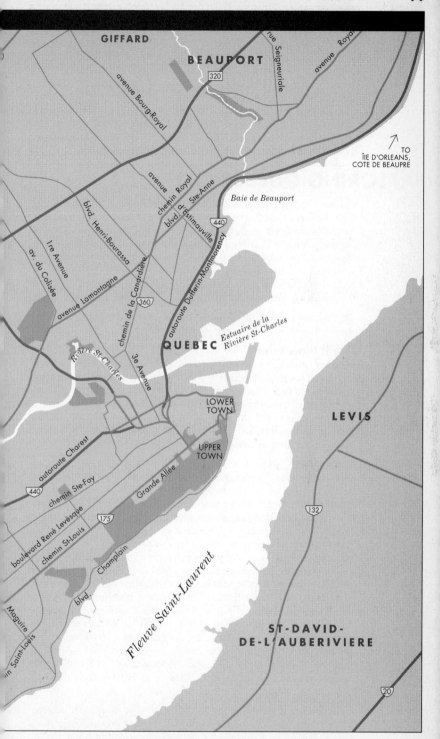

GIFFARD

BEAUPORT

320

rue Seigneuriale

avenue Royal

avenue Bourg-Royal

TO
ÎLE D'ORLEANS,
COTE DE BEAUPRÉ

avenue

chemin Royal

blvd. Henri-Bourassa

blvd. d. Ste-Anne

blvd. d. Estimauville

Baie de Beauport

440

1re Avenue

av. du Colisée

avenue Lamontagne

chemin de la Canardière

autoroute Dufferin-Montmorency

360

QUEBEC

*Estuaire de la
Rivière St-Charles*

Rivière St-Charles

3e Avenue

LOWER
TOWN

LEVIS

autoroute Charest

UPPER
TOWN

chemin Ste-Foy

Grande Allée

440

boulevard René Lévesque

175

132

chemin St-Louis

Champlain

blvd.

Maguire

min Saint-Louis

Fleuve Saint-Laurent

**ST-DAVID-
DE-L'AUBERIVIERE**

20

Walking

Québec City is a wonderful place to wander on foot. From Parc Mont-morency (Montmorency Park), you can see the Laurentian Mountains jutting majestically above the St. Lawrence River. Even more impressive vistas are revealed if you walk along the walls or climb to the city's highest point, Cap Diamant (Cape Diamond). You can spend days investigating the narrow cobblestone streets of the historic Old City, visiting historic sites or browsing for local arts and crafts in the boutiques of quartier Petit-Champlain. Strolling the Promenade des Gouverneurs and the Plains of Abraham, you are offered a view of the river as well as the Laurentian foothills and the Appalachian mountains.

EXPLORING QUÉBEC CITY

Québec City's split-level landscape divides the Upper Town on the cape from the Lower Town, along the shores of the St. Lawrence. If you look out from the Terrasse Dufferin boardwalk in Upper Town, you will see the rooftops of Lower Town buildings directly below. Separating these two sections of the city is steep and precipitous rock, against which were built the city's more than 25 *escaliers* (staircases). Today you can also take the *funiculaire* (funicular), a cable car that climbs and descends the cliff between Terrasse Dufferin and the Maison Jolliet in Lower Town.

The first two tours primarily focus on the oldest sections of town, while the third explores the modern part of the city.

Great Itineraries

Whether you take a weekend or a week, there's enough history, scenery, and entertainment to delight the most seasoned traveler. A weekend visitor might enjoy the historic sights of the Old City, strolling along ancient streets and the boardwalk by the river in the evening before dining at some of the city's fine restaurants. A week-long stay allows you to wander beyond the city proper, and might include a visit to the shrine of Ste-Anne de Beaupré or to the quiet splendor of Ile d'Orléans.

IF YOU HAVE 3 DAYS

Walk through the Quartier Petit-Champlain, Place Royale, and the Vieux Port. Start by taking the funicular from Terrasse Dufferin to the Quartier, which resembles a quaint riverside village. Visit the Maison Chevalier, a historic home; then on to Place Royale, the earliest site of French civilization in North America, which, in the summer, has a wide variety of entertainment. Stop at Notre-Dame-des-Victoires church, its magnificent high altar sculpted in the form of a castle. On rue Dal-housie, visit Explore, a multimedia sound and light show. Further along, at number 85, the Musée de la Civilization has an assortment of dynamic exhibitions that can easily occupy a visitor for part of a day. A visit to the Vieux Port, just beyond the Musée, provides a window on the maritime activities of yesteryear. The Old Port interpretation center and the fascinating l'Ilot des Palais, an archaeological dig, are both worth a visit. Visit the antique shops on rue St-Paul and, at the foot of côte de la Montagne, walk down escalier Casse-cou (break-neck stairs) and take the funicular back up to Terrasse Dufferin.

IF YOU HAVE 5 DAYS

Vieux Québec was the first North American city to be included on UN-ESCO's prestigious World Heritage list. To understand its importance, take a walking tour starting at the Tourist Information Bureau at 60 rue d'Auteuil, then go south in the direction of St-Louis. Near the St-Louis gate, you can visit the Poudrière de l'Esplanade, a former pow-derhouse and initiation center on the fortifications. Farther along rue St-Louis, find rue Donnacona, the site of the museum and chapel of the Ursulines order, who arrived in Québec in 1639. In the museum, thematic exhibits evoke the daily life of the sisters while the chapel preserves its original 1723 interior decor. The mortal remains of the founder, Blessed Marie de l'Incarnation, rest in the adjacent oratory. The Anglican Cathedral of the Holy Trinity on rue des Jardins is modeled after London's St. Martin-in-the-Fields and houses numerous precious objects. Back along St-Louis, visit Place d'Armes, under the French regime a site for military parades and public speeches, and admire the majestic Chateau Frontenac to the south. Then it is on to the Terrasse Dufferin, where you can visit some of the sites listed in the two-day tour.

IF YOU HAVE 7 DAYS

A full week provides an opportunity to view the impressive fortifications in Québec, since the city was, during the 17th, 18th, and 19th centuries, instrumental in the ultimate defense of all northeastern America. Begin at the Citadelle, a national historic site atop Cap Diamant. Visit the star-shape fortifications and then walk along the Fortifications of Québec, a rampart of nearly 4½ kilometers (3 miles) that encircles the old city. Other outdoor sites worth a visit are Artillery Park and Battlefield Park, home of the famous Plains of Abraham and the Musée du Québec, just a few steps from the Wolfe Monument. The Terrasse Earl Grey offers a splendid view of the river, and you can stroll the Promenade des Gouverneurs, which runs along the edge of the cliff to Terrasse Dufferin. Pick up some of the shorter tours at that point and, if time permits, save a day to visit the destination of 1.5 million pilgrims annually, the Basilica of Ste-Anne-de-Beaupré, taking the route of the historic avenue Royale or Route 360. Or enjoy the farms and woodlands of Ile d'Orléans, a 15-minute drive from Vieux Québec, connected to the mainland by a bridge.

Haute-Ville (Upper Town)

Numbers in the text below correspond to numbers in the margin and on the maps.

The most prominent buildings of Québec City's earliest European inhabitants, who set up political, educational, and religious institutions, stand here. Upper Town became the political capital of the colony of New France and, later, of British North America. Historic buildings with thick stone walls, large wood doors, glimmering copper roofs, and majestic steeples fill the heart of the city.

A Good Walk

Start where rue St-Louis meets rue du Fort at **Place d'Armes** ①, a large plaza bordered by government buildings. To your right is the colony's former treasury building, **Maison Maillou,** interesting for its 18th-century architecture. A little farther along, at number 25, is **Maison Kent,** where the capitalization of Québec was signed in 1759. South of Place d'Armes's towers Québec City's most celebrated landmark, **Château Frontenac** ②, an imposing green-turreted castle once the administrative and military headquarters of New France and now a hotel. As you head to the boardwalk behind the Frontenac, notice the glorious bronze statue of Samuel de Champlain, standing where he built his residence.

Walk south along the boardwalk called the **Terrasse Dufferin** ③ for a panoramic view. At the boardwalk's western tip begins the **Promenade des Gouverneurs**, which skirts along the cliff and leads up to the Citadelle and Québec's highest point, Cap Diamant (Cape Diamond).

As you pass to the southern side of the Frontenac, you will come to a small park called **Jardin des Gouverneurs** ④. From the north side of

82

Upper and Lower Towns

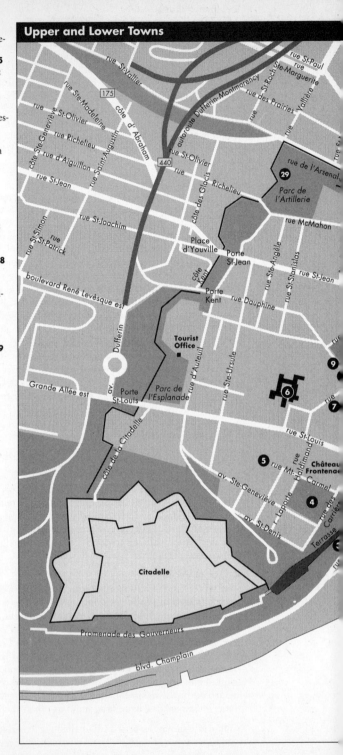

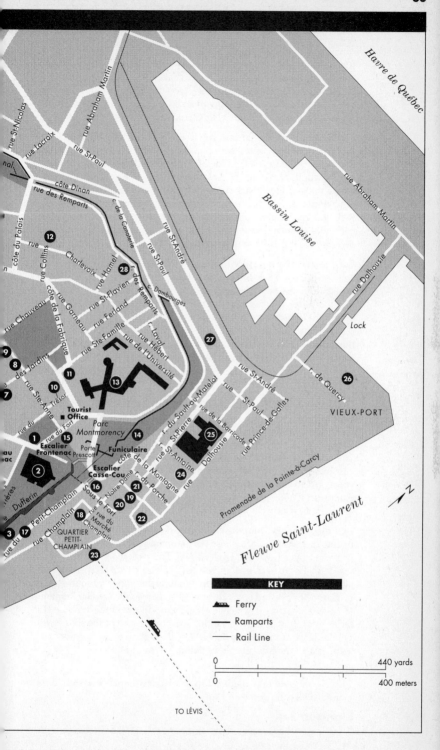

Havre de Québec

rue St-Nicolas

rue Lacroix

rue St-Paul

rue Abraham Martin

côte Dinan

rue des Remparts

Bassin Louise

rue Abraham Martin

côte du Palais

rue

12

Charlevoix

rue Collins

côte de la Canoterie

rue St-André

rue Dalhousie

28

rue Hamel

rue St-Flavien

rue St-Paul

Lock

côte de la Fabrique

rue Chauveau

côte de la Fabrique

rue Garneau

rue Ferland

c. Dambourges

rue des Remparts

9

des Jardins

rue Ste-Famille

rue Ferland

rue Hébert

rue de l'Université

rue Laval

27

r. de Quercy

26

8

11

Tresor

13

VIEUX-PORT

7

rue Ste-Anne

10

rue St-André

St-Paul

rue de la Barricade

**Tourist
Office**

rue du Fort

*Parc
Montmorency*

rue du Sault-au-Matelot

rue St-Pierre

rue St-André

rue Prince-de-Galles

1

15

14

**Escalier
Frontenac**

Porte
Prescott

Funiculaire

côte de la Montagne

rue St-Antoine

25

Dalhousie

au

2

**Escalier
Casse-Cou**

rue St-Antoine

24

Promenade de la Pointe-à-Carcy

Dufferin

16

Notre Dame

r. du Porche

21

19

rue du Fort

3

17

Petit-Champlain

18

Sous-le-Fort

20

r. du
Marché
Champlain

22

rue Champlain

**QUARTIER
PETIT-
CHAMPLAIN**

23

Fleuve Saint-Laurent

N

KEY
🚢 Ferry
▬ Ramparts
— Rail Line

0 — 440 yards

0 — 400 meters

TO LÉVIS

the park follow rue Mont Carmel until you come to another small park landscaped with flower beds interlaced with footpaths, **Cavalier du Moulin** ⑤. After 1693, it was used as a fortification.

Retrace your steps down rue Mont Carmel, turn left on rue Haldimand and left again on rue St-Louis; then make a right and follow rue du Parloir until it intersects with a tiny street called rue Donnacona where ★ you'll find the **Couvent des Ursulines** ⑥, a private school that houses a museum and has a lovely chapel next door.

On the nearby rue des Jardins, you'll see the **Holy Trinity Anglican Cathedral** ⑦ a dignified church with precious objects on display. Next come two buildings with Art Deco details: the **Hôtel Clarendon** ⑧ just east of the cathedral, at rue des Jardins and rue Ste-Anne and, next door, the ★ **Edifice Price** ⑨. Head back on rue Ste-Anne past the cathedral and continue until the street becomes a narrow, cobblestone thoroughfare lined with boutiques and restaurants. In summer, activity here starts early and continues until late: Stores stay open, artists paint, and street musicians perform as long as there is an audience.

Turn left onto the outdoor art gallery of **rue du Trésor** ⑩ and at its end, turn left on rue Buade. At the corner of côte de la Fabrique is **Basilique Notre-Dame-de-Québec** ⑪ and the beginning of Québec City's **Latin Quarter,** which extends to the streets northwest of the ☞ **Seminaire de Québec**—rue Buade, rue des Remparts, côte de la Fabrique, and côte du Palais—as far as rue St-Jean. This district was dubbed the Latin Quarter because Latin was once a required language course at the seminary. Latin is no longer compulsory and Québec Seminary–Laval University has moved to Ste-Foy, but students still cling to this neighborhood.

Head down côte de la Fabrique and turn right when it meets rue Collins. The cluster of old stone buildings sequestered at the end of the street is the **Monastère des Augustines de l'Hôtel-Dieu de Québec** ⑫. Retrace your steps on Collins Street and côte de la Fabrique. When you reach rue Ste-Famille on the left, you will find the wrought-iron entrance gates of the **Séminaire du Québec** ⑬. Head north across the courtyard to the **Musée de l'Amérique Française** (Museum of North American Francophones). Next, you can visit Québec Seminary's **Chapelle Extérieure** (Outer Chapel), at the seminary's west entrance.

Exit the seminary from the east at rue de l'Université and head south to côte de la Montagne, where **Parc Montmorency** ⑭ straddles the hill between Upper Town and Lower Town. This park marks the spot where Canada's first wheat was grown in 1618 and where the colony's first legislation was passed in 1694 in a building no longer standing. Walk through the park and cross côte du Montagne to the **Escalier Frontenac** (Frontenac Stairway), which leads to the north end of the Terrasse Dufferin. Turn right at the top for the 30-minute recap of the six sieges of Québec City at the **Musée du Fort** ⑮. As you leave the museum, head southeast to the funicular booth along Terrasse Dufferin.

TIMING
This tour should take the better part of a day. Lunchtime should find you at the Basilique Notre-Dame.

Sights to See
Numbers in the margin correspond to points of interest on the Upper and Lower Towns map.

⑪ **Basilique Notre-Dame-de-Québec** (Our Lady of Québec Basilica). This basilica has the oldest parish in North America, dating from 1647. It's been rebuilt three times: in the early 1700s, when François de Montmorency Laval was the first bishop; in 1759, after cannons at Lévis fired upon it during the siege of Québec; and in 1922, after a fire. The basilica's somberly ornate interior includes a canopy dais over the episcopal throne, a ceiling of clouds decorated with gold leaf, richly colored stained-glass windows, and a chancel lamp that was a gift of Louis XIV. The large and famous crypt was Québec City's first cemetery; more than 900 people are interred here, including 20 bishops and four governors of New France. The founder of the city, Samuel de Champlain, is believed to be buried near the basilica: Archaeologists have been searching for his tomb since 1950. ⊠ *16 rue Bade,* ☎ *418/692–2533.* ⊡ *Free.* ⊙ *Oct.–May, daily 7–4:30; June–Sept., daily 8–6.*

❺ **Cavalier du Moulin.** A small park landscaped with flower beds interlaced with footpaths, the Cavalier du Moulin is the former site of a stone windmill that became part of the French fortifications. The windmill was strategically placed so that its cannons could destroy the Cap-Diamant Redoubt (near Promenade des Gouverneurs) and the St-Louis Bastion (near St-Louis Gate) in the event that New France was captured by the British. ⊠ *Between rue St. Louis and av. Ste.-Geneviève.* ⊡ *Free.* ⊙ *May–Nov., daily 7 AM–9 PM.*

Centre Marie-de-l'Incarnation. Next to the Musée des Ursulines (☞ *below*), is this bookstore with an exhibit on the life of the Ursulines' first superior, who came from France and cofounded the convent. ⊠ *10 rue Donnacona,* ☎ *418/692–1569.* ⊡ *Free.* ⊙ *Feb.–Nov., Tues.–Sat. 10–11:30 and 1:30–4:30, Sun. 1:30–4:30.*

Chapelle des Ursulines (Ursuline Chapel). On the grounds of the Couvent des Ursulines (☞ *below*), is this little chapel where French General Montcalm was buried after he died in the 1759 battle. The exterior was rebuilt in 1902, but the interior contains the original chapel, which took sculptor Pierre-Noël Levasseur from 1726 to 1736 to complete. The votive lamp was lit in 1717 and has never been extinguished. ⊠ *12 rue Donnaconna.* ⊡ *Free.* ⊙ *May–Oct., Tues.–Sat. 10–11:30 and 1:30–4:30, Sun. 12:30–4:30.*

★ ❷ **Château Frontenac.** This imposing green-turret castle with its slanting copper roof, Québec City's most celebrated landmark, was once the administrative and military headquarters of New France. It owes its name to the Comte de Frontenac, governor of the French colony between 1672 and 1698. Looking at the magnificence of the château's location, you can see why Frontenac said, "For me, there is no site more beautiful nor more grandiose than that of Québec City."

Samuel de Champlain, who founded Québec City in 1608, was responsible for Château St-Louis, the first structure to appear on the site of the Frontenac; it was built between 1620 and 1624 as a residence for colonial governors. In 1784, Château Haldimand was constructed here, but it was demolished in 1892 to make way for Château Frontenac (☞ Lodging, *below*). The latter was built as a hotel in 1893, and it was considered to be remarkably luxurious at that time: Guest rooms contained fireplaces, bathrooms, and marble fixtures, and a special commissioner traveled to England and France in search of antiques for the establishment. The hotel was designed by New York architect Bruce Price, who also worked on Québec City's Gare du Palais (rail station) and other Canadian landmarks, such as Montréal's Windsor Station. The Frontenac was completed in 1925 with the addition of a 20-story central tower. Owned by Canadian Pacific Hotels, it has accumulated a star-studded guest roster, including Queen Elizabeth, Madame Chiang Kai-shek, Ronald Reagan, and François Mitterrand, as well as

Franklin Roosevelt and Winston Churchill, who convened here in 1943 and 1944 for two wartime conferences. ⊠ *1 rue des Carrières,* ☎ *418/692–3861.*

6 Couvent des Ursulines (Ursuline Convent). The site of North America's oldest teaching institution for girls, still a private school, was founded in 1639 by two French nuns. The convent has many of its original walls still intact. On its property are a museum (☞ Musée des Ursulines, *below*) and a chapel (☞ Chapelle des Ursulines, *above*) that you may visit. Next door is an interesting bookstore (☞ Centre Marie-de-l'Incarnation, *above*). ⊠ *12 rue Donnacona.*

★ **9 Edifice Price** (Price Building). The city's first skyscraper, the 15-story Art Deco Edifice Price, was built in 1929 and served as headquarters of the Price Brothers Company, the lumber firm founded in Canada by Sir William Price. Today the building is owned by the provincial government and houses the offices of Québec City's mayor. Don't miss the interior: Exquisite copper plaques depict scenes of the company's early pulp and paper activities, while the two artfully carved maple-wood elevators are '30s classics. It is next door to the Hôtel Clarendon (☞ *below*). ⊠ *65 rue Ste-Anne.*

7 Holy Trinity Anglican Cathedral. This stone church dates from 1804 and was one of the first Anglican cathedrals built outside the British Isles. Its simple and dignified facade is reminiscent of London's St. Martin-in-the-Fields. The cathedral's land was originally given to the Recollet fathers (Franciscan monks from France) in 1681 by the king of France for a church and monastery. When Québec came under British rule, the Recollets made the church available to the Anglicans for services. Later, King George III of England ordered construction of the present cathedral, with an area set aside for members of the royal family. A portion of the north balcony still remains exclusively for the use of the reigning sovereign or her representative. The church houses precious objects donated by George III; wood for the oak benches was imported from the Royal Forest at Windsor. The cathedral's impressive rear organ has more than 2,500 pipes. ⊠ *31 rue des Jardins,* ☎ *418/692–2193.* ▣ *Free.* ☉ *May–June, daily 9–5; July and Aug., daily 9–9; Sept. and Oct., weekdays 10–4; Nov.–May, offices only; Sun. services in English 8:30 and 11 AM and in French 9:30 AM.*

8 Hôtel Clarendon. One of Québec City's finest Art Deco structures is the Clarendon, Québec's oldest hotel (☞ Lodging, *below*). Although the Clarendon dates from 1866, it was reconstructed in its current Art Deco style—geometric patterns of stone and wrought iron decorating its interior—in 1930. ⊠ *57 rue Ste-Anne, at rue des Jardins,* ☎ *418/692–2480.*

4 Jardin des Gouverneurs (Governors' Park). This small park on the southern side of the Frontenac is home to the **Wolfe-Montcalm Monument,** a 50-foot obelisk that is unique because it pays tribute to both a winning (English) and a losing (French) general. The monument recalls the 1759 battle on the Plains of Abraham, which ended French rule of New France. British General James Wolfe lived only long enough to hear of his victory; French General Louis-Joseph Montcalm died shortly after Wolfe with the knowledge that the city was lost. During the French regime, the public area served as a garden for the governors who resided in Château St-Louis. On the south side of the park is **avenue Ste-Geneviève,** lined with well-preserved Victorian houses dating from 1850 to 1900 that have been converted to quaint old-fashioned inns.

Maison Maillou. The colony's former treasury building typifies the architecture of New France with its sharply slanted roof, dormer windows, concrete chimneys, shutters with iron hinges, and limestone walls. Built between 1736 and 1753, it stands at the end of ☞ **rue du Trésor.** Maison Maillou now houses the Québec City Chamber of Commerce and is not open for tours. ✉ *17 rue St-Louis.*

⑫ **Monastère des Augustines de l'Hôtel-Dieu de Québec** (Augustine Monastery). Augustine nuns arrived from Dieppe, France, in 1639 with a mission to care for the sick in the new colony; they established the first hospital north of Mexico, the **Hôtel-Dieu hospital,** the large building west of the monastery. The **Musée des Augustines** (Augustine Museum) is in hospital-like quarters with large sterile corridors leading into a ward that has a small exhibit of antique medical instruments, such as a pill-making device from the 17th century. Upon request, the Augustines also offer guided tours of the **chapel** (1800) and the cellars used by the nuns as a shelter, beginning in 1659, during bombardments by the British. ✉ *32 rue Charlevoix,* ☎ *418/692–2492.* 🎫 *Free.* ☉ *Tues.–Sat. 9:30–noon and 1:30–5, Sun. 1:30–5.*

Musée de l'Amérique Française. Housed in a former student residence of the Québec Seminary–Laval University (☞ Séminaire du Québec, *below*), this museum focuses on the history of the French presence in North America. There are more than 400 landscape and still-life paintings dating from as long ago as the 15th century, rare Canadian money that was used in colonial times, and scientific instruments acquired through the centuries for the purposes of research and teaching. A former chapel has been renovated and is used for exhibits and cultural activities. The museum was expected to close during the summer of 1996 and reopen in October 1996 after extensive renovations. ✉ *9 rue Université,* ☎ *418/692–2843.* 🎫 *$3, free Tues.* ☉ *Tues.–Sun. 10–5.*

Musée des Ursulines (Ursuline Museum). Within the walls of the Couvent des Ursulines (☞ *above*) is this former residence of one of the convent's founders, Madame de la Peltrie. It offers an informative perspective on 120 years of the Ursulines' life under the French regime, from 1639 to 1759. For instance, you'll discover that because the Ursulines were without heat in winter, their heavy clothing sometimes weighed as much as 20 pounds. You'll also see why it took an Ursuline nun nine years of training to attain the level of a professional embroiderer; the museum contains magnificent pieces of ornate embroidery, such as altar frontals with gold and silver threads intertwined with precious jewels. ✉ *12 rue Donnacona,* ☎ *418/694–0694.* 🎫 *$3.* ☉ *Feb. 7–Dec. 1, Tues.–Sat. 9:30–noon and 1:30–5, Sun. noon–5.*

NEED A BREAK?   At the neon-lit **Bistro Taste-Vin** (✉ 32 rue St-Louis, ☎ 418/692–4191), on the corner of rue des Jardins and rue St-Louis, sample delicious salads, pastries, and desserts.

⑮ **Musée du Fort** (Fort Museum). This museum's sole exhibit is a sound-and-light show that reenacts the region's most important battles, including the Battle of the Plains of Abraham and the 1775 attack by American generals Arnold and Montgomery. ✉ *10 rue Ste-Anne,* ☎ *418/692–2175.* 🎫 *$5.50.* ☉ *June–Aug., daily 10–6; Apr.–May, Sept. and Oct., daily 10–5; Nov.–Mar., weekdays 11–noon and 1:45–3:30, weekends 11–5; English presentation every hr on the hr.*

❶ **Place d'Armes.** For centuries, this square atop a cliff has been a gathering place for parades and military events. Upper Town's most central location, the Place is bordered by government buildings; at its west side is the majestic **Ancien Palais de Justice** (Old Courthouse), a Renaissance-style building from 1887. The Place stands on land that was occupied by a church and convent of the Recollet missionaries (Franciscan monks), who in 1615 were the first order of priests to arrive in New France. The Gothic-style fountain at the center of Place d'Armes pays tribute to their arrival. ⊠ *rue St. Louis and rue du Fort.*

⑩ Rue du Trésor. The road colonists took on their way to pay rent to the king's officials is now a narrow alley where hundreds of colorful prints, paintings, and other artworks are on display. You won't necessarily find masterpieces here, but this walkway is a good stop for a souvenir sketch or two. On this street is the **Québec Experience,** a multimedia sound-and-light show that takes you into the heart of Québec's history, from the first explorers until modern days. ⊠ *8 rue du Trésor,* ☎ *418/694–4000.* ☞ *$6.50.* ⊙ *Mid-May–mid-Oct., daily 10– 10; mid-Oct.–mid-May, daily 10–5.*

⑬ Séminaire du Québec (Québec Seminary). Behind these gates lies a tranquil courtyard surrounded by austere stone buildings with rising steeples; these structures have housed classrooms and student residences since 1663. The seminary was founded by François de Montmorency Laval, the first bishop of New France, to train priests of the new colony. In 1852 the seminary became Université Laval (Laval University), the first Catholic university in North America. The university eventually outgrew these cramped quarters; in 1946 it moved to a larger, modern campus in the suburb of Ste-Foy. The **Musée du Séminaire** offers guided tours of the seminary during the summer. The small Roman-style chapel, **Chapelle Extérieure** (Outer Chapel), at the west entrance of Québec Seminary, was built in 1888 after fire destroyed the first chapel, which dated from 1750. ⊠ *2 Cote de la Fabrique,* ☎ *418/694–1020.*

③ Terrasse Dufferin. The Terrasse, a wide boardwalk with an intricate wrought-iron guardrail, allows a panoramic view of the St. Lawrence River, the town of Lévis on the opposite shore, Ile d'Orléans, and the Laurentian Mountains. It was named for Lord Dufferin, governor of Canada between 1872 and 1878, who had this walkway constructed in 1878. At its western end begins the **Promenade des Gouverneurs,** which skirts the cliff and leads up to Québec's highest point, Cap Diamant, and also to the Citadelle (☞ *below*).

Basse-Ville (Lower Town)

New France first began to flourish in the streets of Lower Town along the banks of the St. Lawrence River. These streets became the colony's economic crossroads, where furs were traded, ships came in, and merchants established their residences.

Despite the status of Lower Town as the oldest neighborhood in North America, its narrow and time-worn thoroughfares have a new and polished look. In the 1960s, after a century of decay as the commercial boom moved west and left Lower Town abandoned, the Québec government committed millions of dollars to restore the district to the way it had been during the days of New France. Today modern boutiques, restaurants, galleries, and shops catering to tourists occupy the former warehouses and residences.

A Good Walk

Begin this tour on the northern tip of rue du Petit-Champlain at **Maison Louis-Jolliet** ⑯, the lower station of the funicular. You can also wander down the **Escalier Casse-Cou** (Breakneck Steps) instead of taking the funicular from the Upper to the Lower towns. Heading south on **rue du Petit-Champlain** ⑰, the city's oldest street, you'll notice the cliff on the right that borders this narrow thoroughfare, with Upper Town on the heights above. At the point where rue du Petit-Champlain intersects with boulevard Champlain, make a U-turn to head back north on rue Champlain. One block farther, at the corner of rue du Marché-Champlain, you'll find **Maison Chevalier** ⑱, an old stone house. Walk east to rue Notre-Dame, which leads directly to **Place Royale** ⑲, formerly the heart of New France. The small stone church at the south side of the Place Royale is the **Eglise Notre-Dame-des-Victoires** ⑳, the oldest church in Québec. Then, on the northwest corner of the square, look for the cool, dark, and musty cellars of the **Maison des Vins** ㉑, a wine store.

On the east side of Place Royale, take rue de la Place, which leads to an open square, **Place de Paris** ㉒ At this point of the tour you may conveniently catch the 15-minute **Lévis–Québec ferry** ㉓ to the opposite shore of the St. Lawrence River for the view. Back on the Québec side of the river, stop at **Explore** ㉔, a sound-and-light show. Continue north on rue Dalhousie until you come to the **Musée de la Civilisation** ㉕, devoted to Québecois culture and civilization. Head east toward the river to the **Vieux-Port de Québec** ㉖, at one time the busiest on the continent. The breezes here from the St. Lawrence provide a cool reprieve on a hot summer's day, and you can browse through the **Marché du Vieux-Port** (Farmer's Market). You are now in the ideal spot to explore Québec City's **antiques district** ㉗.

Walk west along rue St-Paul and turn left onto a steep brick incline called côte Dambourges; when you reach côte de la Canoterie, take the stairs back on the cliff to rue des Remparts. Continue approximately a block west along rue des Remparts until you come to the last building in a row of purple houses, **Maison Montcalm** ㉘, the former home of General Montcalm. Continue west on rue des Remparts and turn left on côte du Palais and then immediately right on rue de l'Arsenal, which brings you to the **Parc de l'Artillerie** ㉙, a complex of 20 military, industrial, and civilian buildings.

TIMING

A morning of strolling will take you to two of the city's most famous squares, Place Royale and Place de Paris. Take the time for a brisk 15-minute ferry ride to Lévis and back and you'll be ready for a mid-morning snack. After the Explore light show, tour the Musée de la Civilisation before a late lunch in the antiques district. After browsing along rue St-Paul, explore Parc de l'Artillerie and its adjoining buildings.

Sights to See

㉗ **Antiques district.** Antiques shops cluster along rue St-Pierre and rue St-Paul. Rue St-Paul was once part of a business district where warehouses, stores, and businesses abounded. After World War I, shipping and commercial activities plummeted; low rents attracted antiques dealers. Today numerous cafés, restaurants, and art galleries have turned this area into one of the town's more fashionable sections.

⑳ **Eglise Notre-Dame-des-Victoires** (Our Lady of Victory Church). The oldest church in Québec was built on the site of Samuel de Champlain's first residence, which also served as a fort and trading post. The church was built in 1688 and was restored twice. Its name comes from two French victories against the British: one in 1690 against Admiral William Phipps and another in 1711 against Sir Hovendon Walker. The interior contains copies of paintings by such European masters as Van Dyck, Rubens, and Boyermans; its altar resembles the shape of a fort. A scale model suspended from the ceiling represents *Le Brezé,* the boat that transported French soldiers to New France in 1664. The side chapel is dedicated to Ste-Geneviève, the patron saint of Paris. ✉ *Pl. Royale,* ☎ *418/692–1650.* ✍ *Free.* ☉ *Daily 9–4:30, Sat. 9–4, except during Mass (Sun. 9:30, 11, and noon; May–Oct., Sat. 7 PM), marriages, and funerals; Oct.–mid-May, Tues.–Sat. 9–4:30.*

Escalier Casse-Cou. The steepness of the city's first iron stairway, an ambitious 1893 design by Charles Baillairgé, a city architect and engineer, is ample evidence of how it got its name. It was built on the site of the original 17th-century stairway that linked Upper Town and Lower Town during the French regime. Today, shops, quaint boutiques, and restaurants are at various levels.

㉔ Explore. This 30-minute sound-and-light show uses high-tech visual art to relive the story of the founding of the city. Sail up the St. Lawrence River with Jacques Cartier and Samuel de Champlain to Québec and witness their first encounter with native Indians. ⊠ *63 rue Dalhousie,* ☎ *418/692–2063.* ☞ *$5.50.* ⊙ *May–Sept., daily 10–6; Apr., May, Oct., and Nov., daily 10–5; Dec., daily 11–3.*

㉓ Lévis–Québec ferry. En route to the opposite shore of the St. Lawrence River, you get a striking view of Québec City's skyline, with the Château Frontenac and the Québec Seminary high atop the cliff. The view is even more impressive at night. ⊠ *Rue Dalhousie, 1 block south of Place de Paris,* ☎ *418/644–3704,* ☞ *$1.25.* ⊙ *1st ferry leaves at 6:30 AM; crossings every ½ hr 7:30 AM–6:30 PM, every hr 7:30 PM–2:30 AM; final crossing 3:45 AM.*

NEED A
BREAK?

Café du Monde (⊠ 57 rue Dalhousie, ☎ 418/692–4455), with an impressive view of the St. Lawrence River, specializes in brunch on Saturday and Sunday. Croissants, sausages, waffles with maple syrup, and *moules et frites* (mussels with French fries) are popular.

---

⑱ Maison Chevalier. This old stone house was built in 1752 for shipowner Jean-Baptiste Chevalier; the house's style, of classic French inspiration, clearly reflects the urban architecture of New France. Fire walls, chimneys, vaulted cellars, and original wood beams and stone fireplaces are some of its noteworthy features. ⊠ *50 rue du Marché-Champlain,* ☎ *418/643–2158.* ☞ *Free.* ⊙ *Mid-June–Sept., daily 10–6.*

㉑ Maison des Vins. In this former warehouse dating from 1689, the Québec Société des Alcools sells more than 1,000 kinds of rare and vintage wines, which range in price from $10 to $1,000. ⊠ *1 Pl. Royale,* ☎ *418/643–1214.* ⊙ *Tues. and Wed. 9:30–5:30, Thurs. and Fri. 9:30–9, Sat. 9:30–5.*

⑯ Maison Louis-Jolliet. Built in 1683, this house, now a souvenir shop at the lower station of the funicular, was used by the first settlers of New France as a base for further westward explorations. A monument commemorating Louis Jolliet's discovery of the Mississippi River in 1672 stands in the park next to the house. At the north side of the house is Escalier Casse-Cou (☞ *above*), the city's first iron stairway. ⊠ *16 rue du Petit-Champlain,* ☎ *418/692–1132.*

㉘ Maison Montcalm. This was the home of French General Louis-Joseph Montcalm from 1758 until the capitulation of New France. A plaque dedicated to the general is on the right side of the house. ⊠ *rue des Remparts between rues Hamel and St. Flavien.*

☙ ㉕ Musée de la Civilisation (Civilization Museum). Wedged into the foot of the cliff, this spacious museum with a striking limestone and glass facade has been artfully designed by architect Moshe Safdie to blend into the city landscape. Its campanile echoes the shape of church steeples throughout the city. The museum has innovative, entertaining, and sometimes playful exhibits devoted to aspects of Québec's culture and civilization. Several of the shows, with their imaginative use of artwork, video screens, computers, and sound, will appeal to both adults and children. Its thematic approach, which focuses on participation and interaction, also extends to exhibits of an international nature. ✉ *85 rue Dalhousie,* ☎ *418/643–2158.* 🎟 *$6; free Tues. in winter.* ☉ *June 24–Sept. 2, daily 10–7; Sept. 3–June 23, Tues.–Sun. 10–5, Wed. 10–9.*

㉙ Parc de l'Artillerie (Artillery Park). This national historic park is a complex of 20 military, industrial, and civilian buildings, so situated to guard the St. Charles River and the Old Port. Its earliest buildings served as headquarters for the French garrison and were taken over in 1759 by the British Royal Artillery soldiers. The defense complex was used as a fortress, barracks, and cartridge factory during the American siege of Québec in 1775 and 1776. The area served as an industrial complex providing ammunition for the Canadian army from 1879 until 1964. One of the three buildings you can visit is a former **powder magazine,** which in 1903 became a shell foundry. The building houses a detailed model of Québec City in 1808, rendered by two surveyors in the office of the Royal Engineers Corps. Sent to Britain in 1813, it was intended to show British officials the strategic importance of Québec so that more money would be provided to expand the city's fortifications. The model details the city's houses, buildings, streets, and military structures. The powder magazine is open daily 10–5, and admission is $2.75. The **Dauphin Redoubt,** named in honor of the son of Louis XIV (the heir apparent), was constructed from 1712 to 1748. It served as a barracks for the French garrison until 1760, when it became an officers' mess for the Royal Artillery Regiment. It's open late June–early September, daily 10–5. The **Officers' Quarters,** a dwelling for Royal Artillery officers until 1871 when the British army departed, is now a museum for children, with shows on military life during the British regime. The Officers' Quarters are open late June–early September, daily 10–5. ✉ *2 rue d'Auteuil,* ☎ *418/648–4205.*

㉒ Place de Paris. This square, a newcomer to these historic quarters, is dominated by a black-and-white geometric sculpture, *Dialogue avec l'Histoire* (Dialogue with History), a gift from France positioned on the site where the first French settlers landed. ✉ *rue Dalhousie.*

⑲ Place Royale. This cobblestone square is encircled by the former homes of wealthy merchants, which have steep Normandy-style roofs, dormer windows, and several chimneys. Until 1686 the area was called Place du Marché, but its name was changed when a bust of Louis XIV, *"le Roi Soleil"* (the Sun King), was erected at its center. During the late 1600s and early 1700s, when Place Royale was continually under threat of attacks from the British, the colonists progressively moved to higher and safer quarters atop the cliff in Upper Town. Yet after the French colony fell to British rule in 1759, Place Royale flourished again with shipbuilding, logging, fishing, and fur trading. ✉ *Place Royale Information Centre, 215 Marche Finlay,* ☎ *418/646–3167.* ☉ *June 3–Sept. 29.*

⑰ Rue du Petit-Champlain. This street was the main street of a former harbor village, with trading posts and the homes of rich merchants. Today it has pleasant boutiques and cafés. Natural-fiber weaving, Inuit carvings, hand-painted silks, and enameled copper crafts are some of the local specialties that are good buys here.

㉖ Vieux-Port de Québec (Old Port of Québec). The old harbor dates from the 17th century, when ships first arrived from Europe bringing supplies and settlers to the new colony. At one time this port was among the busiest on the continent: Between 1797 and 1897, Québec shipyards turned out more than 2,500 ships, many of which passed the 1,000-ton mark. The port saw a rapid decline after steel replaced wood and the channel to Montréal was deepened to allow larger boats to reach a good port upstream. In 1984, the 72-acre port was restored with a $100 million grant from the federal government; today it encompasses several parks. You can stroll along the riverside promenade, where merchant and cruise ships are docked. At the port's northern end, where the St. Charles meets the St. Lawrence, a lock protects the marina in the Louise basin from the generous Atlantic tides that reach even this far up the St. Lawrence. In the northwest section of the port, an exhibition center, **Port de Québec in the 19th Century** (✉ 100 rue St-André, ☎ 418/648–3300), presents the history of the port in relation to the lumber trade and shipbuilding. Admission to the center is $2.50, and it is open May–August, daily 10–5; September–October, daily noon–4; and October–May by reservation. At the port's northwestern tip is the **Marché du Vieux-Port** (Old Port Market), where farmers sell their fresh produce. The market is open May–October, daily 8–8.

Outside the Walls

Numbers in the text below correspond to numbers in the margin and on the maps.

In the 20th century, Québec City grew into a modern metropolis outside the historic confines of the city walls. Yet beyond the walls lies a great deal of the city's military history, in the form of its complex fortifications and battlements.

A Good Walk

★ Start close to St-Louis Gate at **Parc de l'Esplanade** ㉚, the site of a former military drill and parade ground. Esplanade Park is also the starting point for walking the city's 4½ kilometers (3 miles) of walls; in summer, guided tours begin here. From the **Powder Magazine** in the park, head south on côte de la Citadelle, which leads directly to the **Citadelle** ㉛, the largest fortified base in North America still occupied by troops. Retrace your steps down côte de la Citadelle to Grande Allée. Continue west until you come to the Renaissance-style **Parliament Buildings** ㉜, which mark Parliament Hill, headquarters of the provincial government. Across from the Parliament on the south side of Grande Allée is the **Manège Militaire**, a turreted granite armory built in 1888, four years after the Parliament Buildings. Also designed by Taché, it is still a drill hall for the 22nd Regiment.

Continue along **Grande Allée** ㉝, Québec City's version of the Champs-Elysées, with its array of trendy cafés, clubs, and restaurants. If you turn left on Place Montcalm, you'll be facing the **Montcalm Monument** ㉞. Continue south on Place Montcalm to one of North America's largest and most scenic parks, **Parc des Champs-de-Bataille** ㉟, or Battlefields Park. This 250-acre area of gently rolling slopes offers unparalleled views of the St. Lawrence River. Within the park and just west of the Citadelle are the **Plains of Abraham** ㊱, the site of the famous 1759 battle that decided the fate of New France.

Take avenue Laurier, which runs parallel to Battlefields Park, a block west until you come to a neatly tended garden called **Parc Jeanne d'Arc** ㊲. If you continue west on avenue Laurier, you'll see a stone oval defense tower, **Tour Martello no. 2** ㊳; on the left, toward the south end of the park, stands **Tour Martello no. 1** ㊴. Continue a block west on rue de Bernières and then follow avenue George V along the outskirts of Battlefields Park until it intersects with avenue Wolfe-Montcalm. You'll come to the tall **Wolfe Monument** ㊵, which marks the place where the British general died. Turn left on avenue Wolfe-Montcalm for a leisurely stroll through the **Musée de Québec** ㊶. From the museum head north on avenue Wolfe-Montcalm, turning right on Grande Allée and walk-

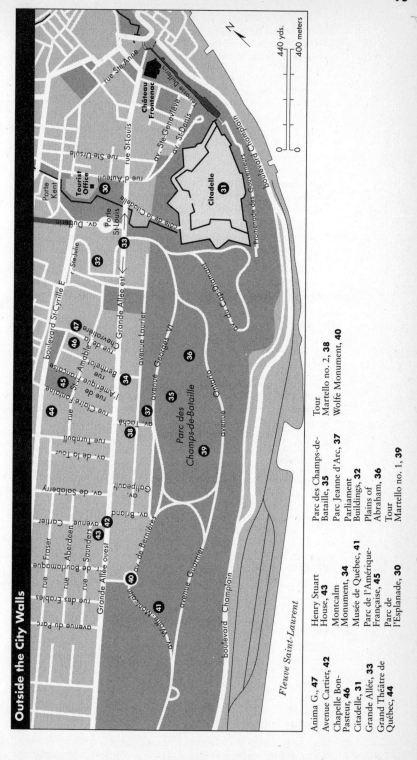

Outside the City Walls

Anima G., **47**
Avenue Cartier, **42**
Chapelle Bon-
Pasteur, **46**
Citadelle, **31**
Grande Allée, **33**
Grand Théâtre de
Québec, **44**

Henry Stuart
House, **43**
Montcalm
Monument, **34**
Musée de Québec, **41**
Parc de l'Amérique-
Française, **45**
Parc de
l'Esplanade, **30**

Parc des Champs-de-
Bataille, **35**
Parc Jeanne d'Arc, **37**
Parliament
Buildings, **32**
Plains of
Abraham, **36**
Tour
Martello no. 1, **39**

Tour
Martello no. 2, **38**
Wolfe Monument, **40**

ing a block to avenue Cartier. Head north on **avenue Cartier** ㊷ to indulge in the pleasures offered by the many good restaurants, clubs, and cafés lining the block. At the corner of avenue Cartier is the **Henry Stuart House** ㊸, home to the same family from 1918 to 1987.

If you continue north along avenue Cartier, the first major intersection is boulevard René-Lévesque Est. Turn right and walk two blocks to the concrete modern building of the **Grand Théâtre de Québec** ㊹, a center for the city's performing arts. High-waving flags east of the Grand Théâtre are displayed in the **Parc de l'Amérique-Française** ㊺, dedicated to places in North America with a French-speaking population. Take rue Claire-Fontaine a block south, turn left on rue St-Amable, and then left again on rue de la Chevrotière. On the west side of the street you'll see the **Chapelle Bon-Pasteur** ㊻, which is surrounded by modern office complexes. Across rue de la Chevrotière is the entrance of **Edifice Marie-Guyart,** whose observation tower, **Anima G.** ㊼, allows a great view. Two sights not in walking distance are the **Aquarium du Québec** (Québec Aquarium) and the **Jardin Zoologique du Québec.**

TIMING
Take in Esplanade Park and the Citadelle in the morning, with time out for a 30-minute tour of the Parliament Buildings (call ahead; reservations are required). Then stroll the Grande Allée to the scenic and sprawling Battlefields Park, site of the famous Plains of Abraham. Before lunch visit the Musée de Québec and, if you want to eat outdoors, stop at the Halles Petit-Cartier to pick up some bread and cheese. Visit the Henry Stuart House. Spend more time on avenue Cartier, then visit the Grand Théâtre du Québec or continue exploring the Plains of Abraham.

Sights to See
Numbers in the margin correspond to points of interest on the Outside the City Walls map.

㊼ **Anima G.** This observation gallery is on top of Edifice Marie-Guyart, Québec City's tallest office building. The gray, modern concrete tower, 31 stories high, has the best view of the city. There's an express elevator. ✉ *1037 rue de la Chevrotière,* ☎ *418/644–9841.* ▨ *Free.* ☻ *Late Jan.–early Dec., weekdays 10–4, weekends and holidays 1–5.*

☙ **Aquarium du Québec.** About 10 kilometers (6 miles) from the city center, this aquarium contains more than 300 species of reptiles, fish, and seals from the lower St. Lawrence River. A wooded picnic ground makes this spot ideal for a family outing. The Québec City transit system, Société de Transport de la Communauté Urbaine de Québec, or STCUQ (☎ 418/627–2511), runs buses 13 and 25 here. ✉ *1675 av. des Hôtels, Ste-Foy,* ☎ *418/659–5264; reservations, 418/659–5266.* ▨ *$7.50.* ☻ *Daily 9–5; seals are fed and put on a show at 10:15 and 3:15.*

㊻ **Chapelle Bon-Pasteur** (Bon-Pasteur Chapel). This slender church with a steep sloping roof was designed by Charles Baillargé in 1868. Its ornate baroque-style interior has carved wood designs painted elaborately in gold leaf. The chapel houses 32 religious paintings done by the nuns of the community from 1868 to 1910. Classical concerts are performed here between October and June. ✉ *1080 rue de la Chevrotière,* ☎ *418/641–1069 or 418/648–9710.* ▨ *Free.* ☻ *July and Aug., Tues.–Sun. 1:30–4; Sept.–June by reservation; musical artists' Mass Sun. 10:45.*

㉛ **Citadelle** (Citadel). Built at the city's highest point, on Cap Diamant, the Citadelle is the largest fortified base in North America still occupied by troops. The 25-building fortress was intended to protect the port, prevent the enemy from taking up a position on the Plains of Abraham,

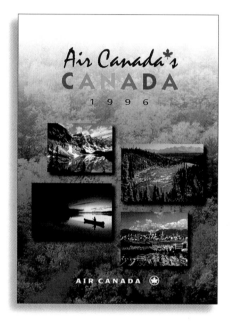

Use your MCI Card®

for the easy way to

call when traveling.

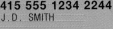

MCI☆   **Calling Card**

415 555 1234 2244
J.D. SMITH

Convenience on the road

• Your MCI Card® number is your
  home number, guaranteed.

• Pre-programmed to
  speed dial to your home.

• Call from any phone in
  the U.S.

MCI☆

1 - 8 0 0 - 7 5 4 - 8 9 4 1

http://www.mci.com

and provide a last refuge in case of an attack. Having inherited incomplete fortifications, the British sought to complete the Citadelle to protect themselves against retaliations from the French. By the time the Citadelle was completed in 1832, the attacks against Québec City had ended. Since 1920 the Citadelle has served as a base for the Royal 22nd Regiment. Firearms, uniforms, and decorations from the 17th century are displayed in the **Royal 22nd Regiment Museum,** in the former powder house, built in 1750. If weather permits, you can watch the Changing of the Guard, an elaborate ceremony in which the troops parade before the Citadelle resplendent in red coats and black fur hats. Admission is by guided tour only. ⊠ *1 côte de la Citadelle,* ☎ *418/648–2815.* ⚏ *$4.50.* ☉ *Mid-Mar.–Apr., daily 10–3; May and June, daily 9–4; July–early Sept., daily 9–6; Sept., daily 9–4; Oct., daily 10–3, Nov.–early Feb. and mid-Feb.–mid-Mar., groups only (reservations required); early Feb.–mid-Feb., daily 11–3; Changing of the guard mid-June–Labor Day, daily 10 AM. Tattoo July and Aug., Tues., Thurs., and weekends 6 PM.*

�33 **Grande Allée.** One of the city's oldest streets, Grande Allée was the route people took from outlying areas to sell their furs in town. Now there are trendy cafés, clubs, and restaurants here. The street actually has four names: in the old city, it is rue St-Louis; outside the walls, Grande Allée; farther west, chemin St-Louis; and farther still, boulevard Laurier.

🅐44 **Grande Théâtre de Québec.** Opened in 1971, the theater incorporates two main halls, both named for 19th-century Canadian poets. The Grande Salle of Louis-Frechette, named for the first Québec poet and writer to be honored by the French Academy, holds 1,800 seats and is used for concerts, opera, and theater. The Petite Salle of Octave-Crémazie, used for experimental theater and variety shows, derives its name from the poet who stirred the rise of Québec nationalism in the mid-19th century.

As the complex was being constructed, Montréal architect Victor Prus commissioned Jordi Bonet, a Québec sculptor, to work simultaneously on a three-wall mural. The themes depicted in the three sections are death, life, and liberty. Bonet wrote "La Liberté" on one wall to symbolize the Québécois' struggle for freedom and cultural distinction. The theater has a full repertory in winter, but no shows in summer. ⊠ *269 blvd. René-Lévesque Est,* ☎ *418/646–0609.* ☉ *Guided tours (reservations required) daily 9–5.*

🅐43 **Henry Stuart House.** Built in 1849, this English-style cottage was home to the Stuart family from 1918 to 1987 when it was designated a historic monument by the Ministry of Culture. Its decor has remained unchanged since 1930. Most of the furniture was imported from England in the second half of the 19th century. ⊠ *82 Grande Allée Ouest,* ☎ *418/647–4347.* ⚏ *$5.* ☉ *June–Aug., Wed.–Mon. 11–5; Sept.–May, Thurs. and Sun. 11–5 or by reservation.*

NEED A BREAK?   **Halles Petit-Cartier** (⊠ 1191 av. Cartier, ☎ 418/688–1630), a food mall, has restaurants and shops that sell French delicacies—cheeses, pastries, breads, vegetables, and candies.

☾ **Jardin Zoologique du Québec.** This zoo is especially scenic because of the DuBerger River, which traverses the grounds. About 250 animal species live here, including bears, wildcats, primates, and birds of prey. There are farm animals and horse-drawn carriage rides, and you can cross-country ski here in winter. The zoo is 11 kilometers (7 miles) west of Québec City on Route 73. Québec City transit (☎ 418/627–2511) operates Bus 801 here. ⊠ *9141 av. du Zoo, Charlesbourg,* ☎ *418/622–0313.* ⚏ *$4.50 June–Oct.; Nov.–May $4.50 weekends, free weekdays.*

34 **Montcalm Monument.** France and Canada joined together to erect this monument honoring Louis-Joseph Montcalm, who claimed his fame by winning four major battles in North America—but his most famous battle was the one he lost, when the British conquered New France on September 13, 1759. Montcalm was north of Québec City at Beauport when he learned that the British attack was imminent. He quickly assembled his troops to meet the enemy and was wounded in battle in the leg and stomach. Montcalm was carried into the walled city, where he died the next morning. 🚇 *Pl. Montcalm.*

41 **Musée de Québec** (Québec Museum). This neoclassical beaux-arts showcase has more than 18,000 traditional and contemporary pieces of Québec art. The portraits by artists well known in the area, such as Ozias Leduc (1864–1955) and Horatio Walker (1858–1938), are particularly notable. This museum's very formal and dignified building in Battlefields Park was designed by Wilfrid Lacroix and erected in 1933 to commemorate the tricentennial of the founding of Québec. The museum has renovated the original building, incorporating the space of an abandoned prison dating from 1867. A hallway of cells, with the iron bars and courtyard still intact, has been preserved as part of a permanent exhibition of the prison's history. ✉ *1 av. Wolfe-Montcalm,* ☎ *418/643–2150.* 🎫 *$4.75; free Wed.* ☉ *June–Aug., Thurs.–Tues. 10–5:45, Wed. 10–9:45; Sept.–May, Tues. and Thurs.–Sun. 11–5:45, Wed. 11–8:45.*

45 **Parc de l'Amérique-Française.** Inaugurated in 1985 by former Québec premier, the late René Lévesque, the park is dedicated to places in North America with a French-speaking population. Flags are flown from Acadia, British Columbia, Louisiana, Manitoba, Saskatchewan, and Ontario, but Québec's own Fleur de Lys leads the way. Blue and white, the colors of Sun King Louis XIV, constitute a reminder of Québec's French origins, culture, and language. ✉ *rues St. Amable and Claire-Fontaine.*

30 **Parc de l'Esplanade** (Esplanade Park). In the 19th century, this was a clear space surrounded by a picket fence and poplar trees. Today you'll find the **Poudrière de l'Esplanade** (Powder Magazine), which the British constructed in 1820; it houses a model depicting the evolution of the wall surrounding the Old City. The French began building ramparts along the city's natural cliff as early as 1690 to protect themselves from British invaders. The colonists had trouble convincing the French government back home, though, to take the threat of invasion seriously, and by 1759, when the British invaded for control of New France, the walls were still incomplete; the British, despite attacks by the Americans during the War of Independence and the War of 1812, took a century to finish them. ✉ *Powder Magazine, 100 rue St-Louis,* ☎ *418/ 648–7016.* 🎫 *$2.50.* ☉ *Daily 10–5.*

37 **Parc Jeanne d'Arc** (Joan of Arc Park). This park, bright with colorful flowers, has an equestrian statue of Jeanne d'Arc as its focal point. A symbol of courage, the statue stands in tribute to the heroes of 1759 near the place where New France was lost to the British. The park also commemorates the Canadian national anthem, "O Canada"; it was played here for the first time on June 24, 1880. ✉ *avs. Laurier and Taché.*

32 **Parliament Buildings.** The Parliament Buildings, erected between 1877 and 1884, are the seat of L'Assemblée Nationale (the National Assembly) of 125 provincial representatives. Québec architect Eugène-Étienne Taché designed the classic and stately buildings in the late 17th-century Renaissance style of Louis XIV, with four wings set in a square around an interior court. In front of the Parliament, statues pay tribute to important figures of Québec history: Cartier, Champlain, Frontenac,

Wolfe, and Montcalm. There's a 30-minute tour (in English or French) of the President's Gallery, the Legislative Council Chamber, and the National Assembly Chamber, which is green, white, and gold—colors that correspond to the House of Commons in both London and Ottawa. ✉ *Av. Dufferin and Grande Allée Est, door 3,* ☎ *418/643–7239.* ☜ *Free.* ☉ *Guided tours (reservations required) Jan.–May and Sept.–Nov., weekdays 9–5; late June–Aug., daily 9–5.*

㊱ Plains of Abraham. This park is the site of the famous 1759 battle that decided the fate of New France. It was named after the river pilot Abraham Martin. People cross-country ski here in winter. The interpretation center is open year-round. A bus serves as shuttle and guided tour, with commentary in French and English, around the Plains of Abraham, making 11 stops. Call Pavillon Baillargé, Musée de Québec (☎ 418/648–4071) for departure times. ☜ *Tour $1.* ☉ *Tours Mid-June–1st Mon. in Sept., daily 10–6.*

Tour Martello nos. 1 and 2 (Martello Towers 1 and 2). Of the 16 Martello towers in all of Canada, four were built in Québec City because the British government feared an invasion after the American Revolution. **㊴ Tour Martello no. 1** (✉ South end of Parc Jeanne d'Arc), which exhibits the history of the four structures, was built between 1802 and **㊳** 1810. **Tour Martello no. 2** (✉ av. Taché and av. Laurier), which has an astronomy display, was built in the early 19th century to slow an enemy approach. **Tour no. 3** guarded westward entry to the city, but it was demolished in 1904. **Tour no. 4** is on rue Lavigueur overlooking Rivière St-Charles (St. Charles River) but is not open to the public.

㊵ Wolfe Monument. This tall monument marks the place where the British general died. Wolfe landed his troops about 3 kilometers (less than 2 miles) from the city's walls; the 4,500 English soldiers scaled the cliff and opened fire on the Plains of Abraham. Wolfe was mortally wounded in battle and was carried behind the lines to this spot. ✉ *Rue de Bernières and av. Wolfe-Montcalm.*

DINING

$$$$ ✗ **À la Table de Serge Bruyère.** This restaurant has put Québec on the
★ map of great gastronomic cities. The city's most famous culinary institution serves classic French cuisine presented with plenty of crystal, silver, and fresh flowers and with relentless attention to detail. Only one sitting is offered each night. Opened in 1980 by the late chef Serge Bruyère, native of Lyon, France, the restaurant is now run by Henriette Barré. The *menu gourmand* is a five-course meal for about $50. Specialties include scampi in puff pastry with fresh tomatoes, scallop stew with watercress, and duckling supreme with blueberry sauce. The 1843 Livernois building now includes a café, a food store, and a catering service—all serving food from Bruyère's celebrated kitchen. If the main restaurant is out of your price range, **À la Petite Table** is less formal and less expensive, with such dishes as seafood terrine and pork with tarragon sauce. ✉ *1200 rue St-Jean,* ☎ *418/694–0618. Reservations essential. Jacket required. AE, DC, MC, V.*

$$$$ ✗ **Café de la Paix.** An evening spent at this local favorite takes you back to a dining experience in Paris circa 1930. The tables could not get closer or the lights dimmer amid the Art Deco extravagance of lamps in Venetian glass, wood sculpted in geometric patterns, and stained-glass windows. The food is on a par with other fine restaurants in the city, but there are hints that the chefs are relying on their reputations (the restaurant dates from 1952). The table d'hôte includes such tasty dishes as pheasant with peaches. Salmon comes with four sauces: rasp-

Dining

Lodging

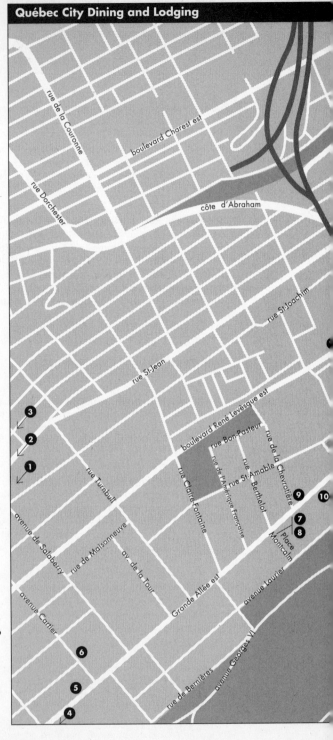

Québec City Dining and Lodging

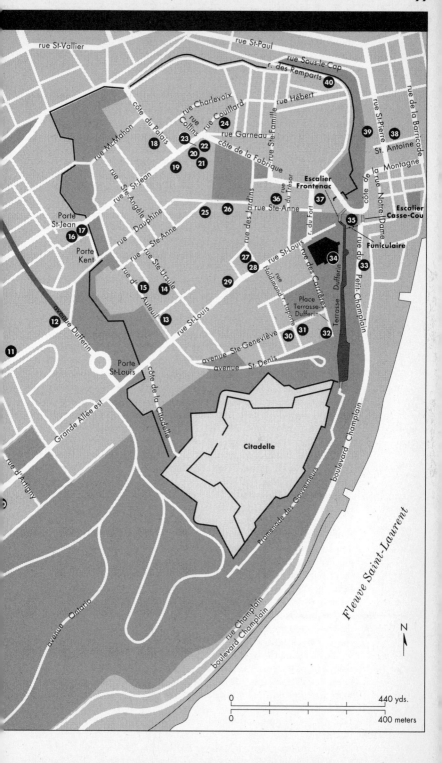

rue St-Vallier

rue St-Paul

rue Sous-le-Cap

r. des Remparts

40

rue St-Charlevoix

rue Couillard

rue Collins

24

rue Hébert

rue Garneau

rue St-Pierre

39

rue de la Barricade

38

St. Antoine

18

côte du Palais

rue McMahon

23

22

côte de la Fabrique

rue Ste-Famille

20

21

19

rue Ste-Jean

rue Ste-Angèle

rue Dauphine

rue d'Auteuil

rue Ste-Anne

rue Ste-Ursule

25

26

rue des Jardins

rue du Trésor

36

rue Ste-Anne

côte de la Montagne

rue St-Pierre

côte de la Montagne

Escalier Frontenac

37

côte de la Montagne

rue Notre-Dame

Escalier Casse-Cou

35

Funiculaire

Porte St-Jean

17

16

Porte Kent

15

14

13

27

28

29

rue St-Louis

r. du Fort

rue des Carrières

34

rue du Petit-Champlain

33

12

avenue Dufferin

11

Porte St-Louis

côte de la Citadelle

avenue Ste-Geneviève

avenue St-Denis

rue Haldimand

rue de l'apôtre

Place Terrasse-Dufferin

30

31

32

Terrasse Dufferin

rue d'Artigny

Grande Allée est

Citadelle

Promenade des Gouverneurs

boulevard Champlain

avenue Ontario

rue Champlain

boulevard Champlain

Fleuve Saint-Laurent

N

| 0 | | | | 440 yds. |
| 0 | | | | 400 meters |

berry vinegar, hollandaise, tarragon, and mustard. The meat entrées, including filet mignon and leg of lamb, are also recommended. You choose your dessert from a cart; try the fresh fruit and the chocolate truffle cake. The service is prompt and attentive. ⌧ *44 rue des Jardins,* ☎ *418/692–1430. Reservations essential. AE, DC, MC, V. No lunch Sun. in winter.*

$$$$ ✕ **La Fenouillère.** Here, in a bright wood room, views of the Pierre Laporte bridge can accompany your dinner. Chef Yvon Godbout has served a constantly rotating table d'hôte since 1986, going out of his way to offer seasonal products. The house specialty is salmon, but you may want to ask for the lamb, as it is done to a turn, and very popular among the restaurant's regular customers. ⌧ *Hotel Best Western Aristocrate, 3100, chemin St-Louis, Ste-Foy,* ☎ *418/653–3886. AE, DC, MC, V.*

$$$$ ✕ **Le Marie Clarisse.** Wood-beam ceilings, stone walls, sea-blue decor, and a lit fireplace make this dining spot one of the coziest in town. In an ancient building on the bottom of Escalier Casse-Cou near Place Royale, Le Marie Clarisse is well known for its unique seafood dishes, such as halibut with nuts and honey and scallops with port and paprika. Occasionally, the menu includes a good game dish, such as caribou with curry. The *menu du jour* has about seven entrées to choose from; dinner includes soup, salad, dessert, and coffee. ⌧ *12 rue du Petit-Champlain,* ☎ *418/692–0857. Reservations essential. AE, DC, MC, V. No lunch Sat. Closed Sun.*

$$$$ ✕ **Le Saint-Amour.** This restaurant has all the makings of a true haute-
★   cuisine establishment without the pretentious atmosphere. A light and airy atrium, with a retractable roof for outdoor dining in summer, creates a relaxed dining ambience. Chef Jean-Luc Boulay returns regularly to France for inspiration; his studies pay off in such specialties as stuffed quail in port sauce and salmon with chive mousse. Sauces here are light, with no flour or butter. The *menu de decouvert* has nine courses, and the *menu de dégustation* has seven. If you plan to order one of these menus, it's a good idea to mention it when you make your reservation. The chef's true expertise shines in his diverse dessert menu— try the crème brûlée sweetened with maple syrup or the royal chocolate cake made with caramelized hazelnuts. ⌧ *48 rue Ste-Ursule,* ☎ *418/694–0667. AE, DC, MC, V.*

$$$ ✕ **Aux Anciens Canadiens.** This establishment is named for a book by
★   Philippe-Aubert de Gaspé, who once resided here. The house, dating from 1675, has five dining rooms with different themes. The *vaisselier* (dish room) is bright and cheerful, with colorful antique dishes, a fireplace, and an antique stove. Come for the authentic French Canadian cooking; hearty specialties include duck in maple glaze and caribou with blueberry wine sauce. The restaurant also serves the best caribou (a local beverage made with sweet red wine and whiskey, known for its kick) drink in town. ⌧ *34 rue St-Louis,* ☎ *418/692–1627. AE, DC, MC, V.*

$$$ ✕ **Gambrinus.** This comfortable and convenient restaurant near rue
★   du Trésor and the Château Frontenac serves excellent Continental cuisine in two elegant, mahogany-paneled, plant-filled dining rooms with windows facing the street. The reliable menu includes a range of meat, fish, and pasta entrées, with such specialties as rack of lamb with herbs and caribou medallions. The table d'hôte is a good bet and provides generous portions and delectable desserts. Service here is unrushed and thoroughly professional. ⌧ *15 rue du Fort,* ☎ *418/692–5144. AE, DC, MC, V. No lunch weekends.*

$$$ ✕ **L'Astral.** This circular restaurant on the 29th floor of the Hôtel Loews Le Concorde revolves high above Battlefields Park and the Old City. The food is not the best in town and the service can be slow, but the views are excellent. The modern and uninspired decor does not detract from the view, either; there's no room for anything besides the dining

tables next to large windows. On Saturday nights, a vast buffet—organized around a theme such as Mediterranean food—is served. Sunday brunch consists of more than 30 items. ✉ *1225 Pl. Montcalm,* ☎ *418/647–2222. AE, DC, MC, V.*

$$$ ✕ **Le Graffiti.** A good alternative to Old City dining, this restaurant housed in a modern gourmet food mall serves the cuisine of Provence. It's a romantic setting, with dark mahogany-paneled walls and large bay windows that look out onto the passersby along avenue Cartier. The distinctive seasonal menu includes such dishes as scampi spiced with basil and red pepper, and chicken liver mousse with pistachios. There's a reasonably priced table d'hôte. ✉ *1191 av. Cartier,* ☎ *418/529–4949. AE, DC, MC, V.*

$$$ ✕ **Le Paris Brest.** This busy restaurant on Grande Allée serves a gre-
★ garious crowd attracted to its tastefully prepared French dishes. Its angular halogen lighting and soft yellow walls add a fresh, modern touch to this historic building. Traditional fare, such as *escargots au Pernod* (snails with Pernod) and steak tartare, are presented artistically. Popular dishes include lamb with *herbes de Provence* and beef Welling-ton. À la carte and main-course dishes are accompanied by a generous side platter of vegetables. Wine prices range from $22 to $250. ✉ *590 Grande Allée Est,* ☎ *418/529–2243. AE, DC, MC, V.*

$$$ ✕ **Portofino Bistro Italiano.** By joining two 18th-century houses, owner James Monti has created a cozy restaurant with a bistro flavor. The room is distinctive: burnt sienna walls, a wood pizza oven set behind a semicircular bar, deep blue tablecloths and chairs. Service in this lively restaurant is excellent. Not to be missed: the thin-crust pizza and its accompaniment of oils flavored with pepper and oregano, and *pennini al'arrabiata*—tubular pasta with a spicy tomato sauce. Don't miss the homemade *tiramisù*—ladyfingers dipped in espresso with a whipped cream and mascarpone-cheese filling. There's a fixed price meal of the day, and from 3 to 7 PM the restaurant serves a beer and pizza meal for $9.95. ✉ *54 rue Couillard,* ☎ *418/692–8888. Reservations essential. AE, D, DC, MC, V.*

$$ ✕ **Café Suisse.** This large chalet close to Place d'Armes serves Swiss cuisine, including 25 different varieties of fondue—the Gruyère and the chocolate fondues are especially recommended. Another popular item is *raclette,* a dish with melted cheese, served with bread, potatoes, onions, pickles, and ham. The spacious chalet looms three stories high with clichéd murals of alpine scenes. In the summer, there are umbrella-shaded café tables outside. ✉ *32 rue Ste-Anne,* ☎ *418/694–1320. AE, DC, MC, V.*

$$ ✕ **L'Apsara.** The Cambodian family that owns this restaurant near the St-Louis Gate excels at using both subtle and tangy spices to create unique flavors. It's ideal if you're seeking a reprieve from French fare. Decor combines Western and Eastern motifs, with flowered wallpaper, Oriental art, and small fountains. Innovative dishes from Vietnam, Thailand, and Cambodia include such starters as *fleur de pailin* (a rice paste roll filled with fresh vegetables, meat, and shrimp) and *mou sati* (pork kebabs with peanut sauce and coconut milk). The assorted miniature Cambodian pastries are delicious with tea served from a little elephant container. ✉ *71 rue d'Auteuil,* ☎ *418/694–0232. AE, MC, V.*

$$ ✕ **Le Café de la Terrasse.** This restaurant in the landmark Château Fron-tenac does not share the hotel's opulence, but it does have a view of Terrasse Dufferin and the St. Lawrence River. Standard but dependable Continental dishes are served à la carte and at buffets throughout the day. Between 2:30 and 5 PM you can have tea, complete with watercress sandwiches and pastries. ✉ *Château Frontenac, 1 rue Car-rières,* ☎ *418/692–3861. AE, DC, MC, V.*

$$ ✕ **Le Commensal.** At Le Commensal, diners serve themselves from an
★ outstanding informal vegetarian buffet (plates are weighed to deter-
mine the price). Hot and cold dishes running the gamut of health-con-
scious cooking include stir-fry tofu and ratatouille (vegetables in mild
sauce with couscous). In a mix of modern and ancient atmospheres,
the restaurant has plenty of space. ✉ *860 rue St-Jean,* ☎ *418/647–
3733. AE, DC, MC, V.*

$$ ✕ **L'Echaudé.** This chic black-and-white bistro attracts a mix of business
★ and tourist clientele because of its location between the financial and an-
tiques districts in Lower Town. The modern decor consists of a stark dining area with a mirrored wall and a stainless-steel bar where you dine
atop high stools. Lunch offerings include *cuisse de canard confit* (duck
confit) with French fries and fresh seafood salad. The three-course
brunch for Sunday antiques shoppers includes giant croissants and a tan-
talizing array of desserts. ✉ *73 Sault-au-Matelot,* ☎ *418/692–1299. Reservations essential. AE, DC, MC, V. No dinner Sun. or Mon. Sept.–May.*

$$ ✕ **Paparazzi.** An Italian restaurant a 15-minute drive west of the Old
City, Paparazzi has a sleek, bistro ambience—bare wood tables, halo-
gen lighting, and wrought-iron accents. Its food competes with that of
many of the finer dining establishments in town, but without the high
prices. The imaginative menu changes twice a year. Specialties include
pizza paparazzi, with wild mushrooms, fresh tomatoes, and a mix of
cheeses. The dessert list is interesting. ✉ *1365 av. Maguire, Sillery,* ☎
418/683–8111. AE, DC, MC, V.

$ ✕ **Casse-Crêpe Breton.** Crepes in generous proportions are served in
this diner-style restaurant on rue St-Jean. From a menu of 15 fillings,
pick your own chocolate or fruit combinations, or design a larger
meal with cheese, ham, and vegetables. The tables surround three
round hot plates at which you watch your creations being made.
Crêpes made with two to five fillings cost under $5. ✉ *1136 rue St-
Jean.* ☎ *418/692–0438. No credit cards.*

$ ✕ **Chez Temporel.** Tucked behind rue St-Jean and côte de la Fabrique,
★ this homey café is an experience *très français.* The aroma of fresh cof-
fee fills the air. The rustic decor incorporates wooden tables, chairs,
and benches, and a tiny staircase winds to an upper level. Croissants
are made in-house; the staff will fill them with Gruyère and ham or
anything else you want. Try the equally delicious croque-monsieur and
quiche Lorraine. ✉ *25 rue Couillard,* ☎ *418/694–1813. No credit cards.*

$ ✕ **Le Cochon Dingue.** Across the street from the ferry in Lower Town
is the boulevard Champlain location of this chain, a cheerful café
(whose name translates to "The Crazy Pig"), with sidewalk tables and
indoor dining rooms, which artfully blend the chic and the antique.
Black-and-white checkerboard floors contrast with ancient stone walls.
Café fare includes dependably tasty homemade quiches, thick soups,
and such desserts as fresh raspberry tart and maple-sugar pie. ✉ *46
blvd. Champlain,* ☎ *418/692–2013;* ✉ *46 blvd. René Lévesque,* ☎
418/523–2013; ✉ *1326 av. Maguire, Sillery,* ☎ *418/684–2013. AE,
DC, MC, V.*

$ ✕ **Les Frères de la Côte.** This pizza house, despite being in the heart
of the tourist district, is a favorite for many locals. The friendly, bois-
terous atmosphere flows from its doors into the foyer, where you will
find hundreds of snapshots documenting happy dining experiences. There
are 17 kinds of pizza and a full range of other dishes—pasta with blue
cheese, lamb with *herbes de Provence,* or grilled spicy Italian sausage
with fries. For dessert, try the apple pie with orange caramel glaze and
cream. When it comes time to leave, don't overlook the tempting bas-
ket of homemade bread for sale. ✉ *1190 rue St-Jean,* ☎ *418/692–
5445. AE, MC, V.*

LODGING

$$$$ ⊞ **Château Frontenac.** Towering above the St. Lawrence River, the
★ Château Frontenac is Québec City's most renowned landmark. Its
public rooms—from the intimate piano bar to the 700-seat ballroom
reminiscent of the Versailles Hall of Mirrors—have the opulence of years
gone by, and almost all the guest rooms have excellent views. Reserve
well in advance, especially from the end of June to mid-October. An
extensive renovation was completed in 1993, in time for the hotel's
100th birthday. The Frontenac has one of the finer restaurants in
town, Le Champlain, where classic French cuisine is served by waiters dressed in traditional French costumes. ⊠ *1 rue des Carrières, G1R
4P5,* ☎ *418/692–3861 or 800/441–1414,* ℻ *418/692–1751. 610
rooms. 2 restaurants, bar, snack bar, indoor pool, health club, hair salon,
art gallery. AE, DC, MC, V.*

$$$$ ⊞ **Hilton International Québec.** Just outside St-Jean Gate, the Hilton
rises from the shadow of Parliament Hill. It has spacious facilities and
efficient services and hosts groups as well as tourists. The lobby, which
can be chaotic at times, has a bar and an open-air restaurant. The hotel,
next to the Parliament Buildings, is in the middle of the activity of the
Winter Carnival and is connected to a mall, Place Québec, which has
40 shops. Standard yet ultramodern rooms have tall windows; those
on upper floors have fine views of the Old City. Guests on executive
floors are offered a free breakfast and an open bar from 5 to 6 PM. ⊠
3 Pl. Québec, G1K 7M9, ☎ *418/647–2411 or 800/445–8667,* ℻
*418/647–6488. 565 rooms, 36 suites. Restaurant, piano bar, outdoor
pool, sauna, health club. AE, D, DC, MC, V.*

$$$$ ⊞ **Hôtel Loews Le Concorde.** When Le Concorde was built in 1974,
★ the shockingly tall concrete structure aroused controversy because it
supplanted 19th-century Victorian homes. Yet for visitors, it is especially convenient for city touring and nightlife. Inside the hotel there's
almost as much going on as at the cafés and restaurants along the nearby
Grande Allée; Le Concorde houses the revolving restaurant L'Astral
(☞ Dining, *above*), a sidewalk café, and a bar. Rooms have good
views of Battlefields Park and the St. Lawrence River, and nearly all
have been redone in modern decor combined with traditional furnishings. Amenities for business travelers have expanded; one of the
VIP floors is reserved for female executives. ⊠ *1225 Pl. Montcalm,
G1R 4W6,* ☎ *418/647–2222 or 800/463–5256; in the U.S., 800/235–
6397;* ℻ *418/647–4710. 424 rooms. 2 restaurants, bar, outdoor pool,
sauna, health club. AE, D, DC, MC, V.*

$$$$ ⊞ **Hôtel Radisson Gouverneurs Québec.** Opposite the Parliament
Buildings, this large, full-service establishment is part of a Québec
chain. Its light and spacious rooms have luminous pastel decor, wood
furniture, and marble bathrooms. VIP floors were designed to lure the
business traveler, but there is also plenty of room for tourists. The hotel
occupies the first 12 floors of a tall office complex; views of the Old
City are limited to the higher floors. ⊠ *690 blvd. René-Lévesque Est,
G1R 5A8,* ☎ *418/647–1717 or 800/333–3333,* ℻ *418/647–2146.
377 rooms with bath. Restaurant, piano bar, outdoor pool, sauna, health
club. AE, D, DC, MC, V.*

$$$ ⊞ **Auberge Saint-Antoine.** This charming little find is within com-
fortable walking distance of all the old town's attractions. Although
modernly built, it seems much older because it is installed in an old
maritime warehouse and has a generally rustic atmosphere. Each room
is styled differently; all have a combination of antiques and contem-
porary pieces. Some have river views; others have terraces. ⊠ *10 rue
St-Antoine, G1K 4C9,* ☎ *418/692–2211 or 800/267–0525,* ℻
418/692–1177. 29 rooms. CP. AE, DC, MC, V.

$$$ ☒ **Château Bonne Entente.** This sprawling resort is 10 minutes from the airport and 20 minutes from the walled city. It's commonly called "The Other Château," the country cousin of the urban Frontenac. A private mansion until 1940, it has evolved into a popular spot for the well heeled. In the newest wing, rooms are decorated in contemporary style with fine wood, plush carpeting, and all the modern amenities. Other rooms have antiques and a rustic atmosphere. The property encompasses 11 acres of land, with separate cottage rooms behind the main complex. ☒ *3400 chemin Ste-Foy, Ste-Foy G1X 1S6,* ☎ *418/653–5221 or 800/463–4390,* FAX *418/653–3098. 109 rooms, 50 cottages. Restaurant, bar, pool, health club, tennis, badminton, volleyball, fishing, ice-skating. AE, D, DC, MC, V.*

$$$ ☒ **Germain des Près.** One of the newly popular hotels for the business crowd is in Ste-Foy, close to Place Laurier and with easy access to Québec City and the airports. Its ultramodern rooms—in black and white or black and tan—have white comforters on the beds. ☒ *1200 av. Germain-des-Près, Ste-Foy, G1V 3M7,* ☎ *418/658–1224,* FAX *418/658–8846. 126 rooms with shower or bath. Restaurant, business services, meeting room. AE, DC, MC, V.*

$$$ ☒ **Hôtel Clarendon.** Built in 1870 and considered the oldest hotel in Québec, the Clarendon has been entirely refurbished in its original Art Deco and Art Nouveau styles. Most rooms have excellent views of old Québec. ☒ *57 rue Ste-Anne, G1R 3X4,* ☎ *418/692–2480 or 800/463–5250,* FAX *418/692–4652. 96 rooms with bath. Restaurant, café, air-conditioning, meeting rooms. AE, D, DC, MC, V.*

$$$ ☒ **Hôtel Manoir Victoria.** This European-style hotel with an excellent fitness center is well situated near the train station. Its discreet, old-fashioned entrance gives way to a large, wood-paneled foyer. A substantial buffet breakfast is included in some packages. ☒ *4 Côte du Palais, G1R 4H8,* ☎ *418/692–1030,* FAX *418/692–3822. 145 rooms and suites. Restaurant, bistro, meeting rooms, health club, indoor pool, sauna, beauty salon. AE, D, DC, MC, V.*

$$$ ☒ **Hôtel Marie Rollet.** This intimate little inn in the heart of Old Québec, built in 1876 by the Ursulines Order, is an oasis of warm woodwork and antique charm. Two rooms have working fireplaces. A rooftop terrace has a garden view. ☒ *81 rue Ste-Anne, G1R 3X4,* ☎ *418/694–9271. 10 rooms with bath. Indoor parking. MC, V.*

$$$ ☒ **Le Château de Pierre.** Built in 1853, this tidy Victorian manor on a picturesque street has kept its English origins alive. The high-ceilinged halls have ornate chandeliers and Victorian rooms are imaginatively decorated with floral themes; some have either a balcony, fireplace, or vanity room. Several rooms in the front have bay windows with a view of Governor's Park. ☒ *17 av. Ste-Geneviève, G1R 4A8,* ☎ *418/694–0429,* FAX *418/694–0153. 15 rooms. AE, MC, V.*

$$$ ☒ **L'Hôtel du Théâtre.** There's much history that accompanies this hotel in the Capitole Building just outside the St-Jean Gate. In 1903 it opened as an avant-garde theater, then it was a movie house before closing in the 1980s. In 1992 it came back to life, following a $15 million restoration that transformed it into an exclusive 40-room lodging, an Italian bistro, and an elaborate 1920s cabaret-style dinner theater, Théâtre Capitole (☞ Nightlife and the Arts, *below*). A glitzy showbiz theme is prevalent throughout the hotel, with stars on carpets, doors, and keys. Rooms are small and simple, highlighted with a few rich details. Ceilings are painted within sculpted moldings with a blue-and-white sky motif and beds have white down-filled comforters. ☒ *972 rue St-Jean, G1R 1R5,* ☎ *418/694–4040 or 800/363–4040,* FAX *418/694–1916. 40 rooms. Restaurant, bar, theater. AE, DC, MC, V.*

$$$ ⊞ **L'Hôtel du Vieux Québec.** In the heart of the Latin Quarter on rue St-Jean, this brick hotel is surrounded by striking historic structures. Once an apartment building, it still has the long-term visitor in mind. The interior design is simple, with sparsely furnished but comfortable rooms decorated in pastel colors. Many rooms have kitchens (dishes and cooking utensils can be rented for $10); some have air-conditioning. ⊠ *1190 rue St-Jean, G1R 1S6,* ☎ *418/692–1850,* FAX *418/692–5637. 38 units with bath. AE, MC, V.*

$$$ ⊞ **Manoir d'Auteuil.** Originally a private home, this lodging is one of
★ the more lavish manors in town. At press time it was undergoing a renovation that will reinstate many of its former Art Deco and Art Nouveau details. An ornate sculpted iron banister wraps around four floors; guest rooms have detailed trimmings and blend modern design with the Art Deco structure. Each room is different; one room was formerly a chapel, and another has a tiny staircase leading to its bathroom. Of special interest is the room with blue bathroom—the shower has seven showerheads. Some rooms look out onto the wall between the St-Louis and St-Jean gates. ⊠ *49 rue d'Auteuil, G1R 4C2,* ☎ *418/694–1173,* FAX *418/694–0081. 16 rooms with bath. Breakfast room. CP. AE, DC, MC, V.*

$$$ ⊞ **Manoir Ste-Geneviève.** This quaint and elaborately decorated hotel dating from 1880 stands near the Château Frontenac, on the southwest corner of the Jardin des Gouverneurs. A plush Victorian ambience is created with fanciful wallpaper and rooms decorated with precious stately English manor furnishings, such as marble lamps, large wooden bedposts, and velvet upholstery; you'll feel as if you are staying in a secluded country inn. Service here is personal and genteel. Some rooms have air-conditioning. ⊠ *13 av. Ste-Geneviève, G1R 4A7,* ☎ FAX *418/694–1666. 9 rooms with bath. No credit cards.*

$$ ⊞ **Château de la Terrasse.** Although this four-story inn may not have the same charm as others in the city, it does have something that many lack: a view of the St. Lawrence River from rooms in the front. While the interior hints at having once possessed a refined and elegant decor, with its high ceilings and stained glass lining the large bay windows, the furnishings these days are plain and unremarkable. ⊠ *6 Pl. Terrasse Dufferin, G1R 4N5,* ☎ *418/694–9472,* FAX *418/694–0055. 18 rooms. Breakfast room. AE, MC, V.*

$$ ⊞ **L'Auberge du Quartier.** This small, amiable inn in a house dating
★ from 1852 benefits from a personal touch. The cheerful rooms are modestly furnished but well maintained. A suite of rooms on the third floor can accommodate a family at a reasonable cost. A 20-minute walk west from the Old City, L'Auberge du Quartier is convenient to avenue Cartier and Grande Allée nightlife; joggers can use Battlefields Park across the street. ⊠ *170 Grande Allée Ouest, G1R 2G9,* ☎ *418/525–9726. 14 rooms with bath. Breakfast room, free parking. CP. AE, DC, MC, V.*

$$ ⊞ **L'Auberge St-Louis.** If you're looking for convenience, this inn's central location on the main street of the city can't be beat. A lobby resembling a European pension and tall staircases lead to small guest rooms with comfortable but bare-bones furniture. Six budget rooms are on the fourth floor. The service here is friendly. ⊠ *48 rue St-Louis, G1R 3Z3,* ☎ *418/692–2424,* FAX *418/692–3797. 27 rooms, 14 with bath. MC, V.*

$$ ⊞ **Manoir Lafayette.** In 1882, this gray stone building was a lavish, private home; over a century later, it is a simple hotel. Considering the location on Grande Allée—a street crowded with restaurants and trendy bars—the clean, comfortable accommodations are reasonably priced. The lobby is open and welcoming, with floral sofas surrounding a fireplace and television. Rooms in the newer wing—although fresher—resemble those in the old part: All are quite small, with high ceilings, wooden furniture, floral bedspreads and drapes, televisions, and phones. Rooms facing Grande Allée may be noisy; older rooms cost a little less. ✉ *661 Grande Allée Est, G1R 2K4,* ☎ *418/522–2652 or 800/363–8203,* FAX *418/522–4400. 67 rooms. Bistro, baby-sitting. AE, DC, MC, V.*

$ 🏨 **Manoir des Remparts.** There's nothing fancy about this hotel on a residential street bordering the north side of Québec City's natural cliff. Guest rooms with private bath have telephone and TV. ✉ *3½ rue des Remparts, G1R 3R4,* ☎ *418/692–2056,* FAX *418/692–1125. 36 rooms. Breakfast room. CP. AE, DC, MC, V.*

NIGHTLIFE AND THE ARTS

For a place its size, Québec City has a wide variety of cultural institutions, from the reputed Québec Symphony Orchestra to several small theater companies. The arts scene changes significantly depending on the season. From September to May, a steady repertory of concerts, plays, and performances is presented in theaters and halls around town. In summer, indoor theaters close to make room for outdoor stages.

For arts and entertainment listings in English, consult the *Québec Chronicle-Telegraph,* published on Wednesday. The French-language daily newspaper, *Le Soleil,* has listings on a page called "Où Aller à Québec" ("Where to Go in Québec"). *Voilà Québec* and *Hospitalité Québec* are bilingual quarterly entertainment guides distributed free in tourist information areas. Also, *Voir,* a weekly devoted to arts listings and reviews, appears on the street every Thursday.

Tickets for most shows can be purchased through **Billetech,** with outlets at the Grand Théâtre de Québec (✉ 269 blvd. René-Lévesque Est, ☎ 418/643–8131), Bibliothèque Gabrielle-Roy (☎ 418/691–7400), Colisée (☎ 418/691–7211), Théâtre Périscope (☎ 418/529–2183), Palais Montcalm (☎ 418/670–9011), Salle Albert-Rousseau (☎ 418/659–6710), La Baie department store, (✉ Pl. Laurier, 2nd level, ☎ 418/627–5959), and Provigo supermarkets. Hours vary and in some cases tickets must be bought at the outlet.

The Arts

Dance

Grand Théâtre de Québec (✉ 269 blvd. René-Lévesque Est, ☎ 418/643–8131) presents a dance series with both Canadian and international companies. Dancers also appear at Bibliothèque Gabrielle-Roy, Salle Albert-Rousseau, and the Palais Montcalm (☞ Theater, *below*).

Film

Most theaters present French films and American films dubbed into French. Two popular theaters are **Cinéma de Paris** (✉ 966 rue St-Jean, ☎ 418/694–0891) and **Cinéma Place Charest** (✉ 500 rue du Pont, ☎ 418/529–9745). **Cinémas Ste-Foy** (✉ Pl. Ste-Foy, Ste-Foy, ☎ 418/656–0592) almost always shows films in English. **Le Clap** (✉ 2360 chemin Ste.-Foy, Ste-Foy, ☎ 418/650–2527) has a repertoire of foreign, offbeat, and art films. **Imax Theatre** (✉ Galeries de la Capitale, 5401 blvd. des Galeries, Galeries de la Capitale, ☎ 418/627–4629 or 800/643–4629) has extra-large-screen movies.

Music

L'Orchestre Symphonique de Québec (Québec Symphony Orchestra) is Canada's oldest. It performs at Louis-Frechette Hall in the **Grand Théâtre de Québec** (✉ 269 blvd. René-Lévesque Est, ☎ 418/643–8131).

Tickets for children's concerts at the **Joseph Lavergne auditorium** and classical concerts at the **Salle de l'Institut** (✉ 42 rue St-Stanislaus) must be purchased in advance at the **Bibliothèque Gabrielle-Roy** (✉ 350 rue St-Joseph Est, ☎ 418/691–7400).

Popular music concerts are often booked at the **Colisée de Québec** (✉ Parc de l'Exposition, 2205 av. du Colisée, Parc de l'Exposition, ☎ 418/691–7211).

Theater

All theater productions are in French. The following theaters schedule shows from September through April.

Grand Théâtre de Québec (✉ 269 blvd. René-Lévesque Est, ☎ 418/643–8131) is a theater where classic and contemporary plays are staged by the leading local theater company, le Théâtre du Trident (☎ 418/643–5873). **Palais Montcalm** (✉ 995 Pl. d'Youville, ☎ 418/670–9011), a municipal theater outside St-Jean Gate, presents a broad range of productions. A diverse repertory, from classical to comedy, is staged at **Salle Albert-Rousseau** (✉ 2410 chemin Ste-Foy, Ste-Foy, ☎ 418/659–6710). **Théâtre Capitole** (✉ 972 rue St-Jean, ☎ 418/694–4444), a restored turn-of-the-century cabaret-style theater, offers a broad repertory of classical and pop music, plays, and comedy shows. **Théâtre de la Bordée** (✉ 1143 rue St-Jean, ☎ 418/694–9631) presents small-scale productions. **Théâtre Périscope** (✉ 2 rue Crémazie Est, ☎ 418/529–2183), a multipurpose theater, stages about 200 shows a year, including performances for children.

SUMMER THEATER

Place d'Youville. During the summer, open-air concerts are presented here, just outside St-Jean Gate.

Nightlife

Nightlife in Québec City is centered on the clubs and cafés of rue St-Jean, avenue Cartier, and Grande Allée. In winter, evening activity is livelier toward the end of the week, beginning on Wednesday. But as warmer temperatures set in, the café-terrace crowd emerges, and bars are active seven days a week. Most bars and clubs stay open until 3 AM.

Bars and Lounges

Le Pub Saint-Alexandre (✉ 1087 rue St-Jean, ☎ 418/694–0015), a popular English-style pub, was formerly a men-only tavern. It's a good place to look for your favorite brand of beer—there are approximately 200 kinds, 20 on tap. You'll find mainly yuppies at **Vogue** and **Sherlock Holmes** (✉ 1170 d'Artigny, ☎ 418/529–9973), two bars stacked one atop the other. Sherlock Holmes is a pub-restaurant downstairs; for dancing, try Vogue upstairs.

Discos

There's a little bit of everything—live rock bands to loud disco—at **Chez Dagobert** (✉ 600 Grande Allée Est, ☎ 418/522–0393), a large and popular club. **Merlin** (✉ 1179 av. Cartier, ☎ 418/529–9567), a second-story disco with an English pub below, is packed nightly.

Folk, Jazz, and Blues

Maison de la Chanson (✉ Théâtre Petit Champlain, 78 rue du Petit-Champlain, ☎ 418/692–2613) is an excellent spot for contemporary Québec music. French-Canadian folk songs fill **Chez Son Père** (✉ 24 St-Stanislas, ☎ 418/692–5308), a smoky pub on the second floor of an old building in the Latin Quarter. Singers perform nightly. At **Le d'Auteuil** (✉ 35 rue d'Auteuil, ☎ 418/692–2263), a converted church across from Kent Gate, rhythm and blues, jazz, and blues emanate. The first jazz bar in Québec City, **L'Emprise at Hôtel Clarendon** (✉ 57 rue

Ste-Anne, ☎ 418/692–2480), is the preferred spot for enthusiasts. The Art Deco decor sets the mood for Jazz Age rhythms.

OUTDOOR ACTIVITIES AND SPORTS

Two parks are central to Québec City: the 250-acre Battlefields Park, with its panoramic views of the St. Lawrence River, and Cartier-Brébeuf Park, which runs along the St. Charles River. Both are favorite spots for such outdoor sports as jogging, biking, and cross-country skiing. Scenic rivers and mountains close by (no more than 30 minutes by car) make this city ideal for the sporting life. For information about sports and fitness, contact **Québec City Tourist Information Office** (✉ 60 rue d'Auteuil, G1R 4C4, ☎ 418/692–2471) or **Québec City Bureau of Parks and Recreation** (✉ 65 rue Ste-Anne, 5th Floor, G1R 3X5, ☎ 418/691–6278).

Participant Sports

Bicycling

Bike paths along rolling hills traverse Battlefields Park, at the south side of the city. For a longer ride over flat terrain take the path north of the city skirting the St. Charles River; this route can be reached from rue St-Roch, rue Prince Edouard, and Pont Dorchester (Dorchester Bridge). Paths along the côte de Beaupré, beginning at the confluence of the St. Charles and St. Lawrence rivers, are especially scenic. They begin northeast of the city at rue de la Verandrye and boulevard Montmorency or rue Abraham-Martin and Pont Samson (Samson Bridge) and continue 10 kilometers (6 miles) along the coast to Montmorency Falls.

You can rent bicycles by the day at **Auberge de la Paix** (✉ 31 rue Couillard, ☎ 418/694–0735).

Boating

Lakes in the Québec City area have facilities for boating. Take Route 73 north of the city to St-Dunstan de Lac Beauport, then take Exit 157, boulevard du Lac, to **Lac Beauport** (☎ 418/849–2821), one of the best nearby resorts. Boats and boards can be rented at **Campex** (✉ 8 chemin de l'Orée, Lac Beauport, ☎ 418/849–2236) for canoeing, kayaking, and windsurfing.

Dogsledding

Learn how to mush in the forest with **Adventure Nord-Bec** (✉ 665 rue St. Aimé, St. Lambert de Lévis G0S 2W0, ☎ 418/889–8001), 20 minutes from the city. Overnight camping trips are available.

Fishing

Permits are needed for hunting and fishing in Québec. They are available from the **Ministry of Wildlife and the Environment** (✉ Pl. de la Capitale, 150 blvd. René-Lévesque Est, ☎ 418/643–3127). The ministry also publishes a pamphlet on fishing regulations that is available at tourist information offices.

Réserve Faunique des Laurentides (☎ 418/848–2422) is a wildlife reserve with good lakes for fishing, approximately 48 kilometers (30 miles) north of Québec City via Route 73.

Golf

The Québec City region has 18 golf courses, and several are open to the public. Reservations during summer months are essential. **Club de Golf de Cap Rouge** (✉ 4600 rue St-Felix, ☎ 418/653–9381) in Cap Rouge, with 18 holes, is one of the courses closest to Québec City. **Club de Golf de Beauport** (✉ 3533 rue Clemenceau, ☎ 418/663–1578), a nine-hole course, is 20 minutes by car via Route 73 North. **Parc du Mont Ste-Anne** (⊠ Rte. 360, C.P. 653 Beaupré, ☎ 418/827–3778), a half-hour drive north of Québec, has one of the best 18-hole courses in the region.

Health and Fitness Clubs

One of the city's most popular health clubs is **Club Entrain** (⊠ Pl. de la Cité, 2600 blvd. Laurier, ☎ 418/658–7771). Facilities include a weight room with Nautilus, a sauna, a whirlpool, aerobics classes, and squash courts. Nonguests at **Hôtel Radisson des Gouverneurs** (⊠ 690 blvd. René-Lévesque Est, ☎ 418/647–1717) can use the health club facilities, which include weights, a sauna, a whirlpool, and an outdoor heated pool, for a $5 fee. **Hilton International Québec** (⊠ 3 Pl. Québec, ☎ 418/647–2411) has a smaller health club with weights, a sauna, and an outdoor pool available to nonguests for a $10 fee. **YMCA du Vieux-Québec** (⊠ 650 av. Wilfred Laurier, ☎ 418/522–0800) has facilities that include squash, badminton, a health club, volleyball, and access to a pool for a $2.28 fee. Pool facilities cost $2.25 at the **YWCA** (855 av. Holland, ☎ 418/683–2155).

Hiking and Jogging

The Parc Cartier-Brébeuf, north of the Old City along the banks of the St. Charles River, has about 13 kilometers (8 miles) of hiking trails. For more mountainous terrain, head 19 kilometers (12 miles) north on Route 73 to Lac Beauport. For jogging, Battlefields Park, Parc Cartier-Brébeuf, and Bois-de-Coulonge park in Sillery are the most popular places in the area.

Horseback Riding

Jacques Cartier Excursions (⊠ 978 av. Jacques-Cartier Nord, Tewkesbury, ☎ 418/848–7238), also known for rafting, offers summer and winter horseback riding. An excursion includes an hour of instruction and three hours of riding; the cost is $49 on weekends and $35 weekdays in spring and fall, and $55 on weekends and $39 on weekdays in winter. Reservations are required.

Horticulture

Visitors who enjoy gardening will delight in the botanical **Jardin Roger-Van den Hende.** Included is a water garden, more than 2,000 plant species from North and South America, Europe, and Asia and a collection of trees, small shrubs, and remarkable rhododendrons. The Metrobus and buses 11 and 16 run to the gardens. ⊠ *Pavillon de l'Environtron, 2480 blvd. Hochelaga, Ste-Foy,* ☎ *418/656–3410.* ▧ *Free.* ☉ *May–Oct., daily 9–8.*

Villa Bagatelle is an interpretation center on the villas and garden estates of Sillery. Its English garden, where you can have tea, has more than 350 varieties of indigenous and exotic plants. ⊠ *1563 chemin St-Louis, Sillery,* ☎ *418/688–8074.* ▧ *$2.* ☉ *Mar.–Dec., Tues.–Sun., 11–5.*

Ice Canoeing

Hey, if people windsurf on the ice, why not canoe? This exhilarating sport entails propelling the vessel (a cross between a canoe and a rowboat) over the uneven ice of the St. Lawrence, dipping and sliding and rocking and dragging until you (hopefully) get to open water, at which time you jump in the boat and row. When you return, just hop on the nearest iceberg. To propel the boat on the ice, you straddle it, one knee in a padded rest inside, the other leg pushing like a skateboard. The professional guides at **Le Mythe des Glaces** (⊠ 737 Blvd. du Lac, Charlesbourg, ☎ 418/849–6131) will suit you up from head to toe. Half-day, full-day, and overnight trips are available. This sport is not for the unfit.

Rafting

Jacques Cartier River, about 48 kilometers (30 miles) northwest of Québec City, provides good rafting.

Jacques Cartier Excursions (✉ 978 av. Jacques-Cartier Nord, Tewkesbury, ☎ 418/848−7238) offers rafting trips on the Jacques Cartier River. Tours originate from Tewkesbury, a half-hour drive from Québec City, from May through September. A half-day tour costs $30. A full day is $68 on weekends, $49 on weekdays. Wet suits are $15 extra. In winter, snow-rafting excursions are available and include a two-hour sleigh ride and all-day mountain sliding in river rafts. The total cost is $49. Reservations are required.

Nouveau Monde, Adventure–O–Max (✉ 960 av. Jacques-Cartier Nord, Tewkesbury, ☎ 418/848−4144 or 800/267−4144) has excursions on the Jacques Cartier River from mid-May through September. A 3-hour excursion costs $44, a two-day package $99. Reserve one month in advance for weekends, two weeks in advance for weekdays.

Skating

The ice-skating season runs December through March. There is a 4-kilometer (2½ mile) stretch for skating along the St. Charles River, between the Dorchester and Lavigueur bridges, January through March, depending on the ice. Rentals and changing rooms are nearby. ✉ *Marina St-Roch*, ☎ *418/691−7188.* ☉ *Skating weekdays noon–10, weekends 10–10.*

Place d'Youville, just outside St-Jean Gate, has an outdoor skating rink open from November to April. From December to March, try the Patinoire de la Terrasse adjacent to the Chateau Frontenac (☎ 418/692−2955). Open from 11 AM to 11 PM, skates can be rented for $4 daily. Nighttime skating can also be done at **Village des Sports** (✉ 1860 blvd. Valcartier, St-Gabriel-de-Valcartier, ☎ 418/844−3725).

Skiing

CROSS-COUNTRY

You can ski cross-country on many trails; Battlefields Park on Québec City's south side, which you can reach from Place Montcalm, has scenic marked trails. Thirty-two ski centers in the Québec area offer 1,700 kilometers (1,050 miles) of groomed trails and heated shelters; for information, call **Regroupement des stations de ski de fond** (☎ 418/653−5875). Lac Beauport, 19 kilometers (12 miles) north of the city, has more than 20 marked trails (250 kilometers, or 155 miles); contact **Les Sentiers du Moulin** (✉ 99 chemin du Moulin, ☎ 418/849−9652). **Parc du Mont Ste-Anne** (✉ Rte. 360, C.P. 400 Beaupré, ☎ 418/827−4561), which is 40 kilometers (25 miles) northeast of Québec City, has 215 kilometers (133 miles) of cross-country trails. **Le Centre de Randonnée à Skis de Duchesnay** (✉ 143 rue de Duchesnay, St-Catherine-de-Jacques-Cartier, ☎ 418/875−2147), just north of Québec City, has 11 marked trails totaling 125 kilometers (77 miles).

DOWNHILL

Four alpine ski resorts, all with night skiing, are within a 30-minute drive of Québec City. **Station Mont Ste-Anne** (✉ Rte. 360, C.P. 400 Beaupré, ☎ 418/827−4561; lodging, 800/463−1568) is the largest resort in eastern Canada, with 50 downhill trails, 12 lifts, and a gondola. **Station Touristique Stoneham** (✉ 1420 av. du Hibou, Stoneham, ☎ 418/848−2411) is known for its long, easy slopes with 25 downhill runs and 10 lifts. Two smaller alpine centers can be found at Lac Beauport: 15 trails at **Mont St-Castin** (✉ 82 chemin du Tour du Lac, Box 1129, Lac Beauport, ☎ 418/849–6776 or 418/849–1893) and 25 trails at **Le Relais** (✉ 1084 blvd. du Lac, Lac Beauport, ☎ 418/849–1851).

Upon request and for a fee, most major hotels arrange ski-bus service for guests. **Visite Touristique de Québec** (☎ 418/653–9722) offers a bus service to Mont Ste-Anne and Stoneham. It leaves from major hotels in Québec City and from the information center in Ste-Foy daily between 7:30 AM and 8:30 AM and returns from the slopes at 4 PM. It costs $9 each way; $15 round-trip. Telephone for reservations.

Brochures about ski centers in Québec are available at the Québec Tourism and Convention Bureaus or by calling 800/363–7777.

Snow Slides

At **Glissades de la Terrasse,** adjacent to the Château Frontenac, a wooden toboggan takes you down a 700–foot snow slide. ☎ *418/692–2955.* ▱ *$1 per ride.* ⊙ *Daily 11 AM–11 PM.*

Visitors to **Village des sports** can use inner tubes or carpets on the two 300-foot snow slides, or join 6–12 others for a snow raft ride down one of seven groomed trails. ✉ *1860 blvd. Valcartier, St-Gabriel-de-Valcartier,* ☎ *418/844–3725.* ▱ *Rafting and sliding $16.50 per day, with skating $18.50.* ⊙ *Weekdays 10–10, weekends 10 AM–10:30 PM.*

Tennis

At **Montcalm Tennis Club** (✉ 901 blvd. Champlain, Sillery, ☎ 418/687–1250), south of Québec City in Sillery, four indoor and seven outdoor courts are open daily from 8 AM to 10 PM. At **Tennisport** (✉ 6280 blvd. Hamel, Ancienne Lorette, ☎ 418/872–0111) there are 11 indoor tennis courts, two squash courts, seven raquetball courts, and eight badminton courts.

Winter Carnival

One of the highlights of the winter season in Québec is the **Québec Winter Carnival** (✉ 290 rue Joly, ☎ 418/626–3716), famous for its joie de vivre. The whirl of activities over 3 weekends in January and/or February includes night parades, a snow-sculpture competition, and a canoe race across the St. Lawrence River. You can participate in or watch every activity imaginable in the snow from dogsledding to ice climbing. Dates for 1997 are January 31 to February 16.

Spectator Sports

Tickets for sporting events can be purchased at **Colisée de Québec** (✉ Québec Coliseum, 2205 av. du Colisée, ☎ 418/691–7211) or through **Billetech** (☞ Nightlife and the Arts, *above*).

Harness Racing

There's horse racing at **Hippodrome de Québec.** ✉ *Parc de l'Exposition,* ☎ *418/524–5283.* ▱ *$2.50 grandstand, $5 club house; half price Mon., Tues., and Fri. nights, when Montréal and Ontario races are shown only on TV.*

SHOPPING

Shopping is European-style on the fashionable streets of Québec City. The boutiques and specialty shops clustered along narrow streets (such as rue du Petit-Champlain, and rue Buade and rue St-Jean in the Latin Quarter) have one of the most striking historic settings on the continent.

Prices in Québec City tend to be on a par with those in Montréal and other North American cities, so you won't have much luck hunting for bargains. When sales occur, they are usually listed in the French daily newspaper, *Le Soleil*.

Stores are generally open Monday through Wednesday 9:30–5:30, Thursday and Friday until 9, Saturday until 5, and Sunday noon–5. In summer, shops may be open seven days a week, and most have later evening hours.

Department Stores

Large department stores can be found in the malls of the suburb of Ste-Foy, but some have outlets inside Québec City's walls.

Holt Renfrew & Co., Ltd. (⊠ Pl. Ste-Foy, Ste-Foy, ☎ 418/656–6783), one of the country's more exclusive stores, carries furs, perfume, and tailored designer collections for men and women. **La Baie** (⊠ Pl. Laurier, Ste-Foy, ☎ 418/627–5959) is Québec's version of the Canadian Hudson's Bay Company conglomerate, founded in 1670 by Montréal trappers Pierre Radisson and Medard de Groseillers; the company established the first network of stores in the Canadian frontier. Today, La Baie carries both men's and women's clothing and household wares. **Simons** (⊠ 20 côte de la Fabrique, ☎ 418/692–3630), one of Québec City's oldest family stores, used to be its only source for fine British woolens and tweeds; now the store also has a large selection of designer clothing, linens, and other household items.

Food and Flea Markets

At **Marché du Vieux-Port,** farmers from the Québec countryside sell fresh produce in the Old Port near rue St-André, from May through October, 8–8.

Rue du Trésor hosts a flea market near the Place d'Armes that features sketches, paintings, and etchings by local artists. Fine portraits of the Québec City landscape and region are plentiful. Good, inexpensive souvenirs also may be purchased here.

Shopping Centers

Place Québec (⊠ 5 Pl. Québec, ☎ 418/529–0551), the mall closest to the Old City, is a multilevel shopping complex and convention center with 40 stores; it is connected to the Hilton International Hotel. **Halles Petit-Cartier** (⊠ 1191 av. Cartier, ☎ 418/688–1630), off Grande Allée and a 15-minute walk from St-Louis Gate, is a food mall for gourmets, with everything from utensils to petits fours.

The following shopping centers are approximately a 15-minute drive west along Grande Allée. **Place Ste-Foy** (⊠ 2450 blvd. Laurier, Ste-Foy, ☎ 418/653–4184) has 125 specialty stores. Next door to Place Ste-Foy is **Place de la Cité** (⊠ 2600 blvd. Laurier, Ste-Foy, ☎ 418/657–6920), with 125 boutiques. The massive **Place Laurier** (⊠ 2700 blvd. Laurier, Ste-Foy, ☎ 418/653–9318) has more than 350 stores.

Quartier Petit-Champlain (☎ 418/692–2613) in Lower Town is a pedestrian mall with some 40 boutiques, local businesses, and restaurants. This popular district is the best area to find native Québec arts and crafts, such as wood sculptures, weaving, ceramics, and jewelry. Try **Pot-en-Ciel** (⊠ 27 rue du Petit-Champlain, ☎ 418/692–1743) for ceramics. **Pauline Pelletier** (⊠ 38 rue du Petit-Champlain, ☎ 418/692–4871) has porcelain.

Specialty Stores

Antiques

Québec City's antiques district is on rue St-Paul and rue St-Pierre, across from the Old Port. French Canadian, Victorian, and Art Deco furniture, along with clocks, silverware, and porcelain, are some of the rare collectibles that can be found here. Authentic Québec pine furniture, characterized by simple forms and lines, is becoming increasingly rare and costly.

L'Héritage Antiquités (✉ 110 rue St-Paul, ☎ 418/692–1681) specializes in precious Québécois furniture from the 18th century. **Antiquités Zaor** (✉ 112 rue St-Paul, ☎ 418/692–0581), the oldest store on rue St-Paul, is still the best place in the neighborhood to find excellent English, French, and Canadian antiques.

Art

Aux Multiples Collections (✉ 43 rue Buade, ☎ 418/692–4298) has Inuit art and antique wood collectibles. **Galerie Brousseau et Brousseau** (✉ Château Frontenac, 1 rue des Carrières, ☎ 418/694–1828) has Inuit art. **Galerie Madeleine Lacerte** (✉ 1 côte Dinan, ☎ 418/692–1566), in Lower Town, sells contemporary art and sculpture.

Books

English-language books are difficult to find in Québec. One of the city's first bookstores, **Librairie Garneau** (✉ 24 côte de la Fabrique, ☎ 418/692–4262), near City Hall, carries mostly volumes in French. **La Maison Anglaise** (✉ Pl. de la Cité, Ste-Foy, ☎ 418/654–9523), has English-language titles only, specializing in fiction. **Librairie du Nouveau-Monde** (✉ 103 rue St-Pierre, ☎ 418/694–9475), stocks general-interest titles in French and English. **Librairie Smith** (✉ Pl. Laurier, blvd. Laurier, ☎ 418/653–8683) is popular.

Clothing

François Côté Collections (✉ 35 rue Buade, ☎ 418/692–6016) is a chic boutique with fashions for men. **La Maison Darlington** (✉ 7 rue Buade, ☎ 418/692–2268) carries well-made woolens, dresses, and suits for women by fine names in couture. **Louis Laflamme** (✉ 1192 rue St-Jean, ☎ 418/692–3774) has a large selection of stylish men's clothes.

Crafts

Les Trois Colombes Inc. (✉ 46 rue St-Louis, ☎ 418/694–1114) sells handmade items on two floors filled with such goods as clothing made from handwoven fabric, Indian and Inuit carvings, jewelry, pottery, and paintings.

Fur

The fur trade has been an important industry here for centuries. Québec City is a good place to purchase high-quality furs at fairly reasonable prices. Since 1894, one of the best furriers in town has been **Jos Robitaille** (✉ 1500 des Taneurs, ☎ 418/681–7297). The department store **J. B. Laliberté** (✉ 595 rue St-Joseph Est, ☎ 418/525–4841) also carries furs.

Gifts

Collection Lazuli (✉ 774 rue St-Jean, ☎ 418/525–6528; ✉ Pl. de la Cité, Ste. Foy, ☎ 418/652–3732) offers a good choice of unusual art objects and international jewelry.

Jewelry

Joaillier Louis Perrier (✉ 48 rue du Petit-Champlain, ☎ 418/692–4633) has Québec-made gold and silver jewelry. Exclusive jewelry can also be found at **Zimmermann** (✉ 46 côte de la Fabrique, ☎ 418/692–2672).

SIDE TRIPS

Côte de Beaupré and Montmorency Falls

As legend tells it, when explorer Jacques Cartier first caught sight of the north shore of the St. Lawrence River in 1535, he exclaimed, *"Quel beau pré!"* ("What a lovely meadow!"), because the area was the first inviting piece of land he had spotted since leaving France. Today this fertile meadow, first settled by French farmers, is known as Côte de Beaupré (Beaupré Coast), stretching 40 kilometers (25 miles) northeast from Québec City to the famous pilgrimage site of Ste-Anne-de-Beaupré. The impressive Montmorency Falls are midway between these two points.

Montmorency Falls, as they cascade down the side of a 274-foot cliff, are one of the most beautiful sights in the province. These falls are 50% higher than Niagara Falls, which is wider. More than half a million people each year make spiritual pilgrimages to the monumental and inspiring basilica at Ste-Anne-de-Beaupré, along the historic route 360 or chemin Royal, that winds its way from Beauport to St-Joachim. Ste. Anne is the patron saint of those in shipwrecks.

Montmorency Falls

As it cascades over a cliff into the St. Lawrence River, the Montmorency River (named for Charles de Montmorency, who was a governor of New France) is one of the most beautiful sights in the province. The falls, at 274 feet, are higher than Niagara Falls. During very cold weather, the falls's heavy spray freezes and forms a giant loaf-shape ice cone (hill) known to Québécois as the Pain du Sucre (Sugarloaf); this phenomenon attracts sledders and sliders from Québec City. Ice climbers come scale the falls; a school trains novices for only a few days to make the ascent. In the warmer months, a park in the river's gorge leads to an observation terrace that is continuously sprayed by a fine drizzle from water pounding onto the cliff rocks. The top of the falls can be observed from avenue Royale.

The park is also a historic sight. The British general Wolfe, on his way to conquer New France, set up camp here in 1759. In 1780, Sir Frederick Haldimand, then the governor of Canada, built a summer home—now a good restaurant called Manoir Montmorency—on top of the cliff. Prince Edward, Queen Victoria's father, rented this villa from 1791 to 1794. Unfortunately, the structure burned several years ago; what now stands is a re-creation. ☎ 418/663–2877. ⌖ *Free, parking $6.* ☺ *May–mid-June, daily 8:30–6; mid-June–July, daily 9 AM–11 PM; Aug., daily 9–9; Sept. and Oct., daily 9–6; Nov.–May, weekends 8:30–4:30.*

NEED A BREAK?
Restaurant Baker (✉ 8790 av. Royale, Château-Richer, ☎ 418/824–4478), on the way to Ste-Anne-de Beaupré on Route 360, is a good, old-fashioned rustic restaurant that serves such hearty traditional French Canadian dishes as meat pie, pea soup, pâtés, and maple-sugar pie.

Basilique Ste-Anne-de-Beaupré

The monumental and inspiring **Basilique Ste-Anne-de-Beaupré** (Ste-Anne-de-Beaupré Basilica) is in a small town with the same name. The basilica has become a popular attraction as well as an important shrine: More than half a million people visit the site each year.

The French brought their devotion to St. Anne with them when they sailed across the Atlantic to New France. In 1650, Breton sailors caught in a storm vowed to erect a chapel in honor of this patron saint at the exact spot where they landed. The present-day neo-Roman basilica constructed in 1923 was the fifth to be built on the site where the sailors first touched ground.

According to local legend, St. Anne was responsible over the years for saving voyagers from shipwrecks in the harsh waters of the St. Lawrence. Tributes to her miraculous powers can be seen in the shrine's various mosaics, murals, altars, and ceilings. A bas-relief at the entrance depicts St. Anne welcoming her pilgrims, and ceiling mosaics represent her life. Numerous crutches and braces posted on the back pillars have been left by those who have felt the saint's healing powers.

The basilica, which is in the shape of a Latin cross, has two granite steeples jutting from its gigantic structure. Its interior has 22 chapels and 18 altars, as well as round arches and numerous ornaments in the Romanesque style. The 214 stained-glass windows by Frenchmen Auguste Labouret and Pierre Chaudière, finished in 1949, tell a story of salvation through personages who were believed to be instruments of God over the centuries. Other features of the shrine include intricately carved wood pews decorated with various animals and several smaller altars (behind the main altar) that are dedicated to different saints.

The original, 17th-century wood chapel in the village of Ste-Anne-de-Beaupré was built too close to the St. Lawrence and was swept away by river flooding. In 1676, the chapel was replaced by a stone church that was visited by pilgrims for more than a century, but this structure was also demolished in 1872. The first basilica, which replaced the stone church, was destroyed by a fire in 1922. The following year architects Maxime Rosin from Paris and Louis-N. Audet from Québec province designed the basilica that now stands. Tours are given daily in summer at 1 and begin at the information booth at the southwest corner of the courtyard outside the basilica. ✉ *10,018 av. Royale, Ste-Anne-de-Beaupré,* ☎ *418/827–3781.* 🎫 *Free.* ☉ *Reception booth mid-May–mid-Oct., daily 8:30–7:30; guided tours Sept.–mid-May can be arranged by calling in advance.*

Across from the basilica on avenue Royale is the **Commemorative Chapel,** designed by Claude Bailiff and built in 1878. The memorial chapel was constructed on the location of the transept of a stone church built in 1676 and contains the old building's foundations. Among the remnants housed here are the old church's bell dating from 1696, an early 18th-century altar designed by Vezina, a crucifix sculpted by François-Noël Levasseur in 1775, and a pulpit designed by François Baillargé in 1807.

Beaupré Coast Interpretation Center, in the old mill Petit-Pré, built in 1695, has displays on the history and development of the region. ✉ *7007 av. Royale, Château-Richer,* ☎ *418/824–3677.* 🎫 *$1.* ☉ *Late June–Labor Day, daily 9–noon and 1–5.*

Côte de Beaupré A to Z

ARRIVING AND DEPARTING

By Car. To reach Montmorency Falls, take Route 440 (Dufferin-Montmorency Autoroute) northeast from Québec City approximately 9½ kilometers (6 miles) to the exit for Montmorency Falls. To drive directly to Ste-Anne-de Beaupré, continue northeast on Route 440 for approximately 29 kilometers (18 miles) and exit at Ste-Anne-de-Beaupré.

An alternative way to reach Ste-Anne-de-Beaupré is to take Route 360 or avenue Royale. Take Route 440 from Québec City, turn left at d'Estimauville, and right on boulevard Ste-Anne until it intersects with Route 360. Also called "le chemin du Roi" (the King's Road), this panoramic route is one of the oldest in North America, winding 30 kilometers (20 miles) along the steep ridge of the Côte de Beaupré. The road borders 17th- and 18th-century farmhouses, historic churches, and Normandy-style homes with half-buried root cellars. Route 360 goes past the Ste-Anne-de-Beaupré Basilica.

GUIDED TOURS

Companies such as **Gray Line** (☎ 418/653–9722, FAX 418/653–9834), which charge $13–$80 per tour, and **Maple Leaf Sightseeing Tours** (☎ 418/649–9226), lead day excursions along the Côte de Beaupré, with stops at Montmorency Falls and the Ste-Anne-de-Beaupré Basilica.

Beau Temps, Mauvais Temps (✉ 22 rue du Quai, Suite 101, Ste-Pétronille, Ile d'Orléans, ☎ 418/828–2275) offers guided bus tours of the Côte de Beaupré.

Ile d'Orléans

Ile d'Orléans, an island slightly downstream in a northeasterly direction from Québec City, exemplifies the historic charm of rural Québec province with its quiet, traditional lifestyle. A drive around the island will take you past stone churches that are among the oldest in the region and centuries-old houses amid acres of lush orchards and cultivated farmland. Horse-drawn carriages are still a means of transport. Ile d'Orléans is also an important marketplace that provides fresh produce daily for Québec City; roadside stands on the island sell a variety of local products, such as crocheted blankets, woven articles, maple syrup, homemade breads and jams, and fruits and vegetables. The island is known for its superb fruits, and you won't find better strawberries anywhere else in the province. There are about two dozen spots where you can pick your own.

The island was discovered at about the same time as Québec City in 1535. Explorer Jacques Cartier noticed an abundance of vines on the island and called it the "Island of Bacchus," after the Greek god of wine. In 1536, Cartier renamed the island in honor of the duke of Orléans, son of the king of France, François I. Long considered part of the domain of Côte de Beaupré, the island was not given its seignorial autonomy until 1636.

Ile d'Orléans, about 9 kilometers (5½ miles) wide and 34 kilometers (21 miles) long, is now composed of six small villages. These villages have sought over the years to remain relatively private residential and agricultural communities; the island's bridge to the mainland was built only in 1935.

Numbers in the margin correspond to points of interest on the Ile d'Orléans map.

Ste-Pétronille

Start your tour heading west on chemin Royal to Ste-Pétronille, the first village to be settled on the island. Founded in 1648, the community was chosen in 1759 by British General James Wolfe for his headquarters. With 40,000 soldiers and a hundred ships, the English bombarded French-occupied Québec City and Côte de Beaupré.

During the late 19th century, the English population of Québec developed Ste-Pétronille into a resort village. This region is considered by many to be the island's most beautiful, not only because of the spectacular views it offers of Montmorency Falls and Québec City but also for the stylish English villas and exquisitely tended gardens that can be seen from the roadside.

After crossing the bridge to the island, and turning right on chemin Royal, on the left at 20 chemin Royal is the **Plante family farm,** where

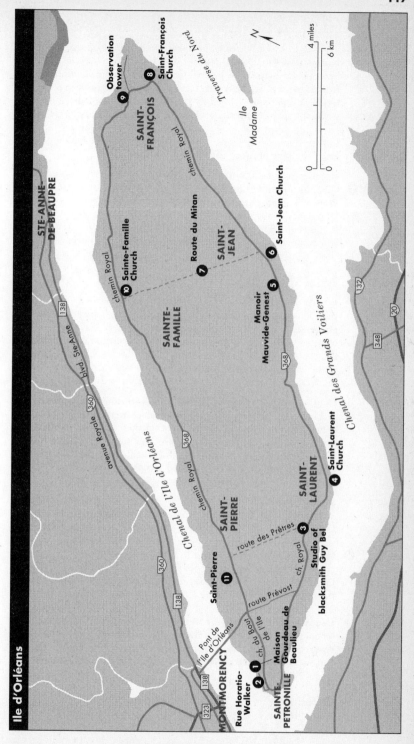

Ile d'Orléans

MONTMORENCY

STE-ANNE-DE-BEAUPRE

SAINT-FRANÇOIS

SAINTE-FAMILLE

SAINT-JEAN

SAINT-PIERRE

SAINT-LAURENT

SAINTE-PETRONILLE

Observation tower

Saint-François Church

Sainte-Famille Church

Route du Mitan

Saint-Jean Church

Manoir Mauvide-Genest

Saint-Laurent Church

Studio of blacksmith Guy Bel

Saint-Pierre

Maison Goudeau de Beaulieu

Rue Horatio-Walker

Pont de l'Ile d'Orléans

route des Prêtres

route Prévost

ch. du Bout de l'Ile

ch. Royal

chemin Royal

Chenal de l'Ile d'Orléans

Chenal des Grands Voiliers

Traverse du Nord

Ile Madame

avenue Royale

blvd. Ste-Anne

138

360

368

323

132

20

348

N

4 miles

6 km

1 2 3 4 5 6 7 8 9 10 11

you can stop to pick apples (in season) or buy some of the island's fresh fruits and vegetables.

Coming from the Plante family farm, farther along on the right is the
1 **Maison Gourdeau de Beaulieu** (⊠ 137 chemin Royal), the island's first home, built in 1648 for Jacques Gourdeau de Beaulieu, who was the first seigneur of Ste-Pétronille. Today this white house with blue shutters is still privately owned by his descendants. Remodeled over the years, it now incorporates both French and Québécois styles. Its thick walls and dormer windows are characteristic of Breton architecture, but its sloping bell-shape roof, designed to protect buildings from large amounts of snow, is typically Québécois.

Coming from Maison Gordeau de Beaulieu, after you descend an incline, turn right beside the river on the tiny street called **rue Horatio-**
2 **Walker,** named after the turn-of-the-century painter known for his landscapes of the island. Walker lived on this street from 1904 until his death in 1938. At 11 and 13 rue Horatio-Walker are his home and workshop. During the summer, his paintings are exhibited in the workshop. Designed by Harry Staveley, the home is a good example of English Arts & Crafts architecture. To tour the house, contact Beau Temps, Mauvais Temps (☎ 418/828–2275).

Farther along chemin Royal, at the border of Ste-Pétronille and St-Laurent, look for a large boulder in the middle of nowhere. The **roche à Maranda** (to the left, just before the intersection of chemin Royal and route Prévost), named for the owner of the property where the rock was discovered in the 19th century, is one of the oldest such rock formations in the world. When the glaciers melted in 9,000 BC, such rocks as this one rolled down with glacial water from the Laurentians onto lower land.

Continue east along chemin Royal, and as you approach the village of
3 St-Laurent, you'll find the **studio of blacksmith Guy Bel** (⊠ 2200 chemin Royal, ☎ 418/828–9300), a talented and well-known local artisan who has done ironwork restoration for Québec City. He was born in Lyon, France, and studied there at the Ecole des Beaux Arts. In summer, you can watch him hard at work; his stylish candlesticks, mantels, and other ironworks are for sale.

St-Laurent

St-Laurent, founded in 1679, is one of the island's maritime villages. Until as late as 1935, residents here used boats as their main means of transportation. Next to the village's marina stands the tall, inspiring
4 **St-Laurent Church.** It was built in 1860 on the site of an 18th-century church that, because of its poor construction, had to be torn down. One of the church's procession chapels is a miniature stone replica of the original. ⊠ 1532 chemin Royal. 🆓 Free. ☉ Summer, daily.

NEED A   **Moulin de Saint-Laurent** (⊠ 754 chemin Royal, ☎ 418/829–3888) is
BREAK?   an early 18th-century stone mill where you can dine in the herb-and-flower garden out back. Scrumptious snacks, such as quiches, bagels, and salads, are available at the café-terrace. The restaurant is closed November–April.

St-Jean

If you continue on chemin Royal, you'll come to the southernmost point of the island, St-Jean, a village whose inhabitants were once river pilots and navigators. Most of its small, homogeneous row houses were built between 1840 and 1860. Being at sea most of the time, the sailors did not need large homes and plots of land as did the farmers. The island's sudden drop in elevation is most noticeable in St-Jean.

❺ St-Jean's beautiful Normandy-style manor, **Manoir Mauvide-Genest,** was built in 1734 for Jean Mauvide—surgeon to Louis XV—and his wife, Marie-Anne Genest. Most notable about this house, which still has its original thick walls, ceiling beams, and fireplaces, is the degree to which it has held up over the years, in spite of being targeted by English guns during the 1759 siege of Québec City. The home is a pleasure to roam; all rooms are furnished with original antiques from the 18th and 19th centuries. It also offers an exhibit on French architecture and a downstairs restaurant that serves French cuisine. ✉ *1451 chemin Royal,* ☎ *418/829–2630.* ⊙ *June–Aug., daily 10–5; Sept.–mid-Oct., weekends by reservation.*

❻ At the opposite end of the village, you'll see **St-Jean Church,** a massive granite structure with large red doors and a towering steeple built in 1749. The church bears a remarkable resemblance to a ship; it is big and round and appears to be sitting right on the St. Lawrence River. Paintings of the patron saints of seamen line the interior walls. The church's cemetery is also intriguing, especially if you can read French. Back in the 18th century, piloting the St. Lawrence was a dangerous profession; the boats could not easily handle the rough currents. The cemetery tombstones recall the tragedies of lives lost in these harsh waters. ✉ *2001 chemin Royal,* ☎ *418/829–3182.* ✐ *Free.* ⊙ *Summer, daily.*

❼ As you leave St-Jean, chemin Royal mounts the incline and crosses **route du Mitan.** In old French, *mitan* means "halfway." This road, dividing the island in half, is the most direct route from north to south. It is also the most beautiful on the island, with acres of tended farmland, apple orchards, and maple groves. If you're running out of time and want to end the tour here, take route du Mitan, which brings you to St-Pierre and the bridge to the mainland.

St-François

When you come to 17th-century farmhouses separated by sprawling open fields, you know you've reached the island's least-toured and most rustic village, St-François. At the eastern tip of the island, this community was originally settled mainly by farmers. St-François is also the perfect place to visit one of the island's *cabanes à sucre* (maple-sugaring huts) found along chemin Royal. Stop at a hut for a tasting tour; sap is gathered from the maple groves and boiled until it turns to syrup. When it is poured on ice, it tastes like a delicious toffee. The maple syrup season is late March through April.

❽ Straight on chemin Royal is **St-François Church,** built in 1734 and one of eight provincial churches dating from the French regime. At the time the English seized Québec in 1759, General Wolfe knew St-François to be among the better strategic points along the St. Lawrence. Consequently, he stationed British troops here and used the church as a military hospital. In May 1988, a fatal car crash set the church on fire, and most of the interior treasures were lost.

❾ About a mile down the road from the St-François Church is a picnic area with a wood **observation tower** situated for perfect viewing of the majestic St. Lawrence at its widest point, 10 times as wide as it is near Québec City. During the spring and autumn months, you can observe wild Canada geese here.

Ste-Famille

Heading west now on chemin Royal, you'll come to one of the island's earliest villages, Ste-Famille, which was founded in 1661. The scenery is exquisite here; there are abundant apple orchards and strawberry fields with views of Côte de Beaupré and Mont Ste-Anne in the distance. But the village also has plenty of historic charm; it has the area's highest concentration of stone houses dating from the French regime.

⑩ Take a quick look at **Ste-Famille Church,** which was constructed in 1749, later than some of the others on the island. This impressive structure is the only church in the province to have three bell towers at the front. Its ceiling was redone in the mid-19th century with elaborate designs in wood and gold. The church also holds a famous painting, *L'Enfant Jésus Voyant la Croix,* done in 1670 by Frère Luc (Father Luc), who was sent from France to decorate churches in the area. ⊠ *3915 chemin Royal.* ☎ *Free.* ☺ *Summer, daily.*

St-Pierre

⑪ The village after Ste-Famille on the northwest side of the island, **St-Pierre,** was established in 1679. Its church, dating from 1717, is the oldest on the island. **St-Pierre Church** is no longer open for worship, but it was restored during the 1960s and is open to tourists. Many of its original components are still intact, such as benches with compartments below, where hot bricks and stones were placed to keep people warm during winter services. ⊠ *1243 chemin Royal.* ☎ *Free.* ☺ *Summer, daily.*

Because St-Pierre is situated on a plateau with the island's most fertile land, the village has long been the center of traditional farming industries. The best products grown here are potatoes, asparagus, and corn, and the many dairy farms have given the village a renowned reputation for butter and other dairy products. At 2370 chemin Royal is the **former home of Felix Leclerc,** one of the many artists who have made the island their home. Leclerc, the father of Québécois folk singing, lived here until he died in August 1988.

If you continue west on chemin Royal, just up ahead are the bridge back to the mainland and Route 440.

DINING AND LODGING

$$$ ✕ **L'Atre.** After you park your car, you'll be driven in a 1954 Chevy to the 17th-century Normandy-style house furnished with Québécois pine antiques. True to the establishment's name, which means "hearth," all the traditional dishes are cooked and served from a fireplace. The menu emphasizes hearty fare, such as beef Bourguignon and tourtière, with maple-sugar pie for dessert. La Grande Fête (the Big Feast) is a nine-course dinner that costs about $60. Halfway through the meal, guests visit the attic for a nip of maple-syrup liqueur. ⊠ *4403 chemin Royal, Ste-Famille,* ☎ *418/829–2474. Reservations essential. AE, MC, V. Closed Nov.–Apr.*

$$–$$$ ✕🏠 **La Goéliche.** This 1890 rustic Victorian country inn stands just steps away from the St. Lawrence River. Québécois antiques decorate light and spacious rooms with their original wood floors. Rooms have telephones; half look out across the river to Québec City. The first rule of this classic French kitchen is that only the freshest ingredients from the island's farms can be used. Lunch is a moderately priced à la carte selection of salads, quiches, and omelets. The evening's menu is more expensive and features such specialties as quail with red vermouth and chicken with pistachio mousseline. The desserts, such as maple syrup mousse with strawberry syrup, have a regional flavor. The romantic dining room has windows overlooking the St. Lawrence River. ⊠ *22 chemin du Quai, Ste-Pétronille,* ☎ *418/828–2248,* ℻ *418/828–2745. 24 rooms. 2 restaurants. AE, MC, V.*

$$ ✕⊞ **Auberge le Chaumonot.** This medium-size hotel in rural St-François is right near the St. Lawrence River's widest point. The inn's large bay windows capitalize on the view of the river and neighboring islands, but the decor is uninspired, with simple wood furniture of the island. The service here is efficient and friendly. The restaurant serves Continental cuisine, with table d'hôte and à la carte menus. ⊠ *425 chemin Royal, St-François, G0A 3S0,* ☎ *418/829–2735. 8 rooms with bath. Restaurant, air-conditioning, pool. AE, MC, V. Closed Nov.–Apr.*

Ile d'Orléans A to Z

ARRIVING AND DEPARTING

By Car. Ile d'Orléans has no public transportation; cars are the only way to get to and around the island, unless you take a guided tour (☞ Guided Tours, *below*). Parking on the island is never a problem; you can always stop and explore the villages on foot. The main road, chemin Royal (Route 368), extends 67 kilometers (40 miles) through the island's six villages; street numbers along chemin Royal begin at No. 1 for each municipality.

From Québec City, take Route 440 (Dufferin-Montmorency Autoroute) northeast. After a drive of about 10 kilometers (6 miles) take the bridge, Pont de l'Ile d'Orléans, to the island.

B&B RESERVATION SERVICE

You can get to know the island by staying at one of its 30 B&Bs. Reservations are necessary. The price for a room, double occupancy, runs about $45–$90. **Beau Temps, Mauvais Temps** (☎ 418/828–2275) is a referral service for these accommodations.

EMERGENCIES

Centre Médical (⊠ 1015 Rte. Prévost, St-Pierre, ☎ 418/828–2213) is the only medical clinic on the island.

GUIDED TOURS

Beau Temps, Mauvais Temps (⊠ 22 rue du Quai, Suite 101, Ste-Pétronille, ☎ 418/828–2275) leads guided walking tours of three villages: Ste-Pétronille, St-Jean, and St-Laurent. River excursions departing from St-Laurent are available from mid-May–mid-September.

Québec City touring companies, including **Maple Leaf Sightseeing Tours** (☎ 418/649–9226), **Gray Line** (☎ 418/653–9722, 𝖥𝖠𝖷 418/653–9834) and **Visite Touristiques de Québec** (☎ 418/653–9722) offer full- and half-day bus tours of the western tip of the island, combined with sightseeing along the Côte de Beaupré.

Any of the offices of the **Québec City Region Tourism and Convention Bureau** (☞ Québec City A to Z, *below*) can provide information on tours and accommodations on the island.

VISITOR INFORMATION

Beau Temps, Mauvais Temps has a tourist office in Ste-Pétronille. ⊠ *22 rue du Quai, Suite 101, Ste-Pétronille,* ☎ *418/828–2275.* ☉ *May–Oct., weekdays 8:30–4; Nov.–Apr., leave message on answering machine.*

The island's **Chamber of Commerce** operates a tourist information kiosk situated at the west corner of côte du Pont and chemin Royal. ⊠ *490 côte du Pont, St-Pierre,* ☎ *418/828–9411.* ☉ *June–Sept., daily 8:30–7, Oct.–May, daily 8:30–noon, 1–4.*

QUÉBEC CITY A TO Z

Arriving and Departing

By Bus

Voyageur Inc. provides regular service from Montréal to Québec City daily, departing hourly 6 AM–9 PM, with an additional bus at 11 PM. The cost of the three-hour ride is $35 one way, round-trip is double that; but a round-trip costs $52.13 if you return within 10 days and do not travel on Friday. Senior citizens travel for $26.46 each way, good for any day. You can purchase tickets only at the terminal.

BUS TERMINALS

Montréal: Terminus Voyageur (⊠ 505 blvd. de Maisonneuve Est, ☎ 514/842–2281). **Québec:** Downtown Terminal (⊠ 320 rue Abraham-Martin, ☎ 418/525–3000); Ste-Foy Terminal (⊠ 2700 blvd. Laurier, ☎ 418/651–7015).

By Car

Montréal and Québec City are linked by Autoroute 20 on the south shore of the St. Lawrence River and by Autoroute 40 on the north shore. On both highways, the ride between the two cities is about 240 kilometers (150 miles) and takes some three hours. U.S. I–87 in New York, U.S. I–89 in Vermont, and U.S. I–91 in New Hampshire connect with Autoroute 20. Highway 401 from Toronto also links up with Autoroute 20.

Driving northeast from Montréal on Autoroute 20, follow signs for Pont Pierre-Laporte (Pierre-Laporte Bridge) as you approach Québec City. After you've crossed the bridge, turn right onto boulevard Laurier (Route 175), which becomes the Grande Allée leading into Québec City.

It is necessary to have a car only if you are planning to visit outlying areas. The narrow streets of the Old City leave few two-hour metered parking spaces available. However, there are several parking garages at central locations in town, with rates running approximately $10 a day. Main garages are at City Hall, Place d'Youville, Edifice Marie Guyart, Complex G, Place Québec, Château Frontenac, Québec Seminary, rue St-Paul, and the Old Port.

By Plane

Québec City has one airport, **Jean Lesage International Airport,** in the suburb of Ste-Foy, about 19 kilometers (12 miles) from downtown. Few U.S. airlines fly directly to Québec City. You usually have to stop in Montréal, Toronto, or Ottawa and take one of the regional and commuter airlines, such as Air Canada's **Air Alliance** (☎ 418/692–0770 or 800/361–8620) or **Canadian Airlines International** (☎ 418/692–1031). **Air Alliance** has a daily direct flight between Newark, New Jersey, and Québec City.

BETWEEN THE AIRPORT AND QUÉBEC CITY

The ride from the airport into town should be no longer than 30 minutes. Most hotels do not have an airport shuttle, but they will make a reservation for you with a bus company. If you're not in a rush, a shuttle bus offered by Maple Leaf Sightseeing Tours (☞ *below*) is convenient and half the price of a taxi.

By Bus. Maple Leaf Sightseeing Tours (⊠ 240 3e rue, ☎ 418/649–9226) has a shuttle bus that runs from the airport to hotels and costs under $10 one-way. Reservations are necessary for the trip to the airport.

By Car. If you're driving from the airport, take Route 540 (Autoroute Duplessis) to Route 175 (blvd. Laurier), which becomes Grande Allée and leads right to the Old City. The ride is about 30 minutes and may be only slightly longer (45 minutes or so) during rush hours (7:30–8:30 AM into town, and 4–5:30 PM leaving town).

By Limousine. Private limo service is expensive, starting at $50 for the ride from the airport into Québec City. Try **Groupe Limousine A-1** (✉ 361, rue des Commissaires Est, ☎ 418/523–5059). **Maple Leaf Sightseeing Tours** (✉ 240 3e rue, ☎ 418/649–9226) acts as a referral service for local companies offering car service.

By Taxi. Taxis are always available immediately outside the airport exit near the baggage claim area. Two local taxi firms are **Taxi Québec** (✉ 975 8e av., ☎ 418/522–2001) and **Taxi Coop de Québec** (✉ 496 2e av., ☎ 418/525–5191), the largest company in the city. A ride into the city costs about $25.

By Train

VIA Rail (☎ 418/692–3940; 800/361–5390 in Québec province), Canada's passenger rail service, runs trains from Montréal to Québec City four times daily on weekdays, three times a day on Saturday, and twice on Sunday. The trip takes less than three hours, with a stop in Ste-Foy. Tickets must be purchased in advance at any VIA Rail office or travel agent. The basic one-way rate is about $40, but it may be reduced to $23 at certain times of year (not including Friday, Sunday, or holidays). Reservations must be made and tickets bought at least five days in advance. First-class service costs about $70 each way, and includes early boarding and a three-course meal with wine.

The train arrives in Québec City at the 19th-century **Gare du Palais** (✉ 450 rue de la Gare du Palais, ☎ 418/524–6452), in the heart of the Old City.

Getting Around

Walking is the best way to explore the city. The Old City measures 11 square kilometers (about 4 square miles), and most historic sites, hotels, and restaurants are within the walls or a short distance outside. City maps are available at tourist information offices.

By Bus

The city's transit system, **Société de Transport de la Communauté Urbaine de Québec (STCUQ)** (☎ 418/627–2511) runs buses approximately every 15 or 20 minutes that stop at major points around town. The cost is $1.85; you'll need exact change. Bus tickets are available for $1.50 ($3.75 for day pass) at major convenience stores. All buses stop in Lower Town at Place Jacques-Cartier or outside St-Jean Gate at Place d'Youville in Upper Town. Transportation maps are available at tourist information offices.

By Ferry

The **Québec–Lévis ferry** (☎ 418/644–3704, 🚢 $1.25) makes a 15-minute crossing of the St. Lawrence River to the town of Lévis. The first ferry leaves daily at 6:30 AM from the pier at rue Dalhousie, across from Place Royale. Crossings run every half hour from 7:30 AM until 6:30 PM, then hourly until 2:30 AM, with a final crossing at 3:45 AM.

By Horse-Drawn Carriage

Hire a calèche on rue d'Auteuil between the St-Louis and Kent gates from **André Beaurivage** (☎ 418/687–9797), **Balades en Calèche** (☎ 418/624–3062), or **Promenades en Calèche** (☎ 418/683–9222). The cost is about $50 without tax or tip for a 45-minute tour of the Old City. Some drivers talk about Québec's history and others don't; if you want a storyteller, ask in advance.

By Limousine

Groupe Limousine A-1 (✉ 361 rue des Commissaires Est, ☎ 418/523–5059) has 24-hour service.

By Taxi

Taxis are stationed in front of major hotels and the Hôtel de Ville (City Hall), along rue des Jardins, and at Place d'Youville outside St-Jean Gate. For radio-dispatched cars, try **Taxi Coop de Québec** (☎ 418/525–5191) and **Taxi Québec** (☎ 418/522–2001). Passengers are charged an initial $2.25, plus $1 for each kilometer.

Contacts and Resources

B&B Reservation Service

Québec City has a large number of B&B and hostel accommodations. To guarantee a room during peak season, be sure to reserve in advance. **Québec City Tourist Information** (✉ 60 rue d'Auteuil, G1R 4C4, ☎ 418/692–2471, ⏰ June–Sept. 5, daily 8:30–8; Sept. 5–Oct. 9, daily 8:30–5:30; Oct. 10–Apr. 15, weekdays 9–5, Apr. 17–May, weekdays 8:30–5:30) has B&B listings.

Car Rentals

Hertz Canada (Québec City Airport: ☎ 418/871–1571; Vieux-Québec, ✉ 44 Côte du Palais, ☎ 418/694–1224 or 800/654–3131), **Via Route** (✉ 2605 Hamel Blvd., ☎ 418/682–2660), **Tilden** (Airport: ☎ 418/871–1224, ✉ 295 St. Paul St., ☎ 418/694–1727).

Consulate

The **U.S. Consulate** (✉ 2 Pl. Terrasse Dufferin, ☎ 418/692–2095) faces the Governor's Park near the Château Frontenac.

Dentists and Doctors

Clinique Dentaire Darveau, Dablois and Tardis (✉ 1175 rue Lavigerie, Edifice Iberville 2, Room 100, Ste-Foy, ☎ 418/653–5412) is open Monday and Tuesday 8–8, Wednesday and Thursday 8–5, and Friday 8–4.

Hôtel-Dieu Hospital (✉ 11 côte du Palais, ☎ 418/691–5042) is the main hospital inside the Old City. **Hale Hospital** (✉ 1250 chemin Ste-Foy, ☎ 418/683–4471) is opposite St. Sacrament Church.

Emergencies

Distress Center (☎ 418/683–2153). **24-hour Poison Center** (☎ 418/656–8090). **Police and fire** (☎ 911 or 418/691–6911). **Provincial police** (☎ 418/623–6262).

English-Language Bookstore

La Maison Anglaise (✉ Pl. de la Cité, Ste-Foy, ☎ 418/654–9523).

Guided Tours

EXCURSIONS

Le Bateau Mouche (✉ 132 rue St-Pierre, No. 100, ☎ 418/692–4949 or 800/361–0130) offers 90-minute boat trips four times a day and a three-hour dinner cruise from mid-May to mid-October. **Croisières AML Inc.** (✉ Pier Chouinard, 10 rue Dalhousie, across the street from the funicular, ☎ 418/692–1159) runs cruises on the St. Lawrence River aboard the MV *Louis-Jolliet*. One- to three-hour cruises from May through mid-October cost $19.

ORIENTATION

Tours cover such sights as Québec City, Montmorency Falls, and Ste-Anne-de-Beaupré; combination city and harbor cruise tours are also available. Québec City tours operate year-round; other excursions to outlying areas may operate only in summer.

Tickets for **Gray Line** bus tours (⊠ 720 rue des Rocailles; departure from Château Frontenac terrace, ☎ 418/622–7420) can be purchased at most major hotels or at the kiosk at Terrasse Dufferin at Place d'Armes. Tours run year-round and cost $13–$70. **Maple Leaf Sightseeing Tours** (⊠ 240 3e rue, ☎ 418/649–9226) offers guided tours in a minibus. Call for a reservation, and the company will pick you up at your hotel. Prices are $20–$91. **Visite Touristique de Québec** (⊠ C.P. 246, ☎ 418/653–9722) gives tours (in English or French) in a panoramic bus, and charges $20–$35. Smaller companies offering tours include **La Tournée du Québec Inc.** (☎ 418/836–8687) and **Fleur de Lys** (418/831–0188).

Late-Night Pharmacy

Pharmacie Brunet (⊠ Les Galeries Charlesbourg, 4266 1re av., north of Québec City in Charlesbourg, ☎ 418/623–1571) is open daily, 24 hours a day.

Opening and Closing Times

Most **banks** are open Monday through Wednesday 10–3 and close later on Thursday and Friday. **Bank of Montréal** (⊠ Pl. Laurier, 2700 blvd. Laurier, Ste-Foy, ☎ 418/525–3786) is open on Saturday 9:30–2. For currency exchange, **Echange de Devises Montréal** (⊠ 12 rue Ste-Anne, Québec, ☎ 418/694–1014) is open September–mid-June, daily 9–5, and mid-June–Labor Day, daily 8:30–7:30.

Museum hours are typically 10–5, with longer evening hours during summer months. Most are closed on Monday.

Shopping hours are Monday through Wednesday 9:30–5:30, Thursday and Friday 9:30–9, Saturday 9:30–5, and Sunday noon–5. Stores tend to stay open later during summer months.

In winter, many attractions and shops change their hours; visitors are advised to call ahead.

Road Conditions

☎ 418/643–6830 (Nov.–Apr.).

Travel Agency

Inter-Voyage (⊠ 1095 rue de l'Amérique Française, ☎ 418/524–1414) is on the first floor of the Édifice Bon Pasteur (Bon Pasteur Building), near the Parliament. It's open weekdays 8:30–5.

Visitor Information

Québec City Region Tourism and Convention Bureau has two tourist information centers, both of which are open year-round:

Québec City (⊠ 60 rue d'Auteuil, ☎ 418/692–2471). The office is open June–early September, daily 8:30–8; early September–mid-October, daily 8:30–5:30; mid-October–mid-April, weekdays 9–5; and mid-April–May, weekdays 8:30–5:30.

Ste-Foy (⊠ 3005 blvd. Laurier, near Québec and Pierre-Laporte bridges, ☎ 418/651–2882). The office is open June–August, daily 8:30–8; September–mid-October, daily 8:30–6; mid-October–mid-April, daily 9–5; and mid-April–May, daily 8:30–6.

Québec Government Tourism Department (⊠ 12 rue Ste-Anne [Place d'Armes], ☎ 418/643–2280 or 800/363–7777). The office is open fall–winter, daily 9–5, and summer, daily 8:30–7:30.

4 Province of Québec

*The Laurentians, l'Estrie,
Charlevoix, and the
Gaspé Peninsula*

*Québec is set apart by its strong French
heritage, a matter not only of language
but of customs, religion, and political
structure. Defining the land outside the
cities are innumerable lakes, streams,
and rivers; farmlands and villages;
great mountains, such as the
Laurentians with their ski resorts, and
deep forests; and a rugged coastline
along the Gulf of St. Lawrence.*

By Dorothy
Guinan

Updated by
Donna
Nebenzahl

AMONG THE PROVINCES OF CANADA, Québec is set apart by its strong French heritage, a matter not only of language but of customs, religion, and political structure. Québec covers a vast area—almost one-sixth of Canada's total—although the upper three-quarters is only sparsely inhabited. Most of the population lives in the southern cities, especially Montréal (☞ Chapter 2) and Québec City (☞ Chapter 3). Outside the cities, however, you'll find serenity and natural beauty in the province's innumerable lakes, streams, and rivers; in its farmlands and villages; in its great mountains and deep forests; and in its rugged coastline along the Gulf of St. Lawrence. Though the winters are long, there are plenty of winter sports to while away the cold months, especially in the Laurentians, with its many ski resorts.

The first European to arrive in Québec was French explorer Jacques Cartier, in 1534; another Frenchman, Samuel de Champlain, arrived in 1603 to build French settlements in the region, and Jesuit missionaries followed in due course. Louis XIV of France proclaimed Canada a crown colony in 1663, and the land was allotted to French aristocrats in large grants called seigneuries. As tenants, known as habitants, settled upon farms in Québec, the Roman Catholic church took on an importance that went beyond religion. Priests and nuns also acted as doctors, educators, and overseers of business arrangements between the habitants and between French-speaking fur traders and English-speaking merchants. An important doctrine of the church in Québec, one that took on more emphasis after the British conquest of 1759, was "survivance," the survival of the French people and their culture. Couples were told to have large families, and they did—up until the 1950s families with 10 or 12 children were the norm.

Québec's recent threats to secede from the Canadian union are part of a long-standing tradition of independence. Although the British won control of Canada in the French and Indian War, which ended in 1763, Parliament passed the Québec Act in 1774, which ensured the continuation of French civil law in Québec and left provincial authority in the hands of the Roman Catholic church. In general, the law preserved the traditional French-Canadian way of life. Tensions between French- and English-speaking Canada continued throughout the 20th century, however, and in 1974 the province proclaimed French its sole official language, much the same way the provinces of Manitoba and Alberta had taken steps earlier in the century to make English their sole official language. In 1990 the Canadian government failed to add Québec's signature to changes it had brought about in the Canadian Constitution, and in 1992 failed to have its proposed constitutional changes accepted by the Canadian population in a referendum. Today Québec is part of the Canadian union and a signatory to its constitution, but it has not accepted the changes made in that document during the 1980s. Trying to engage French- or English-speaking Canadians in a conversation on politics or the constitution, however, usually brings yawns.

Being able to speak French can make your visit to the province more pleasant—many locals do not speak English. If you don't speak French, arm yourself with a phrase book or at least a knowledge of some basic phrases. It's also worth your while to sample the hearty traditional Québécois cuisine, for this is a province where food is taken seriously.

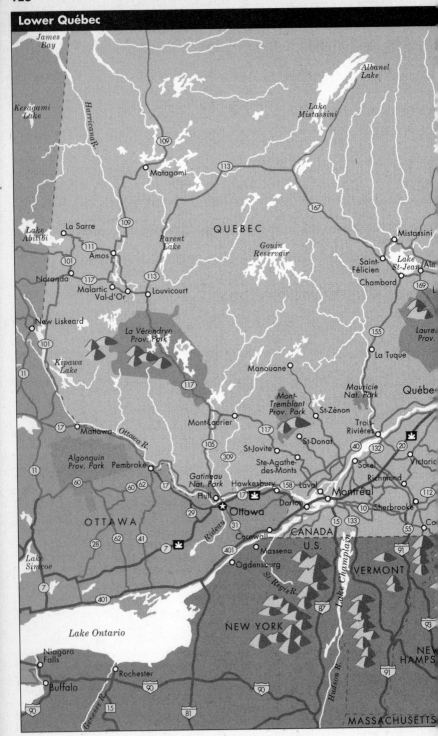

James Bay

Kesagami Lake

Harricana R.

109

Matagami

113

Albanel Lake

Lake Mistassini

167

QUEBEC

La Sarre

Lake Abitibi

111

Amos

109

Parent Lake

Gouin Reservoir

Mistassini

Saint-Félicien

Lake St-Jean

Alm

101

Noranda

117

Malartic

Val-d'Or

113

Louvicourt

Chambord

169

L

155

New Liskeard

101

La Vérendrye Prov. Park

La Tuque

Kipawa Lake

11

Manouane

Mauricie Nat. Park

Québe

17

Mattawa

Ottawa R.

117

Mont-Laurier

Mont-Tremblant Prov. Park

St-Zénon

Trois-Rivières

Algonquin Prov. Park

Pembroke

11

60

60

62

17

105

309

St-Jovite

St-Donat

40

132

20

Victoric

Gatineau Nat. Park

Ste-Agathe-des-Monts

Sorel

Richmond

112

29

Hull

Hawkesbury

158

Laval

Montréal

Sherbrooke

Ottawa

17

Dorion

10

OTTAWA

28

62

41

31

Rideau

Cornwall

CANADA

U.S.

15

133

55

Co

7

Lake Simcoe

401

Massena

Ogdensburg

St. Regis R.

Lake Champlain

91

VERMONT

7

401

87

NEW YORK

93

Lake Ontario

Niagara Falls

Rochester

90

Hudson R.

91

NEW HAMPS

Buffalo

90

Genesee R.

15

90

81

MASSACHUSETTS

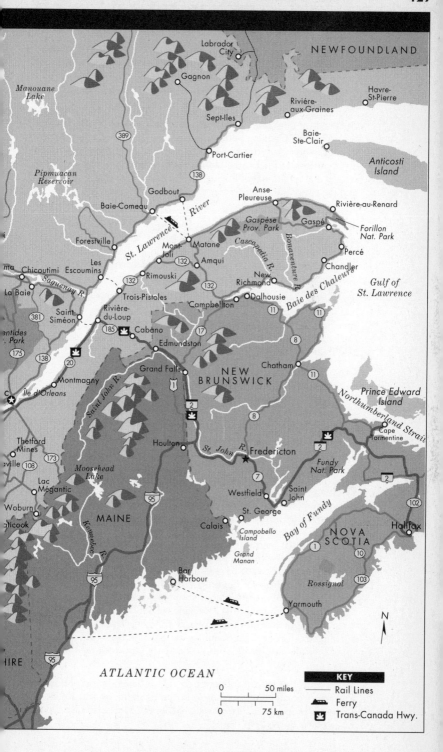

Labrador City

Gagnon

Rivière-aux-Graines

Havre-St-Pierre

NEWFOUNDLAND

Manouane Lake

Sept-Iles

Baie-Ste-Clair

Anticosti Island

389

Port-Cartier

Pipmuacan Reservoir

138

Godbout

St. Lawrence River

Anse-Pleureuse

Rivière-au-Renard

Baie-Comeau

Gaspése Prov. Park

Gaspé

Forillon Nat. Park

Forestville

Mont-Joli

Matane

Cascapédia R.

Percé

Chicoutimi Escoumins

Les Escoumins

132

Amqui

132

New Richmond

Chandler

Gulf of St. Lawrence

ma

La Baie

Saguenay R.

Rimouski

132

Dalhousie

Baie des Chaleurs

Saint Siméon

381

Trois-Pistoles

Campbellton

11

11

Rivière-du-Loup

entides , Park

175

138

185

Cabano

17

8

20

Edmundston

Chatham

11

Montmagny

Grand Falls

NEW BRUNSWICK

Prince Edward Island

Northumberland Strait

Île d'Orleans

1

2

Cape Tormentine

Thetford Mines

aville

108

173

Houlton

St. John R. Fredericton

8

Fundy Nat. Park

2

Moosehead Lake

7

2

Lac Mégantic

Woburn

95

Westfield

Saint John

102

aticook

MAINE

Kennebec R.

Saint John R.

St. George

Calais

Campobello Island

Bay of Fundy

NOVA SCOTIA

Halifax

1

10

Grand Manan

Bar Harbour

Rossignol

103

Yarmouth

95

ATLANTIC OCEAN

N

KEY

—— Rail Lines

Ferry

Trans-Canada Hwy.

0   50 miles

0   75 km

Pleasures and Pastimes

Dining

Whether you enjoy a croissant and espresso at a sidewalk café or order *poutine* (a streetwise mix of homemade French fries—*frites*—and curd cheese and gravy) from a fast-food emporium, you won't soon forget your meals in Québec. There is no such thing as simply "eating out" in the province; restaurants are an integral slice of Québec life.

Outside Montréal and Québec City, you can find both good value and classic cuisine. Cooking in the province tends to be hearty, with such fare as cassoulet, *tourtières* (meat pies), onion soup, and apple pie heading up menus. In the Laurentians, chefs at some of the finer inns have attracted international followings. Local blueberries and maple syrup find their way into a surprising number of dishes.

Granby and its environs are one of Québec's foremost regions for traditional Québécois cuisine, here called *la fine cuisine estrienne*. Specialties include such mixed-game meat pies as *cipaille* and such sweet, salty dishes as ham and maple syrup. Actually, maple syrup—on everything and in all its forms—is a mainstay of Québécois dishes. L'Estrie is one of Québec's main maple-sugaring regions.

In addition to maple sugar, the flavorings cloves, nutmeg, cinnamon, and pepper—spices used by the first settlers—have never gone out of style here, and local restaurants make good use of them in their distinctive dishes. The full country experience of l'Estrie includes warm hospitality at area lodges and inns.

Early reservations are essential. Monday or Tuesday is not too soon to book weekend tables at the best provincial restaurants.

CATEGORY	COST*
$$$$	over $35
$$$	$25–$35
$$	$15–$25
$	under $15

per person, excluding drinks, service, 7% federal tax, and 6.5% provincial tax

Fishing

There are more than 60 outfitters (also known as innkeepers) in the northern Laurentians area, where provincial parks and game sanctuaries abound. Pike, walleye, and lake and speckled trout are plentiful just a three-hour drive north of Montréal. Outfitters provide the dedicated angler with accommodations and every service wildlife and wilderness enthusiasts could possibly require. Open year-round in most cases, their lodging facilities range from the most luxurious first-class resorts to log cabins. As well as supplying trained guides, all offer services and equipment to allow neophytes or experts the best possible fishing in addition to boating, swimming, river rafting, windsurfing, ice fishing, cross-country skiing, hiking, or just relaxing amid the splendor of this still spectacularly unspoiled region.

Lodging

Weary travelers have a full spectrum of accommodation options in Québec: from large resort hotels in the Laurentians and Relais & Châteaux properties in l'Estrie to shared dormitory space in rustic youth hostels near the heart of Gaspé.

CATEGORY	COST*
$$$$	over $125
$$$	$90–$125
$$	$50–$90
$	under $50

Prices are for a standard double room, excluding 10% service charge, 7% federal tax.

River Rafting

Rivière Rouge in the Laurentians rates among the best in North America, so it's not surprising that this river has spawned a miniboom in the sport. Just an hour's drive north of Montréal, the Rouge cuts across the rugged Laurentians through canyons and alongside beaches. From April through October, the adventurous can experience what traversing the region must have meant in the days of the voyageurs, though today's trip, by comparison, is much safer and more comfortable. For outfitter information, see Contacts and Resources at the end of this chapter.

Skiing

CROSS-COUNTRY

Cross-country skiing is popular throughout the Laurentians from December to the end of March, especially at Val David, Val Morin, and Ville l'Estérel. Each has a cross-country ski center and at least a dozen groomed trails.

L'Estrie has more than 900 kilometers (560 miles) of cross-country trails. Three inns—Manoir Hovey, Auberge Hatley, and the Ripplecove Inn—offer the Skiwippi, a week-long package of cross-country treks from one inn to another. The network covers some 32 kilometers (20 miles) of l'Estrie.

DOWNHILL

L'Estrie is a scenic and increasingly popular ski center. Although it is still less crowded and commercialized than the Laurentians, it boasts ski hills on four mountains that dwarf anything the Laurentians have to offer, with the exception of lofty Mont-Tremblant. And, compared to those in Vermont, ski-pass rates are still a bargain. Owl's Head, Mont-Orford, Mont-Sutton, and Bromont have interchangeable lift tickets.

Charlevoix has three main ski areas, with excellent facilities for both the downhill and cross-country skier.

Sugar Huts

Every March the combination of sunny days and cold nights causes the sap to run in the maple trees. *Cabanes à sucre* (sugar huts) go into operation boiling the sap collected from the trees in buckets (now, at some places, complicated tubing and vats do the job). The many commercial shacks scattered over the area host "sugaring offs" and tours of the operation, including the tapping of maple trees, the boiling of the sap in vats, and *tire sur la neige,* when hot syrup is poured over cold snow to give it a taffy consistency just right for "pulling" and eating. A number of cabanes offer hearty meals of ham, baked beans, and pancakes, all drowned in maple syrup. We recommend two cabanes near Sherbrooke.

Exploring Québec

There are two major attractions beyond the city limits of Montréal: l'Estrie (the Eastern Townships), where city folk retreat in summer, and Les Laurentides (the Laurentians), where they escape in winter.

The Laurentians have thousands of miles of unspoiled wilderness and world-famous ski resorts, which can be visited for a weekend, a week, or, for the avid skier, a two-week stay to enjoy the great outdoors. In l'Estrie, rolling hills and farmland make it a major vacation area in both winter and summer, with outdoor activities on ski slopes and lakes and in their provincial parks. Charlevoix is often called the Switzerland of Québec because of its landscape, and the knobby Gaspé Peninsula is where the St. Lawrence River meets the Gulf of St. Lawrence.

Great Itineraries

IF YOU HAVE 2 DAYS
Visit the **Basses Laurentides,** or lower Laurentians, which begin almost immediately outside Montréal. Include in your visit one of the historic seigneuries in the region, or buy renowned Oka cheese from the Cistercian Abbey at **Oka.**

IF YOU HAVE 5 DAYS
Add the **Hautes Laurentides,** or Upper Laurentians, to the two-day itinerary, and enjoy the natural surroundings at **St-Jérome**'s Parc Régional de la Rivière-du-Nord and the quaint resort area of **St-Sauveur-des-Monts.**

IF YOU HAVE 10 DAYS
Summer or winter, your visit can begin in the bustling ski town of **St-Sauveur-des-Monts** and end as far away as **Mont-Tremblant.** For the first-time visitor, the hills and resorts around **Morin Heights, Val Morin,** and **Val David,** up to **Ste-Agathe,** form a pleasant hodgepodge of villages, hotels, and inns. If you have kids in tow, drop in to Val David for a visit to the Santa Claus Village, the summer residence of old St. Nick. Your final destination might be **Parc Mont-Tremblant,** a vast wildlife sanctuary of more than 500 lakes and rivers.

When to Tour Québec

The Laurentians are mainly a winter ski destination, but Montréalers can drive up to enjoy the fall foliage or engage in spring skiing and still get home before dark. The only slow periods are early October, when there is not much to do, and June, when there is plenty to do but the area is beset by blackflies.

LES LAURENTIDES

The Laurentians are divided into two major regions—les Basses Laurentides (the Lower Laurentians) and les Hautes Laurentides (the Upper Laurentians). But don't be fooled by the designations; they don't signify great driving distances.

Avid skiers might call Montréal a bedroom community for the Laurentians; just 56 kilometers (35 miles) to the north, they are home to some of North America's best-known ski resorts. The Laurentian range is ancient, dating to the Precambrian era (more than 600 million years ago). These rocky hills are relatively low, worn down by glacial activity, but they include eminently skiable hills, with a few peaks above 2,500 feet. World-famous Mont-Tremblant, at 3,150 feet, is the tallest.

The P'tit Train du Nord made it possible to easily transport settlers and cargo to the Upper Laurentians. It also opened them up to skiing by the turn of the century. Before long, trainloads of skiers replaced settlers and cargo as the railway's major trade. The Upper Laurentians soon became known worldwide as the number-one ski center in North America—a position they still hold today. Initially a winter weekend getaway for Montréalers who stayed at boardinghouses and fledgling resorts while skiing its hills, the Upper Laurentians began attracting an international clientele, especially with the advent of the Canadian National Railway's special skiers' train, begun in 1928. (Its competitor, the Canadian Pacific Railway, jumped on the bandwagon soon after, doubling the number of train runs bringing skiers to the area.)

Ski lodges, originally private family retreats for wealthy city dwellers, were accessible only by train until the 1930s, when the highway was built. Once the road opened up, cottages became year-round family retreats. Today, there is an uneasy alliance between the longtime cottagers and resort-driven entrepreneurs. Both recognize the other's historic role in developing the Upper Laurentians, but neither espouses the other's cause. At the moment, commercial development seems to be winning out. A number of large hotels have added indoor pools and spa facilities, and efficient highways have brought the country closer to the city—45 minutes to St-Sauveur, 1½–2 hours to Mont-Tremblant.

The Lower Laurentians start almost immediately outside Montréal. Considered the birthplace of the Laurentians, this area is rich in historic and architectural landmarks. Beginning in the mid-17th century, the governors of New France, as Québec was then called, gave large concessions of land to its administrators, priests, and top-ranking military, who became known as seigneurs. In the Lower Laurentians, towns like Terrebonne, St-Eustache, Lac-des-Deux-Montagnes, and Oka are home to the manors, mills, churches, and public buildings these seigneurs had built for themselves and their habitants—the inhabitants of these quasi-feudal villages.

The resort vacation area truly begins at St-Sauveur-des-Monts (Exit 60) and extends as far north as Mont-Tremblant, where it turns into a wilderness of lakes and forests best visited with an outfitter. Laurentian guides planning fishing and hunting trips are concentrated around St-Donat near Parc Mont-Tremblant.

To the first-time visitor, the hills and resorts around St-Sauveur, Ste-Marguerite Station, Morin Heights, Val Morin, and Val David, up to Ste-Agathe, form a pleasant hodgepodge of villages, hotels, and inns that seem to blend one into another.

La Seigneurie de Terrebonne

Numbers in the margin correspond to points of interest on the Laurentians map.

❶ *30 km (20 mi) north of Montréal. From Montréal take blvd. Pie-IX to the bridge of the same name then Highway 25 N. Exit at Terrebonne to Hwy. 440.*

La Seigneurie de Terrebonne, one of the most famous seigneuries, is on l'Ile-des-Moulins, about 20 minutes from Montréal.

Governor Frontenac gave the land to Sieur André Daulier in 1673. Terrebonne was maintained by a succession of seigneurs until 1832, when Joseph Masson, the first French-Canadian millionaire, bought it. He and his family were the last seigneurs de Terrebonne; their reign ended in 1883.

Today, Terrebonne offers visitors a bona fide glimpse of the past. Now run by the Corporation de l'Ile-des-Moulins rather than a French aristocrat, the seigneurie's mansions, manors, and buildings have all been restored. Take a walk through Terrebonne's historical center and then stop at the **Centre d'Interprétation Historique de Terrebonne Museum.**

The Laurentians

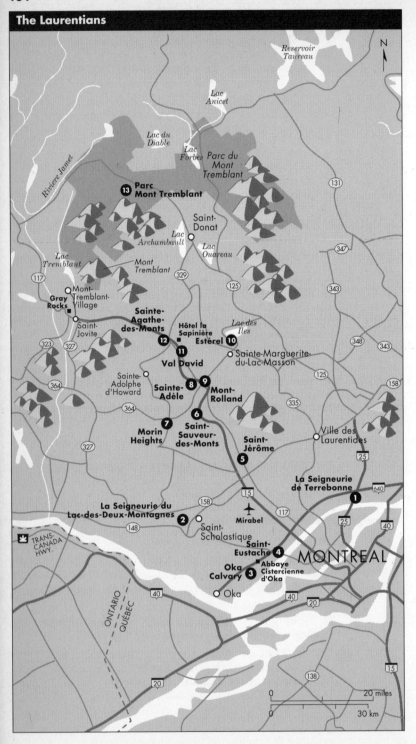

Reservoir Taureau

Lac Anicet

Lac du Diable

Lac Forbes

Parc du Mont Tremblant

Rivière Jamet

13 Parc Mont Tremblant

Saint-Donat

Lac Archambault

Lac Ouareau

Lac Tremblant

Mont Tremblant

329

125

117

Mont-Tremblant-Village

Gray Rocks

Saint-Jovite

323   327

Sainte-Agathe-des-Monts

Hôtel la Sapinière

Lac des Îles

12   **Estérel 10**

11

Val David

Sainte-Marguerite-du-Lac-Masson

348   343

Sainte-Adolphe d'Howard

8 **9**

Sainte-Adèle   **Mont-Rolland**

158

364

335

364

7

Morin Heights

6

Saint-Sauveur-des-Monts

Saint-Jérôme

Ville des Laurentides

327

5

La Seigneurie de Terrebonne

1   640

La Seigneurie du Lac-des-Deux-Montagnes

158

2

148

Saint-Scholastique

Mirabel

15

117

125

25

25   40

MONTREAL

Saint-Eustache **4**

Oka Calvary   **3**   **Abbaye Cistercienne d'Oka**

Oka

40

40   20

TRANS-CANADA HWY.

ONTARIO QUÉBEC

40

20

138

15

0   20 miles

0   30 km

It features three exhibits: the Seigneurial Regime; the water, saw, flour, and wool mills of the region that gave the island its name; and the beginning of the Industrial Revolution in Terrebonne. ⊠ *Blvd. des Braves and rue St-Pierre,* ☎ *514/471–0619.* ☞ *Free.* ☉ *Mid-May–late June, Tues.–Sun. 1–5; late June–early Sept., Tues.–Sun. 10–8.*

La Seigneurie du Lac-des-Deux-Montagnes

❷ *30 km (20 mi) west of Montréal. Take Hwy. 13 or 15 North out of Montréal to Hwy. 640 West. Exit from Hwy. 640 West at Hwy. 148. Take this road into the town of St-Scholastique.*

La Seigneurie du Lac-des-Deux-Montagnes, in St-Scholastique, is 40 minutes from Montréal. It was allotted to the Sulpician priests in 1717. Already appointed the seigneurs of the entire island of Montréal, the priests used this as the base from which to establish an Amerindian mission. A highlight of the seigneury is the Sulpicians' seignorial manor on rue Belle-Rivière, erected between 1802 and 1808. The manor was part of the set for the late Claude Jutra's acclaimed film, *Kamouraska,* based on the novel by Québec's prize-winning author Anne Hébert.

Dining and Lodging

$$$ ✕▧ **Hotel du Lac Carling.** This new hotel caters to the athletic crowd: In addition to its sports center, there's a golf course next door, and there's cross-country skiing and downhill skiing nearby. The rooms are done in a rustic theme, and a stay includes breakfast and supper in their award-winning restaurant, the Lis. ⊠ *Rte. 327, Pinehill, Brownsburg, 21 km/13 mi north of St-Scholastique J0V 1A0,* ☎ *514/533–9211 or 800/661–9211,* ℻ *514/533–9197. 100 rooms. Restaurant, bar, pool, sauna, exercise room, racquetball, squash. EP, MAP. AE, DC, MC, V.*

Oka Calvary

❸ *12 km (8 mi) southeast of La Seigneurie du Lac-des-Deux-Montagnes.*

To promote piety among the Amerindians, the Sulpicians erected the Oka Calvary (Stations of the Cross) between 1740 and 1742. Three of the seven chapels are still maintained, and every September 14 since 1870, Québécois pilgrims have congregated here from across the province to participate in the half-hour ceremony that proceeds on foot to the Calvary's summit. A sense of the divine is inspired as much by the magnificent view of Lac-des-Deux-Montagnes as by religious fervor.

In 1887, the Sulpicians gave about 865 acres of their property near the Oka Calvary to the Trappist monks, who had arrived in New France in 1880 from Bellefontaine Abbey in France. Within 10 years they had built their monastery, the **Abbaye Cistercienne d'Oka,** and they transformed this land into one of the most beautiful domains in Québec. The abbey is one of the oldest in North America. Famous for creating Oka cheese, the Trappists established the Oka School of Agriculture, which operated until 1960. Today, the monastery is a noted prayer retreat. The gardens and chapel are open to visitors. ⊠ *1600 chemin d'Oka,* ☎ *514/479–8361.* ☞ *Free.* ☉ *Chapel daily 8–12:15 and 1–8; gardens and boutique weekdays 9:30–11:30 and 1–4:30, Sat. 9–4.*

Kanestake, a Mohawk Indian reserve near Oka, made headlines during the summer of 1990 when a 78-day armed standoff between Mohawk Warriors (the reserve's self-proclaimed police force) and Canadian and provincial authorities took place. The Mohawks of Kanestake said they opposed the expansion of the Oka golf course, claiming the land was stolen from them 273 years before. When the standoff ended peacefully, the golf course was not expanded. As was the case when Indians opposed logging in British Columbia during the early 1990s, the Canadian media turned the affair into a cause célèbre. But the Oka incident, like the others, has since died down.

St-Eustache

4 *25 km (16 mi) northeast of Oka Calvary.*

St-Eustache is another must for history buffs. One of the most important and tragic scenes in Canadian history took place here: the 1837 Rebellion. Since the British conquest of 1759, French Canadians had been confined to preexisting territories while the new townships were allotted exclusively to the English. Adding to this insult was the government's decision to tax all imported products from England, which made them prohibitively expensive. The result? In 1834, the French Canadian Patriot party defeated the British party locally. Lower Canada, as it was then known, became a hotbed of tension between the French and English, with French resistance to the British government reaching an all-time high. Rumors of rebellion were rife, and in December 1837, some 2,000 English soldiers led by General Colborne were sent in to put down the "army" of North Shore patriots by surrounding the village of St-Eustache. Jean-Olivier Chénier and his 200 patriots took refuge in the local church, which Colborne's cannons bombed and set afire. Chénier and 80 of his comrades were killed during the battle, and more than 100 of the town's houses and buildings erected during the seignorial regime were looted and burned down by Colborne's soldiers. Traces of the bullets fired by the English army cannons are visible on the facade of St-Eustache's church at 123 rue St-Louis. Most of the town's period buildings are open to the public. For a guided tour or for a free brochure that serves as a good walking-tour guide, visit the town's **Arts and Cultural Services Center** (✉ 235 rue St-Eustache, ☎ 514/974–5000, Ext. 282). Tours are offered from April until November.

NEED A   Before heading north, stop at **Pâtisserie Grande-Côte** (✉ 367A chemin
BREAK?   de la Grande-Côte, ☎ 514/473–7307) to sample the wares of St-Eustache's most famous bakery and pastry shop.

St-Jérôme

5 *25 km (16 mi) north of St-Eustache.*

Rivaling St-Eustache in Québec's historic folklore is St-Jérôme, in the Upper Laurentians. Founded in 1834, it is today a thriving economic center and cultural hub. It first gained prominence in 1868 when Curé Antoine Labelle became pastor of this parish on the shores of Rivière du Nord. Curé Labelle devoted himself to opening up northern Québec to French Canadians. Between 1868 and 1890, he founded 20 parish towns—an impressive achievement given the harsh conditions of this vast wilderness. But his most important legacy was the famous P'tit Train du Nord railway line, which he persuaded the government to build in order to open St-Jérôme to travel and trade.

Follow St-Jérôme's **promenade,** a 4-kilometer-long (2½-mile-long) boardwalk alongside the Rivière du Nord from rue de Martigny bridge to rue St-Joseph bridge for a walk through the town's history. Descriptive plaques en route highlight episodes of the Battle of 1837. The **Centre d'Exposition du Vieux-Palais** housed in St-Jérôme's old courthouse has changing exhibits of contemporary art, featuring mostly Québec artists.

✉ *185 rue du Palais,* ☎ *514/432–7171.* ✉ *Free.* ☉ *Tues.–Fri. noon–5, weekends 1–5.*

Parc Régional de la Rivière-du-Nord was created as a nature retreat. Trails through the park lead to the spectacular **Wilson Falls** (*chutes*). The **Pavillon Marie-Victorin** has summer weekend displays and workshops devoted to nature, culture, and history. You can hike, bike, cross-country ski, snowshoe, or snow slide; bike and ski rentals are available. ✉ *1051 blvd. International (R.R. 2),* ☎ *514/431–1676.* ✉ *$3 per car.* ☉ *Fall–spring, daily 9–5; summer, daily 9–7.*

St-Sauveur-des-Monts

❻ *25 km (16 mi) north of St-Jérôme.*

St-Sauveur-des-Monts is the focal point for area resorts. It has gone from a 1970s sleepy Laurentian village of 4,000 residents that didn't even have a traffic light to a thriving year-round town attracting some 30,000 cottagers and visitors on weekends. Its main street, rue Principale, once dotted with quaint French restaurants, now boasts *brochetteries,* and the narrow strip is so choked in summertime with cars and tourists that it has earned the sobriquet "Crescent Street of the North," borrowing its name from the well-known, action-filled street in Montréal. Despite all this development, St-Sauveur has managed to maintain some of its charming, rural character.

For those who like their vacations—winter or summer—lively and activity-filled, St-Sauveur is the place where the action rolls nonstop. In winter, skiing is the main thing. (Mont-St-Sauveur, Mont-Avila, Mont-Gabriel, and Mont-Olympia all offer special season passes and programs, and some ski-center passes can be used at more than one center in the region.) From Mont-St-Sauveur to Mont-Tremblant, the area's ski centers (most situated in or near St-Sauveur, Ste-Adèle, Ste-Agathe, and St-Jovite) offer night skiing. All have ski instructors—many are members of the Canadian Ski Patrol Association.

☺ Just outside St-Sauveur, the Mont-St-Sauveur **Water Park** and tourist center will keep children occupied with slides, a giant wave pool, a shallow wading pool, snack bars, and more. The rafting river attracts the older, braver crowd; the nine-minute ride follows the natural contours of steep hills and requires about 12,000 gallons of water to be pumped per minute. The latest attraction is tandem slides where plumes of water flow through figure-eight tubes. ✉ *350 rue St-Denis,* ☎ *514/871–0101 or 800/363–2426.* ✉ *Full day $22, half-day $17, evening (after 5) $9; cost includes access to all activities.* ☉ *June 3–June 21, daily 10–4; June 22–Aug. 25, daily 10–7; Aug. 26–Sept. 2, daily 11–6.*

Dining

$$$ ✕ **Auberge St-Denis.** This classic Québec inn has a fine restaurant serving French cuisine; game is a specialty. Artfully presented dishes are served in one of three dining rooms, one with a huge stone fireplace. Try the *arrivage de gibier,* an assortment of wild game with an exotic fruit sauce. ✉ *61 St-Denis,* ☎ *514/227–4602. Reservations essential. AE, DC, MC, V.*

Nightlife

Les Vieilles Portes (✉ 185 rue Principale, ☎ 514/227–2662) is a popular pub where you can relax, order your favorite beer, and have a bite to eat.

Shopping

Rue Principale has shops, fashion boutiques, and outdoor café terraces decorated with bright awnings and flowers. Housed in a former bank,

Solo Mode (✉ 239B rue Principale, ☎ 514/227–1234) carries such international labels as Byblos. **Les Factoreries St-Sauveur** (✉ 100 rue Guindon, Exit 60 from Hwy. 15, ☎ 514/227–1074) is a factory outlet mall with 12 boutiques. Canadian, American, and European manufacturers sell a variety of goods at reduced prices, from designer clothing to household items.

Morin Heights

❼ *10 km (6 mi) west of St-Sauveur-des-Monts.*

The town's architecture and population reflect its English settlers' origins, and most residents are English-speaking. Morin Heights has escaped the overdevelopment of St-Sauveur but still offers the visitor a good range of restaurants, bookstores, boutiques, and crafts shops to explore. During the summer months, windsurfing, swimming, and canoeing on the area's two lakes are popular pastimes.

There's a new spin on an old sport at **Ski Morin Heights** (✉ Exit 60, Autoroute 15 N, ☎ 514/227–2020 or 800/661–3535), where snowboarding is the latest craze. Although it doesn't have overnight accommodations, Ski Morin Heights has a 44,000-square-foot chalet with hospitality services and sports-related facilities, eateries, après-ski activities, a pub, and a day-care center. There are special ski-lesson programs for children ages 2 and up.

In the summer, vacationers head for the region's golf courses (two of the more pleasant are the 18-hole links at Ste-Adèle and Mont-Gabriel), campgrounds at Val David, Lacs Claude and Lafontaine, and beaches; in the fall and winter, they come for the foliage as well as alpine and Nordic skiing.

The Arts

Théâtre Morin Heights (☎ 514/226–1944) presents productions at a local elementary school during summer. Popular musicals, lighthearted comedies, mysteries, and children's plays are in the repertoire. Reservations are a must.

Lodging

$$ 🏠 **Auberge Swiss Inn.** This moderately priced inn is within 4 kilometers (2½ miles) of Ski Morin Heights, and is a bargain to boot. The Swiss-style chalet exudes coziness, with wood paneling and a fireplace lounge. ✉ *796 Rte. St-Adolphe, J0R 1H0,* ☎ *514/226–2009,* FAX *514/226–5709. 10 rooms. Restaurant, lounge, boating, cross-country skiing. MC, V.*

Ste-Adèle

❽ *12 km (7 mi) north of Morin Heights.*

The busy town of Ste-Adèle is full of gift and Québec-crafts shops, boutiques, and restaurants. It also has an active nightlife, including a few discos.

The reconstructed **Village de Seraphin**'s 20 small homes, grand country house, general store, and church recall the settlers who came to Ste-Adèle in the 1840s. This award-winning historic town also has a train tour through the woods. ✉ *Hwy. 117,* ☎ *514/229–4777.* 🎫 *$8.75.* ☺ *Late May–late June and early Sept.–mid-Oct., weekends 10–5; late June–early Sept., daily 10–5.*

Dining and Lodging

$$$$ ✕ **La Clef des Champs.** This family-owned hillside restaurant, with its gourmet French cuisine and cozy, romantic atmosphere, is tucked away among trees and faces a mountain. Elegant dishes include *noisette d'agneau en feuilleté* (lamb in pastry) and poached salmon in red wine sauce. Top off your meal with the *gâteau aux deux chocolats* (two-chocolate cake). ⊠ *875 chemin Ste-Marguerite,* ☎ *514/229–2857. AE, DC, MC, V. Closed Mon. Oct.–May, except holidays.*

$$$$ ✕⊡ **L'Eau à la Bouche.** This elegant inn has superb service, luxurious
★ appointments, and a terrace with a flower garden. The auberge faces Le Chantecler's ski slopes, so skiing is literally at the door. Tennis, sailing, horseback riding, and a golf course are nearby. The highly recommended restaurant superbly marries nouvelle cuisine and traditional Québec dishes. The care and inventiveness of chef-proprietor Anne Desjardins is extraordinary. Try the marinated salmon and smoked scallops on a bed of julienned cucumber with a blend of mustards, or a warm salad of quail breast, with an emulsion of olive oil and citrus fruit. ⊠ *3003 blvd. Ste-Adèle, J0R 1L0,* ☎ *514/229–2991,* ⁏AX *514/229–7573. 25 rooms. Restaurant, pool. EP, MAP. AE, DC, MC, V.*

$$$$ ⊡ **Le Chantecler.** This Montréaler favorite on Lac Ste-Adèle is nestled at the base of a mountain with 22 downhill ski runs. Skiing is the obvious draw—trails begin almost at the hotel entrance. The condominium units, hotel rooms, and chalets all have a rustic appeal, furnished with Canadian pine. ⊠ *1474 chemin Chantecler, C.P. 1048, J0R 1L0,* ☎ *514/229–3555; in Québec, 800/363–2420;* ⁏AX *514/229–5593. 300 rooms, 20 suites. Restaurant, indoor pool, spa, golf course, beach, tennis, boating. EP, MAP. AE, D, DC, MC, V.*

$$ ⊡ **Auberge aux Croissants.** This inn at the foot of the Laurentian Mountains is only a five-minute drive from Mont-St-Sauveur. Although most rooms have no TV or telephone, such conveniences are found in one of the two cozy lounges, and an impressive buffet-breakfast is included with the price of the room. One room has a whirlpool bath. ⊠ *750 chemin Ste-Marguerite, J0R 1L0,* ☎ *514/229–3838. 13 rooms, 1 suite. 2 lounges, outdoor pool. MC, V.*

Outdoor Activities and Sports

GOLF

Club de Golf Chantecler (⊠ Exit 67, 2520 chemin du Golf, ☎ 514/229–3742) has 18 holes.

Mont-Rolland

❾ *3 km (2 mi) east of Ste-Adèle.*

Mont-Rolland is the jumping-off point for the Mont-Gabriel ski area, about 16 kilometers (10 miles) to the northeast.

Dining and Lodging

$$$ ✕⊡ **Auberge Mont-Gabriel.** At this deluxe resort spread out on a 1,200-acre estate, you can relax in one of the cozy, modern rooms with a view of the valley or be close to nature in one of the log cabins with fireplaces. The dining is superb here. Tennis, golf, and ski-week and -weekend packages are available. ⊠ *Autoroute 15 (Exit 64), J0R 1G0,* ☎ *514/229–3547 or 800/668–5253,* ⁏AX *514/229–7034. 127 rooms, 10 suites. Restaurant, indoor and outdoor pools, 18-hole golf course, 6 tennis courts. EP, MAP. AE, DC, MC, V.*

Nightlife

If live music is what you want, head to **Bourbon Street** (✉ 2045 Rte. 117, ☎ 514/229–2905).

Outdoor Activities and Sports

DELTAPLANING

If white-water rafting isn't adventure enough, there is always delta-planing, in which human and machine become one. The **Vélidelta Free-Flying School** (✉ C.P. 631, ☎ 514/229–6887) offers lessons on free-flying, and the more advanced tricks of the trade you'll need to earn the required deltaplane pilot's license, including flight maneuvers, speed, and turns. Equipment is provided. You can choose a one-day initiation flying lesson, or a four-day course.

SKIING

Ski Mont-Gabriel (☎ 514/227–1100) has 12 superb downhill trails primarily for intermediate and advanced skiers. The most popular runs are the Tamarack and the O'Connell trails for advanced skiers and Ober-gurgl for intermediates.

Estérel

🔟 *12 km (7 mi) north of Mont-Rolland.*

The permanent population of the town of Estérel is a mere 80 souls. But visitors to **Hotel l'Estérel,** a resort off Autoroute 370, at Exit 69, near Ste-Marguerite Station, swell that number into the thousands. Founded in 1959 on the shores of Lac Dupuis, this 5,000-acre domain was bought by Fridolin Simard from Baron Louis Empain. Named Estérel by the baron because it evoked memories of his native village in Provence, Hotel l'Estérel soon became a household word for holiday vacationers in search of a first-class resort area.

Lodging

$$$$ 🏨 **Hôtel l'Estérel.** If this all-inclusive resort were in the Caribbean, it would probably be run by Club Med, given the nonstop activities. Comfortable rooms offer a view of either the lake or the beautiful flower gardens. ✉ *39 blvd. Fridolin Simard, J0T 1E0,* ☎ *514/228–2571 or 800/363–3623,* ꜰᴀx *514/228–4977. 135 rooms. Restaurant, indoor pool, exercise room, tennis courts, 18-hole golf course, beach, marina, downhill and cross-country skiing, ice-skating disco. EP, MAP. AE, DC, MC, V.*

Val David

⑪ *18 km (11 mi) west of Estérel.*

Val David is a rendezvous for mountain climbers, ice scalers, dogsledders, hikers, and summer or winter campers.

� Children know Val David for its **Santa Claus Village.** This is Santa Claus's summer residence, where children can sit upon Santa's knee and speak to him in either French or English. On the grounds is a petting zoo, with goats, sheep, horses, and colorful birds. Bumper boats and games are run here, as well. ✉ *987 rue Morin,* ☎ *819/322–2146.* 🎟 *$7.* ☉ *Late May–early June, weekends 10–6; early June–late Aug., daily 10–6.*

Dining and Lodging

$$$$ ✕🏨 **Hôtel La Sapinière.** Comfortable accommodations are offered in this homey, dark brown frame hotel with its bright country flowers. The rooms, with country-style furnishings and pastel floral accents, come with such luxurious little extras as thick terry-cloth bathrobes and hair dryers. Relax in front of a blazing fire in one of several cozy lounges.

The property is best known for its fine dining room and wine cellar. ✉ *1244 chemin de la Sapinière, J0T 2N0,* ☎ *819/322–2020 or 800/567–6635,* FAX *819/322–6510. 70 rooms. Dining room, lounge. MAP. AE, DC, MC, V.*

Shopping

Val David is a haven for artists, many of whose studios are open to the public. The **Atelier Bernard Chaudron, Inc.** (✉ 2449 chemin de l'Ile, ☎ 819/322–3944), sells hand-shaped and hammered lead-free pewter objets d'art.

Ste-Agathe-des-Monts

⑫ *5 km (3 mi) north of Val David, 96 km (60 mi) northwest of Montréal.*

Overlooking Lac des Sables is Ste-Agathe-des-Monts, the largest commercial center for ski communities farther north.

The **Village du Mont-Castor,** about 1 kilometer (½ mile) north of Ste-Agathe-des-Monts, is an attractive re-creation of a turn-of-the-century Québécois village; more than 100 new homes have been built here in the traditional fashion of full-length logs set *pièce sur pièce* (one upon the other).

Dining and Lodging

$$–$$$ ✕ **Chatel Vienna.** Run by Eberhards Rado and his wife, who is also ★ the chef, this Austrian restaurant serves Viennese and other Continental dishes in a lakeside setting. You may want to try the prize-winning home-smoked trout, served with an herb and spice butter and garden-fresh vegetables. You may also opt for a variety of schnitzels, a sauerkraut plate, or venison. Try the hot spiced wine, Czech pilsner beer, or dry Austrian and other international white wines. A Sunday buffet brunch tempts the palate with approximately 35 dishes and is served from 11:30 until 2 for under $20. ✉ *6 rue Ste-Lucie,* ☎ *819/326–1485. Reservations essential. MC, V.*

$$–$$$ ✕ **Chez Girard.** Excellent French cuisine is the hallmark of this restaurant-auberge on the shores of Lac des Sables. The airy dining room has windows facing the lake and pastel colors that create a soft, romantic atmosphere. Some of the house specialties include *saumon au champagne* (salmon with champagne), rack of lamb with *herbes de Provence,* ostrich patand *magret de canard.* A Sunday brunch is offered for $16.95. ✉ *18 rue Principale Ouest,* ☎ *819/326–0922. Reservations essential. AE, DC, MC, V.*

$$$ ⊡ **Auberge du Lac des Sables.** A favorite with couples, this inn offers a quiet, relaxed atmosphere in a country setting with a magnificent view of Lac des Sables. All rooms have contemporary decor and a balcony. ✉ *230 St-Venant, J8C 2Z7,* ☎ *819/ 326–3994,* FAX *819/326–9159. 19 rooms. Dining room. CP. MC, V.*

$ ⚠ **Au Parc des Campeurs.** This lively resort area attracts campers with this spacious campground. ✉ *Tour du Lac and Rte. 329, J8C 1M9,* ☎ *819/324–0482 or 800/561–7360.*

Outdoor Activities and Sports

BOATING

The **Alouette** touring launch (✉ Municipal dock, rue Principal, ☎ 819/326–3656) has guided tours of Lac des Sables. Sailing is the favorite summer sport, especially during the "24 Heures de la Voile," a weekend sailing competition (☎ 819/326–0457) that takes place each year in June.

Mont-Tremblant

25 km (16 mi) north of Ste-Agathe-des-Monts.

Mont-Tremblant, one of Canada's best-known ski resorts, is also car-racing country. Racing champion Jackie Stewart has called Mont-Tremblant "the most beautiful racetrack in the world." The **Formula 2000 "Jim Russell Championships"** of the Canadian Car Championships (☎ 819/425–2739) take place here on weekends in June, July, August, and September.

❶ The mountain and the hundreds of square miles of wilderness beyond it constitute **Parc Mont-Tremblant.** Created in 1894, this was once the home of the Algonquin Indians, who called this area Manitonga Soutana, meaning "mountain of the spirits." Today it is a vast wildlife sanctuary of more than 500 lakes and rivers protecting about 230 species of birds and animals, including moose, deer, bear, and beaver. In the winter, its trails are used by cross-country skiers, snowshoers, and snowmobile enthusiasts. Moose hunting is allowed in season, and camping and canoeing are the main summer activities.

Dining and Lodging

$$$–$$$$ ✕⊞ **Club Tremblant.** Across the lake from Station Mont-Tremblant, this hotel was built as a private retreat in the 1930s by a wealthy American. The original large, log-cabin lodge is furnished in colonial style, with wooden staircases and huge stone fireplaces. The rustic but comfortable main lodge has excellent facilities and a dining room serving four-star cuisine. Both the main lodge and the 122-unit deluxe condominium complex—fireplaces, private balconies, kitchenettes, and split-level design de rigueur—built just up the hill from the lodge, offer magnificent views of Mont-Tremblant and its ski hills. There is a golf course nearby. ⊠ *av. Cuttle, J0T 1Z0,* ☎ *819/425–2731,* FAX *819/425–9903. 121 rooms. Restaurant, indoor pool, exercise room, swimming, fishing, boating, tennis. EP, MAP. AE, MC, V.*

$$–$$$$ ✕⊞ **Auberge du Coq de Montagne.** Owners Nino and Kay Faragalli have earned a favorable reputation for their auberge on Lac Moore. The cozy, family-run inn is touted for its friendly service, great hospitality, and modern accommodations. Kudos have also been garnered for the great Italian cuisine served up nightly, which also draws a local crowd; reservations are essential. Year-round facilities and activities, on-site or nearby, include canoeing, kayaking, sailboarding, fishing, badminton, tennis, horseback riding, skating, and skiing. ⊠ *2151 chemin Principale, C.P. 208, J0T 1Z0,* ☎ *819/425–3380 or 800/895–3380,* FAX *819/425–7846. 16 rooms. Restaurant, sauna, exercise room, beach. MAP in winter; EP, MAP in summer. AE, MC, V.*

$$$–$$$$ ⊞ **Station Mont-Tremblant.** On 14-kilometer-long (9-mile-long) Lac
★ Tremblant, this is the northernmost resort that is easily accessible in the Upper Laurentians. Accommodations include a rustic lodge and modern condo units with kitchenettes. The partying is lively in winter, with lots of après-ski bars in the hotel and in the immediate area. ⊠ *3005 chemin Principale, J0T 1Z0,* ☎ *819/425–8711 or 800/461–8711,* FAX *819/681–5590. Restaurant, bars, golf course, tennis courts, horseback riding, beach, swimming, windsurfing, sailing, dance club. EP, MAP. AE, MC, V.*

$$–$$$$ ⊞ **Gray Rocks.** This sprawling wood hotel is the oldest ski resort in the Laurentians and has its own private mountain ribboned by 20 ski runs. The modern chalets and condominium units overlook Lac Ouimet. Some of the rooms share baths. Winter ski packages, including cross-country skiing, are good value for the money, as are the summer ten-

nis packages. A private airstrip and seaplane anchorages are available. ⊠ *Rte. 327 N, 525 rue Principale, J0T 1Z0,* ☎ *819/425–2771 or 800/567–6767,* ℻ *819/425–3474. 306 rooms. Restaurant, indoor pool, health club, horseback riding, spa, 22 tennis courts, children's programs. EP, MAP. AE, MC, V.*

$$$ 🏨 **Auberge Villa Bellevue.** This equally venerable and less expensive alternative to Gray Rocks (☞ *above*) is on Lac Ouimet. Supporting its reputation as a family resort, the inn invites children under 18 who share a room with their parents to stay free and pay for meals only during the summer. In winter, weekend packages include transportation to nearby Mont-Tremblant. The hotel has a list of local baby-sitters, and offers a full summer program of children's activities. Accommodations range from hotel rooms to chalets and condominiums. ⊠ *845 rue Principale, J0T 1Z0,* ☎ *819/425–2734 or 800/567–6763,* ℻ *819/425–9360. 86 rooms, 14 suites. Restaurant, indoor pool, tennis courts, exercise room, beach, sailing, windsurfing, waterskiing, children's programs. EP, MAP. AE, DC, MC, V.*

Outdoor Activities and Sports

SKIING

With the longest vertical drop (2,131 feet) in eastern Canada, **Mont-Tremblant** (☎ 819/425–8711 or 819/681–2000) offers 74 downhill trails, 10 lifts, and 90 kilometers (56 miles) of cross-country trails. Downhill beginners favor the 6-kilometer (3-mile) Nansen trail; intermediate skiers head for the Beauchemin run. Experts choose the challenging Flying Mile on the south side and Duncan and Expo runs on the mountain's north side. The speedy Duncan Express is a quadruple chair lift.

L'ESTRIE

L'Estrie (also known as the Eastern Townships) refers to the area in the southeast corner of the province of Québec, bordering Vermont, New Hampshire, and Maine. Its northern Appalachian hills, rolling down to placid lakeshores, were first home to the Abenaki natives, long before "summer people" built their cottages and horse paddocks here. The Abenaki are gone, but the names they gave to the region's recreational lakes remain—Memphremagog, Massawippi, Mégantic.

L'Estrie was populated by United Empire Loyalists fleeing the Revolutionary War and, later, the newly created United States of America, to continue living under the English king in British North America. It's not surprising that l'Estrie is reminiscent of New England with its covered bridges, village greens, white church steeples, and country inns. The Loyalists were followed, around 1820, by the first wave of Irish immigrants—ironically, Catholics fleeing their country's union with Protestant England. Some 20 years later the potato famine sent more Irish pioneers to the townships.

The area became more Gallic after 1850, as French Canadians moved in to work on the railroad and in the lumber industry. Around the turn of the century, English families from Montréal and Americans from the border states discovered the region and began summering at cottages along the lakes. During the Prohibition era, the area attracted even more cottagers from the United States. Lac Massawippi became a favorite summer resort of wealthy families whose homes have since been converted into gracious inns.

Today the summer communities fill up with equal parts French and English visitors, though the year-round residents are primarily French. Nevertheless, the locals are proud of both their Loyalist heritage and Québec roots. They boast of "Loyalist tours" and Victorian gingerbread homes and in the next breath direct visitors to the snowmobile museum in Valcourt, where, in 1937, native son Joseph-Armand Bombardier built the first *moto-neige* (snowmobile) in his garage. (Bombardier's inventions were the basis of one of Canada's biggest industries, supplying New York City and Mexico City with subway cars and other rolling stock.)

Over the past two decades, l'Estrie has developed from a series of quiet farm communities and wood-frame summer homes to a thriving all-season resort area. In winter, skiers flock to eight downhill centers and some 90 kilometers (56 miles) of cross-country trails. By early spring, the sugar huts are busy with the new maple syrup. L'Estrie's southerly location makes this the balmiest corner of Québec, notable for its spring skiing. In summer, boating, swimming, sailing, golfing, and bicycling take over. And every fall the inns are booked solid with "leaf peepers" eager to take in the brilliant foliage.

Granby

Numbers in the margin correspond to points of interest on the L'Estrie (Eastern Townships) and Montérégie map.

🕙 *80 km (50 mi) east of Montréal.*

Granby is the gateway to l'Estrie. This town is best known for its zoo, the **Jardin Zoologique de Granby.** It houses some 800 animals from 225 species. There are two rare snow leopards here on loan from Chicago's Lincoln Park Zoo and New York's Bronx Zoo. The complex includes amusement park rides and souvenir shops as well as a playground and picnic area. ⊠ *347 rue Bourget,* ☎ *514/372–9113.* 🎟️ *$15.* ⊙ *Late May–early Sept., daily 9:30–5; Sept., weekends 9–5.*

Granby is also the townships' gastronomic capital. Each October, the month-long Festival Gastronomique attracts more than 10,000 *gastronomes* who use the festival's "gastronomic passport" to sample the cuisines at several dining rooms. To reserve a passport, contact **Festival Gastronomique de Granby et Région** (⊠ 650 rue Principle, J2G 8L4, ☎ 514/378–7272).

Dining and Lodging

$$$–$$$$ ✕🏨 **Hostellerie les Trois Tilleuls.** This romantic little inn on a quiet country road is a lovely spot to hole up and investigate the surrounding Montérégie region, or to return to after a hard day exploring the big city—Montréal is 20 minutes away. The rooms are modern, and well equipped with hair dryers and magnifying mirrors; each has a balcony or terrace facing the lovely Rivière Richelieu just outside. Packages are available for theatergoers and cross-country skiers, among others. Montréalers come to savor the cuisine of chef Jean-Francois Methot—and in the hopes of taking home one of his recipes. ⊠ *290 Richelieu, St-Marc-sur-Richelieu, J0L 2E0,* ☎ *514/584–2231 or 800/263–2230; in Québec, 800/856–7787;* 🖷 *514/584–3146. 24 rooms, 1 suite. Restaurant, bar, pool, 2 tennis courts, meeting rooms. AE, DC, MC, V.*

Outdoor Activities and Sports

BIKING

Cyclists will find outdoor bliss on the paved l'Estriade path, which links Granby to Waterloo, and the Montérégiade between Granby and Farnham, both 21 km (13 miles) long.

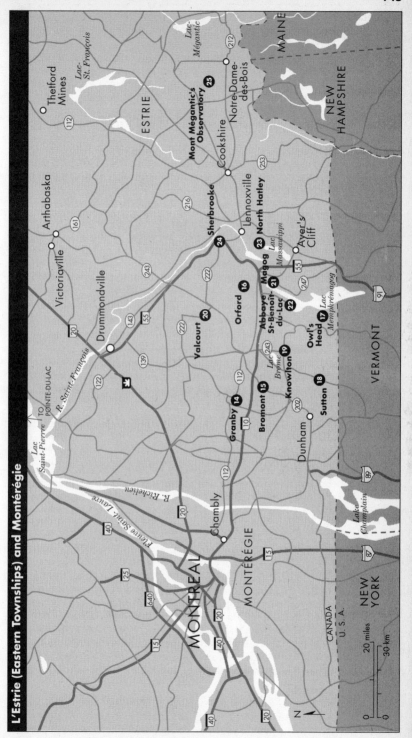

L'Estrie (Eastern Townships) and Montérégie

Bromont

⓯ *8 km (5 mi) south of Granby.*

Bromont, closest to Montréal, is as lively at night as during the day. It offers the only night skiing in l'Estrie and a slope-side disco, Le Bromontais, where the après-ski action continues into the night. Bromont and Orford are *stations touristiques* (tourist centers), meaning that they offer a wide range of activities in all seasons—boating, camping, golf, horseback riding, swimming, tennis, water parks, trail biking, canoeing, fishing, hiking, cross-country and downhill skiing, and snowshoeing. As the former Olympic equestrian site, Bromont is horse country, and every year in late June it holds a riding festival (☎ 514/534–3255). **Bromont Aquatic Park** (✉ Exit 78 from Autoroute 10, ☎ 514/534–2200) is a water-slide park.

Lodging

$$$–$$$$ 🏨 **Le Château Bromont Resort Spa.** Massages, electropuncture, algae wraps, facials, and aromatherapy are just a few of the pampering services at this European-style resort spa. Rooms are large and comfortable, with contemporary furniture, but those facing the Atrium are a little somber. L'Equestre Bar, named for Bromont's equestrian interests, has a cocktail hour and live entertainment. ✉ *90 rue Stanstead, J0E 1L0,* ☎ *514/534–3433, 800/304–3433,* FAX *514/534–0514. 147 rooms. Restaurant, bar, indoor pool, sauna, spa, hot tubs, squash, racquetball, badminton. EP, MAP. AE, D, DC, MC, V.*

Outdoor Activities and Sports

BIKING, CANOEING, AND HORSEBACK RIDING

Base de Plein Air Davignon (✉ 319 chemin Gale, ☎ 514/534–2277 or 800/363–8952) rents mountain bikes, canoes, and horses.

SKIING

Bromont (☎ 514/534–2200), which has 22 trails, was the site of the 1986 World Cup.

Shopping

Factory outlet shopping is gaining popularity in l'Estrie—especially in Bromont, where **Les Versants de Bromont** (✉ 120 blvd. Bromont, Exit 78 from Hwy. 10, ☎ 819/843–8300) houses 27 boutiques. Shoppers can save between 30% and 70% on items carrying such national and international labels as Liz Claiborne, Vuarnet, and Oneida.

Orford

⓰ *25 km (16 mi) northeast of Bromont.*

Orford's regional park is the site of an annual arts festival highlighting classical music, pops, and chamber orchestra concerts. Since 1951, thousands of students have come to the **Orford Arts Center** (✉ Box 280, ☎ 819/843–3981; in Canada May–Aug., 800/567–6155) to study and perform classical music in the summer. Canada's internationally celebrated Orford String Quartet originated here. Festival Orford also includes jazz and folk music.

Lodging

$$$ 🏨 **Auberge Estrimont.** An exclusive complex in cedar combining hotel rooms, condos, and larger chalets, Auberge Estrimont is close to ski hills, riding stables, and golf courses. Every room, whether in the hotel or in an adjoining condo unit, has a fireplace and a private balcony. ✉ *44 av. de l'Auberge, C.P. 98, Orford-Magog J1X 3W7,* ☎ *819/843–1616 or 800/567–7320,* FAX *819/843–4909. 76 rooms, 7 suites. Restau-*

rant, bar, indoor and outdoor pools, hot tub, sauna, tennis, exercise room, squash, racquetball. AE, DC, MC, V.

Outdoor Activities and Sports
SKIING

Mont-Orford Ski Area (☎ 819/843–6548), at the center of a provincial park, offers plenty of challenges for alpine and cross-country skiers, from novices to veterans. It has 41 trails and the steepest drop of all area ski resorts.

Owl's Head

⓱ *25 km (16 mi) south of Magog.*

Owl's Head Ski Area (☎ 514/292–3342) is a mecca for skiers looking for fewer crowds. It has 27 trails and a 4-kilometer (2½-mile) intermediate run, the longest in l'Estrie. Aside from superb skiing, Owl's Head has tremendous scenery. From the trails you can see nearby Vermont and Lac Memphrémagog. (You might even see the lake's legendary sea dragon, said to have been sighted around 90 times since 1816.)

Sutton

⓲ *40 km (25 mi) southwest of Magog.*

Sutton is a well-established community with crafts shops, cozy eateries, and bars (La Paimpolaise is a favorite among skiers).

The Arts
Arts Sutton (⊠ 7 rue Academy, ☎ 514/538–2563) is a long-established mecca for the visual arts.

Lodging
$$–$$$ 🏠 **Auberge la Paimpolaise.** This auberge is right on Mont-Sutton, 50 feet from the ski trails. Nothing fancy is offered, but the location is hard to beat. Rooms are simple, comfortable, and clean, with a woodsy appeal. All-inclusive weekend ski packages are available. A complimentary breakfast is served. ⊠ *615 rue Maple, J0E 2K0,* ☎ *514/538–3213 or 800/263–3213,* 🖷 *514/538–3970. 28 rooms. EP, MAP. AE, MC, V.*

Outdoor Activities and Sports
BICYCLING

Vélo Sutton (⊠ 33 rue Principale Nord, ☎ 819/538–2561) rents bicycles.

GOLF

Reservations must be made in advance at **Les Rochers Bleus** (⊠ 550 Rte. 139, ☎ 514/538–2324), an 18-hole course.

SKIING

Mont-Sutton (☎ 514/538–2339), where you pay to ski by the hour, has 53 trails. This ski area attracts a diehard crowd of mostly Anglophone skiers from Québec. It's also one of the area's largest resorts, with trails that plunge and wander through pine, maple, and birch trees slope-side.

Knowlton

⓳ *15 km (9 mi) northeast of Sutton.*

Along the shore of Lac Brome is the village of Knowlton, a pleasant place to shop for antiques and gifts. In summer check to see what's
★ playing at Knowlton's popular **Théâtre Lac Brome** (☞ *below*). In win-

ter many Montréalers come here to ski at **Glen Mountain** (⊠ off Rte. 243, ☎ 514/243–6142).

The Arts

Théâtre Lac Brome (☎ 514/243–0361) is an English-language theater company that stages productions of classic Broadway and West End hits. The 175-seat, air-conditioned theater is behind Knowlton's popular pub of the same name.

Valcourt

⑳ *32 km (20 mi) north of Knowlton.*

Valcourt is the birthplace of the inventor of the snowmobile, so it follows that this is a world center for the sport, with more than 1,500 kilometers (1,000-plus miles) of paths cutting through the woods and meadows. The **Musée Joseph-Armand Bombardier** displays this innovator's many inventions. ⊠ *1001 av. Joseph-Armand Bombardier,* ☎ *514/532–5300.* ⚏ *$5.* ☉ *Late June–Aug., daily 10–5:30; Sept.–late June, Tues.–Sun. 10–5.*

Lodging

$$$ ⊞ **L'Auberge du Lac St-Pierre.** This small, modern hotel on the lake
★   near Trois Rivières, halfway between Montréal and Québec City, has high ratings for cuisine and accommodations. The luxurious rooms are done in soothing pastels, with televisions, telephones, and whirlpool baths in many. Lake views from the dining room, the conservatory, and many of the guest rooms add to the tranquillity. It's an ideal stop on a tour of southern Québec. ⊠ *Box 10, 1911 rue Notre-Dame (Rte. 138), Pointe-du-Lac (about 160 km/100 mi north of Valcourt) G0X 1Z0,* ☎ *819/377–5971 or 888/377–5971,* ℻ *819/377–5579. 30 rooms. Restaurant, pool, tennis court, business services, meeting rooms. EP, MAP. AE, DC, MC, V.*

Magog

㉑ *32 km (20 mi) south of Valcourt.*

At the northern tip of Lac Memphrémagog, a large body of water reaching into northern Vermont, lies the bustling resort town of Magog. A once sleepy village, the town has grown into a four-season resort destination. Two sandy beaches, great bed-and-breakfasts, hotels and restaurants, boating, ferry rides, bird-watching, sailboarding, aerobics, horseback riding, and snowmobiling are just some of the activities offered.

The streets downtown are lined with century-old homes and churches, some of which have been converted into stores, galleries, and theaters.

NEED A   **La Source** (⊠ 420 rue Principale Ouest, ☎ 819/843–0319) is a small
BREAK?   tearoom with an array of cheeses, pâtés, and Swiss chocolates.

Dining and Lodging

$$ ✕ **Auberge de l'Étoile Sur-le-lac.** This popular restaurant serves three meals a day in casual surroundings. Its somber interior, decorated in dark colors, is brightened by the windows facing Lac Memphrémagog. House specialties include wild game and Swiss fondue. ⊠ *1150 rue Principale Ouest,* ☎ *819/843–6521. Reservations essential. AE, DC, MC, V.*

$$$ ✕⊞ **Ripplecove Inn.** The Ripplecove vies with the Hatley and Hovey inns for best in the region. Its accommodations, service, and dining room are consistently excellent. The English pub–style room combines classical and French cuisine in such dishes as *petit timbale de sole et* *saumon fumé a l'algue nori* (timbale of sole and smoked salmon with seaweed), and the *gâteau de foie de volaille à la creme de porto* (gâteau of chicken livers in a port-flavored sauce). ⊠ *700 chemin Ripplecove, C.P. 246, Ayer's Cliff (11 km/7 mi south of Magog) J0B 1C0,* ☎ *819/ 838–4296 or 800/668–4296,* ⊠ *819/838–5541. 25 rooms with bath. Restaurant, 2 beaches, pool, windsurfing, sailing, cross-country skiing, meeting facilities. MAP. AE, MC, V.*

$$$–$$$$ 🏨 **Centre de Santé Eastman.** This four-season resort offers respite to the bone-weary and bruised skier. Accommodations are in three houses: the rustic Maison Canadienne, the country-style Volet Bleu, and the modern Pavillon Kaufman. There are holistic spa treatments, massage, and stretch workouts. Top off an already healthy day with fine vegetarian cuisine or light seafood and chicken dishes in the dining room. ⊠ *895 chemin Diligence, Eastman (15 km/9 mi west of Magog) J0E 1P0,* ☎ *514/297–3009 or 800/665–5272,* ⊠ *514/297–3370. 19 rooms. Dining room, spa, cross-country skiing. MAP. AE, MC, V.*

$$$ 🏨 **Club Azur.** Fireplaces warm these condominiums, many of which have kitchens. The units accommodate from two to eight people. ⊠ *81 rue des Jardins, R.R. 4, J1X 5X8,* ☎ *819/868–6681 or 800/823– 6681,* ⊠ *819/868–4484. Indoor and outdoor pool, badminton, 3 tennis courts, ice-skating, cross-country skiing. MC, V.*

Nightlife and the Arts

Théâtre le Vieux Clocher (⊠ 64 rue Merry Nord, ☎ 819/847–0470) presents pop and rock concerts, and occasionally French plays.

Magog is lively after dark, with a variety of bars, cafés, bistros, and great restaurants to suit every taste and pocketbook. **La Grosse Pomme** (⊠ 270 rue Principale Ouest, ☎ 819/843–9365) is a multilevel complex with huge video screens, dance floors, and restaurant service. An outdoor summer terrace has live entertainment. **Au Chat Noir** (⊠ 266 rue Principale Ouest, ☎ 819/843–4337) features jazz music, dinner theater, and dancing. **The Auberge Orford** (⊠ 20 rue Merry Sud, ☎ 819/843–9361) is another outdoor summer terrace that doesn't stop. There's often live entertainment.

Shopping

Stroll along Magog's **rue Principale** for a look at boutiques, art galleries, and crafts shops with local artisans' work. **Amandine** (⊠ 499 rue Principale Ouest, ☎ 819/847–1346) is a lovely gift shop with unusual dishes, bath items, and Belgian chocolates.

Abbaye St-Benoît-du-Lac★

㉒ *21 km (13 mi) west of Magog. From Magog to St-Benoît, take the road to Austin and then follow the signs for the side road to the abbey.*

This abbey's slender bell tower juts up above the trees like a fairy-tale castle. Built on a wooded peninsula in 1912 by the Benedictines, the abbey is home to some 60 monks, who sell apples and apple cider from their orchards as well as distinctive cheeses: Ermite, St-Benoît, and ricotta. Gregorian masses are sung daily and are open to the public (☎ 819/843–4080). The abbey was once known as a favorite retreat for some of Québec's best-known politicians.

North Hatley

㉓ *15 km (9 mi) east of Magog.*

North Hatley, the town on the tip of Lac Massawippi, is home to **The Pilsen** (☎ 819/842–2971), Québec's earliest microbrewery. Although the beer is no longer brewed on-site, the Pilsen still serves Massawippi pale ale on tap. The pub also has great food, loads of atmosphere, and a convivial crowd year-round.

The Arts

★ **The Piggery** (✉ Box 390, ☎ 819/842–2432 or 819/842–2431), a theater that was once a pig barn, reigns supreme in l'Estrie cultural life. The venue is renowned for its risk taking, often presenting new plays by Canadian playwrights and even experimenting with bilingual productions. The season runs June–August.

Naive Arts Contest (✉ Galerie Jeannine-Blais, 100 rue Main, ☎ 819/842–2784) shows the work of more than 100 painters of naive art from some 15 countries. This show takes place every two years; the next year is 1998.

L'Association du Festival du Lac Massawippi (☎ 819/563–4141) presents an annual antiques and folk-arts show in July. The association also sponsors a series of classical music concerts performed at the Eglise Ste-Catherine in North Hatley, on Sundays starting in late April and continuing through June.

Dining and Lodging

$$$$ ✕⛫ **Manoir Hovey.** Overlooking the perfectly pristine Lac Massawippi,
★   this retreat has the ambience of a private estate, while offering the activities of a resort. Built in 1900, Hovey Manor resembles George Washington's home at Mount Vernon, Virginia. Each wallpapered room has personality, with a mix of antiques and newer wood furniture, richly printed fabrics, and lace trimmings; many have fireplaces and private balconies. The dining room serves exquisite Continental and French cuisine; if in season, try warm roulades of Swiss chard with spring lamb, preserved apricots, and roasted hazelnuts or grilled tenderloin of beef marinated with juniper berries and a sauce of tarragon and horseradish. Dinner, breakfast, and most sports facilities are included in room rates. ✉ *C.P. 60, J0B 2C0*, ☎ *819/842–2421 or 800/661–2421* ⅎⱯⅩ *819/842–2248. 40 rooms, 1 suite, 1 4-bedroom cottage. Dining room, 2 bars, pool, tennis court, 2 beaches, ice fishing, mountain bikes, cross-country skiing, library, meeting rooms. MAP. AE, DC, MC, V.*

$$$ ✕⛫ **Auberge Hatley.** Chef Alain Labrie specializes in regional dishes at this restaurant/inn, which has three times been voted the best in Québec. The menu changes seasonally, but the rich foie gras and *canard de Barbarie* are recommended if available. The antique yellow room has a panoramic view of Lake Massawippi; linger over your coffee or sip your selection from the wine cellar, which has more than 3,000 bottles. Guest rooms in this 1903 country manor are charmingly decorated; some have a whirlpool and a fireplace. ✉ *325 chemin Virgin, C.P. 330, J0B 2C0*, ☎ *819/842–2451*, ⅎⱯⅩ *819/842–2907. 25 rooms. Restaurant. MAP. AE, DC, MC, V. Closed last 2 wks in Nov.*

Sherbrooke

㉔ *16 km (10 mi) north of North Hatley.*

The region's unofficial capital and largest city is Sherbrooke, named in 1818 for Canadian Governor General Sir John Coape Sherbrooke. Founded by Loyalists in the 1790s along the St-François River, it has a number of art galleries, including the **Musée des Beaux-Arts de Sherbrooke** (✉ 174 rue du Palais, ☎ 819/821–2115). This gallery is open Tuesday and Thursday–Sunday 1–5 and Wednesday 1–9. Admission is $2; the charge is waived on Wednesday evening. The **Sherbrooke Tourist**

Information Center (⊠ 48 rue Dépôt, ☎ 819/564–8331) conducts city tours from late June through early September. Call for reservations.

The Arts

The **Centennial Theatre** (☎ 819/822–9692) at Bishop's University in Lennoxville, 5 kilometers (3 miles) south of Sherbrooke, presents a roster of international, Canadian, and Québécois jazz, classical, and rock concerts, as well as dance, mime, and children's theater.

Dining and Lodging

$$ ✕ **La Falaise St-Michel.** Chef and part-owner Patrick Laigniel offers up French cuisine in a warm redbrick and wood room that takes off any chill even before you sit down. A large selection of wines complements the table d'hôte. ⊠ *Rue Webster and Wellington North, behind Banque National,* ☎ *819/346–6339. AE, DC, MC, V.*

$$ ✕ **Restaurant au P'tit Sabot.** Specialties include dishes featuring wild boar, quail, and bison. The cozy room is a pleasant refuge from the bustle of Sherbrooke's main drag. With a piano in the corner, pink decor, and room for only 35 patrons, a romantic atmosphere prevails. ⊠ *1410 rue King Ouest,* ☎ *819/563–0262. AE, DC, MC, V.*

$ 🏨 **Bishop's University.** If you are on a budget, this is a great place to stay. The prices can't be beat, and the location near Sherbrooke is good for touring. The university's grounds are lovely, with a river cutting through the campus and its golf course. Much of the architecture is reminiscent of stately New England campuses. Visit the university's 136-year-old chapel, and also look for the butternut tree, an endangered species in l'Estrie. Facilities include a sports complex with an Olympic-size indoor pool and tennis courts. Reservations for summer guests are accepted as early as September, so it's a good idea to book in advance. ⊠ *Rue College, Lennoxville (5 km/3 mi south of Sherbrooke) J1M 1Z7,* ☎ *819/822–9651,* ℻ *819/822–9615. 564 beds. Indoor pool, tennis courts, exercise room. MC, V. Closed Sept.–mid May.*

Sugar Huts

There are two sugar huts near Sherbrooke that give tours of their maple-syrup producing operations in the spring: It's best to call before visiting. **Erablière Patoine** (⊠ 1105 chemin Beauvoir, ☎ 819/563–7455) is in Fleurimont. **Bolduc** (⊠ 525 chemin Lower, ☎ 819/875–3022) is in Cookshire.

Mont-Mégantic's Observatory

㉕ *74 km (46 mi) east of Sherbrooke.*

Both amateur stargazers and serious astronomers are drawn to this site, in a beautifully wild and mountainous part of l'Estrie. The observatory is at the summit of l'Estrie's second-highest mountain (3,601 feet), whose northern face records annual snowfalls rivaling any in North America. The observatory is a joint venture by the Université de Montréal and Université Laval. Its powerful telescope allows resident scientists to observe celestial bodies 10 million times smaller than the human eye can detect. There's a welcome center, called the Astrolab, on the mountain's base, where visitors can view an exhibition, a mulitmedia show, and learn about the night sky. ⊠ *189 Route du Parc, Notre-Dame-des-Bois,* ☎ *819/888–2822.* 🎫 *Astrolab $8, night tour to summit $8.* ☉ *Astrolab late June–Labor Day, daily 10–6; night tour to summit late June–Labor Day, daily 8 PM.*

Dining and Lodging

$$$ ⬚ **Aux Berges de l'Aurore.** Although this tiny bed-and-breakfast has attractive furnishings and spectacular views, as it sits at the foot of Mont-Mégantic, the draw here is the inn's cuisine. The award-winning restaurant has a five-course meal with ingredients supplied from the inn's huge fruit, vegetable, and herb garden, as well as wild game from the surrounding area: boar, fish, hare, and quail. ⬚ *51 chemin de l'Observatoire, Notre-Dame-des-Bois,* ☎ *819/888–2715. MC, V. Closed Jan.–May.*

CHARLEVOIX

Stretching along the St. Lawrence River's north shore, east of Québec City from Ste-Anne-de-Beaupré to the Saguenay River, Charlevoix embraces mountains rising from the sea and a succession of valleys, plateaus, and cliffs cut by waterfalls, brooks, and streams. The roads wind into villages of picturesque houses and huge tin-roof churches.

New France's first historian, the Jesuit priest François-Xavier de Charlevoix, gave his name to the region. Charlevoix (pronounced sharle-vwah) was first explored by Jacques Cartier, who landed in 1535, although the first colonists didn't arrive until well into the 17th century. They developed a thriving shipbuilding industry, specializing in the sturdy schooner they called a *goelette,* which they used to haul everything from logs to lobsters up and down the coast in the days before rail and paved roads. Shipbuilding has been a vital part of the provincial economy until recent times, though wrecked and forgotten goelettes are visible from many beaches in the region.

Ste-Anne-de-Beaupré

Numbers in the margin correspond to points of interest on the Charlevoix map.

26 *33 km (20 mi) east of Québec City.*

Charlevoix begins in the tiny town of Ste-Anne-de-Beaupré (named for Québec's patron saint). Each year more than a million pilgrims visit the
★ region's most famous religious site, the **Basilique Ste-Anne-de-Beaupré,** (☞ Chapter 3), which is dedicated to the mother of the Virgin Mary.

At the **Cap Tourmente Wildlife Reserve,** about 8 kilometers (5 miles) northeast of Ste-Anne-de-Beaupré, more than 100,000 greater snow geese gather every October and May.

Outdoor Activities and Sports

SKIING

Parc du Mont-Ste-Anne (☞ Chapter 3), outside Québec City, is on the World Cup downhill ski circuit. **Le Massif** (⬚ 1350 rue Principale, C.P. 47, Petite Rivière St-François, ☎ 418/632–5876) is a three-peak ski resort that has the province's highest vertical drop—2,500 feet.

WHALE-WATCHING

Whale-watching cruises (in St-Joachim, ☎ 418/827–3776) are highly recommended. You can, on occasion, spot whales, seals, and dolphins from ferries and from land, so nature lovers are encouraged to bring their binoculars.

Baie-St-Paul

27 *60 km (37 mi) northeast of Ste-Anne-de-Beaupré.*

Baie-St-Paul, Charlevoix's earliest settlement after Beaupré, is popular with hang gliders and artists. Here, the high hills circle a wide plain

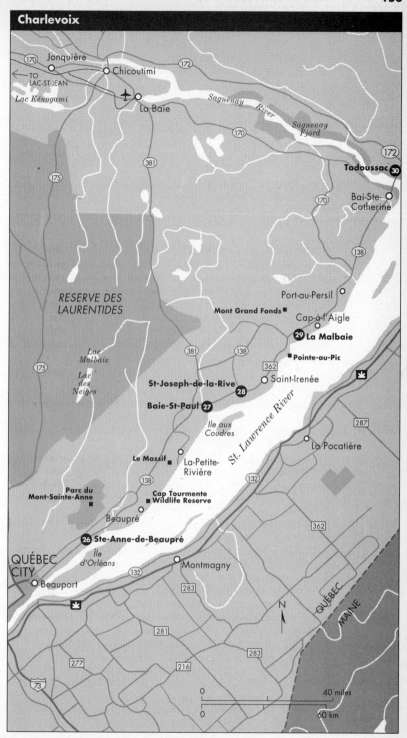

170 Jonquière

172

← TO
LAC-ST-JEAN

Chicoutimi

Lac Kénogami

La Baie

Saguenay River

170

Saguenay Fjord

381

172

175

Tadoussac 30

170

Bai-Ste-
Catherine

138

*RESERVE DES
LAURENTIDES*

Port-au-Persil

Mont Grand Fonds■

Cap-à-l'Aigle

29 **La Malbaie**

*Lac
Malbaie*

381

138

■ Pointe-au-Pic

175

*Lac
des
Neiges*

362

Saint-Irenée

St-Joseph-de-la-Rive 28

287

Baie-St-Paul 27

*Ile aux
Coudres*

St. Lawrence River

Le Massif ■

La-Petite-
Rivière

La Pocatière

138

132

*Parc du
Mont-Sainte-Anne* ■

Cap Tourmente
■ Wildlife Reserve

362

Beaupré

**QUÉBEC
CITY**

26 **Ste-Anne-de-Beaupré**

*Île
d'Orléans*

Beauport

132

Montmagny

283

287

N

QUÉBEC
MAINE

281

277

216

283

73

0   40 miles

0   60 km

holding the village beside the sea. Many of Québec's greatest landscapists portray the area, and their work is on display year-round at the **Centre d'Art Baie-St-Paul** (⊠ 4 rue Ambroise-Fafard, ☎ 418/435–5654) and the **Centre d'Exposition de Baie-St-Paul** (⊠ 23 rue Ambroise-Fafard, ☎ 418/435–3681).

Dining and Lodging

$$$ ✕ **Auberge la Maison Otis.** Try creative Québec-oriented French cuisine like *ballotine de faisan* (pheasant), stuffed with quail and served in a venison sauce followed by a delicious assortment of cheeses. The restaurant is a 150-year-old Norman-style house, elegantly decorated in pastel pink, centered around a huge stone fireplace. ⊠ *23 rue St-Jean-Baptiste,* ☎ *418/435–2255. MC, V.*

$$ ✕ **Mouton Noir.** French cuisine is served amid flowers on the terrace in the summer or in a cozy rustic setting in the winter. You'll always find a varied menu, with pasta, fish, and meat, for very reasonable prices. ⊠ *43 rue Ste-Anne,* ☎ *418/435–3075. AE, MC, V.*

$$$$ ⌂ **Auberge la Maison Otis.** This inn offers calm and romantic ac-
★   commodations in three buildings, including an old stone house, in the center of the village. Some of the 30 country-style rooms have whirlpools, fireplaces, and antique furnishings. Summer lunches are served amid flowers on an outdoor terrace. Skiing and ice-skating are possible nearby. ⊠ *23 rue St-Jean-Baptiste, G0A 1B0,* ☎ *418/435–2255,* ℻ *418/435–2464. 30 rooms with bath, 4 suites. Restaurant, lounge, piano bar, air-conditioning, indoor pool, sauna, health club. MAP available. AE, MC, V.*

En Route   From Baie-St-Paul, you can take the open, scenic coastal drive (Route 362) or the faster Route 138 to Pointe-au-Pic, La Malbaie, and Cap-à-l'Aigle. This section of Route 362 has memorable views of rolling hills—green, white, or ablaze with fiery hues, depending on the season—meeting the broad expanse of the "sea" as the locals like to call the St. Lawrence estuary.

St-Joseph-de-la-Rive

❷❽   *15 km (9 mi) northeast of Baie-St-Paul.*

A secondary road leads sharply down into St-Joseph-de-la-Rive, with its line of old houses hugging the mountain base on the narrow shore road. The town is host to peaceful inns and inviting restaurants, such as l'Auberge sous les Pins (⊠ 362 rue F.A. Savard, Box 4, G0A 3Y0, ☎ 418/635–2583), which means "inn under the pines." Nearby Papeterie St-Gilles (⊠ 304 rue F.A. Savard, ☎ 418/635–2430) produces unusual handcrafted stationery, using a 17th-century process. Across rue F.A. Savard from Papeterie St-Gilles is the small **Exposition Maritime** (Maritime Museum), which commemorates the days of the St. Lawrence goelettes.

OFF THE   **ILE AUX COUDRES –** From St-Joseph you can catch a ferry (☎ 418/438–
BEATEN PATH   2743) to Ile aux Coudres, an island where Jacques Cartier's men gathered *coudres* (hazelnuts) in 1535. Since then, the island has produced many a goelette, and former captains now run several small inns. Larger inns feature folk-dance evenings. Many visitors like to bike around the 16-kilometer (10-mile) island taking in windmills, inns, water mills, and old schooners, as well as boutiques selling paintings and local handicrafts, such as household linen.

Lodging

$$ ⊞ **Hôtel Cap-aux-Pierres.** This hotel provides top-notch accommoda-
★ tions in both a traditionally Canadian main building and a motel sec-
tion open in the summer only. About a third of the rooms have river
views. The restaurant serves a mix of Québec standards and nouvelle
cuisine, and entertainment includes folk dancing on summer Saturday
evenings. ⊠ *246 rue Principale, La Baleine, Ile aux Coudres, G0A 2A0,*
☎ *418/438–2711 or 800/463–5250,* FAX *418/438–2127. 98 rooms.*
Restaurant, bar, indoor and outdoor pool. MAP. AE, DC, MC, V.

La Malbaie

㉙ *35 km (22 mi) northeast of St-Joseph.*

La Malbaie is one of the most elegant and historically interesting re-
sort towns in the province. It was known as Murray Bay in an earlier
era when wealthy Anglophones summered here and in the neighbor-
ing villages of Pointe-au-Pic and Cap-à-l'Aigle. Once called the "sum-
mer White House," this area became popular with both American and
Canadian politicians in the late 1800s when Ottawa Liberals and
Washington Republicans partied decorously through the summer with
members of the Québec judiciary. William Howard Taft built the first
of three summer residences in Pointe-au-Pic in 1894, when he was the
American civil governor of the Philippines. He became the 27th pres-
ident of the United States in 1908, and later chief justice of the Supreme
Court. Locals still fondly remember the Tafts and the parties they
threw in their elegant summer homes.

Now many Taft-era homes serve as handsome inns, guaranteeing an old-
fashioned coddling, with such extras as breakfast in bed, gourmet
meals, whirlpools, and free shuttles to the ski areas in winter. Many serve
lunch and dinner to nonresidents, so you can tour the area going from
one gourmet's delight to the next. The cuisine, as elsewhere in Québec,
is genuine French, rather than a hybrid invented for North Americans.

Musée de Charlevoix traces the region's history as a vacation spot in
a series of exhibits and is developing an excellent collection of local
paintings and folk art. ⊠ *1 rue du Havre, Pointe-au-Pic (3 km/2 mi
south of La Malbaie),* ☎ *418/665–4411.*

The **Casino de Charlevoix,** styled after European casinos, welcomes vis-
itors year-round. The minimum age is 18. ⊠ *183 av. Richelieu,* ☎ *418/
665–5300 or 800/965–5355.* ⊘ *Sun.–Thurs. 10 AM–2 AM, Fri. and
Sat. 10 AM–3 AM.*

The Arts

Domaine Forget is a music and dance academy that presents concerts
on summer evenings by international-caliber musicians, many of whom
are teaching or learning at the school. The Domaine also functions as
a stopover for traveling musicians, who take advantage of its rental
studios. The season runs from the beginning of May through August.
⊠ *St-Irenée (15 km/9 mi south of La Malbaie),* ☎ *418/452–8111 or
418/452–2535,* FAX *418/452–3503.*

Dining and Lodging

$$$$ ✕ **Auberge des 3 Canards.** This inn has made a name for itself in the
region, not only for its accommodations but also for its award-winning
restaurant. The menu may include *gratin d'escargots aux bluets* (snails
with a blueberry and grapefruit sauce baked au gratin) as an appetizer,
and stuffed pheasant—the breasts smothered in mustard sauce and the
legs seasoned with spicy maple sauce—as a main course. Homemade
desserts include *Pomme de l'Ile aux Coudres*—cheese-topped apples with

a touch of honey. Meals are elegantly presented in a rustic setting. The warmth of the natural wood contrasts with the pale and deep blue touches throughout. ☒ *49 côte Bellevue, Pointe-au-Pic (3 km/2 mi south of La Malbaie)*, ☎ *418/665–3761. AE, MC, V.*

$$$–$$$$ ✕ **Auberge sur la Côte.** Simple white tablecloths, natural wood, and stone walls create a rustic setting for fine French cuisine. A house specialty is *agneau de Charlevoix*, lamb seasoned with lemon and thyme, served with fresh vegetables. Lunch is served in summer only, but the dining room is open in the evening year-round. ☒ *205 chemin des Falaises, La Malbaie*, ☎ *418/665–3972. AE, MC, V.*

$$$$ 🏨 **Auberge la Pinsonnière.** An atmosphere of country luxury prevails,
★ and each room is decorated differently; some have fireplaces, whirlpools, and king-size four-poster beds. Rooms offer a commanding view of Murray Bay on the St. Lawrence River. ☒ *124 rue St-Raphael, Cap-à-l'Aigle (3 km/2 mi south of La Malbaie), G0T 1B0*, ☎ *418/665–4431*, FAX *418/665–7156. 21 rooms, 6 suites. 2 restaurants, 3 lounges, indoor pool, sauna, tennis court, beach, spa. MAP. AE, MC, V.*

$$$$ 🏨 **Hôtel Manoir Richelieu.** The Manoir Richelieu, an imposing castle nestled amid trees on a cliff overlooking the St. Lawrence River, has been offering first-class accommodations to vacationers for centuries. It was founded in 1776 as a haven for wealthy travelers. Although still rich in elegance and charm, the resort has adapted to the needs of today's visitor and is now an affordable vacation spot. Whale-watching and snowmobile packages are available. ☒ *181 rue Richelieu, Pointe-au-Pic (3 km/2 mi south of La Malbaie), G0T 1M0*, ☎ *418/665–3703 or 800/463–2613*, FAX *418/665–3093. 372 rooms. Restaurant, indoor and outdoor pools, sauna, golf course, tennis courts, cross-country skiing, snowmobiling. AE, DC, MC, V.*

$$ 🏨 **Les Studios du Domaine.** This unique retreat at the foot of the Charlevoix Mountains facing the St. Lawrence River is a music and dance academy in the summer but is open to tourists during the winter season. Studio apartments, each with one or two bedrooms, and a kitchenette, are available for reasonable prices. In the summer, weekly concerts are open to the public, and Les Studios also offers a Sunday brunch complete with a musical ensemble. Golf, cross-country and downhill skiing, and the Charlevoix casino are all nearby. Concerts are held June–August on Wednesday, Friday, and Saturday at 8:30; admission is $20 per person. Sunday brunch is served 11–2 and costs $22 per person. ☒ *398 chemin les Bains, St-Irenée (15 km/9 mi south of La Malbaie), G0T 1V0*, ☎ *418/452–3535*, FAX *418/452–3503. 28 apartments. MC, V.*

Outdoor Activities and Sports

GOLF

Club de Golf de Manoir Richelieu (☒ 181 av. Richelieu, Pointe-au-Pic, ☎ 418/665–2526 or 800/463–2613) has 18 holes.

SKIING

Mont-Grand Fonds (☒ 1000 chemin des Loisirs, ☎ 418/665–0095) has 14 slopes and 125 kilometers (80 miles) of cross-country trails.

Tadoussac

30 *71 km (44 mi) north of La Malbaie.*

The road, the views, and the villages continue all the way up to Baie-Ste-Catherine, which shares the view up the magnificent Saguenay Fjord with the small town of Tadoussac. Jacques Cartier made a stop at this point in 1535, and it became an important meeting site for fur traders in the French Territory until the mid-19th century. Whale-watching excursions and cruises of the fjord now depart from Tadoussac, as well as from Chicoutimi, farther up the deep fjord. As the Sague-nay River flows from Lac St-Jean south toward the St. Lawrence, it has a dual character: Between Alma and Chicoutimi, the once rapidly flowing river has been turned into hydroelectric power; in its lower sec-tion, it becomes wider and deeper and flows by steep mountains and cliffs, en route to the St. Lawrence. The white beluga whale breeds in the lower portion of the Saguenay in summer, and in the confluence of the fjord and the seaway are many marine species, which attract other whales, such as pilot, finback, humpback, and blues.

Sadly, the beluga is an endangered species; the whales, along with 27 species of mammals and birds and 17 species of fish, are being threat-ened by pollution in the St. Lawrence River. This has inspired a $100 million project funded by both the federal and provincial govern-ments. An 800-square-kilometer (496-square-mile) marine park (☎ 418/235–4703) at the confluence of the Saguenay and St. Lawrence rivers has been created to protect its fragile ecosystem in the hope of reversing some of the damage already done.

Outdoor Activities and Sports
WHALE-WATCHING

Croisières Navimex Canada, Inc. (✉ 25 Pl. Marché Champlain, Suite 400, Québec City G1K 4H2, ☎ 418/692–4643), offers three-hour whale-watch-ing cruises ($30) and 4½-hour dinner cruises on the Saguenay Fjord ($40). Cruises depart from Baie-Ste-Catherine, Tadoussac, and Rivière du Loup (the departure from Rivière du Loup costs an additional $5).

THE GASPÉ PENINSULA

Jutting into the stormy Gulf of St. Lawrence like the battered prow of a ship, the Gaspé Peninsula remains an isolated region of unsurpassed wild beauty, an area where the land ends. Sheer cliffs tower above broad beaches, and tiny coastal fishing communities cling to the shoreline. Inland rise the Chic-Choc Mountains, eastern Canada's highest, the realm of woodland caribou, black bear, and moose. Townspeople in some Gaspé areas speak mainly English.

Jacques Cartier landed on the Gaspé in 1534, but it wasn't until the early 1800s that the first settlers arrived. Today, the area still seems unspoiled and timeless, a blessing for travelers dipping and soaring along the spectacular coastal highways or venturing on river-valley roads to the interior. Geographically, the peninsula is among the oldest lands on earth. A vast, mainly uninhabited forest covers the hilly hinterland. Local tourist officials can be helpful in locating outfitters and guides to fish and hunt large and small game. The Gaspé's four major parks—Port Daniel, Forillon, Causapscal, and Gaspé—cover a total of 2,292 square kilometers (885 square miles).

The Gaspé was on Jacques Cartier's itinerary—he first stepped ashore in North America in the town of Gaspé—but Vikings, Basques, and Portuguese fisherfolk had come long before. The area's history is told in countless towns en route. Acadians, displaced by the British from New Brunswick in 1755, settled Bonaventure; Paspébiac still has a gun-powder shed built in the 1770s to help defend the peninsula from Amer-ican ships; and United Empire Loyalists settled New Carlisle in 1784.

Carleton

Numbers in the margin correspond to points of interest on the Gaspé Peninsula map.

 201 km (125 mi) southeast of Mont-Joli.

Gaspé Peninsula

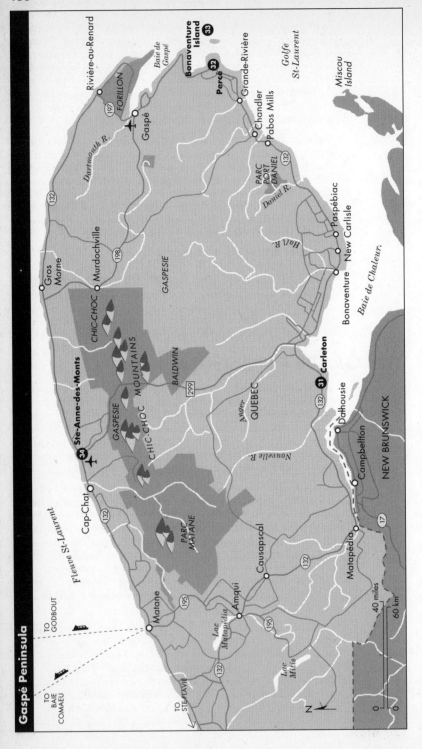

In case you want to be welcomed there.

We're here to see that you're always welcomed at establishments everywhere. That's why millions of people carry the American Express® Card – for peace of mind, confidence, and security, around the world or just around the corner.

do more

Cards

In case you're running low.

We're here to help with more than 118,000 Express Cash locations around the world. In order to enroll, just call American Express before you start your vacation.

do more

Express Cash

And just in case.

We're here with American Express® Travelers Cheques
and Cheques *for Two*.® They're the safest way to carry
money on your vacation and the surest way to get a
refund, practically anywhere, anytime.

Another way we help you...

do more ®

AMERICAN
EXPRESS

**Travelers
Cheques**

The **Notre Dame Oratory** on Mont-St-Joseph dominates this French-speaking city. The view from this point, almost 2,000 feet above Baie de Chaleurs, is spectacular on a clear day.

Dining and Lodging

$$–$$$ ✕📷 **Motel Hostelerie Baie-Bleue.** This motel is snuggled up against a mountain beside the Baie des Chaleurs and offers great views. Daily guided bus tours leave from the hotel June–September. The large restaurant, La Seignerie, has been recognized for excellence. Chef Simon Bernard prepares regional dishes, especially seafood. The table d'hôte won't break your budget and the wine list is extensive and well chosen. ✉ *482 blvd. Perron, Rte. 132, G0C 1J0,* ☎ *418/364–3355 or 800/463–9099,* FAX *418/364–6165. 95 rooms. Restaurant, pool, tennis courts, beach. AE, MC, V.*

Outdoor Activities and Sports

WATER SPORTS

Windsurfers and sailors enjoy the breezes around the Gaspé; there are windsurfing marathons in Baie-des-Chaleurs each summer.

Percé

㉜ *193 km (120 mi) east of Carleton.*

The most famous sight in the region is the huge fossil-embedded rock off the town of Percé that the sea "pierced" thousands of years ago. The largest colony of gannets in the world summers off Percé on ★ **㉝ Bonaventure Island.**

Dining and Lodging

$ ✕ **La Sieur de Pabos.** Boasting the best seafood in the province, this rustic restaurant overlooks Pabos Bay, south of Chandler, about 40 kilometers (25 miles) south of Percé. The chef suggests *crêpe de la seigneurie,* a seafood crepe with a delicately seasoned white sauce. ✉ *325 Rte. 132, Pabos Mills,* ☎ *418/689–2281. AE, MC, V.*

$$–$$$ 📷 **La Bonaventure-sur-Mer Hotel.** The waterfront location with views of Percé Rock and Bonaventure Island makes up for the motel-standard decor. Some motel units have kitchenettes. ✉ *Rte. 132, C.P. 339, G0C 2L0,* ☎ *418/782–2166. 90 rooms. Dining room, beach. AE, DC, MC, V. Closed Nov.–May.*

$$–$$$ 📷 **La Normandie Hotel/Motel.** All but four rooms of this split-level motel face the ocean, with views of Percé Rock and Bonaventure Island. The location in the center of town puts shops and restaurants within walking distance; a beach and a municipal pool are also nearby. Third-floor rooms are more spacious. ✉ *221 Rte. 132 Ouest, C.P. 129, G0C 2L0,* ☎ *418/782–2112 or 800/463–0820. 45 rooms. Restaurant, lounge, sauna, exercise room. EP, MAP. AE, DC, MC, V. Closed Nov.–Apr.*

$$ 📷 **La Côte Surprise Motor Hotel.** Most of the rooms of this motel have views of Percé Rock and the village. Decor is standard in both motel and second-floor hotel units, but the private balconies and terraces are a plus. ✉ *Rte. 132, C.P. 339, G0C 2L0,* ☎ *418/782–2166,* FAX *418/782–5323. 36 rooms. Dining room, snack bar, lounge. AE, D, DC, MC, V. Closed Oct.–May.*

Ste-Anne-des-Monts

㉞ *282 km (175 mi) northwest of Percé.*

The region boasts Québec's longest ski season and highest peaks. Ste-Anne-des-Monts, on the north shore of the peninsula, offers the only heli-skiing east of the Rockies, with deep powder, open bowl, and glade skiing clear into June on peaks that rise to 2,700 feet. Other centers operate from mid-November through May.

Dining and Lodging

$$ ✕ **Cabillaud.** In this bright restaurant, chef Yvan Belzile serves the local specialty—seafood—as well as his own—duck. This is a good place to unwind with a wine from their fine selection and a view of the ever-present ocean. ⊠ *268 rue Notre-Dame Est, Cap-Chat,* ☎ *418/786–2480. MC, V.*

$$ ⊡ **Gîte du Mont-Albert.** In Gaspé Provincial Park, this property is 40 kilometers (25 miles) south of Ste-Anne, nestled in the middle of the Chic-Choc Mountains. It's a perfect retreat for hiking, bicycling, horseback riding, or salmon fishing on the Ste-Anne River. ⊠ *Rte. 299, C.P. 1150, G0E 2G0,* ☎ *418/763–2288 or 888/270-4483. 48 rooms. Dining room, bar. AE, MC, V.*

PROVINCE OF QUÉBEC A TO Z

Arriving and Departing

By Bus

Most major bus lines in the province connect with **Voyageur** (☎ 514/842–2281).

By Car

The major highways are Autoroute des Laurentides 15, a six-lane highway from Montréal to the Laurentians; Autoroute 10 East from Montréal to l'Estrie; U.S. 91 from New England, which becomes Autoroute 55 as it crosses the border to l'Estrie; and Highway 138, which runs from Montréal along the north shore of the St. Lawrence River.

By Plane

Most airlines fly into either of Montréal's airports (Mirabel or Dorval) or Québec City's airport (☞ Chapters 2 and 3).

By Train

Regular **VIA Rail** (800/665–0200) passenger service connects all the province with Montréal and Québec City and offers limited service to the Gaspé Peninsula.

Getting Around

Québec

BY BUS

Most bus traffic to the outer reaches of the province begins at the bus terminal in downtown Québec City (⊠ 225 blvd. Charest Est, ☎ 418/524–4692).

BY CAR

The province has fine roads, along which drivers insist on speeding. Road maps are available at any of the numerous seasonal or permanent Québec tourist offices (call 800/363–7777 for the nearest location). Major entry points are Ottawa/Hull, U.S. 87 from New York State south of Montréal, U.S. 91 from Vermont into l'Estrie area, and the Trans-Canada Highway just west of Montréal.

The Laurentians

BY BUS

Frequent bus service is available from the **Terminus Voyageur** (⊠ 505 blvd. de Maisonneuve Est, ☎ 514/842–2281) in downtown Montréal. **Limocar Laurentides'** service (☎ 514/435–8899) departs regularly for

L'Annonciation, Mont-Laurier, Ste-Adèle, Ste-Agathe-des-Monts, and St-Jovite, among other stops en route. Limocar also has a service to the Basses Laurentides (Lower Laurentians) region, departing from the Laval bus terminal at the Métro Henri-Bourassa stop in north Montréal, stopping in many towns, and ending in St-Jérôme.

BY CAR

Autoroute des Laurentides 15, a six-lane highway, and the slower but more scenic secondary road, Route 117, lead to this resort country. Try to avoid traveling to and from the region on Friday evening or Sunday afternoon, as you're likely to sit for hours in bumper-to-bumper traffic.

L'Estrie

BY BUS

Buses depart daily from the **Terminus Voyageur** (✉ 505 blvd. de Maisonneuve Est, ☎ 514/842–2281) in Montréal, to Granby, Lac-Mégantic, Magog, and Sherbrooke.

BY CAR

Take Autoroute 10 Est from Montréal; from New England take U.S. 91, which becomes Autoroute 55 as it crosses the border at Rock Island.

Gaspé Peninsula

BY CAR

Take the Trans-Canada Highway northeast along the southern shore of the St. Lawrence River to just south of Rivière-du-Loup, where you pick up the 270-kilometer (150-mile) Route 132, which hugs the dramatic coastline. At Ste-Flavie, follow the southern leg of Route 132. Note that the entire distance around the peninsula is 848 kilometers (527 miles).

Contacts and Resources

Camping

For information on camping in the province's private trailer parks and campgrounds, write for the free publication "Québec Camping," available from **Tourisme Québec** (✉ 12 rue Ste-Anne, Québec City G1X 3X2, ☎ 418/643–2280). Inquiries about camping in Québec's three national parks should be directed to **Parks Canada Information Services** (✉ 3 rue Buade, Box 6060, Haute Ville, Québec City G1R 4V7, ☎ 418/648–4177).

Emergencies

Dial 911 to reach the **police, fire,** and **ambulance.**

Fishing

More than 20 outfitters are members of the Laurentian tourist association; several recommendations follow. **Pourvoirie des 100 Lacs Nords** (☎ 514/444–4441). **Lac Beauregard Outfitters** (✉ Mont-Laurier, ☎ 819/326–0269). **Pourvoirie Boismenu** (✉ Lac-du-Cerf, ☎ 819/597–2619). Before setting off into the wilds, consult the **Fédération des Pourvoyeurs du Québec** (✉ Québec Outfitters Federation, 2485 blvd. Hamel, Québec City G1P 2H9, ☎ 418/527–5191) or ask for its list of outfitters available through tourist offices.

Don't forget: Fishing requires a permit, available from the regional offices of the **Ministère du Loisir, de la Chasse et de la Pêche** (✉ 6255 av. 13, Montréal H1X 3E6, ☎ 514/374–2417), or inquire at any Laurentians sporting-goods store displaying an "authorized agent" sticker.

Guest Farms

Agricotours (✉ 4545 av. Pierre de Coubertin, C.P. 1000, Succursale M, Montréal H1V 3R2, ☎ 514/252–3138), the Québec farm-vacation association, can provide lists of guest farms in the province.

Mountain Climbing

Perhaps the best way to view the scenery of the Upper Laurentians is to mountain climb. The **Fédération Québécoise de la Montagne** (✉ 4545 rue Pierre-de-Coubertin, C.P. 1000, Succursale M, Montréal H1V 3R2, ☎ 514/252–3004) can give you information about this sport, as can the region's tourist offices.

Nature Tours

The **Montréal Zoological Society** (✉ 2055 rue Peel, Montréal H3A 1V4, ☎ 514/845–8317) is a nature-oriented group that offers lectures, field trips, and weekend excursions. Tours include whale watching in the St. Lawrence estuary, and hiking and bird-watching in national parks throughout Québec, Canada, and the northern United States.

River Rafting

Four companies specializing in white-water rafting at Rivière Rouge are on-site at the trip's departure point near Calumet. (Take Route 148 past Calumet; turn onto chemin de la Rivière Rouge until you see the signs for the access road to each rafter's headquarters.) **Aventures en Eau Vive** (☎ 819/242–1916), **Nouveau Monde** (☎ 819/242–7238), **Propulsion** (☎ 800/461–3300), and **W-3 Rafting** (☎ 514/334–0889) all offer four- to five-hour rafting trips and provide transportation to and from the river site, as well as guides, helmets, life jackets, and, at the end of the trip, a much-anticipated meal. Most have facilities on-site or nearby for dining, drinking, camping, bathing, swimming, hiking, and horseback riding.

Skiing

For information about ski conditions, telephone the **Maison du Tourisme des Laurentides** (☎ 800/463–9777) and ask for the ski report.

Snowmobiling

Point de Vue Canada (✉ 1227 av. St-Hubert, Suite 200, Montréal H2L 3Y8, ☎ 514/843–8161) offers snowmobile tours in the Laurentians, in Charlevoix, and as far north as the James Bay region. The group also has such adventure packages as "The Magic of the Nunavik Arctic," a weeklong adventure in Québec's Grand Nord, where participants spend one night in an igloo, travel on dogsleds, and go ice fishing.

Visitor Information

QUÉBEC

Tourism Québec (✉ 12 rue Ste-Anne, Québec City, G1R 3X2, ☎ 418/643–2280 or 800/363–7777) can provide information on provincial tourist bureaus throughout the province.

THE LAURENTIANS

The major tourist office is the **Maison du Tourisme des Laurentides** (✉ 14142 rue de Lachapelle, R.R. 1, St-Jérôme J7Z 5T4, ☎ 514/436–8532 or 800/561–6673), just off the Autoroute des Laurentides 15 at Exit 39. The office is open mid-June–Aug., daily 8:30–8; Sept.–mid-June, Sat.–Thurs. 9–5, Fri. 9–7.

Year-round regional tourist offices are in the towns of Labelle, Mont-Laurier, Mont-Tremblant, St-Antoine, St-Sauveur-des-Monts, St-Jovite, Ste-Adèle, Ste-Agathe-des-Monts, Val David, and Piedmont. **Seasonal tourist offices** (mid-June–Labor Day) are in Bois Briand, Grenville,

Lachute, L'Annonciation, Ste-Marguerite-du-Lac-Masson, Notre-Dame-du-Laus, and St-Adolphe-Howard.

L'ESTRIE

Year-round regional provincial tourist offices are in the towns of Bromont, Danville, Eastman, Granby, Lac Mégantic, Magog, Sherbrooke, Sutton, Mansonville, and Waterloo. **Seasonal tourist offices** (June–Labor Day) are in Coaticook, La Patrie, Pike River, East Angus, Eaton-Corner, Freliohsburg, Lac Brome, and Stanstead. Seasonal bureaus' schedules are irregular, so contact the **Association Touristique de l'Estrie** (⊠ 25 Brocage, Sherbrooke, J1L 2J4, ☎ 819/820–2020) before visiting. This association also provides lodging information.

FRENCH VOCABULARY

One of the trickiest French sounds to pronounce is the nasal final *n* sound (whether or not the *n* is actually the last letter of the word). You should try to pronounce it as a sort of nasal grunt—as in "huh." The vowel that precedes the *n* will govern the vowel sound of the word, and in this list we precede the final *n* with an *h* to remind you to be nasal.

Another problem sound is the ubiquitous but untransliterable *eu*, as in *bleu* (blue) or *deux* (two), and the very similar sound in *je* (I), *ce* (this), and *de* (of). The closest equivalent might be the vowel sound of "stood."

English	French	Pronunciation

Basics

English	French	Pronunciation
Yes/no	Oui/non	wee/nohn
Please	S'il vous plaît	seel voo play
Thank you	Merci	mair-**see**
You're welcome	De rien	deh ree-**ehn**
That's all right	Il n'y a pas de quoi	eel nee ah pah de kwah
Excuse me, sorry	Pardon	pahr-**dohn**
Sorry!	Désolé(e)	day-zoh-**lay**
Good morning/ afternoon	Bonjour	bohn-**zhoor**
Good evening	Bonsoir	bohn-**swahr**
Goodbye	Au revoir	o ruh-**vwahr**
Mr. (Sir)	Monsieur	muh-**syuh**
Mrs. (Ma'am)	Madame	ma-**dam**
Miss	Mademoiselle	mad-mwa-**zel**
Pleased to meet you	Enchanté(e)	ohn-shahn-**tay**
How are you?	Comment allez-vous?	kuh-mahn-tahl-ay-**voo**
Very well, thanks	Très bien, merci	tray bee-ehn, mair-**see**
And you?	Et vous?	ay voo?

Numbers

one	un	uhn
two	deux	deuh
three	trois	twah
four	quatre	**kaht**-ruh
five	cinq	sank
six	six	seess
seven	sept	set
eight	huit	wheat
nine	neuf	nuf
ten	dix	deess
eleven	onze	ohnz
twelve	douze	dooz
thirteen	treize	trehz
fourteen	quatorze	kah-torz

8

fifteen	quinze	kanz
sixteen	seize	sez
seventeen	dix-sept	deez-**set**
eighteen	dix-huit	deez-**wheat**
nineteen	dix-neuf	deez-**nuf**
twenty	vingt	vehn
twenty-one	vingt-et-un	vehnt-ay-**uhn**
thirty	trente	trahnt
forty	quarante	ka-**rahnt**
fifty	cinquante	sang-**kahnt**
sixty	soixante	swa-**sahnt**
seventy	soixante-dix	swa-sahnt-**deess**
eighty	quatre-vingts	kaht-ruh-**vehn**
ninety	quatre-vingt-dix	kaht-ruh-vehn-**deess**
one-hundred	cent	sahn
one-thousand	mille	meel

Colors

black	noir	nwahr
blue	bleu	bleuh
brown	brun/marron	bruhn/mar-**rohn**
green	vert	vair
orange	orange	o-**rahnj**
pink	rose	rose
red	rouge	rouge
violet	violette	vee-o-**let**
white	blanc	blahnk
yellow	jaune	zhone

Days of the Week

Sunday	dimanche	dee-**mahnsh**
Monday	lundi	luhn-**dee**
Tuesday	mardi	mahr-**dee**
Wednesday	mercredi	mair-kruh-**dee**
Thursday	jeudi	zhuh-**dee**
Friday	vendredi	vawn-druh-**dee**
Saturday	samedi	sahm-**dee**

Months

January	janvier	zhahn-vee-**ay**
February	février	feh-vree-**ay**
March	mars	marce
April	avril	a-**vreel**
May	mai	meh
June	juin	zhwehn
July	juillet	zhwee-**ay**
August	août	ah-**oo**
September	septembre	sep-**tahm**-bruh
October	octobre	awk-**to**-bruh
November	novembre	no-**vahm**-bruh
December	décembre	day-**sahm**-bruh

Useful Phrases

Do you speak English?	Parlez-vous anglais?	par-lay **voo** ahn-**glay**
I don't speak French	Je ne parle pas français	zhuh nuh parl pah frahn-**say**
I don't understand	Je ne comprends pas	zhuh nuh kohm-**prahn** pah
I understand	Je comprends	zhuh kohm-**prahn**
I don't know	Je ne sais pas	zhuh nuh say **pah**
I'm American/British	Je suis américain/anglais	zhuh sweez a-may-ree-**kehn**/ahn-**glay**
What's your name?	Comment vous appelez-vous?	ko-mahn voo za-pell-ay-**voo**
My name is . . .	Je m'appelle . . .	zhuh ma-**pell** . . .
What time is it?	Quelle heure est-il?	kel air eh-**teel**
How?	Comment?	ko-**mahn**
When?	Quand?	kahn
Yesterday	Hier	yair
Today	Aujourd'hui	o-zhoor-**dwee**
Tomorrow	Demain	duh-**mehn**
This morning/afternoon	Ce matin/cet après-midi	suh ma-**tehn**/set ah-pray-mee-**dee**
Tonight	Ce soir	suh **swahr**
What?	Quoi?	kwah
What is it?	Qu'est-ce que c'est?	kess-kuh-**say**
Why?	Pourquoi?	poor-**kwa**
Who?	Qui?	kee
Where is . . .	Où est . . .	oo ay
the train station?	la gare?	la gar
the subway station?	la station de métro?	la sta-**syon** duh may-**tro**
the bus stop?	l'arrêt de bus?	la-**ray** duh **booss**
the terminal (airport)?	l'aérogare?	lay-ro-**gar**
the post office?	la poste?	la post
the bank?	la banque?	la bahnk
the . . . hotel?	l'hôtel . . .?	lo-**tel**
the store?	le magasin?	luh ma-ga-**zehn**
the cashier?	la caisse?	la **kess**
the . . . museum?	le musée . . .?	luh mew-**zay**
the hospital?	l'hôpital?	lo-pee-**tahl**
the elevator?	l'ascenseur?	la-sahn-**seuhr**
the telephone?	le téléphone?	luh tay-lay-**phone**
Where are the restrooms?	Où sont les toilettes?	oo sohn lay twah-**let**
Here/there	Ici/là	ee-**see**/la
Left/right	A gauche/à droite	a goash/a drwaht
Straight ahead	Tout droit	too drwah

Is it near/far?	C'est près/loin?	say pray/lwehn
I'd like . . .	Je voudrais . . .	zhuh voo-**dray**
a room	une chambre	ewn **shahm**-bruh
the key	la clé	la clay
a newspaper	un journal	uhn zhoor-**nahl**
a stamp	un timbre	uhn **tam**-bruh
I'd like to buy . . .	Je voudrais acheter . . .	zhuh voo-**dray** ahsh-**tay**
a cigar	un cigare	uhn see-**gar**
cigarettes	des cigarettes	day see-ga-**ret**
matches	des allumettes	days a-loo-**met**
dictionary	un dictionnaire	uhn deek-see-oh-**nare**
soap	du savon	dew sah-**vohn**
city plan	un plan de ville	uhn plahn de **veel**
road map	une carte routière	ewn cart roo-tee-**air**
magazine	une revue	ewn reh-**vu**
envelopes	des enveloppes	dayz ahn-veh-**lope**
writing paper	du papier à lettres	dew pa-pee-**ay** a **let**-ruh
airmail writing paper	du papier avion	dew pa-pee-**ay** a-vee-**ohn**
postcard	une carte postale	ewn cart pos-**tal**
How much is it?	C'est combien?	say comb-bee-**ehn**
It's expensive/ cheap	C'est cher/pas cher	say share/pa share
A little/a lot	Un peu/beaucoup	uhn peuh/bo-**koo**
More/less	Plus/moins	plu/mwehn
Enough/too (much)	Assez/trop	a-say/tro
I am ill/sick	Je suis malade	zhuh swee ma-**lahd**
Call a doctor	Appelez un docteur	a-play uhn dohk-**tehr**
Help!	Au secours!	o suh-**koor**
Stop!	Arrêtez!	a-reh-**tay**
Fire!	Au feu!	o fuh
Caution!/Look out!	Attention!	a-tahn-see-**ohn**

Dining Out

A bottle of . . .	une bouteille de . . .	ewn boo-**tay** duh
A cup of . . .	une tasse de . . .	ewn tass duh
A glass of . . .	un verre de . . .	uhn vair duh
Ashtray	un cendrier	uhn sahn-dree-**ay**
Bill/check	l'addition	la-dee-see-**ohn**
Bread	du pain	dew pan
Breakfast	le petit-déjeuner	luh puh-**tee** day-zhuh-**nay**
Butter	du beurre	dew burr
Cheers!	A votre santé!	ah vo-truh sahn-**tay**

Cocktail/aperitif	un apéritif	uhn ah-pay-ree-**teef**
Dinner	le dîner	luh dee-**nay**
Dish of the day	le plat du jour	luh plah dew **zhoor**
Enjoy!	Bon appétit!	bohn a-pay-**tee**
Fixed-price menu	le menu	luh may-**new**
Fork	une fourchette	ewn four-**shet**
I am diabetic	Je suis diabétique	zhuh swee dee-ah-bay-**teek**
I am on a diet	Je suis au régime	zhuh sweez o ray-**jeem**
I am vegetarian	Je suis végétarien(ne)	zhuh swee vay-zhay-ta-ree-**en**
I cannot eat . . .	Je ne peux pas manger de . . .	zhuh nuh **puh** pah mahn-**jay** deh
I'd like to order	Je voudrais commander	zhuh voo-**dray** ko-mahn-**day**
I'm hungry/thirsty	J'ai faim/soif	zhay fahm/swahf
Is service/the tip included?	Est-ce que le service est compris?	ess kuh luh sair-**veess** ay comb-**pree**
It's good/bad	C'est bon/mauvais	say bohn/mo-**vay**
It's hot/cold	C'est chaud/froid	say sho/frwah
Knife	un couteau	uhn koo-**toe**
Lunch	le déjeuner	luh day-zhuh-**nay**
Menu	la carte	la cart
Napkin	une serviette	ewn sair-vee-**et**
Pepper	du poivre	dew **pwah**-vruh
Plate	une assiette	ewn a-see-**et**
Please give me . . .	Donnez-moi . . .	doe-nay-**mwah**
Salt	du sel	dew sell
Spoon	une cuillère	ewn kwee-**air**
Sugar	du sucre	dew **sook**-ruh
Waiter!/Waitress!	Monsieur!/ Mademoiselle!	muh-**syuh**/ mad-mwa-**zel**
Wine list	la carte des vins	la cart day **van**

MENU GUIDE

French	English
Garniture au choix	Choice of vegetable accompaniment
Menu à prix fixe	Set menu
Plat du jour	Dish of the day
Selon arrivage	When available
Supplément/En sus	Extra charge
Sur commande	Made to order

Breakfast

Confiture	Jam
Miel	Honey
Oeuf à la coque	Boiled egg
Oeufs au bacon	Bacon and eggs
Oeufs au jambon	Ham and eggs
Oeufs sur le plat	Fried eggs
Oeufs brouillés	Scrambled eggs
Omelette (nature)	Omelet (plain)
Petits pains	Rolls

Starters

Anchois	Anchovies
Andouille(tte)	Chitterling sausage
Assiette de charcuterie	Assorted pork products
Assiette anglaise	Assorted cold cuts
Crudités	Mixed raw vegetable salad
Escargots	Snails
Hors-d'oeuvres variés	Assorted appetizers
Jambon (de Bayonne)	Ham (Bayonne)
Jambon de Campagne	Country-style ham (air-cured or smoked)
Jambonneau	Cured pig's knuckle
Mortadelle	Bologna sausage
Oeufs à la diable	Deviled eggs
Pâté	Liver purée blended with meat
Quenelles	Light dumplings (fish, fowl, or meat)
Saucisson	Dried sausage
Terrine	Pâté sliced and served from an earthenware pot
Viande séchée	Cured dried beef

Salads

Salade d'endives	Endive salad
Salade de thon	Tuna salad
Salade mixte	Mixed salad
Salade niçoise	Riviera combination salad
Salade russe	Diced vegetable salad
Salade verte	Green salad

Soups

Bisque	Seafood stew
Bouillabaisse	Fish and seafood stew

Crème de . . .	Cream of . . .
Potage	Light soup
julienne	shredded vegetables
parmentier	potato
Pot-au-feu	Stew of meat and vegetables
Soupe	Hearty soup
du jour	of the day
à l'oignon gratinée	French onion soup
au pistou	Provençal vegetable soup
Velouté de . . .	Cream of . . .
Vichyssoise	Cold leek and potato cream soup

Fish and Seafood

Anguille	Eel
Bar	Bass
Bigorneaux	Winkles
Bourride	Fish stew from Marseilles
Brandade de morue	Creamed salt cod
Brochet	Pike
Cabillaud	Fresh cod
Calmar	Squid
Carpe	Carp
Coquille St-Jacques	Scallops in creamy sauce
Crabe	Crab
Crevettes	Shrimp
Cuisses de grenouilles	Frogs' legs
Daurade	Sea bream
Ecrevisses	Prawns
Ecrevisses	Crayfish
Eperlans	Smelt
Harengs	Herring
Homard	Lobster
Huîtres	Oysters
Langouste	Spiny lobster
Langoustines	Dublin bay prawns (scampi)
Lotte	Burbot
Lotte de mer	Angler
Loup	Catfish
Maquereau	Mackerel
Matelote	Fish stew in wine
Merlan	Whiting
Morue	Cod
Moules	Mussels
Palourdes	Clams
Perche	Perch
Poulpes	Octopus
Raie	Skate
Rascasse	Fish used in bouillabaisse
Rouget	Red mullet
Saumon	Salmon
Sole	Sole
Thon	Tuna
Truite	Trout

Meat

Agneau	Lamb
Boeuf	Beef
pavé	Thick slice of boned beef
Boulettes de viande	Meatballs
Brochette	Kabob
Cassoulet toulousain	Casserole of white beans and meat
Cervelle	Brains
Chateaubriand	Double fillet steak
Chops	Côtelettes
Choucroute garnie	Sausages and cured pork served with sauerkraut
Contre-filet	Loin strip steak
Côte de boeuf	T-bone steak
Côte	Rib
Entrecôte	Rib or rib-eye steak
Epaule	Shoulder
Escalope	Cutlet
Filet	Fillet steak
Foie	Liver
Gigot	Leg
Langue	Tongue
Médaillon	Tenderloin steak
Pieds de cochon	Pig's feet
Porc	Pork
Ragoût	Stew
Ris de veau	Veal sweetbreads
Rognons	Kidneys
Saucisses	Sausages
Selle	Saddle
Steak/steack	Steak (always beef)
Tournedos	Tenderloin of T-bone steak
Veau	Veal

Methods of Preparation

A point	Medium
A l'étouffée	Stewed
Au four	Baked
Bien cuit	Well-done
Bleu	Very rare
Bouilli	Boiled
Braisé	Braised
Frit	Fried
Grillé	Grilled
Rôti	Roast
Saignant	Rare
Sauté/poêlée	Sautéed

Game and Poultry

Blanc de volaille	Chicken breast
Caille	Quail
Canard/caneton	Duck/duckling
Cerf/chevreuil	Venison (red/roe)

Coq au vin	Chicken stewed in red wine
Dinde/dindonneau	Turkey/young turkey
Faisan	Pheasant
Grive	Thrush
Lapin	Rabbit
Lièvre	Wild hare
Oie	Goose
Perdrix/perdreau	Partridge/young partridge
Pigeon/pigeonneau	Pigeon/squab
Pintade/pintadeau	Guinea fowl/young guinea fowl
Poularde	Fattened pullet
Poule au pot	Chicken stewed with vegetables
Poulet	Chicken
Poussin	Spring chicken
Sanglier/marcassin	Wild boar/young wild boar
Volaille	Fowl

Vegetables

Artichaut	Artichoke
Asperge	Asparagus
Aubergine	Eggplant
Carottes	Carrots
Champignons	Mushrooms
Chicorée	Chicory (Endive)
Chou-fleur	Cauliflower
Chou (rouge)	Cabbage (red)
Choux de Bruxelles	Brussels sprouts
Courgette	Zucchini
Cresson	Watercress
Endive	Endive
Epinard	Spinach
Fèves	Broad beans
Haricots blancs/verts	White kidney/French beans
Laitue	Lettuce
Lentilles	Lentils
Oignons	Onions
Petits pois	Peas
Poireaux	Leeks
Poivrons	Peppers
Pomme de terre	Potato
Radis	Radishes
Tomates	Tomatoes

Potatoes, Rice, and Noodles

Nouilles	Noodles
Pâtes	Pasta
Pommes (de terre)	Potatoes
allumettes	matchsticks
dauphine	mashed and deep-fried
duchesse	mashed with butter and egg yolks
en robe des champs	in their skin
frites	French fries
mousseline	mashed
nature/vapeur	boiled/steamed

| Riz | Rice |
| pilaf | boiled in bouillon with onions |

Sauces and Preparations

Béarnaise	Vinegar, egg yolks, white wine, shallots, tarragon
Béchamel	White sauce
Bordelaise	Mushrooms, red wine, shallots, beef marrow
Bourguignon	Red wine, herbs
Chasseur	Wine, mushrooms, onions, shallots
Diable	Hot pepper
Forestière	Mushrooms
Hollandaise	Egg yolks, butter, vinegar
Indienne	Curry
Madère	With Madeira wine
Marinière	White wine, mussel broth, egg yolks
Meunière	Brown butter, parsley, lemon juice
Périgueux	With goose or duck liver purée and truffles
Poivrade	Pepper sauce
Provençale	Onions, tomatoes, garlic
Tartare	Mayonnaise flavored with mustard and herbs
Vinaigrette	Vinegar dressing

Fruits and Nuts

Abricot	Apricot
Amandes	Almonds
Ananas	Pineapple
Banane	Banana
Brugnon	Nectarine
Cacahouètes	Peanuts
Cassis	Blackcurrants
Cerises	Cherries
Citron	Lemon
Citron vert	Lime
Dattes	Dates
Figues	Figs
Fraises	Strawberries
Framboises	Raspberries
Fruits secs	Dried fruit
Groseilles	Red currants
Mandarine	Tangerine
Marrons	Chestnuts
Melon	Melon
Mûres	Blackberries
Myrtilles	Blueberries
Noisettes	Hazelnuts
Noix de coco	Coconut
Noix	Walnuts
Orange	Orange
Pamplemousse	Grapefruit

Pastèque	Watermelon
Pêche	Peach
Poire	Pear
Pomme	Apple
Pruneaux	Prunes
Prunes	Plums
Raisins secs	Raisins
Raisins blancs/noirs	Grapes green/blue

Desserts

Coupe (glacée)	Sundae
Crêpe suzette	Thin pancake simmered in orange juice and flambéed with orange liqueur
Crème caramel	Caramel pudding
Crème Chantilly	Whipped cream
Flan	Custard
Gâteau au chocolat	Chocolate cake
Glace	Ice cream
Mousse au chocolat	Chocolate pudding
Sorbet	Water ice
Tarte aux pommes	Apple pie
Tourte	Layer cake
Vacherin glacé	Ice-cream cake

Alcoholic Drinks

A l'eau	With water
Avec des glaçons	On the rocks
Apéritifs	Cocktails
Kir/blanc-cassis	Chilled white wine mixed with black-currant syrup
Bière	Beer
Blonde/brune	Light/dark
Calvados	Apple brandy
Eau-de-vie	Brandy
Kirsch	Cherry brandy
Liqueur	Cordial
Poire William	Pear brandy
Porto	Port
Sec	Straight
Vin	Wine
sec	dry
brut	very dry
léger	light
doux	sweet
rouge	red
rosé	rosé
mousseux	sparkling
blanc	white

Nonalcoholic Drinks

Café	Coffee
noir	black
crème	cream
au lait	with milk

décaféiné	caffeine-free
express	espresso
Chocolat chaud	Hot chocolate
Eau minérale	Mineral water
gazeuse	carbonated
non gazeuse	still
Jus de . . .	. . . juice (see fruit)
Lait	Milk
Limonade	Lemonade
Limonade gazeuse	Ginger ale
Schweppes	Tonic water
Thé	Tea
crème/citron	with milk/lemon
glacé	iced tea
Tisane	Herb tea

INDEX

NOTES

NOTES

NOTES

NOTES

CNN✈
Airport Network

Your
Window
To The
World
While You're
On The
Road

Keep in touch when you're traveling. Before you take off, tune in to CNN Airport Network. Now available in major airports across America, CNN Airport Network provides nonstop news, sports, business, weather and lifestyle programming. Both domestic and international. All piloted by the top-flight global resources of CNN. All up-to-the minute reporting. And just for travelers, CNN Airport Network features two daily Fodor's specials. "Travel Fact" provides enlightening, useful travel trivia, while "What's Happening" covers upcoming events in major cities worldwide. So why be bored waiting to board? **TIME FLIES WHEN YOU'RE WATCHING THE WORLD THROUGH THE WINDOW OF CNN AIRPORT NETWORK!**

Fodor's Travel Publications

Available at bookstores everywhere, or call 1–800–533–6478, 24 hours a day.

Gold Guides
U.S.

Alaska

Arizona

Boston

California

Cape Cod, Martha's
Vineyard, Nantucket

The Carolinas & the
Georgia Coast

Chicago

Colorado

Florida

Hawai'i

Las Vegas, Reno,
Tahoe

Los Angeles

Maine, Vermont,
New Hampshire

Maui & Lāna'i

Miami & the Keys

New England

New Orleans

New York City

Pacific North Coast

Philadelphia & the
Pennsylvania Dutch
Country

The Rockies

San Diego

San Francisco

Santa Fe, Taos,
Albuquerque

Seattle & Vancouver

The South

U.S. & British Virgin
Islands

USA

Virginia & Maryland

Washington, D.C.

Foreign

Australia

Austria

The Bahamas

Belize & Guatemala

Bermuda

Canada

Cancún, Cozumel,
Yucatán Peninsula

Caribbean

China

Costa Rica

Cuba

The Czech Republic
& Slovakia

Eastern &
Central Europe

Europe

Florence, Tuscany
& Umbria

France

Germany

Great Britain

Greece

Hong Kong

India

Ireland

Israel

Italy

Japan

London

Madrid & Barcelona

Mexico

Montréal &
Québec City

Moscow, St.
Petersburg, Kiev

The Netherlands,
Belgium &
Luxembourg

New Zealand

Norway

Nova Scotia, New
Brunswick, Prince
Edward Island

Paris

Portugal

Provence &
the Riviera

Scandinavia

Scotland

Singapore

South Africa

South America

Southeast Asia

Spain

Sweden

Switzerland

Thailand

Tokyo

Toronto

Turkey

Vienna & the Danube

Fodor's Special-Interest Guides

Caribbean Ports
of Call

The Complete Guide
to America's
National Parks

Family Adventures

Gay Guide
to the USA

Halliday's New
England Food
Explorer

Halliday's New
Orleans Food
Explorer

Healthy Escapes

Kodak Guide to
Shooting Great
Travel Pictures

Net Travel

Nights to Imagine

Rock & Roll Traveler
USA

Sunday in New York

Sunday in
San Francisco

Walt Disney World,
Universal Studios
and Orlando

Walt Disney World
for Adults

Where Should We
Take the Kids?
California

Where Should We
Take the Kids?
Northeast

Worldwide Cruises
and Ports of Call

Special Series

Affordables
Caribbean
Europe
Florida
France
Germany
Great Britain
Italy
London
Paris

Fodor's Bed & Breakfasts and Country Inns
America
California
The Mid-Atlantic
New England
The Pacific Northwest
The South
The Southwest
The Upper Great Lakes

The Berkeley Guides
California
Central America
Eastern Europe
Europe
France
Germany & Austria
Great Britain & Ireland
Italy
London
Mexico
New York City
Pacific Northwest & Alaska
Paris
San Francisco

Compass American Guides
Arizona
Canada
Chicago
Colorado
Hawaii
Idaho
Hollywood
Las Vegas

Maine
Manhattan
Montana
New Mexico
New Orleans
Oregon
San Francisco
Santa Fe
South Carolina
South Dakota
Southwest
Texas
Utah
Virginia
Washington
Wine Country
Wisconsin
Wyoming

Fodor's Citypacks
Atlanta
Hong Kong
London
New York City
Paris
Rome
San Francisco
Washington, D.C.

Fodor's Español
California
Caribe Occidental
Caribe Oriental
Gran Bretaña
Londres
Mexico
Nueva York
Paris

Fodor's Exploring Guides
Australia
Boston & New England
Britain
California
Caribbean
China
Egypt
Florence & Tuscany
Florida

France
Germany
Ireland
Israel
Italy
Japan
London
Mexico
Moscow & St. Petersburg
New York City
Paris
Prague
Provence
Rome
San Francisco
Scotland
Singapore & Malaysia
Spain
Thailand
Turkey
Venice

Fodor's Flashmaps
Boston
New York
San Francisco
Washington, D.C.

Fodor's Pocket Guides
Acapulco
Atlanta
Barbados
Jamaica
London
New York City
Paris
Prague
Puerto Rico
Rome
San Francisco
Washington, D.C.

Mobil Travel Guides
America's Best Hotels & Restaurants
California & the West
Frequent Traveler's Guide to Major Cities
Great Lakes
Mid-Atlantic

Northeast
Northwest & Great Plains
Southeast
Southwest & South Central

Rivages Guides
Bed and Breakfasts of Character and Charm in France
Hotels and Country Inns of Character and Charm in France
Hotels and Country Inns of Character and Charm in Italy
Hotels and Country Inns of Character and Charm in Paris
Hotels and Country Inns of Character and Charm in Portugal
Hotels and Country Inns of Character and Charm in Spain

Short Escapes
Britain
France
New England
Near New York City

Fodor's Sports
Golf Digest's Best Places to Play
Skiing USA
USA Today The Complete Four Sport Stadium Guide

Fodor's Vacation Planners
Great American Learning Vacations
Great American Sports & Adventure Vacations
Great American Vacations
Great American Vacations for Travelers with Disabilities
National Parks and Seashores of the East
National Parks of the West

WHEREVER YOU TRAVEL, *H*ELP IS NEVER FAR AWAY.

From planning your trip to providing travel assistance along the way, American Express® Travel Service Offices are always there to help.

Montreal/Quebec

American Express Travel Service
Centre Eaton, Metro Level
705 St. Catherine Ouest
Montreal
514/282-0445

American Express Vacation Travel Service
800 Rene Levesque Blvd. W.
Suite 1201
Montreal
514/392-4407

American Express Travel Service
Place Versailles
7525 Sherbrook Est
Montreal
514/354-8442

American Express Travel Service
2000 Peel Building
1140 de Maisonneuve W.
Montreal
514/284-3300

Travel

http://www.americanexpress.com/travel

American Express Travel Service Offices are found in central locations throughout Canada.